Paul Britton was born in 1946. Following degrees
obtained in psychology from Warwick and
Sheffield universities, he has spent the last twenty
years working as a consultant clinical and forensic
psychologist. He has advised the Association of
Chief Police Officers' Crime Committee on
offender profiling for many years and currently
teaches postgraduates in clinical and forensic
psychology. He is married with two children. Paul
Britton's previous work, *The Jigsaw Man*, won
the Crime Writers' Association Gold Dagger
Award for Non-Fiction and is also published by
Corgi.

Also by Paul Britton

THE JIGSAW MAN

and published by Corgi Books

PICKING UP
THE PIECES

PAUL BRITTON

CORGI BOOKS

PICKING UP THE PIECES
A CORGI BOOK : 0 552 14718 4

Originally published in Great Britain by Bantam Press,
a division of Transworld Publishers

PRINTING HISTORY
Bantam Press edition published 2000
Corgi edition published 2001

1 3 5 7 9 10 8 6 4 2

Set in 10/12pt Times by
Falcon Oast Graphic Art.

Corgi Books are published by Transworld Publishers,
61–63 Uxbridge Road, London W5 5SA,
a division of The Random House Group Ltd,
in Australia by Random House Australia (Pty) Ltd,
20 Alfred Street, Milsons Point, Sydney, NSW 2061, Australia,
in New Zealand by Random House New Zealand Ltd,
18 Poland Road, Glenfield, Auckland 10, New Zealand
and in South Africa by Random House (Pty) Ltd,
Endulini, 5a Jubilee Road, Parktown 2193, South Africa.

Printed and bound in Great Britain by
Cox & Wyman Ltd, Reading, Berkshire.

DEDICATION

Every day children are grievously damaged by those who are supposed to protect and love them. Even if we can find these children, the harm can rarely be fully undone.

It is always emotionally painful for me to reconstruct, psychologically, the ordeal endured by the victims of crime. However, my discomfort is trivial when compared to the true terror and pain they have suffered, and which their loved ones will suffer always, inescapably.

Front-line clinical staff spend whole careers treating 'forensic' patients. They constantly risk physical injury and emotional burn-out in getting close to some of the most dangerous men and women in our society.

I have worked with these people as patients and colleagues; I'm sure they have affected who I have become. I dedicate *Picking Up the Pieces* to them, and also to Marilyn who, happily for me, is still there, picking up my pieces.

ACKNOWLEDGEMENTS

Through many criminal and other difficult, sensitive cases I have worked with the most able and far-seeing investigators of our day. They have each contributed to changing the ways in which information is gathered, analysed and acted upon. Here I pay particular tribute to:

Detective Superintendent David Cox, Detective Superintendent Michael Short, Detective Inspector John Bradley, Detective Chief Superintendent Ken John, Detective Superintendent Jon Dawson, and Detective Superintendent Gary Copson, who was prepared to direct a light into some particularly ugly corners, just because it seemed right.

My own development as a psychologist was nurtured by men and women who gave more than they realized:

At Warwick, Tom Watson, John Annett, George Kiss, Ian Morley, Richard Skemp, Elizabeth Hitchfield, Christine Hewitt, Keith Hoskin, and Steve Van Toller, who agreed to be my personal tutor even though there were more students than chairs for them to sit on.

At Sheffield, Paul Jackson and Michael West transformed students into researchers and sought-after practitioners.

The National Health Service continues to function because the administrative, clerical, clinical and managerial staff do so much more than should fairly be asked of them. If honours were given on this basis, then Dr James Earp, consultant forensic psychiatrist, would be a worthy recipient, as would Bill Carpenter and Diane Purvis, my NHS secretary.

It is a long, sometimes bumpy journey. My most valued companions have been Mal and Emma and Rufus, and Ian and Katherine; they have taken the load if ever the axle looked as if it might begin to bend.

As before, I acknowledge those men and women who cannot be named for reasons of confidentiality or security. I am glad to have helped, and have learned much from working with you. I hope someone is preparing your successors.

'Good things of day begin to droop and drowse,
While night's black agents to their preys do rouse.
Thou marvell'st at my words: but hold thee still;
Things bad begun make strong themselves by ill:
So, prithee, go with me . . .'

Shakespeare, *Macbeth*, Act III scene ii

A NOTE TO THE READER

In order for us to understand how one person's experiences and personality may lead them to abduct, maim or obliterate others, while other people are made inert and empty by what seem to be similar circumstances, we must be given sufficient detail of what it was in their lives that led them to behave as they did. At the same time, it is important to ensure that the secrets and histories of individuals I have met in the consulting room are not set out in a manner that would enable people to recognize them. To be true to both requirements, I have, with the exception of names that are in the public domain, protected the identities of the people I write about by changing names and altering a number of details when describing case histories.

However, every case is real; no dramatic strands have been added or embellished for effect. Of course those cases which are a matter of public record and criminal investigation are reported in their original detail, in the accepted manner.

I have withheld some aspects of methods of offending and injuries or defilement of victims, where full description would either show how to get away with crime or be more graphic than was necessary to explain the significance of particular behaviour. Nevertheless this book inevitably has sections that will be uncomfortable or distressing to read. I cannot apologize for this, as my intention is not to alarm but to provide a deeper understanding of the psychological processes that underpin some of the most serious and otherwise inexplicable crimes facing us today. I hope that a growing insight into these factors will lead to increasingly early recognition of potential dangers, and the referral of those affected to the clinicians. Where it is too late for this, and a crime has already been committed, I hope that *Picking Up the Pieces* will continue my work of making available to the police and other investigators a more profound knowledge of the psychological functioning of the offender, helping them to direct their scarce resources more effectively and make detection more likely, and prevent even more people from being hurt or killed. I ask you to ride through your discomfort and give your compassion to those who have suffered so terribly.

INTRODUCTION

Over the past twenty-two years I have analysed and treated thousands of patients, each one of them unique as only human beings can be. The range of their problems is as diverse and complicated as human experience itself.

When I began my career as a clinical psychologist, I had no thought of specializing in the forensic (crime-related) area. Given the nature of the work, it was hardly the sort of choice to recommend to anyone.

Forensic psychology is a field of expertise that emerged from two separate strands. First it came from the special hospitals and regional secure units that are used to assess and treat people who offend as a consequence of some mental abnormality. Secondly, it emerged from the prison system, where psychologists have worked for many years with individual inmates, as well as researching the most effective regimes for running the prisons themselves.

This is not pleasant work. Often it involves treating people who have depraved and dangerous minds and who grievously hurt those around them. It also means seeing the vulnerable, deeply wounded victims of crime.

Among my most painful and difficult work has been

examining young children at risk of emotional, sexual and physical injury. I also have to interview their parents and advise the courts on whether the family should remain together or if the children should be sent into the loneliness and, sometimes, ineptitude of the care system.

Very little has been written about these areas of my work. The spotlight has tended to focus on my involvement in criminal investigations, yet, since 1984, when I pioneered the use of psychological profiling in the UK, my clinical practice – my experience as a psychologist – has been the bedrock upon which this work has been built. This first use of psychological profiling resulted in the conviction of Paul Bostock for the murders of Caroline Osborne and Amanda Weedon; it is now acknowledged that Bostock was the first person in Britain to be caught and convicted with the help of a psychological analysis and profile created from evidence left by an *unknown* offender at a crime scene, which, drawing on professional psychological expertise, painstakingly established key characteristics of the offender: his primary motivational driving forces; his intelligence, education and abilities; his emotions, personality structure and employment; his sexual, social and family relationships; the location of his current and previous homes and the geographical range he is comfortable with and will operate in; and, crucially important, the likelihood that he will offend again.

Since that first case I have travelled tens of thousands of miles in my spare time, criss-crossing Britain to assist in over a hundred investigations involving murder, rape, kidnapping, arson and extortion. I have 'walked through the minds' of perpetrators and provided police with the psychological

14

characteristics that would narrow their search for potential suspects and help to stop them killing again. Although psychological profiling remains a relatively new science, it has enabled offenders to be caught in cases of serious crime including murder by strangers – something that may involve the abduction and killing of children. This new science enables a greater understanding of why people behave in this otherwise inexplicable way, so making it possible for us to see if this risk can be reduced by the earlier identification of potential offenders and the treatment of the underlying causes. With a greater understanding of why people offend in these seemingly uncontrollable fashions, it may be possible to treat a number of, for example, rapists or stalkers in a way that would prevent them reoffending when they are released into society.

In *The Jigsaw Man* (1997), I revealed the details of my work for the police and gave an insight into the world of offender profiling. In this book I've returned to certain criminal cases and introduced new crimes to illustrate particular points about how I draw my conclusions.

My two roles have dovetailed effectively because both require an understanding of the broader psychological aspects of offending and offenders. What makes a person abduct, rape, kill, torture or abuse another human being? What were the developmental processes that moulded them and sent them along this particular path?

As a forensic psychologist, I have always known that if I could prevent just one person from committing a crime, then I would be preventing many others from ever becoming victims. For example, by the time many sexual offenders reach the middle years of their 'careers' they will have harmed over 150 separate victims. It seems a lot, but I have examined paedophiles in their early twenties who could trace back more than 400 separate child victims before being caught. Being convicted and punished rarely changes these men. They have to be analysed and treated.

There is a wealth of scientific literature about human behaviour and psychological functioning and this knowledge underpins my work in the consulting room. At the same time, I learn new things every day with each patient I interview.

People often ask me how I can look at a crime scene in all its dreadful detail and know so much about the person responsible without ever having met them. I hope that I have managed to answer this question in the pages that follow by showing how my consulting-room work relates directly to the work I do for the police and the tasks I undertake now.

I have chosen the clinical cases very carefully. They are not sensationalized or meant to shock, but rather to give an insight into a world that very few people ever see.

PROLOGUE

A ring-bound set of photographs slid across the desk towards me. The colour prints began with a sequence of wide-angle shots of a country lane. The trees were bare and etched starkly against the grey skies.

The body was barely visible, showing up only as a splash of white against the hedge. It could have been a discarded shopping bag or an abandoned 'For Sale' sign.

Finally the lens moved closer, zeroing in. There could be no dignity or privacy about the process. The body of a lifeless and naked woman was exposed from every conceivable angle.

The marble coldness accentuated the dull whiteness of her skin. It seemed almost too white – as though somebody had dumped a naked shop-window mannequin, having dragged it backwards across the ground by its armpits.

I had to fight the urge to look away. I knew from experience that such photographs are not easily forgotten. They burn themselves inexorably into the mind and choose unexpected moments to return.

The body had been photographed through each stage of examination and post mortem. I knew the

17

procedure. Every square inch would be photographed, scraped, swabbed or cut open. Body fluids, fingernail dirt and pubic hair would be sealed in plastic or glass and then passed hand-to-hand along the evidential chain; from the pathologist to the laboratory, to the prosecution, to the court and to the jury.

Violent death becomes a very public event. And no matter how much is done later to restore a victim's dignity, for those few days or weeks she (or he) becomes the most important piece of evidence in a murder investigation.

I opened a new folder of photographs of the post mortem. The difference between a person lying at a scene of crime and then washed, weighed and cleaned for the pathologist is quite startling.

Almost unconsciously, I began asking myself questions. Had she been conscious when he strangled her? How quickly did she die? Where was she killed? How did he incapacitate her?

The answers were important because they influenced the much larger issue of motivation. What did the killer seek to achieve when he murdered this poor woman? What went through his mind?

Detective Superintendent David Cox had called me the previous day in the middle of lunch. I closed the doors to the lounge so I could take the call in private.

'I'm sorry to bother you at home, Paul, but I'd like you to look at something.'

My heart sank. I knew where such a statement normally led me.

'We've found a body, but we don't have any ID at all. She's been murdered.'

I made a few notes on a foolscap pad and checked

my diary for the following day. I had an outpatient clinic that couldn't be moved. It would have to be the evening. I arranged for David to meet me at home.

Normally, I tried to keep people connected with my work away from home, for obvious reasons. However, I knew the Leicestershire force well. If David Cox said it was urgent, then I knew it was.

At the dining table, Marilyn had started clearing the plates and I helped her pack the dishwasher. She knew without asking that the telephone call had come from the police. After nearly thirty years of marriage I would swear she is almost telepathic.

It had been a difficult few weeks. Ten days earlier I'd travelled to Gloucester, where police had found three bodies in the garden of 25 Cromwell Street. Frederick West was in custody and his wife Rosemary was helping police with their inquiries. The man heading the investigation, Detective Superintendent John Bennett, asked me if I could give them some insight into what they were dealing with.

The Wests had lived at the house for twenty-two years and came across as a cheerful couple who were outwardly friendly and good neighbours. At the same time, three bodies had been dug out of their garden – all of them dismembered.

Bennett gave me a complete briefing on the case, including statements, pathology reports and the details of a previous offence that dated back to December 1972.

Ultimately, I had to tell him and the interviewing teams that they were looking at evidence of predatory and sadistic sexual psychopathy. I had seen it before and dealt with it clinically, but this case had a particularly dreadful feature – a combined depravity where

19

husband and wife had drawn energy from each other. They hadn't just killed for the sake of taking a life; their victims were playthings who were tortured and abused.

'You are dealing with prolific murderers. You have found only three of their victims.'

'But where are the others?' asked Detective Inspector Terry Moore.

'Everywhere he's lived. Everywhere he's worked. Sometimes sexual psychopathic murderers get comfortable with disposing of bodies in a particular way – some leave them in ditches, some put them in rivers, some bury them. Mr and Mrs West looked after them – they kept them close.'

'So that's why they used the back garden?'

'Not exactly,' I told them. 'They used the garden because the house is full.'

In the ten days since that conversation, four more bodies had been uncovered in the basement of 25 Cromwell Street. Every few days John Bennett had sent me the transcripts of police interviews with Mr and Mrs West. After dinner each evening, I sat down and studied the questions and answers, looking for anything I might have missed.

Now, on top of all this, I had a new case to deal with. Murderers rarely wait in line.

As I finished looking through the last of the albums, I slid them back across the desk. David Cox sat opposite, shuffling several folders to one side as if clearing space between us.

Although not a tall man he was solid and would have been an asset to any rugby team. He had fair hair, a very young face for a man of his rank and a direct but obliging manner.

His briefing was cautious because he didn't quite know if I could help him.

'Four days ago, on Thursday 3 March 1994, a woman's body was found by a man walking his dog in a country lane at Bitteswell, near Lutterworth, about fifteen miles south of Leicester. She was lying on a grass verge at the edge of the village, on a rough dead-end road known locally as Woodby Lane. No attempt had been made to conceal the body.

'The post mortem reveals that she was strangled and killed up to twelve hours before she was found. There is no evidence of sexual assault but she did have sex with someone just before she died. According to the pathologist, she was killed elsewhere and dumped some time on Wednesday night.'

The photographs of the grass verge showed her lying starkly white against the cold winter green of her surroundings.

'How old was she?'

'Anywhere between thirty and fifty-five.'

'You don't know?'

'That's why I've come to see you. We don't even have a name. It's been four days. If she's local then nobody's reported her missing. We've trawled the missing persons files and we've asked other forces to search their records. So far we've drawn a blank.'

'Perhaps she's from overseas.'

'Interpol hasn't come up with a match.'

I could understand his frustration. Conducting a murder investigation without knowing the victim's name is like playing snooker in the dark.

'I'm not quite sure how I can help,' I said, genuinely puzzled.

'I was hoping you might tell us something about her.'

21

If I hadn't known Cox so well, I would probably have laughed. He was asking me to profile an unknown victim psychologically, where the only possible source of clues was her naked body.

Normally when I work on a police investigation, there is already a wealth of detail about the method used in the crime and a reasonable amount known about the victim. This is vital if I'm properly to reconstruct what happened – not just through the eyes of the victim but also of the predator.

I have to answer four questions – what happened, how, to whom and why? And then the fifth question – who did it?

The third of these questions involves the most pain because it means discovering all that I can about the victim – her strengths, weaknesses, loves, hates and fears. Was she a careful person? Did she make friends easily? How did she dress? The closer I get to her, the greater the pain because she becomes real to me. I can walk through her mind and see the world through her eyes.

SIOs have often asked me why this is so important to me.

It's because when I know a victim, I know more about the person who killed her. I can put a precise shape to his personality and behavioural preferences. I can move back through his life from the offence and begin drawing up a picture of his family, friends, relationships and schooling. Then, moving forward, I can draw out his occupation, habits and where he might live, how he'll be affected by the crime and if he'll offend again. If so, how and where.

This is what psychological offender profiling sets out to achieve. It is like having an empty picture frame and filling it with pieces of a jigsaw until the image is clear.

Now, for the first time in my career, I was being asked to profile an unknown victim before I could profile her killer.

The crime scene photographs were all taken in daylight. I wanted to know how it altered in the darkness. How did it look to the killer on that night?

The following evening, I drove to Bitteswell alone in my car. I had a warm overcoat on the passenger seat and the heater at full blast.

Bitteswell is an old village and its buildings look as though they've grown up between the trees like toadstools on the woodland floor. Approaching from the Lutterworth side, the left turn into Woodby Lane is on the far side of the village and is quite awkward.

The Old Royal Oak is a typical Midlands country pub, almost on the corner of Valley Lane and Woodby Lane. In the fading daylight it seemed deserted, but soon it would be a beacon for the locals, drawing them inside. The killer had been within earshot when he stopped his vehicle to dump the body.

Woodby Lane was sometimes used by courting couples and occasionally by suspected drug users, according to David Cox. The narrow strip of bitumen was flanked on both sides by hedges and fences. It was difficult to turn a car and I needed headlights to find a field gateway to reverse into. A mile or so further down, the lane petered out among a cluster of agricultural buildings.

I almost missed the bay where the body had been dumped. It was just a short way into the lane, where the narrow grass verge broadened for a distance of twenty or thirty yards. At its widest point the verge was about fifteen feet across from the edge of the road to a broken hedge and an empty field beyond.

I looked again at the entrance to Woodby Lane. From either direction it came into view quite late on a bend. This was not the place you would select to leave a body hidden, not if you were pre-planning it and not if you were moderately bright.

As I sat in the car, I looked at the photograph of the dead woman's head and shoulders. She had a distinctive face. Whoever she was, I had no doubt that the everyday pressures and tensions of life had shaped her looks. With such strong features and the heavy coverage of the crime in the local media, surely she'd have been recognized if she were a Leicester girl.

Yet nobody had come forward. Five days had passed and instead of a name beneath her photograph there was a question mark. I felt as though David Cox had invited this woman into my home and I couldn't let her leave without finding her name.

Back in my study, I wrote a list of facts about the victim:

5' 1" tall.
Shoulder-length naturally light brown hair, permed at least six months ago and not cut for some time.
Both ears pierced.
Blue-grey eyes.
Sallow complexion.
Bust 46½", bra size 44c.
Plain silver ring on third finger of right hand.
Hips 46½".
Has never given birth to children.
Toenails unkempt.

Lower jaw protrudes causing lower teeth to overlap upper teeth.
Possibly an occasional smoker.
Weighed approximately 13 stone.
Dress size 22–24.
Waist 40".
Bitten nails, fingers not manicured.
Shoe size 2½–3.

What could she tell me about herself? Her immediate personal hygiene was good. She had been frequently sexually active. She had sex shortly before she died. Her most recent partner hadn't used a condom – there were traces of semen found in her vagina. There were no bruises or abrasions to the genitals to indicate the intercourse had been forced.

There were no defence wounds. Whoever garrotted her had been close enough to take her before she could react. There were no indications that she had been bound, gagged or restrained before being strangled.

She was far too heavy for her naked body to have been carried from a house or a flat without a high risk of being seen. There was also no bruising or marking to indicate this had happened.

Nothing about this poor woman or the scene of her disposal signalled a long-drawn-out, control-based interaction with her killer. Instead, the hallmarks of her death were scornfully indifferent expediency and anger.

Her murderer may have thought this way about her, but I didn't and neither did David Cox. One way or another, she was going to tell us who did this.

How does a woman get herself into a situation where she could just disappear from a community and have nobody report her missing?

The answer lay within the parameters of my clinical practice and the women who were sent to me by the courts, or defence solicitors, or sometimes by an alert GP. They came because they had attacked a man, or another girl, or had begun to lose touch with their young child. They were prostitutes.

The lives of such women usually have only a very loose structure. They move around – often staying one week in Kings Cross and the next in Balsall Heath in Birmingham, or Hillfields in Coventry. They disappear from an area for days or weeks at a time and then re-surface again. Some drift out of prostitution and try to get a normal job but eventually find their way back onto the streets again.

The murder victim had sex frequently, and just before she died. The intercourse had not been forced. She was killed soon afterwards and dumped on a roadside verge in an area where nobody knew her. Despite a nationwide search, nobody anywhere had reported her missing.

All of this strongly suggested that she was a prostitute.

If this girl worked as a prostitute, then it was at the lower end of the scale – on the streets, in cars and from motorway service stations. At the other end of the scale, high-class call-girls and escorts can earn as much as professional athletes. They have the looks and bodies of glamour models and actresses and they can pass in glittering company without causing embarrassment. These women don't just sell sex – they sell a fantasy.

By comparison, the woman found in Woodby Lane was significantly overweight for her height. She had a long-standing, uncorrected dental problem that affected her appearance. Her hair wasn't particularly well cut, or cared for with costly conditioners and treatments.

Her complexion hadn't been well looked after by a regime of skin-care products and her fingernails and toenails weren't manicured.

Her make-up was inexpensive and applied without a great deal of subtlety or care. This was in keeping with her overall presentation.

This woman – as harsh as it may sound – did not sell dreams or fantasies. She was merely a facility for sex. She was also careless enough to allow a man who paid for sex at this level to have intercourse without wearing a condom. Girls who work at the higher end of the market tend to be more careful.

How did this particular woman find her level in prostitution? I suspect because she wouldn't have been able to establish herself in a different career. I knew that she had never given birth, so she wasn't left with a child and no other means of support.

Perhaps an unscrupulous boyfriend had wooed her into the job, or a girlfriend had shown her the ropes. She would have been easy to exploit, particularly by people who lived in the same social stratum.

She would be of no more than average intelligence, perhaps a little below, given her inattention to her over-all self-care. Her schooling would have been indifferent. She would be from a working-class family who hadn't been able to compensate for her lack of achievement and poor prospects. Nor could they stop her becoming a prostitute.

A day later, I presented my analysis to David Cox and his senior colleagues. We met in a hot and stuffy room at the new force headquarters on the western edge of Leicester.

As I finished the briefing I asked if there were any questions.

'You're sure she was a prostitute?' asked David.

'As sure as I can be with the information available.'

'And you think she's a traveller, not a local girl?'

'Yes. You'd know her if she was local.'

'So where is she from?'

'I would look at the red-light areas and big motorway service centres with established prostitution. Focus on those areas within an hour or so of Bitteswell. Whoever killed her didn't put her out for display. He dumped her for his own preservation. He wanted to get her a good way off from where he picked her up because he knows that makes it harder for you to trace him. But there's a limit to how long he's willing to drive about with a dead woman in his vehicle. He also had to strip her somewhere en route. That's not easy in a car. I'd say an hour or so – depending on the traffic and the weather. You're probably looking at a radius of fifty miles.'

'Birmingham?' asked a detective.

'Could be. It might be Coventry, Northampton or Nottingham – anywhere with an established red-light area that's also close to trunk roads or the motorways.'

After the briefing David Cox asked if I'd prepare a psychological offender profile of the killer. In the meantime, the murder squad had been following up on the scant number of leads.

Two people, passing in a car, had seen a middle-aged man on the grass verge near Bitteswell Football Club just over an hour before the body was discovered. He was described as being in his forties or fifties, with greying hair and a short-sleeved shirt. He looked either lost or agitated.

The police had been door to door in the area and set up a mobile incident room to question motorists. At the same time, a sketch of the victim was released to the media and printed on a poster.

Despite these efforts, the body still hadn't been identified by 10 March – a week after its discovery. A new artist's impression was prepared, in colour, using a hairdresser and a beautician to give advice on how the victim looked in life.

The impression was shown nationally on GMTV. On the same day an advertisement was placed in the *Sun* newspaper, accompanied by a story asking for public help in identifying the woman. The police revealed that she might have been a prostitute from the Black Country, who worked in the Birmingham or Wolverhampton areas.

Within hours came the breakthrough that David Cox and his team had been hoping for. A family in Stafford saw the artist's impression on TV and thought they recognized the woman. A short time later, police sealed off a nearby flat-fronted terrace cottage.

The victim had a name – Tracy Lyn Turner, aged thirty. She was a prostitute who worked out of motorway service stations and lorry stops, mainly in North London. She was last seen alive at 4.30 p.m. on 2 March, plying for trade on the southbound slip road of a service station on the M6 near Birmingham. Earlier that day she had withdrawn money from a building society and gone shopping.

Tracy was almost totally deaf and relied on an amplifier aid about the size of a personal stereo. There was no sign of it in her house, or where the body had been found.

Cox and his team now had a new challenge – to piece together all they could about Tracy's lifestyle and movements. Did she have regular clients? Who were her friends? Where did she normally work? What were her hours? Did she offer any specialist sexual services?

My role in the murder inquiry was only just starting. I now had to draw up a psychological profile of the killer, telling the police all that I could about him.

He was out there somewhere, remembering what he had done. Although he had taken a risk, he felt good. They wouldn't catch him. The slag had wanted her money, but he'd had her for free. Then he showed her what he thought of her kind. That's the good thing about slags – they know their place and there are always plenty more.

I didn't know this man's name or address, but I had met others exactly like him during consultations. I had examined their minds and listened to their rationalizations and their deviant fantasies.

Sadly, I had also interviewed women like Tracy. There is a stereotyped image in the public's mind whenever the word 'prostitute' is mentioned. People are very quick to jump to conclusions. I make no such judgements. There may be similarities in their occupation and background, but each prostitute is a separate and unique human being. They are someone's daughter, sister, niece, wife or mother.

Yet the sad reality is that most of them suffer dreadful experiences in their daily lives. Prostitutes, as a group, make up the largest number of unsolved murder cases in Britain. I can vouch for this because I've seen more dead prostitutes than I care to remember.

I sometimes ask myself how I ended up where I am, doing what I do.

When I started my career as a clinical psychologist, I had no idea that I'd eventually spend my spare time studying post-mortem photographs and walking murder scenes. My real work is about picking up the pieces of damaged lives and trying to make people whole again.

When I told police the true nature of Frederick and Rosemary West and that Tracy Turner was a prostitute, I could do so because I had seen people with very similar lives in my consulting room – where I gathered my knowledge of human behaviour and psychological functioning.

It is where my story has to start . . .

1

'Mum isn't here. I can't find her. I keep looking.'

'Where is she?'

'I don't know.'

'Is she far away?'

'No. She should be here. I want her.'

'Tell me about your mother.'

He didn't answer immediately. His eyes were closed and the tempo of his breathing had changed slightly. Fingernails dug sharply into the palms of his hands.

'We go on picnics to Stratford-upon-Avon and eat sandwiches by the river and drink orange squash. My brother and me dangle our feet in the water and watch the bubbles where the fish are feeding.

'After lunch, Mum lies back in a deckchair and has her "forty winks" but I don't think she really sleeps. Sometimes I lay my head on her lap and look up at the sky through the leaves. I like that.

'In the afternoon we buy ice creams. I choose strawberry but Tom always has chocolate. You should see his face afterwards. Mum has to spit on a handkerchief and wipe his chin and his cheeks.'

'What day do you go?'

'Sunday. School the next day.'

'Do you like school?'

'I guess.' He shrugged ambivalently.

'What are your best lessons?'

'English.'

'Who's your teacher?'

'Mrs Jenkins.'

'What is she like?'

'Nice. She's always nice. She doesn't shout or get uptight.'

'What about your friends?'

'No, I haven't really got any. Not many.'

'What do you do at playtime?'

'Ordinary stuff. Sometimes there's a fight.'

'What about after school?'

'I stay out as much as possible. I don't go home.'

'Why?'

'I just don't. I go looking for Mum.'

'Why? Where is she?'

'She should be there. I want her to be . . .'

'Does she have a job?'

'Um . . . I don't think so.'

'When do you go home? You can't stay out all day.'

'No.'

'What happens?'

'It's dark inside. I don't like it.'

'What do you do?'

'I try to go to my room. I want to get to my room.'

'What's in your room?'

'Maybe I'll be OK then. Maybe I can go to sleep.'

'It's a bit early to go to sleep.'

'Yeah, I know. I'm frightened. I want Mum.'

'And . . . ?'

'I just want her.'

'But she's not there, you say. Isn't there anybody else to look after you?'

'He's there . . .' His voice shook, and his face had become pale and strained. A long pause followed. Every muscle seemed tense as he sat forward in the chair, but still he wouldn't open his eyes.

'I'm scared. I can hear his footsteps on the stairs. I know he's coming.'

'What happens?'

'The door opens and he's standing there. I'm in the corner. He grabs me by the hair and puts his face up against mine. I can see the spit in the corners of his mouth. "Where is she?" he says. "Where is the bitch?"

' "I don't know, Dad. Don't call her that."

' "Ah, yes, you do know. Where is she? Whose bed is she in now?"

' "No, Dad. She wouldn't . . ."

' "Why are you covering for her, you little bastard? They're all the same – you'll see! Where is she?"

' "I don't—"

' "Lying little bastard!"

' "Please no, Dad, don't hit me."

' "Come with me." He drags me by the hair along the hallway to their bedroom. My head is twisted back so I can only see the ceiling and I have to walk on tiptoes so he doesn't tear my hair out. He shoves me towards the bed and throws back the bedclothes.

'He screams, "Look at it!" I don't know what I'm supposed to do. "Look at what that disgusting slut has left behind!"

'He forces my face against the mattress. What should I see?

' "Smell that! Where is the bitch?"

' "I don't know. Please. I want my mum."

34

'He forces me down and locks my head between his knees. Then he starts hitting me with his belt. "WHERE IS SHE?"

' "I don't know. I don't know."

' "You're not even mine, you little bastard. What do you think of that? Ask the bitch about your father. She won't even remember."

' "No. No."

' "Where is she? You're shielding her. You didn't come home from school because you were out running a message for her."

' "No."

' "Where were you?"

' "Nowhere."

' "Liar!" '

This final accusation echoed off my consulting-room walls. Ray Knox cowered in his chair, as if trying to become smaller. His head had dropped almost apologetically and his voice had trailed off. Slowly he dissolved into tears. I didn't see them. He didn't raise his face. But I watched him wipe them away with his shirtsleeve, as children often do.

Without warning, his eyes snapped open as if spring-loaded. On his feet, he spun away from the desk with clenched fists. Every bit of power in his six-foot frame was put behind the punch. It smashed into the side of a filing cabinet, buckling the metal.

'My life was ruined by that fucking abuser,' he announced in a quiet voice that was nevertheless filled with a driving energy.

The statement seemed to hang in the air between us, as though he'd issued a challenge.

His face was contorted by grief, but his eyes were blazing. He challenged me to contradict him.

35

'Don't you believe me? Don't you believe what I'm saying? Every word of it is true.'

'I can see what it's done to you.'

'And it doesn't matter that he's an old man now. Justice isn't only for the young. You won't talk me out of it. He has to die.'

Outside the sun had turned the parked cars into ovens and the newly surfaced road had become a sticky pudding of tar and gravel. Heat reflected against the windows, and the inside walls were warm to the touch.

I don't particularly enjoy the summer. On hot days I can almost feel the energy being sapped out of me and a headache waiting to happen. The glare hurts my eyes and the mandatory suit, collar and tie only make it worse.

The police have often told me how the heat affects the crime rate, and I've seen it reflected in my own case records. On hot days patience wears thin and tempers fray easily. Overheated motorists hammer steering wheels and patrons stumble out of pubs having had too much to drink.

Raymond Chandler described it best when he wrote about 'those hot dry Santa Anas that come down through the mountain passes and curl your hair and make your nerves jump and your skin itch. On nights like that every booze party ends in a fight. Meek little wives feel the edge of the carving knife and study their husbands' necks. Anything can happen.'

Ray's chair had toppled backwards and now lay on its side. Someone had stuck chewing gum to the bottom. It neatly punctuated a stencilled notice warning of the fire dangers of the foam padding.

The outpatient clinic was in an old schoolhouse, now

used by the local health authority. On the wall it still had a picture of the Queen that must have gazed down upon generations of youngsters.

The consulting room was a good size, with two windows side by side. It overlooked a small garden in which rose bushes were now competing with dandelions for space. Maintenance budgets didn't stretch to hiring a full complement of gardeners. The money was needed elsewhere.

In the distance I could see Portakabins on a building site and the darkened brick of an incinerator chimney that was soon to be demolished. It would no doubt make the evening news. The public has a morbid fascination with seeing things blown up. Someone has probably written a psychological thesis on the subject.

Ray righted his chair and self-consciously sat down. He glanced fleetingly at the filing cabinet and then lowered his eyes. If his punch had landed a fraction nearer to the drawer he'd have broken every knuckle in his fist.

Above his head the ceiling was decorated with plaster squares, each divided by metal strips. A fluorescent light sat in the centre. As with all of my consulting rooms this one was purely functional. There were no decorations or surplus furnishings. A desk, two chairs, a clock, blotter, foolscap pad, case file and a few pens were all I needed. The filing cabinet was optional – particularly now.

A neutral room is like a blank canvas. There was nothing to distract a patient. I work to create a timeless, placeless environment where a patient can eventually relax and talk.

A room such as this may well say something about my working principles. There are no family photographs, books, magazines or diplomas. I don't wear a wedding ring or an old school tie. Nothing that can give any notion of what I might be like. Preconceptions create problems that colour how easily I can establish a rapport with a weary or distressed patient.

Suppose, for example, I had a golfing trophy on my desk. (It's hardly likely, I can promise you.) A patient arrives who was never very good at sport. Perhaps they were mocked or ridiculed at school for their lack of ability. They were always the last to be chosen for teams and were belittled by coaches. They spent years finding excuses to avoid gym and swimming practice.

Now, as they walk into my consulting room, they see a trophy. What do they think? How do they react towards me? It's another hurdle to get across that shouldn't be there.

Ray opened and closed his fist, wincing slightly. Thin white scars ran along the back of his hand. These were knife cuts, possibly self-inflicted. They were likely to cause pain rather than long-term injury. At some point I would have to ask him about them, but that could wait.

For the moment, I had to make sure he was functioning properly before he left the outpatient clinic. I had ten minutes before the next patient was due.

'Is your hand OK?'

He nodded.

'Do you want a few moments?'

'No. I'm OK.'

He moved slowly now. The explosion of anger had drained his energy. Grey flecks of paint from the filing cabinet dusted his knuckles.

His black hair had been combed across his scalp and

edged down his cheeks as sideburns. In his early forties, Ray was above average height and had a physical self-assurance that showed in the way he moved.

He wore a checked shirt with the sleeves rolled up above his elbows and a pair of trousers that stretched beneath the beginnings of a paunch.

I had met Ray Knox only forty minutes earlier. All I knew of him came from a referral letter from his doctor. Apparently he had complained of feeling depressed, stressed and 'out of control'. When asked to explain, he said, 'I think I might hurt someone.'

The local GP wasted no time in passing the case along. Clearly, Ray wasn't the sort of patient a doctor wanted in a crowded waiting room of young mothers and distracted children. It was also impossible to assess such a problem in the eight or ten minutes a GP allocates to each patient.

The case had been referred to the forensic psychology service at its central base in Leicester. According to the referral letter, Ray had seen two psychiatrists over the previous three years. In each case they had vaguely described the problem as a 'difficulty with managing anger'. This covered a huge range of possibilities and was like pointing to a group of haystacks knowing only one of them held the needle.

Despite his own fears, Ray had no recorded history of trouble with the police or of violence. No complaint had ever been made against him. At first glance, I doubted if he'd ever incurred so much as a speeding ticket.

Like any new patient on a first visit, he had seemed slightly self-conscious. He wanted immediate answers or hoped that I could put a hand on his head or give him a pill that would instantly make him better.

Clinical psychologists can't work like this and I had tried to explain that to him at the outset.

'There are two things I need to know, Ray. Who you are. And how you came to be who you are. These are two very general questions but out of them we will learn everything else. We'll discover if you have a clinical problem and whether or not I can do anything to help.'

He nodded.

'So tell me, what brings you to see me?'

Ray pressed his palms against his knees. 'Doesn't the doctor say?'

'I do have a referral letter, but I'd prefer to hear it from you.'

'Well, I'm just depressed. I wake up OK, but then I get bad during the day.'

'What happens?'

'I just feel bad.'

Ray struggled to tell me his thoughts. Partly this came from wariness. He avoided answering even the simplest questions about what was going on in his life. At the same time he put up a wall of measured pleasantness.

In many instances, this first telling of the present-day difficulty is the hardest part of the first consultation. It means establishing trust very early.

Slowly, I managed to glean some details of his life. Ray worked in a brewery moving barrels. He didn't drink – he'd given up four years earlier, although he didn't say why.

'I used to be pretty sociable and outgoing,' he said. 'But I don't feel like it any more. I don't go out. I'm missing days at work. My wife . . .' The sentence trailed off.

'What about your wife?'

'She's wonderful. She's been really patient with me. I'm a lucky man.'

'Do you have any children?'

'Two girls. Julie is thirteen and Rita is ten.'

'The referral letter suggests that you have aggressive feelings.'

'Yeah. I lose my temper.'

'How often does that happen?'

'I don't know really.'

'When was the last time?'

He shrugged.

'So what makes you feel you're going to lose your temper?'

'It's hard to explain. It's just a feeling I get.'

'Tell me about it.'

Again, he struggled to find the words.

Despite his defensiveness, I could see that Ray wanted to engage. Nobody had forced him to come and see me. The courts or the probation service hadn't stipulated he attend. It had been his own choice.

'Tell me about your mum,' I asked.

'She must be in her sixties now.'

'What sort of woman is she?'

'I don't know really . . . I haven't seen her for a long time.'

His voice hadn't faltered, but I could see the tension in his forearms. Physical signs like this are important to a psychologist. Sometimes they tell me just as much as the words spoken by a patient.

'What about when you were little? Was she at work, or at home?'

'Well, it's difficult to say.'

'Why is it difficult? What about your dad? Were you all at home together?'

41

Ray shifted uneasily in his chair and glanced out of the window. His hands were pressing hard on his knees, as though he was forcing himself to stay seated.

I kept probing – asking simple questions about his childhood.

'Where did you grow up?'

'Reading, in Berkshire.'

'Any brothers or sisters?'

'No.'

'What sort of work did your dad do?'

Ray's jaw tightened. He didn't want to answer. I could see a man who was used to holding things away, but I was giving him only two options. He could either say, 'I can't do this,' and walk away; or he could stay with it and let me help him.

Easing the pressure slightly, I changed the subject.

'So tell me more about your mum.'

'What's to tell?'

'You haven't said if she went out to work.'

'Maybe she did.'

He was still trying very hard to hold the door closed on me. But each time he answered a simple question, I pushed it open a crack. I asked him about his father again, probing gently. From being slightly ajar the door suddenly swung open.

In just a few moments I witnessed a transformation. I no longer had a forty-year-old man in front of me. Ray was a little boy again. He was back there, cowering on the floor of his parents' bedroom, feeling the blows and hearing the abuse. He held his arms over his head and pleaded his innocence.

This man had a remarkable ability to visualize scenes internally. He wasn't simply describing events in the past tense or in the abstract. He was back there,

42

reliving them; feeling his face pushed into the bedsheets and seeing the spittle in the corner of his father's mouth. The sounds, colours, smells and sensations were as real to him as they had been over thirty years earlier.

Then came the explosion of rage that nearly destroyed my filing cabinet. The small boy had become a man again – a tortured individual who believed his father deserved to die.

The childhood scene that Ray described wasn't based on an isolated beating. A child has to learn to be that afraid. Instead, everything pointed to a violent, unpredictable father who had battered and tormented his son for years.

'Whose bed is she in now?' his father had screamed. 'You're not even mine, you little bastard!'

Thirty years on and the injured little boy was now a damaged man. What had he shouted? 'My life was ruined by that fucking abuser! . . . You won't talk me out of it. He has to die.'

People say things in the heat of the moment. They get angry and make groundless threats or empty promises. Was this Ray? Is this what he meant by losing his temper? Were these the 'aggressive urges' mentioned in the referral letter?

If so, I asked myself, why now?

Despite a brutal childhood, Ray had obviously managed to put a reasonable life together. He seemed to be happily married, with two children he loved, a secure job and a house. What had happened to upset this so suddenly?

'Can you give me an example of when you lose your temper?'

'You've just seen one.'

'Another example.'

43

He described an incident that had happened the previous week. He and his wife had been having a coffee at a café when a couple of young lads wrestled open the door and loudly jostled their way inside.

They were brash and self-confident, bantering with the middle-aged owner, who admonished them for being so noisy and disruptive. The youths, perhaps recognizing a figure of authority, gave way and left.

Ray didn't hear the actual conversation. He didn't have to.

'I just sort of snapped. I lost it. One second I'm sitting having coffee and the next I'm on my feet screaming at this bloke behind the counter. I wanted to rip his heart out.'

'Why?'

'He was throwing his weight around. How dare he treat those lads like that! Who died and made him God? They were only fooling around. I wanted to hit him. If Stella hadn't been there, I mean, I don't know what would have happened . . .'

'Do you know why you reacted like that?'

'No.'

'Has that sort of thing happened before?'

'A few times.'

'When?'

'In the past couple of years. That's about when my behaviour started.'

'What do you mean when you say "my behaviour"?'

'The pictures in my head. The thoughts.'

'Tell me about the pictures.'

He looked at me nervously. He didn't know whether to say anything more.

'What is it about these thoughts and pictures that worries you?'

44

His voice dropped to a whisper. 'The violence.'

Ray might not have been particularly well educated but he was bright enough to realize that having violent thoughts was unhealthy. But he didn't know what they meant. Did they make him another Frederick West? Would he be locked up for telling me? I didn't know what they meant yet either; 'violent' covers a wide area.

He pulled back and I looked at the clock. Our time was up. It wouldn't be appropriate to press now.

'I hope you'll come and see me next week, Ray.'

'What's wrong with me?' he asked imploringly.

'We've only just started talking. I don't know enough about you yet, or how you came to get here. That's why I want you to come back again.'

He nodded and stood slowly. His muscles had been so taut that they had locked up.

After he'd gone, I made more notes on a foolscap pad. There was something about Ray that worried me. Initially I'd struggled to put my finger on the problem. Then I understood that he had an ambivalent quality; he seemed to be able to separate himself from his actions.

Everything I'd seen and he'd told me suggested that his behaviour and personality might oscillate between extremes. Did that make him a potentially or a truly violent man?

It was too early to tell.

2

Soon after joining the Leicestershire District Psychology Service in 1978, I was politely shanghaied into teaching an adult education class at Daventry, a small town in Northamptonshire. On the first night I arrived feeling incredibly nervous and daunted. I hadn't done much public speaking.

What am I going to tell them? I thought, as I sought refuge in the toilet.

I had never had any desire to teach, yet there I was fresh out of university, with the ink still drying on my degree, having agreed to present an introductory course in psychology. What would they expect? What would happen if I just went home?

At three minutes to eight, I realized that I couldn't stay in the men's room for ever. With a deep breath that did nothing for my fraught nerves, I walked into the classroom, wrote my name on the blackboard and then turned to see about twenty expectant faces. There were men and women, young, old and middle-aged, all with their eyes focused on me.

Is my voice going to work, I wondered.

'Good evening. My name is Paul Britton and I'm a psychologist. I work in the National Health Service.

Have any of you ever had any previous experience or contact with psychology or psychologists?'

The silence that followed threatened to become embarrassing until a young woman near the front said that she'd read several books. This prompted a few others to nod their heads.

'Would anyone risk giving us an idea of what psychology is?' I asked.

A stillness descended and I could hear the shuffling of feet beneath chairs. My hope to ease my own anxiety by getting the class involved straight away didn't seem to be working. I tried once more. 'It's not a trick question or a test. I just want to know what you think psychology is. What is it about?'

None of the class knew each other, which made it difficult to break the ice. Moreover they were there for different reasons. Some, I discovered, passionately wanted to learn more about psychology or wanted to go on and study it further, while others were there because it was a pleasant way to spend an evening, or because they couldn't get into some other class next door.

'It's about people,' said a woman, about forty-five years old, in a linen jacket.

I wrote the word '*people*' on the blackboard beneath the heading '*Psychology*'.

'It's about knowing how to get people to do what you want,' said another woman who had moved her chair closer to the radiator.

I scribbled, '*Getting people to do what we want.*'

Thoughts and ideas now came in a steady flow.

'It's about analysing your dreams and subconscious thoughts.'

'*Analysing dreams.*'

47

'And knowing what people are thinking by looking at their faces.'

'*Analysing body language.*'

'It helps us understand why we do the things we do.'

'*Human behaviour.*'

A young woman with braided hair added, 'And it helps us understand children so we can be better parents.'

I didn't comment on any of these ideas, but simply wrote them on the board.

Eventually, I put down the chalk. 'Well, I can tell you that not one of these suggestions covers it all, except perhaps "*Human behaviour*". Yet every one of them does have something to do with psychology.'

Instead of giving the class a definition, I began to write headings on the blackboard.

'This is what we'll be talking about over the next twelve weeks,' I said, continuing to write. 'People tend to assume that psychology is simply about helping people in the consulting room, without perhaps realizing that there is an enormous submerged iceberg of knowledge that must be dealt with first. They fail to appreciate that the basics – the scientific, experimental and theoretical work done at universities and in research departments – provide the foundation upon which clinical, forensic, organizational and all the other psychological specialities are built.'

Human Learning.
Developmental Psychology.
Memory.
Motivation.
Emotion.
Personality.

48

The Brain and Nervous System.
Social Behaviour.
Research and Statistics.
The World of Work.
Clinical Problems and Treatments – Anxiety, Phobias,
Sexual Difficulties, Anger, Depression and Mental
Illness.
Romance, Dating and General Social Skills.

As soon as I wrote the word 'statistics', the noise level increased.

'I'm no good at maths. I can't do maths,' said the woman in the linen jacket.

'Me neither. I didn't know we needed that,' echoed an intense man in his early twenties.

'Relax, you don't have to be mathematicians,' I re-assured them. 'But you do need to understand how psychological work is conducted and evaluated.'

The experimental study of the human mind is now 130 years old yet it remains largely uncharted. We are unlikely ever to understand it all because the parameters are so broad and encompass everything we do and say; all that has gone before and is still to come in our knowledge of the world and human behaviour.

There have been times when this exploration and experimentation has been rather hit and miss. A lecturer of mine once explained the origins of Electro Convulsive Therapy (ECT) or electric shock treatment.

Many years ago, mental health scientists observed pigs being electrocuted during slaughter. Every so often the power supply varied and some of the pigs survived the electric shock. These animals seemed to be energized and boisterous.

49

The scientists began pondering whether a small electrical charge applied to the heads of very depressed patients might revitalize them.

After a period of trial and error, ECT became widely used across the Western world. It is still used today as a frightening and last-resort treatment for otherwise intractable mental illness. Its decline has been the result of dramatic progress in drug development and also strong opposition from families of patients who became aware of the negative side effects. These included interference with memory and the patient's sense of independence.

This major psychiatric intervention was used for decades without anybody really understanding how it worked. Of course electricity wasn't a mystery, but nobody understood the gross (let alone the detailed) connection between brain function and the mind. How did the electricity revitalize a patient? What happened inside their head?

When brain experts describe how the mind works, they tend to use models based on the technology of the day. Once they talked of mechanics, fluids and 'humours'. Now they refer to circuit boards, processors and neural networks.

I told my class of students to imagine the mind as being like a fishing net formed by a matrix of hundreds of lines with thousands of knots connecting them. Any single knot may be interesting in itself, but if you try to pick it up, all the others come with it. They are all interconnected and you can't truly understand any single knot unless you understand the principles of those around it. That's what makes psychology so fascinating. It's like having a three-dimensional map that you journey upon and through.

According to biologists there are more potential connections between the cells in a single brain than there are stars in the universe. The identification and understanding of what flows from these connections will not be achieved in my lifetime or that of my children; however, the quest is still exhilarating.

After an hour we had a coffee break and then spent the rest of the evening looking at different models and the various approaches to psychology. From the very beginning I tried to balance the lectures with exercises that got the whole class involved.

This started out as a way to ease my own performance anxiety, yet had the effect of galvanizing the whole group so that they grew very committed and excited. It became a challenge for me to keep up with their desire to learn more.

The enthusiasm of beginners is infectious and during those weeks I was often reminded of why I chose a career in psychology. It had been only a handful of years since I too was a beginner.

In the autumn of 1972 I was working as an export liaison officer at Automotive Products, a motor-car parts company in Leamington Spa. The job was reasonably demanding, but it didn't excite me. Nor was it something I imagined doing for the rest of my life.

Psychology fascinated me, but I knew only a limited amount about it. The parameters seemed so broad and challenging that I'd never grow bored or run out of things to investigate.

At the same time I had a wife, a mortgage and two children under the age of five. I also had no O-levels or A-levels – hardly the ideal preparation for higher education.

I left school with none of the badges that most people collect. After the age of eleven I was sent to a secondary modern school, which didn't prepare children for tertiary education. Despite this, I always wanted to go to university. I just had to find a way.

While working full time, I started an O-level course in the same sort of adult education centre that I later lectured in. I sat the exams in the summer of 1973 and then began studying for my A-levels, cramming two years' worth of learning into less than a year.

In 1974, at the age of twenty-eight, I gained a place at Warwick University to study management science. A month after I started, a separate psychology department was established and I was able to transfer across.

For the next three years we lived frugally, surviving on a student grant. I'm still amazed at how far Marilyn could make so little money stretch.

After graduating with a First, I accepted an advanced postgraduate studentship at Leicester University. Soon afterwards I became an unpaid trainee clinical psychologist with the Leicester Health Authority, the largest in the country. By the time I began lecturing in Daventry, I had started working in a full-time post at Carlton Hayes Psychiatric Hospital in Narborough, Leicestershire – a large Edwardian hospital that had been built as the county asylum in 1905.

The psychology department was set away from the main hospital buildings in the former Medical Superintendent's house. Known as The Rosings, this was a two-storey red-brick house with a large bay window overlooking a small stone terrace.

My day-to-day work centred on assessing and treating people who were damaged by unfortunate events in their lives. Some suffered recurring nightmares or acute anxiety. Others had sexual problems or personality disorders. People couldn't sleep, or stop cleansing, or bring themselves to walk out of their front door to post a letter.

There were patients with psychosomatic complaints – genuine bodily symptoms, such as limb paralysis, visual impairment or disabling skin conditions – that had psychological origins. Others came with exotic illnesses and disorders that doctors had failed to diagnose.

One of my patients thought he was paralysed. Another poor woman couldn't go anywhere without having to rush off to the toilet.

I had two interview rooms during my time at The Rosings. One of them had probably been a bathroom in a former life and still had white tiles on the walls and a window so high up that it offered no view other than of passing clouds.

Patients waited wherever they could sit down, usually on a chair in the secretary's office outside.

I was at the beginning, finding my way, and it was amazing to see the textbooks and lectures come to life. With each new patient who arrived in my consulting room, I learned a little bit more about human functioning and motivation.

If I was concerned about reaching a wrong conclusion, I could always find a more senior psychologist and ask advice. Far more worrying was the possibility that I might not *know* that I had it wrong.

One of my first cases involved a young married woman in her late twenties who came to see me suffering from anxiety problems. Claire Brooks was a pretty woman, of medium height, with hair down to her shoulders and not a strand out of place. Everything about her presentation showed neatness and care. Her shoes gleamed and her blouse and skirt were precisely ironed, without so much as a button loose or a thread pulled.

She sat down and looked at me nervously. I began with some of the housekeeping details – name, address and date of birth. This helped us both to discover that her mouth still worked.

'Most people don't know what to expect when they come to see me for the first time,' I told her, trying to put her at ease. 'They don't know who I am or what I am going to talk about. Some try to predict what I'm going to ask them and spend time beforehand working out all the answers. Then as soon as they sit down and I ask them to tell me something about the problem, their minds go blank. It's as though I've wiped a blackboard duster through their heads.'

Claire's hands were pressed tightly into her lap and she smiled weakly.

'Sometimes they're anxious that I'm going to ask them all sorts of terrible questions. I hope I'm not – at least not today. First I want to find out about you and what has brought you here. Then we'll decide how to take things forward.'

She nodded.

'I have a letter from your GP with some sketchy details but I'd prefer it if you'd tell me, in your own words, how you come to be here.'

'Well, my doctor sent me along.'

'Yes.'

'I haven't been able to sleep and the sleeping pills don't seem to help.'

'Are there any other problems?'

'Well, sometimes I get all panicky and . . . frightened.'

'Exactly what feelings do you have?'

I wanted her to relate the physical symptoms so I could be sure they were applicable to anxiety and not something else. She described heart palpitations and feelings of closing and tightening in her throat. Her hands would perspire and the light seemed to grow dimmer.

As Claire straightened in her chair, she quickly put her hands in the pockets of her cardigan. Very briefly I glimpsed the raw, inflamed skin on her fingers.

'What do you feel anxious about?'

She bit her bottom lip, leaving a carmine mark on the skin. 'Well, I'm frightened of someone breaking into the house.'

'Has that happened before?'

'No.'

'Do you live in an area where it happens often?'

'No, not really. The village is really nice. I can't remember even a bicycle being stolen since we moved in seven years ago.'

'When do you get worried about someone breaking in?'

'At night mainly.'

'What do you do?'

'Well, I go around the house and check all the doors and windows are locked.'

'And then?'

'Well, then I double-check them.'

'How many times?'

'I know it sounds silly, but I want to make sure we are safe,' she said.

'OK. And how many times do you check the locks now?'

She smoothed the front of her dress. 'Nine.'

'Doesn't that seem to be quite a few?'

'I just want to be sure I haven't missed any.'

'And how do you check them?'

'I start downstairs and I do the windows in the lounge first, then I check the patio doors, the dining room, the kitchen . . .' She described the circuit of the house.

'What happens when you finish?'

'I do it again to make sure.'

'What happens if you don't do this nine times?'

'Oh, I always do. Otherwise I couldn't sleep. I'd be too worried.'

'But you're not sleeping anyway?'

'No.'

This level of obsessional behaviour is odd, but normally isn't a great problem. Far worse for Claire were the washing rituals. They had begun with cleaning her hands in the kitchen sink and developed into an elaborate routine where each finger had to be washed and the nail carefully cleaned before being dried in a precise order.

The hand-washing had built up into full bathing which happened six times a day. Again, the ritualized nature of the washing meant that soap *had* to be applied so many times and parts of her body cleaned in a particular order. It was classic obsessive-compulsive behaviour.

'Can you make me better?' Claire asked.

'How do you think I might do that?'

'Well, I don't know, maybe hypnotize me. You hypnotize people, don't you?'

'Yes, I do.'

'So you'll put me under; I'll go to sleep and you'll tell me that when I wake up it will all be gone.'

'I'm afraid it doesn't work like that.'

'Well, what about different tablets?'

'They won't really take the problem away either.'

There was an uncertain pause. In common with a lot of people, Claire expected that I could give her some sort of psychological 'magic bullet' and make her well again.

'In order to help you, I have to know the cause of the problem,' I told her. 'And that means asking a lot of questions and finding out all I can about you. I'll try to be gentle and avoid asking questions that are too embarrassing, but ultimately there will almost certainly be some that are.'

I began by asking her about her present situation. Claire had been married for seven years to David, an engineer who worked for a large manufacturing company. They had a nice house in a local village, which Claire had decorated and now looked after. There were no children.

The next step was to take a detailed history of Claire's life, beginning chronologically with her childhood and her relationship with her parents. This was the standard approach I'd been taught, although sometimes things could be taken out of sequence if they came up in the free flow of conversation.

'Is your mother still alive?' I asked.

'No.'

'How long ago did you lose her?'

'Three years.'

'What happened?'

'She had cancer.'

'When you were growing up did she go out to work or stay at home?'

'She stayed at home.'

'What sort of mum was she?'

'What do you mean?'

Sometimes when I ask this question people start describing someone who is five foot tall and grey-haired.

'What was she like as a mother?'

'Good. She loved me. We were close to each other – you know how mothers are with eldest daughters.'

Although the words sounded positive and full of praise, Claire's descriptions and tone of voice were relatively neutral and almost empty. There was an absence of richness. There was no obvious reason for her to try to deceive me, but she certainly didn't want to say much about her mother.

Pressing her for more details, I reframed the question. 'I'm sure your mum was like the rest of us, we're not all perfect human beings. What about the downside, her bad points?'

After a long pause, Claire replied, 'I don't think she had any.'

'OK.'

I moved on, even though her response had been unrealistic. I could always come back to it later.

Claire described having a fairly typical relationship with her father, who doted on his children when he wasn't away working or down at the pub with his friends.

'How did your mother and father get on?'

'OK, I guess.'

'What sort of things did they argue about?'

I deliberately asked a leading question because this helped Claire to understand that even the most loving couples had occasional rows. If I had asked, 'Did your mother and father ever argue?' she would probably have said, 'No.'

Most people tend to have idealized notions of family values and relationships – mother–father, parent–child, sibling–sibling. We attach importance to being seen as part of a 'good' family.

This has consequences in how we are viewed by our community; it influences jobs, the partners we choose, how we're treated by the courts and even, on occasions, where we're placed on NHS waiting lists.

Family *does* matter. For this reason, sometimes we try to convince ourselves that even if we are imperfect our families aren't. We put forward their strengths and ignore or reduce their weaknesses.

We don't talk about their bad points for fear of being disloyal or bringing shame to the family. Usually this has a positive binding effect on the group, but it's also an important reason why abuse can go on inside a family for years before anyone outside discovers the truth.

I'm not suggesting that Claire had been the victim of abuse. The family life she described seemed to be quite nurturing and child-centred. So far nothing had emerged that could explain her anxiety and obsessional behaviour. However, it was still early days.

At our second consultation, a week later, the history-taking continued. We talked about her education; how she coped academically; her best subjects and worst subjects; high points and low points; ambitions and achievements.

Again, nothing out of the ordinary emerged. There were no obvious problem areas, such as truancy, mis-behaviour or bullying.

I moved on to her occupational history, talking about her various jobs. She'd trained as a nurse and become a day-carer for the elderly. When she married she gave up work.

Claire had started to relax and become accustomed to the fine detail I wanted. I knew this would help when I moved her on to more sensitive areas such as her sexual history and relationships.

'How old were you when you had your first boyfriend?' I asked.

'I'm not sure what you mean,' Claire said. 'When I was nine I had a little boy who was my best friend at school. I had my first proper boyfriend when I was fifteen.'

'Tell me about that.'

'He played soccer with my older brother and went to the boys' school. I used to watch him play on a Saturday morning and afterwards we'd go to the pictures.'

'How long were you together?'

'About six months.'

'How serious was it?'

She laughed. 'At the time it felt like true love.'

'Was it a fully intimate relationship?'

'Heavens, no.'

'What about serious boyfriends after that?'

'One or two.'

'When did you first have a completely intimate relationship?'

Her hands nervously stroked and flattened the fabric of her dress on her thighs. 'With my husband. He was . . . ah . . . the first.'

'How old were you?'

'Nineteen.'

'What sort of difficulties were there?'

'What do you mean?'

'Well, sometimes the early attempts can be quite difficult or painful.'

60

'No, it was OK.'

'And since then how have things been?'

She shrugged.

'Most people in long-term relationships find an occasional sexual hiccup along the way. What about you?'

Claire shook her head a little too insistently.

I pressed her gently. 'It may be that one partner likes to have sex much more often than the other. Or perhaps one of you would like to try new things and experiment a little more in the bedroom. Not every partner feels comfortable with this. Sometimes people like to play all sorts of games; to wear different clothes, or role-play, or try different positions or locations; some like oral sex and others don't . . .'

I watched Claire's reaction closely.

'. . . or sometimes people feel they need to change their sexual partner because they don't feel they're happy with one person. Perhaps somebody new arrives in their life and they find themselves having feelings for them. They don't know quite how to deal with these, or what it means, but this person makes them feel excited and more alive . . .'

Claire looked up at me, wide-eyed. Her hands had stopped moving. She suddenly glanced down again as though frightened I would read something in her eyes.

After a long pause, she whispered, 'How did you know?'

'It happens all the time. Was it you or David who met someone else?'

'Me.' She nodded sorrowfully. 'It's finished now. Over.' She wanted to stress the point.

'Who was it?'

Claire looked at me imploringly. She didn't want to talk about it.

I waited. As the silence grew, a pressure developed. She had to say something.

'Our window cleaner,' she whispered. I almost didn't hear her.

'How did you meet him?'

'He came to clean our windows. I can't reach the ones upstairs. We have them done every two months.'

'What is his name?'

'Bill.'

'What happened?'

'I guess he flirted with me a little and I flirted back. It was harmless. I'd never done anything like that before. His van wouldn't start so I gave him a lift home. It meant he had to come back again. Then one of the skylight windows had a cracked pane and he offered to fix it. I made him a sandwich and a cup of tea. He joked about me being housebound. "Locked in my ivory tower," he said, as if I was some sort of princess. Then it just sort of happened . . .'

'What happened?'

'He kissed me. He was handing me his cup in the kitchen and he just leaned close to me. It wasn't that I let him, it just happened . . .'

'Was it just a kiss?'

Claire shook her head tearfully.

'It all sort of snowballed. I'd never met anyone like Bill; so strong and persuasive. Even as we kissed he was undoing the buttons on my blouse – right there! In the kitchen! I know I should have stopped him, but I didn't want to. A part of me did. He sort of swept me away.' Her tears were now welling, waiting to fall. 'It was stupid, stupid, stupid . . .'

'What happened afterwards?'

'He went away.'

'Did you see him again?'

She nodded. 'He would come to the house two or three times a week. It was during the day while David was at work.'

'How did you feel about Bill?'

'I loved him,' she whispered. 'Or at least I thought I did.'

'What did you find attractive about him?'

'He was so energetic and full of life. Nothing seemed to worry him – he didn't care about money, or things. "Forget lunch – let's make love," he'd say.'

'Did David find out?'

She nodded. 'I left him. Bill and I moved into a flat together about three months after we met.'

'How did you feel about that?'

'Guilty.'

'In what way?'

'Well, I left my marriage. It's supposed to be for keeps, isn't it? But Bill made me feel so young and he really wanted me.'

'And this was different to how you felt with David?'

'Yes.'

Like many women, Claire valued closeness rather than the sexual act. As she began describing her marriage there were several major distinctions between her husband and her lover. Psychologically, Bill had been much more overtly physical and direct. He enjoyed sex and it was important to him.

By contrast, David's expectations and wants were far closer to her own. He didn't seem to press his needs upon her. She appeared to have quite limited sexual experience and felt uncomfortable with variation.

Having run off with Bill, Claire discovered an enjoyment of sex that she had never realized was possible. Their lovemaking was passionate and fulfilling. She became more relaxed about experimenting with positions and playing games. As she described these changes her eyes were bright with the memory.

Life with Bill seemed to be so much more romantic, exciting and rewarding than with her husband. Yet for some reason the affair had ended. I wanted to know why, but knew the question could wait.

'When did you go back to your husband?' I asked.

Suddenly, her bodily signals began to change. She seemed to deflate slowly, shrinking before me, and her voice was tinged with a quiet distress, or a sense of resignation.

She didn't answer for a long while. She wrung her hands, as if washing them in her lap.

'How are you getting on with David?' I asked.

'It's not very nice at the moment.'

'What's happening?'

'He can be pretty horrible to me.'

'Yes?'

She stared at her hands. 'He won't let me forget what happened. He keeps bringing it up . . . you know . . . the affair. I feel bad enough already, but he seems to be almost glad. It's like a stick that he can hit me with. Not that he'd really hit me . . . not physically.'

'So what does he do?'

'He just keeps bringing it up in conversation; punishing me. I'm not blaming him. I deserve it. It's only right that he punishes me. He calls me names. I'm a "dirty bitch" and a "filthy whore". He says I only came back because I had nowhere else to go.'

'How does that make you feel?'

'Ashamed . . . Guilty.'

Claire's voice had dropped to barely a whisper. She was trying to cling to her composure. Her every movement had been studied and correct – like a dancer with a perfectly choreographed routine – but now she was struggling to keep her balance.

I decided to change the subject, easing her disquiet. The lock-checking routines and hand-washing had started after she finished the affair.

'How many times do you wash your hands during the day?'

'I don't know. I don't count.'

'Would it be once every hour, or more often than that?'

'I suppose.'

'And you've said that you take a bath five or six times a day.'

She nodded and chewed on her lip.

I knew that obsessive compulsions like this are almost always accompanied by an anxiety-related thought loop, particularly at the beginning. Eventually the rituals take on a life of their own and function independently of any initial logic or reasoning. I needed to know Claire's thought loop.

'What do you think would happen if you didn't wash your hands?'

'I always wash them.'

'Yes, but what would happen if you didn't?'

'I wouldn't.' She shook her head resolutely.

She was an intelligent woman, responding like a preadolescent. There was something she wasn't telling me; something locked up inside her.

'OK. Before you wash your hands, what are you thinking?'

'I don't know.'

'Why are you washing your hands?'

'Well, because they are dirty.'

'How long is it since you last washed your hands?'

'I'm not sure. Maybe an hour.'

'And what have you been doing in that time?'

'I don't understand the question.'

'Have you been cleaning the bathroom, or emptying the dustbins?'

'No.'

'Making pastry or cleaning shoes?'

'No. I've been here with you.'

'So how have your hands got dirty?'

'Well, they haven't really. But I'll be dirty.'

(Interestingly, she didn't say '*they* will be dirty' but '*I* will be dirty'.)

An obvious question to ask next would be: 'Why are you dirty?' but framed in such a way, it would make Claire feel foolish. She was bright enough to know that she was describing irrational actions. She didn't need me to tell her. Instead, I asked the question in a non-challenging way. 'What is it that's made you dirty?'

'I don't know. I just know that I'm not clean.'

'When you wash your hands or take a bath, does that make you clean?'

There was a resigned, disconsolate look on her face. 'Well, no, not really. I just can't stop.'

Again, everything pointed to a classic obsessive-compulsive disorder. However, other things had to be present before I could be sure. Apart from a persistent irrational urge, there had to be an ongoing attempt to resist it which failed because the urge was stronger. If Claire had washed her hands every ten minutes and made no attempt to overcome the urge, this would have suggested a delusional condition rather than an obsession. It's the same as believing you're Napoleon or continually digging up the garden because you're convinced that you'll find a pot of gold.

An important hypothesis had emerged – one that fitted a lot of the evidence quite neatly. According to Claire, her husband reminded her daily that she was 'soiled goods'. Perhaps she had come to believe this. Her washing was symbolic of her trying to become clean again.

It's a neat answer and all the pieces seemed to fit. But still I wasn't sure.

Back in the days before I became a psychologist, when I worked in a sales force, we had a motto: 'Close early, close often, close late.' It meant that no matter what happened, always try to close the deal before leaving a possible customer.

This is exactly the reverse of what I do as a clinical psychologist. You don't close early and you don't close often. Never jump to conclusions and never stop digging.

It had taken three sessions to get this far. As I wrote up my notes, I couldn't make all the pieces fit together. Something was still missing. In particular, I couldn't accept that Claire's husband's behaviour was entirely to blame for her difficulties. For one thing, it didn't explain why she left the window cleaner. Her affair seemed to be so much more romantic, exciting and rewarding than her marriage. The sex had been better than she had ever experienced. She was in love. Why did she go back?

It was a question that had to be asked carefully. I couldn't impose my own value systems upon her.

Nor could I question the wisdom of her decision. I simply wanted to understand why.

A week later, I noticed a subtle change in Claire. She had always been impeccably neat, but this time her make-up had been applied with slightly more care and there was a soft intensity in her eye contact.

'I expect you think I'm pretty immoral for having gone off with another man,' she said, tilting her head to one side.

'I'm not here to judge you.'

'So you don't think I'm a bad person?'

'Of course not.'

'Are you married, Mr Britton?' she asked. 'I hope you don't mind me asking. You don't have to answer . . .' She laughed nervously.

Her posture had altered slightly. She sat forward on her chair, leaning towards me. Her eyes watched mine.

Claire was only a few years younger than me. I could understand why the window cleaner tumbled into bed with her. I could also see why her husband would have wanted her back.

Although new to clinical psychology, I knew how easily clinical rapport could be mistaken for something more. Claire had told me the most intimate secrets of her sexuality; things she had never uttered to another soul. I had listened to her, without judging or criticizing her.

A man's ability to listen can be very attractive to a woman, particularly if she's having problems with her husband. And the same clinical rapport that encourages honesty can easily be misconstrued. That's why I had to be so careful. I didn't want Claire mistakenly hoping or believing that my interest in her went beyond being purely professional.

I'd been told stories about psychologists who had become flattered by the personal admiration of a patient. Some found themselves defending complaints from an irate husband accusing them of alienating his wife's affections. Worse still, they became involved in affairs that destroyed their careers and tainted a patient's life.

For this reason, I'd made a conscious decision never to make physical contact with a patient. No matter how distressed they became, or in need of reassurance, I wouldn't put my arm around them, or pat their hands. Physical gestures such as these can too easily be misconstrued as intimacy. Instead, I used my voice to comfort and reassure them.

Claire tried several times to ask about my wife and if I had any children. Each time, I steered her back onto her own life. When I asked about her affair with Bill, she used words like 'shame' and 'guilt'. Was it because she found sexual pleasure in it?

'It's wrong,' she said, without elaborating.

'People might feel it's wrong for different reasons. What would your feelings be?'

She thought about this for a while. I could see her slowly becoming aware that there wasn't necessarily one answer. Emotional problems rarely have a single cause. Being human is a culmination of all sorts of different inputs and influences.

'Why do you think it was wrong?' I asked again.

'I shouldn't have done it to my husband. He's a decent man – a good provider. It's not his fault if there wasn't any passion or romance between us. It's my fault.'

'Why else do you think it's wrong?'

'Well, it is not right . . .' She paused and I could see her grappling with an internal dilemma. Her hands fluttered on her lap as she locked and unlocked her painfully raw fingers. She glanced from side to side. The long silence added to her misery.

'Why?' I asked gently.

'Because I could never face my mother again,' she blurted, hiding her face in her hands.

In that instant an entirely new possibility emerged. It had been flagged way back in the first session with Claire when I asked about her mother. She had described a flawless woman with no vices, excesses or unpredictable qualities.

Now I began probing again. I needed to find out more about the value system of the mother and how much of this had been passed on to her daughter.

Claire described a true matriarch – the sort of stern figurehead who had held her family together through thick and thin; a woman who adored her children and didn't have a malicious bone in her body. At the same time, she was completely egocentric and could only accept her own interpretation and understanding of the world.

Claire's earliest memory of her mother was having her hair brushed at night.

'She used to pull it back so severely that I almost cried. "Keep your hair tidy," she'd say. "Good girls don't let their hair hang loose." She'd make me wear my school uniform four inches below my knees. She had a ruler that she used. She'd place it upright and measure. If I'd grown a little, she'd take the hem down.'

Claire's mother had been deeply religious. She taught

her daughter that God expected her to be perfect. This might sound like a fairly central and fundamental Christian belief, but it had been impressed upon Claire in a rather unthinking and rigid way. Unless she remained true to God and obeyed his teachings, then he would punish her.

Although mother and daughter were very close, their relationship was mediated by guilt. The words were never spoken, but the message from Claire's mother was clear. 'Of course I love you, but only if you do as I say. I'm sure that you don't want to hurt me; you don't want to make me cry. You want to make me proud of you. Do as I say and I'll be proud ... be an extension of me.'

These were not ideas imparted from one adult to another. Instead they were communicated to a child in thousands of subtle ways from as soon as Claire was old enough to understand.

It was conditional love, based on a value system at odds with the world around her. Unwittingly, when she emphasized the need for an abstemious approach to intimacy, Claire's mother was undermining her daughter's sexuality and planting the seeds that would cause her problems years later.

It wasn't cruelty or abuse in a physical sense. Her mother had no intention of harming Claire. Quite possibly, she took these values from her own mother, during her own childhood. People's lives are enormously complex and interwoven with those of past generations.

Whatever the reason, it didn't alter the result. As Claire grew into adolescence, her religious beliefs and the values she had been given by her mother became tangled up in issues of her sexuality. By the time she married she believed sex was something to fear rather than celebrate or enjoy. She was frightened by its power to corrupt. As a result, her tendency to enjoy and initiate sex was very low.

Although I didn't examine her husband, there was some suggestion that David had similar attitudes towards sex. At the very least he seemed satisfied with the low frequency and the dignified quality of their lovemaking.

All of this changed for Claire when she met Bill. Here was somebody who shared none of her inhibitions – a person who enjoyed sex for sex's sake. He *wanted* Claire and she found that being enjoyed was something that she responded to.

Perhaps for the first time she began to experience physical arousal and this offset many of the repressive ideas that she had taken from her mother.

'How was the sex different?' I asked her.

'We did different things. He would touch me in ways . . . I did things I hadn't done before.'

'How did it make you feel?'

'At first it was quite shocking . . .'

'Yes?'

'It was so exciting.' Her head dropped. 'I shouldn't have done it. I shouldn't have enjoyed it . . .'

Her sense of guilt now overwhelmed the feelings she once had of passion and desire. This made it difficult for her to relate details of the affair. It had obviously been a sexual revelation, but the inhibiting factors from her past had never gone away.

Over time these feelings of 'shame' and 'guilt' had poisoned her affair. It wasn't that it felt dirty or unclean, it simply didn't feel right. When the passion and novelty of their lovemaking began to wear off, Claire had nothing to offset her guilt.

At the same time she began to realize that she and Bill had very little in common. He was a typically robust working man, who loved snooker and rally driving. He enjoyed a pint and the occasional flutter on the horses. Claire came from a different background. She'd gone to private girls' schools and grown up with piano practice and ballet lessons. Could they really spend the rest of their lives together?

The answer, Claire decided, was no. Six months after the affair started, she went back to her husband. His accusations and harsh words only reinforced the guilt that she already felt. This guilt traced back to her child-hood, when her mother had determined the nature of Claire's existence in a powerful and intractable way.

Somehow I had to explain to Claire that a woman who intended her nothing but good had long ago planted the seeds that now caused her so much pain. As a child she hadn't recognized what her mother did as being wrong. Neither will the adult because she will assume that because this is the sort of upbringing that she experienced, other families and other mothers will be the same.

To make Claire well again, I had to help her under-stand that the family setting she grew up in was idiosyncratic. Not bad. The last thing I wanted to do was to drive a wedge between mother and daughter, regardless of whether her mother was still alive or not.

Instead, I had to delicately unpack Claire's memories and provide her with an alternative reference or bench-mark to that provided by her mother. It meant putting my hands, psychologically speaking, into the very essence of her developmental life.

People's lives are enormously complex and intricate. Interfering with some small part may have massive repercussions for an entirely different and unexpected area of a person's life. That's why I had to be so careful.

I began by helping Claire to use her rational thinking to reappraise elements of her past. To do this, we started talking about another young woman, in the abstract.

'She is about your age, Claire, and had a very similar upbringing. The two of you might have been at school together. Now she's come to you for advice.'

'OK.'

'Her mother is very loving, but has strong beliefs and values that she brings to bear on the child. She's not trying deliberately to manipulate or mould her daughter; it just comes out of every aspect of her daily being. Take, for example, when something about sex is mentioned on the radio or in a book, the young girl can see her mother close herself off.'

'What do you mean?'

'Well, she just seems to tighten up. She doesn't talk. She won't answer questions. If the child were to ask her, "Where do babies come from?" she'll see her mum become agitated and her face redden.'

Claire nodded and looked at me intently.

'What effect do you think that might have on this young girl?'

'Well, I suppose she is going to feel there is something not quite right about sex.'

'At home when she sees her mother and father together, they rarely touch each other. Occasionally, her father puts his arm around her mother and kisses her on the cheek, but for some reason she moves away, as if to say, "This is the wrong place. The wrong time." She may admonish him with a look. How is the girl going to make sense of this?'

74

'She might think women shouldn't let men touch them.'

'As she grows a little older and is introduced to her mother's view of Christianity, she overhears snatches of conversation. A girl down the road has got herself pregnant. She's a slut. She's on her way to hell. It's a mortal sin.'

'Yes.'

'And soon afterwards, the young girl begins to menstruate. There's an accident. The blood stains her dress. Her mother treats this as a matter of shame. "You mustn't say anything," she says. "You mustn't tell anybody. It's private." What does the girl make of this?'

'That it's something dirty,' said Claire.

'Nothing is ever said directly to this girl, but she is reminded in countless small ways that sex is wrong and dirty. There is a right place and a right time – during marriage. Boys only want one thing. You must never encourage them. Don't wear make-up or short dresses. Don't drink or smoke . . .

'There is never an explanation of why this should be so, because there is no formal sex education. All the important details are shielded from her. Boys try to do things that are dirty – end of story. What effect do you think that might have on her?'

'She would probably grow up believing that sex was dirty and something she should avoid, or be ashamed about.'

'Would she be right?'

'No, not really.'

'What do you think might happen when she finally experienced sex?'

'She'll probably feel awkward and a little embarrassed. She might not enjoy it.'

'Does that matter?'

'Yes. If it makes her unhappy.'

'How do you think this happened?'

'Well, her mother didn't mean her any harm. She didn't mean . . .' Claire struggled to find the words. She stopped and looked at me intently. Her eyes had filled with tears. 'I know that we're really talking about me. I understand what you're saying.'

Acceptance is a huge step, but I knew that it wouldn't stop Claire feeling soiled or unclean. Insight isn't a cure. The rituals she had adopted had taken on an existence of their own. Even though her intellect could accept that she wasn't to blame for what happened, that her mother's value systems were perhaps inappropriate, her physical symptoms – the hand-washing and lock-checking – lagged behind.

They had to be treated independently with a series of thought-blocking routines. I had already started this process during our third session together. I set Claire several tasks that she had to take home.

The first involved checking the doors that night. Instead of doing nine circuits of the house, she had to do only seven.

This might not seem like a big request, but it was an enormous hurdle for Claire. Her rituals had become all-encompassing. Failure to follow them, absolutely, made her extremely tense. To combat this, I taught her deep relaxation techniques, making a cassette tape that she could play when the strain became too great.

She had to sit in a chair, close her eyes and listen to my voice on the tape. By learning how to relax her body and expel all other thoughts from her mind, she could push away the tension.

Over the coming weeks, using this technique, I had her begin checking the locks six times a night, then five times, then four . . .

Her bathing and hand-washing rituals were treated in a similar way, although this time I added a rather miserable technique designed to interrupt her thought loop. Whenever Claire thought about being dirty she had to silently shout 'STOP!' It's a miserable act because we all know how impossible it is to tell ourselves *not* to think about something. The moment we try, we fail.

Each time Claire silently shouted, 'STOP!' her thoughts of washing would come back to her. Over and over again this happened, until eventually the loop was disrupted or the urge lost its power.

Another little device used in those days, but not any more, was to give the patient a strong elastic band to put around her wrist. Each time she said 'STOP!' she had to flick the band against her skin. Over time, this added to the disruption in her thought loop.

I asked Claire to keep a hand-washing and bathing diary. From an average of cleaning her hands every half hour and bathing six times a day, I began cutting the frequency. Gradually, I moved her to a point where she had one bath a day and washed her hands once in the morning and once in the afternoon, unless doing messy chores around the house or using the toilet.

At the same time, I helped Claire build up a set of cognitive self-statements that would replace such thoughts as 'I'll be dirty'.

Instead she learned to say silently, 'I don't need to wash my hands. It's just an anxiety problem. I know how to cope with that.'

Dealing with the internal psychological conflicts that

77

pushed Claire in this direction was more difficult. Over the next six months I helped her explore her feelings about herself and her mother. She came to understand that the guilt she carried had not just been the result of her extra-marital affair but had been a part of all her relationships and friendships.

All her life she had needed constantly to please people, without ever really understanding why. As a result, she rarely said no to others, or disagreed with them, or argued a point. Instead, she was kind and overly considerate, continually putting herself out to accommodate others.

This might sound admirable, but in reality Claire was living her mother's life and not her own. She was still trying to please the woman who had used guilt to control her and had taught her that her own happiness was secondary to that of others.

If her mother had known, I'm quite sure she would have been heartbroken to see her daughter go through these problems. She had no notion that this could happen. Very few parents realize just how much impact they have on their child's long-term psychological functioning.

It took almost a year before Claire regained control of her life and was no longer enslaved by the rituals of washing and checking locks. The internal psychological conflicts took even longer to resolve.

After eighteen months of coming to see me, she had come to terms with what had happened and led a more or less normal life. I saw her a couple of times for follow-ups over the next six months. On her last visit she told me that she had left her husband and had started seeing someone else.

'How is it going?'

'I feel good,' she said. 'I'm really happy.'

Although I never interviewed Claire's husband, I'm reasonably sure that their marriage involved two people who didn't function particularly well individually. Ultimately, Claire had found someone whom she regarded as a peer – who matched her own new wholeness. I'm sure it proved to be a far healthier relationship.

David Brooks lost his wife for a second time but eventually accepted the break-up. Rather than blame Claire or criticize her, he became a supportive, almost paternalistic figure in her life.

A balance, of sorts, had been struck.

3

Events in childhood can resonate through our lives and shape who we become. The links might not be immediately obvious, but we are products of our experiences as well as our genetic make-up. I am no different. Particular people and incidents in my life have affected me deeply – often in ways that I can't explain.

My grandparents lived in a small village in Ireland that looked like the cover of a holiday brochure. I only ever visited there twice – once when I was about five and my grandfather was still alive and a second time just after his death, when I was perhaps eight or nine.

I had grown up in Royal Leamington Spa in the English Midlands and compared to that my grandparents' village was something from a different era. Milk arrived each morning by horse-drawn cart and huge cast-iron ranges warmed every kitchen. Dry stone walls, stained with lichen, flanked the winding roads.

On the edge of the village was a blacksmith's forge and I spent hours sitting in there, watching the smith work and helping him with the bellows. At other times I'd wander into shops just to fill my lungs with the wonderful smells. The locals were delightful with their seemingly strange accents and soft voices.

My grandparents' cottage had the only fresh-water tap in the street. Everyone else had to carry water from the village pump. There was no electricity. Oil-fired lamps were filled and trimmed each evening; they threw shadows on the walls and turned everything a golden colour.

There was a big steel gate at the side of the cottage, painted dark green, with vertical bars about an inch wide and horizontal cross-strips going up like a ladder. It was wide enough to take a horse-drawn cart and led into the back yard, which had a dog kennel, an outside toilet and a large wooden shed, away from the back door, where the turf for the fire was stored. At the far end there were steps that went up to a vegetable garden.

My grandparents kept goats in the yard and for me as a townie it was a magical experience to play with them and let them suckle my fingers. There were eight or nine kids of different colours and I gave each one of them a name. Soon they were following me around the yard.

One day my grandfather brushed past me as I was petting them. He picked up a kid by the hind legs and swung it savagely in an arc around his head, smashing its head on the stone wall. I can still hear its last scream and the dull crack of bones breaking. He hung it from a post, took a butcher's knife and began to skin the poor creature.

Suddenly I made the connection between this scene and the dinners we'd eaten. I didn't eat that night – I couldn't bear even to be near the large pot that hung over the cooking range.

That night I crept into the yard. I spent hours clearing the turf out of the wooden shed and shepherding the kids inside. I built a high wall of turf around them, behind the door, trying to conceal them and keep them safe.

Of course, it didn't work. I could still hear them bleating. The next morning my bemused grandfather pulled down the turf and swung another kid against the stone wall. He was selling goat meat to the villagers.

Later that day I searched till I found the key for the padlock on the gate, but it wasn't easy to open. Then I ran the goats into the lane, from where they scattered all over the village – they were safe. My joy didn't last, of course. Within a day or so they had all been re-captured. Neither my mother nor my grandparents could understand what had got into me. Why was I acting so strangely?

I don't recall the incident giving me nightmares, but for a time it definitely affected my trust in adults.

This was compounded a few days later when I almost drowned. Playing with my younger brother, I ran out across a stretch of flat grass that looked almost like a newly mown tennis court. It wasn't grass at all. I crashed through the surface of the disused millpond, into a quicksand of silt that began to suck me under. I grabbed at clumps of grass on the bank and managed to drag myself out. I lost my shoes.

Afterwards, fearing that I'd get into trouble, I tried to clean up and dry off before going back to the cottage. Next to the stream I noticed an old stone building with weathered timber beams. It wasn't big enough to be a house and there was a strip of reddened earth running from a hole in the wall.

The door was open and I walked inside. It had a

concrete floor, sloping down towards the middle, with a channel that drained through a hole in the wall. In the centre of the floor, an enormous metal ring had been set into the concrete. A cow had its back to me, but I could see a rope around its neck.

Oblivious to my presence, a man patted the cow and slipped the rope through the ring. He pulled it tighter until the cow dropped to its knees. He tied the rope off and then picked up a sledgehammer. In one movement, he swung the hammer back and pounded it down on the cow's head. It took a dozen blows before it lay still.

Bone, blood and hide flew everywhere. Then he took a knife and ever so gently cut a flap in the neck, like a small door, peeling back the skin. Then he put the knife inside and carved it across the beast's neck.

I turned and ran, stumbling over rocks and scrambling up grassy banks. My idyllic child's playground with its lakes, hills and streams had quite capriciously been revealed as a place of carnage.

These memories come back to me from time to time. I realize now that I was witnessing country life as it was lived. The people hadn't changed – only my perception of them.

Years later I became a vegetarian. This was mainly due to my children's influence, but perhaps a part of it, at least subconsciously, could be traced back to Ireland.

I didn't read *Silence of the Lambs* by Thomas Harris until a long while after the film had come and gone. When I reached the point where the title is explained, a sudden resonance rang down through the years. Clarice Starling, the FBI agent, described listening to the lambs being slaughtered on her uncle's farm when she was just a child. I knew exactly how that sounded.

We are all influenced by events in childhood.

Memories and emotions stay with us and often determine how we see the world and relate to the people around us. As you might expect, this has been reinforced to me frequently in my consulting room as patients reveal their histories.

I first met Tabitha and Danny in a solicitor's office overlooking one of the older streets in Nottingham. She looked barely fifteen, but was actually nineteen. Her cardigan was too big for her and she kept pulling up the sleeves which immediately slipped down again.

We met in the firm's boardroom, which had a long Edwardian table of polished mahogany. A dozen matching chairs were arranged neatly around it. Two walls were taken up with shelves of leather-bound legal volumes, while a third had three sash windows, neatly divided into small square panes.

I ushered Tabitha and Danny to the armchairs at one end of the room. I sat with my back to the window so I could use the natural light and save my eyes. A tray of coffee had been delivered by a secretary.

'Thank you for seeing us, Mr Britton,' said Danny, shaking my hand. He had sharp features and pale blue eyes. He wore a bottle-green suit and, beneath it, his crisp white shirt still bore the creases from its cellophane wrapping.

Tabitha made no eye contact at all. She wore a long, shapeless dress and tugged the cardigan around herself as she sat down. Danny tried to reassure her and sat close, with his knees touching hers.

Tabitha had been charged with grievous bodily harm and wounding her sixteen-month-old baby daughter. She had pleaded guilty. Both of the baby's legs had been fractured, as well as an arm. According to medical records, there were also older fractures to the skull which weren't the subject of any police charges.

Social Services had asked me to assess Tabitha and the family. They needed a psychological report to make sure the child was taken out of danger and put into care.

At the same time, Tabitha's defending lawyers were also looking for an understanding of why she had injured her baby. They hoped it might help them when she went to court to be sentenced. Perhaps there was something the judge could take into account. Even so, she faced a significant number of years in prison.

'I'm a consultant psychologist,' I began. 'Do you know why we're here?'

'You're going to talk to us about the baby,' said Danny.

'Yes, that's right.'

Tabitha sat on the edge of the chair, with her head tilted slightly, sneaking occasional looks at me.

'I have your name as Tabitha, how do you spell that?'

'T, A, B, I, T, H, A,' said Danny.

'And your date of birth?'

'She's just turned nineteen.'

'What is the date of birth?'

Tabitha stared at the floor.

'The seventh of October,' said Danny.

Having finished the housekeeping, I began explaining: 'As you know, your solicitor and the local authority have both asked me to meet with you and prepare a report for the court. I have an outline of what happened, but I really need to know from you exactly what it is that brings you here.'

There was a general silence.

'So what happened? How do you come to be here?'

Danny took a deep breath. 'Well, Tabitha hurt our baby.'

Tabitha continued to stare at the floor, apparently consumed by sadness or regret.

'Tell me what actually happened,' I asked.

'Tabby hurt our little Josie. She broke her arm and her legs.'

Tabitha flinched slightly as he mentioned the injuries. She dug her fingernails into her wrist until I could see pressure marks of reddened skin.

'Tell me about the day it happened.'

'Well, we went to my mother's,' said Danny. 'I took Tabby and Josie. That's where they were going to spend the day. Then I went off to work. That's where I got a call from Mum. She said the baby wouldn't stop crying. They were taking her to the hospital. I went straight there. Tabby was really upset. The doctors said Josie had been hurt. They said it wasn't accidental. I kept asking Tabby about it, but she kept crying.' He patted her hand.

'That sounds like an awful situation. What do you remember, Tabitha? Can you help me to understand what happened?'

She remained silent and toyed with a strand of black wool that had pulled from the sleeve of her cardigan. There was no tension in her shoulders; she hadn't locked up. She was simply passive.

It's often very difficult for a person to talk about things that are sensitive or might leave them open to criticism. I hoped that Tabitha would become more reassured as we went on.

'She is so sorry,' said Danny. 'She cries about it all the time. If only it hadn't happened . . .' He couldn't finish the sentence and tenderly pulled her head to his shoulder.

'I understand and I know this is difficult. But it's important that I know exactly what happened.' Focusing on Tabitha, I asked, 'Can you say how *you* were? How was the baby that day?'

'She doesn't like to talk about it,' said Danny. 'I'll try to help as much as I can.'

Although Tabitha's silence was an issue, it didn't deeply concern me because I planned to see each of them independently. So far she had given me nothing except an overriding impression of passivity and acceptance. Danny, conversely, came across as a pleasant, articulate and open young man. He was clearly very concerned about her.

'We are working against a tight deadline,' I explained. 'You are due in court very soon. In order for me to prepare a report, I'll need to see you quite often in the next two weeks.'

Danny nodded.

'I'll need to see each of you on your own. Then depending on what comes out of those meetings, we'll go from there.'

'Why do you need to see Tabby on her own?' Danny asked.

'People are often more comfortable talking about their lives when it's just them on their own,' I explained.

'But we're married,' he said.

'Yes, I know. That's why I need to see both of you. I need to look at each of your private histories.'

'But Tabby's the one going to court.'

'I know. I need to cross-reference as many details as I can about her. It may be that I also have to see

87

grandparents, or brothers and sisters. I don't know yet. This whole process is about discovering who you are and how you came to be who you are.'

Danny couldn't hide his disquiet. 'No, I don't think that's a good idea. Tabby won't be able to talk to you on her own. She can't talk to men. She's very shy.'

'I appreciate what you're saying, but I do need to see her . . .'

'She's very upset. You can see that. I've made her a promise not to leave her side. You understand.'

Tabitha said nothing. She looked at me like a startled deer. Although clearly attractive, she had a face that seemed almost too childlike to have definable adult characteristics. There were no laughter lines, or milky childhood scars. She was almost like a shop-window mannequin.

'This is really what we have to do,' I told her, quite insistently.

'Can I come along?' asked Danny, still unhappy.

'As long as you wait outside during the interview.'

'Can you see me first?'

'Of course.'

Four days later, I met the couple again. Beforehand, I read the various police statements and case notes from Social Services' staff.

As requested, I saw Danny first. Although slightly nervous, he still had a relaxed charm about him and an easy-going manner.

'How did you meet Tabitha?'

'I knew one of her brothers. We played rugby together at school. Tabby was only fourteen when I first knew her. We didn't start dating until a few years ago.'

'When did you marry?'

'Last year – after Josie was born.'

'Tell me about your relationship.'

'What can I say? We love each other.'

'What are the nicest things about it?'

'Having Tabby all to myself, I suppose. It's nice to come home and have her there waiting for me. You know how it is.'

'What are the things you row about?'

He shrugged. 'Normal stuff, I guess – money, staying out late after rugby practice . . .'

'What sort of things do you do together?'

'Tabby doesn't like rugby. She prefers to stay home and look after the baby.'

I glanced at my notes. According to Josie's X-rays, there were signs of two older fractures, both to her skull.

'Josie was injured once before, wasn't she?'

'It was an accident. She slipped out of Tabby's hands in the bathroom. Her hands were wet.'

'How did you cope with that?'

'It was awful. I hated the thought of Josie being hurt, or upset. But it was an accident. These things happen.'

'It must be very hard for you now. Tabitha might well go to prison and Social Services are going to want to take Josie into care.'

'It hasn't been easy, Mr Britton. I love my wife. I'm going to help her to get through this.' He wrung his hands together and then wiped his eyes.

'How did you and the baby get on?'

'Just brilliant. My mum was so pleased we had a daughter.'

'How did Tabitha and Josie get on?'

'She loved that baby. I don't know what could

have happened . . .' His voice trailed off and he sighed.

'Obviously you're out at work all day. How often did you leave Tabitha and Josie at your mother's house?'

'On most days.'

'Why is that?'

'Tabby likes the company and it's nice for her to have Mum around.'

'Were you worried about leaving her on her own with Josie?'

'No, not at all.'

Another question formed in my mind. Where was his mum when the assault took place? In her statement she'd insisted that Tabitha couldn't have deliberately harmed the baby. 'I would have known,' she'd said. 'Tabitha loved that baby.'

It wasn't much help. Besotted grandmothers aren't always the most reliable witnesses and this woman might have been in unintentional denial.

The interview with Danny ran smoothly. He filled in many of the gaps that I'd noted in the written statements. At the same time, I wasn't entirely happy with some of his answers, or more his general tone. Where was his anger? Where was the resentment? He showed no sign of bitterness towards Tabitha, or fearfulness for the child. Yet he talked openly about a future time when they'd all be back together. Wasn't he worried about it happening again?

While Danny's mother refused to accept that Tabitha could have harmed Josie, Danny didn't question the fact at all. It wasn't even a case of reluctantly acknowledging the assault – it had simply happened.

I thanked Danny for his co-operation and said that I now needed to see Tabitha.

'I really think I ought to stay,' he said. 'She's very nervous. I don't think she can cope.'

'I've explained this already, Danny. I need to see her on her own. If she can't manage, we can ask you to come in and help her.'

Danny paused at the door, as though he wanted to argue the point. Then he gave a shrug of resignation and left.

'I'll be just outside, sweetheart,' he told Tabitha, squeezing her hand reassuringly.

She wore a mauve polo-neck jumper and dark trousers. Her shoulder-length hair was neatly brushed and her face lightly made up.

Her movements were almost exaggerated in their slowness and everything about her posture seemed to say, 'I'm sorry.' She clutched a bag on her lap as though frightened somebody might snatch it away.

She hadn't uttered a word at our first meeting. Unless I could bring down her anxiety level, I knew that I'd struggle to engage her at all. Silence can be a great pressure or a great comfort, depending upon the circumstances. I had to make it work for me, in a gentle but insistent way.

I began by explaining what I hoped we might talk about. Sitting a little distance away, I tried to give Tabitha plenty of personal space. At the same time I used my tone of voice and relaxed posture to make her feel more at ease.

'It must be very difficult at the moment. I can see you're nervous. Some people I talk to are much more uncomfortable than others are. They're afraid that I'm going to be irritated with them, or think they're telling me stories. Some are worried that I might shout at them, or become annoyed if they don't talk to me. I'm not going to do any of those things, Tabitha. I know this is awkward for you. I appreciate that.'

Her eyes hadn't left the floor and I could see the whites of her knuckles where she tightly clutched the bag.

I continued: 'Let's try to look at it from your point of view. You're a young woman who is about to go before the courts to be sentenced for injuring your baby. Most people get very upset and angry when they hear about a child being hurt. They want to punish the person responsible.

'You probably think that's how I feel. I'm almost a complete stranger. I'm someone who has read all the statements. You probably think that I don't like you, or that I think less of you because of the police charges. I promise you that's not so. My job isn't to have feelings about what happened. My job is to try to understand who you are and how you got to be who you are.

'Babies get hurt in lots of ways, Tabitha, and for lots of reasons. There aren't too many people who set out to hurt them intentionally.'

Her hair had become a veil that covered her face and gave her somewhere to hide. She could see me if she wanted, but I couldn't see her eyes.

'I've had a chat with Danny and he explained how difficult you would find this – talking to me on your own. He wanted to be in here to help you. It's nice to have someone who loves you and wants to be with you. But it can also be a hindrance because often there are things that you can't say in front of someone you love. It can also be hard revealing them to a stranger.'

Tabitha still hadn't said a word. She had barely moved at all since sitting in the chair.

Taking a new approach, I began asking a series of closed questions that required very short answers. Barristers often use this technique at the beginning of a witness's evidence to ease them gently into the examination-in-chief.

For Tabitha it was important that the closed questions came with a gentle tone – not as a staccato grilling.

'How old is your mum?'

There was a long pause. I let the silence build.

'Is she about my age?'

Tabitha shook her head. It was the first response that she'd given me so far.

'Well, how old is she?'

'Thirty-seven,' she whispered.

'What is she like?'

Tabitha shrugged.

'Where were you born?'

'In Nottingham.'

'Any brothers and sisters?'

'A brother.'

'Is he older or younger?'

'Older.'

Taking Tabitha's history took a very long time because she offered little detail in her answers. In truth, there was a massive poverty in her descriptions – particularly of her family and early life. Her replies were defensive, stilted and empty.

As I began asking about her schooling and friendships, the history became a little more detailed. She began to relax and her sentences started to connect. Once or twice she smiled. Whatever threat or risk I posed was receding.

It wasn't until I began looking at her sexual history

that she suddenly shut me out again and became massively distressed. Psychologically she began closing down, putting up barriers. She seemed to shrink in front of me, as if trying to disappear. Something was clearly wrong and I could no longer reach her.

Over the course of our two interviews, Tabitha's passivity had gone through a curious curve. From giving nothing at all, she had finally become engaged and then suddenly retreated into silence again.

This sort of behaviour might have suggested schizophrenia or other mental illness, but this wasn't the case with Tabitha. She'd shown herself to be quite bright and able to engage me clearly and sensibly.

Now I had to reach into her mute world and bring her back.

'Can you help me understand what happened to Josie? How did it come about?'

She didn't react.

'How did Josie get hurt?'

Again nothing.

'According to the statement you made to the police, you were in the bedroom when it happened. Is that right?'

I let the silence envelop her. After what seemed like a long time she nodded her head.

'What happened?'

'I hit her.'

'What with?'

'A plastic doll.' Her voice was flat and monotone.

'Why?'

'She wouldn't stop crying.'

'How long had she been crying?'

Tabitha shrugged. Her shame and embarrassment were manifest in every fibre of her being. This young

94

woman was about to go to prison. She had no idea what that truly entailed. When the cell door closed and the key turned in the lock, I doubted she would have the psychological strength to cope.

The interview ended and I stayed behind in the board-room, writing up my notes. Certain things concerned me, particularly Tabitha's empty descriptions of her early life and her passivity. I had seen this before. They were classic symptoms of childhood sexual abuse.

Nothing in the files had flagged this. Tabitha had been through Social Services systems and no concerns had ever been raised.

Yet even without Tabitha's apparent muteness, there would have been enough to set alarm bells ringing. She had given me no colour or evocative detail about her parents or close family. They were almost cardboard cut-outs, or static pieces of stage furniture.

Now I pondered whether her muteness might be a consequence of abuse. Coupled with her clear distress when talking about her sexual history, the bells were deafening.

That night I sat down to review my case notes. The aim of the interviews had been to generate a psycho-logical analysis of Tabitha and her behaviour. By talking to Danny I could cross-reference and check certain facts.

As I looked at their accounts of the assault on Josie, two problems emerged. First, their descriptions were almost identical. People normally use language in different ways. They have their own vocabularies and speaking styles. Yet in this case Tabitha didn't – to the extent that she had spoken at all, she had used exactly the same words as her husband.

The second problem was a serious anomaly between their accounts and the injuries. Several times I had taken Tabitha, moment by moment, through the assault on her daughter. And no matter how many times I reread my notes and looked at the medical and X-ray reports, I couldn't make her account fit with Josie's injuries. I'm not a radiologist, but the gap was too great for me to ignore.

I arranged to see Tabitha again two days later. This time I wanted to explore the areas that she had been keeping hidden. In a sense I had to take her psychologically by the hand and walk back down the years to when she was a little girl.

It's a difficult thing to do. I had to make a judgement as to how much pressure I could exert in order to help her put material on the table. It had to be enough to unlock Tabitha's defences, but not so much as to damage her and leave her defenceless.

It was particularly crucial that I didn't convey any suggestion to her that 'something had happened' in her past that underpinned a present problem. Otherwise Tabitha might spontaneously *feel* that she remembered traumatic events that hadn't occurred because of a belief that it might please me.

This phenomenon, False Memory Syndrome, has caused considerable clinical difficulty whenever it has been clearly shown to have occurred. It remains an area of vociferous controversy between those who believe it lies at the heart of many allegations of childhood abuse that originate from adults who have spent time in therapy, and others who insist that False Memory Syndrome is being used to defend the guilty and protect offenders from apprehension. At the same time it further traumatizes victims, who feel they aren't believed.

Most people find it very difficult to hide a terrible secret. It's like having a dam where sandbags have been piled up to hold back the waters. It takes an enormous amount of psychological energy to hold that dam in place. Often it's far easier to let it go – to release the pressure.

If Tabitha had such a secret, she had kept it under control for years. She had lived a life, albeit an impoverished one, without letting anybody share this burden.

Now I had to use psychological interviewing techniques to break through her defences. To do this meant giving her the freedom as well as the need to put things on the table. I had to be careful not to give her leading cues. She had to make the running, rather than relying on me.

Much of this comes down to trust. Tabitha had to believe that her innermost thoughts, feelings and deeds were not going to be used to hurt her. I wasn't there morally to judge or criticize her. Rather than damage her, the truth might bring her something good.

I tried to explain this to her before asking again about her mother. A long silence followed. I let it build.

'I can see you're having trouble. There may be lots of reasons for this. Sometimes people aren't used to talking about private things. Or perhaps the answer is rather difficult. I can see that you're frightened. Your heart is racing. You don't want to be here. Inside you wish I would just go away. I'm sorry I can't do that. I'm not here to hurt you. I'm not going to shout, or get angry, or make you feel bad.

'I want to help you, Tabitha, but what I can't do is

pretend that I know the answers and simply write something down. I can't make things up and I can't make you talk to me. You are in control.

'The worst that can happen is that I'll write a report saying that you weren't able to speak to me. I don't want to do that. It doesn't serve any useful purpose. But if that happens, I'm not going to blame you, or think worse of you.'

I could see her relax ever so slightly.

'Now, we were talking about your mum. Is that right?'

'Yes.'

This single voluntary comment was the first she had given since this interview began. It was a major step. Much later in my career, when I began to teach hostage negotiation and train people to talk to kidnappers and extortionists, one of the key things I had to help them to do was to secure that first small 'yes'. All communication builds from there in very small increments.

Rather than congratulating Tabitha and making her feel foolish, I moved calmly on to the next equally small question.

'You mentioned that your mum is still alive?'

'Yes.'

'Does she have a job?'

'No.'

'Was she always at home when you were little?'

'Yes.' There was a slight qualification in her voice.

'It sounds as though there may have been a little bit more to it than that.'

'Yes.'

Now taking a risk, I introduced the first open question. 'What do you mean?'

There was a long pause. I mustn't break this silence.

Tabitha stared at the floor. Psychologically, she was standing on the edge of the dam wall. Which way would she go?

'She wasn't always there,' she said wistfully.

'It can be hard when mums and dads aren't around when you need them.'

'Yes.'

'What do you remember of your early days at home? About your mum?'

Another long pause.

'It was all right.'

She glanced up. Her face had a hunted look. I had seen it before – both in my consulting room and in the playground: children of eight, nine or ten who don't wear the soft, gentle, confident expressions that say, 'what a wonderful world this is'. Instead they are eternally vigilant. Yet no amount of vigilance is going to save them from getting hurt, put down or ridiculed. It is in their faces.

These children haven't necessarily been abused. They simply know that, for whatever reason, they are at the bottom of the heap, and life will never be what they want it to be.

Tabitha's eyes were beginning to work. She looked at me after giving each answer, as if expecting a negative outcome. Her shoulders had straightened a little.

It took a long time but the story that she told in stops and starts was truly awful. When this young girl woke each morning and opened her eyes, she didn't have the same feelings most other children have. There was no excitement at the new day. No eagerness to fling open the curtains and go skipping downstairs to breakfast.

As her eyes opened, the first thing she looked at was

the door. It was still closed. Imagine for a moment that you're that little girl. You hear movement downstairs or on the landing outside. You pull the covers over your eyes and pretend to be asleep. If you're asleep maybe nothing will happen.

The door opens. Footsteps sound on the floor. Covers are pulled back. A hand slides beneath your pyjamas. You can't call for help. This isn't a stranger. This is someone you know. And when the pain comes you try not to open your eyes, but they demand that you must. They snarl in your ear, 'Open your eyes, baby sister. Show me how much you love this.'

Who else was in the house? Surely they could hear the bedhead banging against the wall and the mattress springs creaking beneath her. She didn't cry out, or beg for help. She knew what happened last time and the time before that.

Others had been there before her brother. Inside her. Whispering in her ear. 'Tell Grandad how much you like it ... You like it, don't you? I knew you would.'

She didn't tell her mother. It wasn't that she was frightened of not being believed, or thought her mum wouldn't cope. She knew what would happen. Her mother didn't want to know the truth. Her boyfriend was also raping Tabitha and she didn't want to lose him.

In all, three generations of her family were using this eleven-year-old girl for sex. The rapes had been going on for years, with the men passing her around and competing with each other.

Trapped in this cycle of abuse, Tabitha ceased to be the agent of her own feelings or actions. Her abusers ripped her apart psychologically and removed all trace of her self-esteem and worth. She became imprisoned in a world they created for her.

There are times when I can't help taking my work home with me. For all my knowledge of thought-blocking techniques and stress relief, I still have days when I can't get an image out of my head.

Having immersed myself in the intimate details and rhythm of a patient's life, I can't always push away their pain and sadness. This was one of those instances.

As shocking as it was, Tabitha's story wasn't new to me. I had heard similar histories during my clinical training and early career. And the fact that Tabitha had been the victim of sexual abuse didn't make her any more or less likely to have hurt her baby.

It is true that some victims of abuse will go on to become abusers. Yet one of the greatest misunder-standings I confront in my work is the widely held belief that this is a foregone conclusion.

People come into my office greatly distressed because they fear they are going to abuse their children. The grounds for this fear aren't anger or deviant urges; it doesn't have any rational basis. The reason is that they themselves were abused as children and they're afraid their terrible past has tainted them. They imagine they are perpetrators just waiting for the opportunity.

This is garbage! Society has come to believe this myth because it has failed to understand the statistics. The fact that many people who are abusers turn out to have been abused in their past is not the same as say-ing, 'Most people who are abused will become abusers.'

What of Tabitha? Something about this case had bothered me from the beginning, but I couldn't quite put my finger on it. Her passivity and muteness had flagged her own suffering. Each day she dragged herself through the motions of living, without any real sense of purpose.

Sharing this life with her is a loving and caring husband, the sort of man that most mums and dads would be happy to have as their son-in-law. But why did such a sensitive, aware and alert young man show none of the reactions of anger and bitterness I would expect from someone whose child had been so savagely beaten? He didn't even acknowledge ever having had such feelings. When he talked of being distraught, there was no emotion behind the words.

Again I went back over the material, rereading the statements from social workers, police, doctors, relatives and friends.

Something odd became apparent. Nowhere, in all of this material, was there a point where Tabitha had spontaneously said, 'I hurt my baby.'

Going right back to the hospital when Josie was treated, I searched for the first reference to abuse. It came when an aunt approached Tabitha in the corridor and asked, 'How could you do this? Why did you do this?'

Tabitha had allegedly replied, 'I don't know.'

From that moment she was confronted by people who naturally assumed she was responsible. There was no explanation of how or why. Not once did she say the words, 'I did it.'

She was taken into custody and the police used standard interviewing practices. They put a series of questions to her, but she remained mute. So they put a series of propositions. All Tabitha had to do was say yes. And she did.

From then on, this record of interview became the accepted version of events. Nobody bothered to look any further. Why should they? Someone had confessed. Folks don't normally admit to grievously wounding their baby unless they did it.

Tabitha entered the judicial system. At every stage of her journey, the fundamental act was always assumed – even by her solicitor. This allowed her simply to nod and carry on with the lie.

When she did have to speak, each of her admissions was founded on the interviews she had given before, which she had accepted and incorporated. Only by working backwards was it clear that she had never initiated an admission. She had simply agreed.

I looked closely at the X-ray reports on sixteen-month-old Josie. I sketched out the pattern and severity of the fractures to her legs and arm. Tracing my fingers over the sketch, I thought about Tabitha's description of hitting Josie with a plastic doll.

I knew this didn't make sense. Even wielded in anger, there is no way that such an object would break bones like this.

Nobody had bothered to take the doll to a radiologist and ask for an opinion. Why? Because somebody had confessed.

I still had four days left before Tabitha's court appearance. I arranged to see her again, planning to take her back over the details. She had to be lying about the assault – the story didn't fit.

'What you've told me about hurting Josie isn't true,' I told her quite bluntly.

Tabitha stiffened slightly. It was the first time I had ever contradicted her.

'The injuries are inconsistent with what you've said.

I don't believe that you hit Josie with a plastic doll.'

'But that's what I did,' she blurted, growing very agitated.

'No. That wouldn't have been enough. It looks as though the person would have had to stamp on the baby's leg.'

Tabitha looked confused. Why had I suddenly turned on her like this?

'Yes, I did that. I stood on her leg.'

'What were you wearing?'

'I can't remember . . . my sneakers, I think.'

'But this person would have had to be wearing a really heavy pair of work boots.'

She nodded.

'That's right. I was wearing boots.'

'And this person would have had to actually jump on the baby – not once but time and time again.'

There was a long silence.

'Did you do that?'

'Yes.'

As I expected, Tabitha had simply changed her account to agree with me.

I had a real problem now. The whole system was geared up to send this young woman to prison. However, I was no longer satisfied there was a sound basis for it. The fact that Tabitha had admitted the offence was of little evidential value because it couldn't be believed.

I spoke to her defence lawyer and arranged for the trial date to be deferred. This allowed me longer to investigate. I needed time to discover why Tabitha lied about the attack. Why did she risk going to jail and having her child taken away for ever?

I suspected the answer lay in her history as well as her everyday life.

Although I couldn't be sure, I felt confident enough to surmise certain things. This was a young woman who for as long as she had been in the world had taken the definition of that world and her role in it from other people. When her brother came to rape her, or her grandfather, or her mother's boyfriend, they told her, 'You like this.'

She heard this statement three or four times a week for twelve years after each new rape. Of course it wasn't true, but when you hear it repeated often enough you begin thinking, this must be how liking it feels.

What other terms of reference did Tabitha have? She was never able to challenge her abusers. There was no external voice in her life saying, 'You poor child, this is awful, let me help.'

During those early years, Tabitha wasn't raped in silence. She had to follow a script. This wasn't simply a role-play – she had to become the part. She had to be exactly what they wanted her to be.

Three men used her independently, but each knew of the others. Part of their pleasure was in getting her to do things to the others. She had to tell them constantly how much she enjoyed being their 'dirty little slut'.

Not surprisingly, the effect of this on Tabitha was psychologically catastrophic. All traces of her self-esteem and worth were picked apart until her acceptance was unconditional. She had become totally compliant.

Tabitha grew up to accept blame for everything. These were not just her feelings – they were facts. They were inculcated into her belief system in just the same way as children are taught to wash and brush their teeth. She was disgusting, dirty, defiled. She was nothing. Whatever she did was wrong. She was always wrong. She must be responsible for Josie's injuries.

At the hospital, when her aunt said, 'How could you do this?' Tabitha answered, 'I don't know.'

She wasn't trying to protect anybody. In her mind she thought, I am bad. I am soiled. Of course it's me. I am always to blame.

This was how the pseudo-lie started and was what fuelled it through each stage of the interviews. Tabitha was swept along by the same ceaseless tide of acceptance that ran through her life.

Which brings us to the obvious question – who was responsible?

The short answer is I don't know, but I have my suspicions.

I had a surprise visit a few days after last seeing Tabitha. Danny's demeanour had been completely transformed. Instead of being confident and self-assured, he was extremely agitated, refusing to sit down. He paced around my consulting room. 'What have you done to her?'

'I'm sorry?'

'Tabby. What have you done to her?'

'I don't know what you mean.'

'She's different.'

'In what way?'

My politeness seemed to infuriate him even more. 'I'm gonna make a statement against her. She hurt our baby. She can't get away with that.'

'You must do what you think is best.'

Clearly, Tabitha had gone home and been somehow different. Perhaps she wasn't as passive as before. Perhaps she began looking at things in a different way, or refused to accept that certain things had happened.

Danny raged at me about interfering with his

marriage and 'screwing' with his wife's head. In his anger, he wanted to hit out; to punish someone.

I have no proof that Danny hurt baby Josie, but I witnessed his explosive temper first hand.

During my involvement with Tabitha, she never once conceded that she hadn't injured the child. It was only later when, in treatment, her case had passed to somebody else that she eventually changed her position. Even so, she refused to make an accusation against anybody else.

It also emerged afterwards that Tabitha had not been in the house when Josie suffered the earlier fractures to either side of her skull. Danny had given the account to doctors and Tabitha accepted the blame, saying she accidentally dropped the baby on the bathroom floor. If anybody had checked they would have found the floor was carpeted and the injuries were inconsistent with her statement.

I have been asked many times in my job whether I ever see people who are truly evil. The answer is yes, but only very occasionally.

One of those people, I suspect, is Tabitha's husband.

Danny was already a predator when he met his wife as a teenager. That is why he was drawn to her. He didn't have to work hard on her. She was already there. Her resolve and self-worth had been wiped away years earlier.

He would have known this from so many different clues. He would have blamed her for everything from the milk not being cold enough to the postman being late.

'Why didn't you open my beer?'

'I don't know.'

'Why didn't you clean this glass properly?'

'I don't know.'

This sort of acquiescence and passivity is an absolute prize for a manipulator like Danny. It was like having his own personal servant and slave. The only thing lacking perhaps was some small sign of resistance within Tabitha that he could gain pleasure by overcoming.

That's why people like Danny sometimes push their victims on and on, to see if they can't reach some final point of resistance that they can break through. He didn't need to with Tabitha. She had already been completely broken.

The Crown withdrew the charges against Tabitha as a result of my report, but the law couldn't touch Danny. I wish someone could have whispered in his ear, 'We're watching you,' but the system doesn't work like that. He walked away, still oozing the same unctuous charm and outward pleasantness.

Tabitha wanted to have her baby back, but this wasn't likely to happen in the near future. Somebody had hurt her child and she refused to say who. At the same time, a serious question mark remained over her husband. Unless these issues were resolved, it was unlikely that Josie would ever be returned to her family.

I may have succeeded in keeping Tabitha out of prison, but she was still imprisoned in a world of passivity and hurt. My brief had never been to treat her. It wouldn't have been appropriate under the circumstances. For one thing, I had examined her for the defence, but more importantly I was a man of similar age to one of her violators. Treatment fell to a woman much closer to Tabitha's age who could model appropriate ways of understanding.

There are two stages in convincing a victim of child abuse that it is not her fault. One is quite high impact and immediate. You simply go over the real situation for the first time – 'No, this is not your fault. You were a young, innocent child. These were people who should have looked after you. They were wrong to do what they did. You are not to blame. You are the victim.'

As these words are spoken and begin to take effect, you can almost see the wheels in the patient's mind grinding into a new place. The impact is terrible, but necessary. Tears flow and their distress is heartbreaking.

The second stage of the process is an enormous upsurge of rage and anger when the patient's intellectual realization catches up with their emotions. It can take a year or more of treatment to deal with the emotional damage and its impact. This must be taken away and something else put in its place.

Sadly, Tabitha will have to live with the scars; her memories can never be wiped clean. Yet in time and with the right help, she might find some semblance of a normal life. I hope so.

4

Soon after I left school in the early 1960s I spent a year as a police cadet in Warwickshire. I can't remember exactly why I did so, but we had a couple of local bobbies who particularly impressed me.

One day the station sergeant said he wanted me to become familiarized with a part of my new job. He sent me down to the town mortuary to await the arrival of an ambulance.

The old mortuary was a single-storey brick-built hut set back from the road. It didn't look that dissimilar from the nearby boat sheds on the river. The lower panes of the windows had frosted glass and the pathologist's table was a big marble slab with grooves. The ambulance drew up and the crew opened the twin rear doors.

I will never forget seeing my first dead body. A middle-aged man had collapsed and died of a heart attack in the street. They carried him through wooden doors, past a short partition and bench to the post-mortem room. Then they left him on the bench opposite me. To squeeze past the body, I had gingerly to move his arm. His skin had grown cool. I didn't care for that.

I remembered this scene twenty years later when I saw photographs of another dead body. This time the victim was a thirty-three-year-old pet beautician, Caroline Osborne, who had been murdered and mutilated while out walking her dogs.

In August 1983 I was made a senior clinical psychologist at Leicester General Hospital. Several months later, out of the blue, I had a telephone call from the head of Leicestershire CID, Detective Chief Superintendent David Baker.

He came straight to the point. 'Is it possible to glean characteristics of a murderer from looking at a crime scene?'

'I'm not quite sure I understand.'

'If I were to show you the scene of a crime, pretty much unchanged since it happened, is it possible for you to tell me things about the person who was responsible for the murder?'

I took a deep breath. Nobody had ever asked me such a question. What did I know about murderers? At the same time, a kaleidoscope of clinical cases tumbled through my mind – again and again a person's behaviour reflected their personality.

'Depending on what you can show me,' I told him, 'I'd say the answer is yes.'

Over the next three days, I studied the crime scene photographs, statements and post-mortem report. Nothing could prepare me for the horror of seeing Caroline Osborne's injuries – not even memories of a dead man in Leamington morgue.

The police could find no motive for the murder. She had not been sexually assaulted or robbed. Her body had been found in waist-high grass near the Grand Union Canal in Leicester. She had been bound

111

with twine and knifed seven times. Nearby, police found what appeared to be a black magic symbol on a piece of paper.

Almost unconsciously, I began asking myself questions. What sort of knife did he use? Was he right-handed or left-handed? If so, where did he stand when he delivered the blows? How long had she been conscious? How quickly did she die?

The answers were important because they influenced the much larger question of motivation. What did the killer seek to achieve when he murdered Caroline? For instance, a robbery that went wrong has far different implications to a sexually motivated killing.

Whereas detectives had searched for the physical clues and witnesses, I began looking at the overall location and the salience of certain landmarks and features. I also looked at Caroline Osborne. What was she like? What could she tell me about the man who killed her?

Clearly, Caroline's death wasn't an act of the moment. The bindings and the knife were brought along for the purpose, as was the drawing of the penta-gram. This suggested a degree of planning and deliberation.

This man hadn't simply come across an attractive woman, become aroused, been rebuffed and angrily stabbed her before running away. Caroline had been tied up in a particular way and then attacked. The motive was undoubtedly sexual, although not in the way that we normally think of a rape or sexual assault. It displayed evidence of an even more extreme deviance.

Since I became a clinical psychologist, part of my work had been at the sexual dysfunction clinic at

Leicester General Hospital. This had given me a greater understanding of how our sexual functioning can often become tied to and crossed with fetishes and vivid fantasies.

Very occasionally, a person becomes so preoccupied with these things that the sexual act becomes less and less important or valuable. For a man, the woman can cease to be a mutually consenting, eager participant and instead become a depersonalized vehicle for his pleasure.

The death of Caroline Osborne had been just such an expression of a corrupt lust. The bindings, control and choice of victim suggested a killer whose sexual desire had become mixed with anger and the need to dominate. Rather than fantasizing about mutually consenting sexual contact, this man would have fantasies that featured extreme sexual aggression. Over and over, he played out the killing in his mind – the struggle, binding her, mutilating her with the knife.

I wrote all this down in a detailed description of the psychological and demographic characteristics of Caroline's killer.

Up until that point there was no such thing as 'offender profiling' in Britain. The term was unknown. Much later I discovered that the FBI had been evolving an offender-profiling unit for almost a decade.

David Baker and his colleagues accepted my help but were puzzled. How much weight could they place on my conclusions? They were stepping into a terrain apparently without maps, using a guide who followed signs they weren't trained to see. How could they test my advice? Nobody had ever done this before.

The value of the profile I drew up only became apparent over a year later, in April 1985, when another woman, Amanda Weedon, aged twenty-one, was killed close to the hospital where she worked and lived. Her body was found crushed into a hedge at the side of a path. She had been stabbed and there was no sign of a sexual attack or robbery.

Baker contacted me again.

'Could the two crimes be connected?' he asked.

After studying every known detail of the crime, I told him yes. I also listed the psychological features of the killer that I could draw from the material.

I suggested that he was a very young man – in his mid-teens to early twenties – who was sexually immature and struggled to get girlfriends. He probably lived at home with his family.

He was likely to be a manual worker in the sort of job that demanded dexterity and might involve being comfortable with sharp knives. He was physically strong and athletic. He lived close to the murder scene and knew the area.

Pornography would feature strongly in his life, some of it violent and covering satanic themes. He might also regard the knife he used to kill Caroline as a treasured artefact.

Although I was new to criminal investigations and still relatively new to psychology, none of these observations was pulled out of the air. Nor did they involve a leap of faith or having to shoehorn facts into a preconceived plan. Everything about the crime – the location, timing, weapon, victim, degree of planning and ferocity of the attack – said something about the person responsible. It is exactly the same in my consulting room when a patient's behaviour reflects aspects of his or her personality.

This time the murder squad used the profile to

channel its resources and focus on a much smaller pool of suspects who had the relevant characteristics.

Eventually this highlighted a lonely, sexually immature teenager called Paul Bostock. Regarded as a gentle giant by those who knew him, Bostock lived near both murder scenes and had been interviewed three times after Caroline Osborne's death. In each case he gave an apparently satisfactory alibi.

He worked as a meat processor at a local factory and was a fitness fanatic, jogging and cycling before or after work. He had turned his grandmother's garage into a fitness studio.

When police searched his address, they uncovered his morbid fascination with the occult and black magic. Bostock had a collection of knives in his bedroom, along with violent comics and magazines. His walls were plastered with posters and drawings, some of which included black magic symbols and bondage scenes with topless women trussed up and being tortured. One of the symbols matched that found near to Caroline Osborne's body.

David Baker asked for my advice on how they should interview the nineteen-year-old suspect. Again, this was totally new territory for me.

I began to think in terms of my clinical work. If I had Paul Bostock in my consulting room for assessment, what would I do first? Take his history.

To do this I had to build a rapport with him. Not everybody wants to revisit their past and have their deepest secrets unlocked. Some fight against it or build walls that are harder to break down than stone.

I began by helping the police to understand the psychosexual functioning of the killer; his deviation and the nature of his fantasies. I could also tell them how her murderer would behave during the interviews, and compare this with their suspect.

'Imagine the truth is at the centre of a series of concentric circles,' I told the police. 'You can't go straight to the heart – the suspect won't let you – so you begin way off and talk about family, his early life, school holidays and friends. Get him used to talking about these things in fine detail so that later, when you get close to the murders, you don't suddenly have to change gear from talking in general terms to fine detail. The discontinuity would throw him.

'As you do this, a rapport is building and he'll come to feel good about you. He'll come to know he's safe. He still knows there's a consequence, but he doesn't think you'll turn on him and call him an animal or a monster. Instead you want to understand what happened and how it came about.

'When he's comfortable talking about the minutiae of relationships and how things felt, you take him a step further, moving him closer and closer to the week and the day and the hour that Caroline Osborne was killed.

'When you get too close he'll tell you, "I don't know" or "I wasn't there" or "I can't remember." You can batter on that door but he'll push back even more strongly. Give it a rest, have a break and return later. This time backtrack a little, letting him go over old territory before bringing him back again. You must take him through the day in the most minute detail – what time did you leave? Did you turn left or right? Were your hands in your pockets?

'Then let him pick up the story and you'll find he goes a little further and admits, "Yes, I might have seen her on the towpath."'

'Don't look surprised. Don't say, "Hey, hold on, you denied that before." Instead, you say, "OK, that's fine. Where exactly was she standing? What was she wearing?"

'And so you move on until you reach another point where he can't remember or doesn't know. Don't batter on the door. Pull back again. Employ exactly the same approach.'

The interviews began and over the next two days I listened to the tapes. Each time the interrogators moved closer to the truth the barriers got bigger, but following my advice they were able to cross them. Eventually they reached a point where suddenly they crashed through and the interview went straight to the heart of the murders. The truth came spilling out with a sense of relief.

Paul Bostock pleaded guilty to both murders at Leicester Crown Court and was sentenced to life imprisonment. He is now acknowledged as the first person in Britain to have been caught and convicted with the help of a psychological analysis and profile.

At the time I thought it was a one-off. My role was never mentioned publicly and I went back to my consulting room. Although I could see the benefits of using a psychological approach to analyse a crime, I didn't contemplate how it might be taken any further. It wasn't my job.

Yet in the months and years that followed, as more requests arrived from the police, I realized that I had pioneered a new science in Britain. Psychological profiling of an offender could be used to narrow down the number of potential suspects in a crime and allow police to focus their resources more tightly.

After the Caroline Osborne and Amanda Weedon cases, I helped investigate the Narborough murders of schoolgirls Linda Mann and Dawn Ashworth. Then I advised police how to deal with an extortionist, who first threatened to contaminate tins of Pedigree dog food and then targeted Heinz baby food.

There was no payment or contract involved. I can't clearly remember when I realized these weren't just one-off requests and I had a new strand to my career. It just seemed to happen.

In those early days I had mainly treated people who had anxieties, obsessions, phobias and psychosomatic difficulties. Only occasionally did they have the sort of personality disorders or sexual deviancies that lead some people to rape and murder.

Whether in the consulting room or at a crime scene, I was interested in the detailed shape of this person's mind. My questions were also much the same – who are you and how did you get to be who you are?

Everyone is a rich, three-dimensional person – whether a killer or a choirmaster. Caricatures are of no use to me.

What was happening in the offender's mind? What did he see? What did he do and why?

In a sense, when I profiled an offender, it was like having a patient in my consulting room and going through a one-sided interview. What? Why? How?

Only when I knew certain things about him could I begin to move backwards through his life. Once I could put a shape to his personality and functioning, then I could ask myself, 'How did he get to be like that?'

And from there, I could draw conclusions about his background and lifestyle.

What sort of relationship did he have with his mother and father? What would it be like now? What were the different factors that could have led to this?

How did he regard women in general? Did he have a wife or a girlfriend? What were the relationships like?

How intelligent is he? How did he do at primary school and secondary school? What sort of work is he likely to do now? How will he relate to the people around him?

An unknown offender is like a patient who refuses to speak to me. But with enough information from other sources, it's still possible to paint a fairly detailed picture of a person's life.

5

When my son Ian was very young, he came down with a high fever and saw mysterious 'blobs' floating over his sickbed. These frightened him and made the illness much worse than it already was.

It's very hard to explain to a five-year-old that the blobs don't exist, particularly when he can see them above his head.

I came home one evening and as I climbed the stairs I heard Ian exclaiming, 'You've got one, Mum! Well done. There's another one by the door.'

I found Marilyn in his bedroom, wielding a child's fishing net on a bamboo pole.

'Is that the lot of them?' she asked. 'I'll just pop them out of the window. Now you'll be able to sleep.'

The blobs were never a source of fear again and whenever they returned they were fair game for Marilyn's net. I had never seen an incident like this written up in any text, but it should have been.

The human mind is not yet like a road map where the contours have been plotted and printed in detail. For all the studies and psychological experiments conducted throughout history, we're still dealing with broad pointers and categories rather than absolute signposts.

Occasionally a problem surfaces that science can't properly categorize because it doesn't fit easily into our understanding of human behaviour. When confronted with such a problem, we don't have to throw the rule-book out of the window and start again. The framework of investigation remains the same. It's as if a mechanic has to service a model of car that he hasn't seen before. Despite the unfamiliarity, he can be confident that the engine works on pretty similar principles to others he's seen.

The young woman in my waiting room, Susan Fuller, had a casual beauty and freshness that turned heads. The twenty-two-year-old languages graduate wore just a hint of make-up and nursed a leather satchel on her lap.

When Susan sat down opposite me in the consulting room, she pushed a fringe of hair away from her eyes.

'I know this is going to sound stupid,' she said nervously. 'It's just that I keep seeing someone in my room.'

'Oh, yes. Who?'

'I don't know him. He's not flesh and blood. He comes at night, when the bad dreams wake me. I know it can't be real, but he won't go away.'

'What does he want?'

'It sounds ridiculous, but I think he wants to have my body so that he can be here. He wants to push me out . . .'

Susan began describing the physical symptoms of her anxiety – the heart palpitations and tremors, the clamminess and gulping of air. It is almost impossible to convey in words how dreadful and terrifying this experience can be.

She was suffering from an existential anxiety that

was so profound it went right to her core. Some people are frightened of specific stimuli, such as spiders or going outside, and we call these 'phobic anxieties'. They are terrible problems but relatively easy to treat because there is usually a clear focus to them. Existential anxiety is far more difficult to deal with because there doesn't seem to be an obvious explanation and the magnitude of it confounds everything that has been in the patient's life up until that point.

Those who have had similar symptoms will understand, but others may scratch their heads and think, 'Well, I understand she's upset, but why doesn't she just get a grip of herself and carry on? There's nothing actually wrong with her.'

From my very first meeting with Susan, I had to reassure her that I knew exactly how frightened and alone she felt. I didn't doubt her sincerity or question her symptoms. My task was to help her discover what had happened.

I began by taking a history of the presenting problem – when it first manifested itself and how it had changed. Then I took Susan's personal history, beginning with her childhood and moving through her schooling, career and relationships.

The latter seemed to be unexceptional – so much so that it left a question mark hanging in the air. Occasionally it happens that someone has an anxiety-related problem that seems to be coming out of nowhere, but this is unusual. Normally there is something in the history and personality structure that gives some clue.

Susan's childhood had been happy and she spoke of her parents with great affection. At school she had been a promising and successful student, socially well integrated, academically bright and able to balance her studies and social life.

There had been boyfriends but there was nothing in any of these relationships, as she described them, that suggested undue dependence, violence or any of the many worms that can eat into a relationship and make it pathological.

On the face of it, here was a young woman of whom any parent would be proud; a well-grounded, much-loved individual who inexplicably had difficulty coping with the world.

This shouldn't be. I would have to dig deeper.

Retracing our steps, I asked Susan to tell me about university, where she had studied French.

'Where did you live?'

'On campus for the first year. Then I moved out into a student house with three other girls. We had a great group of friends.'

'What sort of things did you do?'

'The usual – drunken parties, nights at the pub, weekends away . . .'

'Anything else?'

Suddenly I noticed the behavioural equivalent of a fibrillation. Susan became sharply tense and uncomfortable. Her colour dropped and her breathing shifted.

The untrained eye might not have picked up on these things, but observation is a vital tool to a psychologist, particularly when it comes to understanding non-verbal communication. The slightest change in colour, breathing, heart rate, posture, muscle tension, pupil dilation and perspiration can help me recognize possible problem areas. At the same time people fidget and stir in thousands of small ways, particularly when they're nervous or frightened.

What had caused the change in Susan? I couldn't simply ask her because she clearly had held something back from me that she didn't want to talk about. I let her move on and we discussed other things while she settled down again. After fifteen minutes I came back to her social life at university, approaching it from a distance and asking her questions in fine detail.

This is a rather similar technique to the one I'd given the police interviewing Paul Bostock. It enables someone to become so accustomed to answering in specifics that the most important questions aren't flagged or easily recognized. There is nothing deceitful about this. It simply provides an opportunity to explore different areas more deeply, particularly if they conceal a problem.

I started asking Susan about particular friendships, boyfriends and girlfriends. These seemed to be quite normal until she mentioned another group of college friends who she spent time with.

'What sort of things did you do?'

'We'd go out together. Sometimes we'd go and see a band, or just go to the pub.'

'Anything else?'

Susan shifted uncomfortably. 'We went away for weekends.'

'Where did you go?'

'To Wales mainly. We did go to the Isle of Wight once. We hired a cottage near the sea.' She looked up at me, not wanting to continue, hoping that I would change the subject or move the conversation onwards.

I let the silence build a pressure in her. Finally she took a deep breath and her shoulders seemed to sag.

'I know this is going to sound stupid. I know it is. Really, we should have known better. We were all at university.'

'What happened?'

'Well, one night we decided to have a seance.'

'OK, tell me about that. A seance can be various things. Some people believe deeply in life after death and to them a seance is a way of staying in touch with folks who have gone before. Other people can regard a seance as a party game, or an opportunity to poke fun at someone . . .'

'I guess it wasn't really a proper seance. Jenny found a Ouija board in one of the cupboards in the cottage, and some of the others thought it might be a laugh.'

'Did everyone feel that way?'

'No. Wendy was pretty freaked out by the whole idea. She said something about opening a doorway to the devil. She didn't want to play.'

'What about the others?'

'The guys were laughing at her and saying things like, "You don't believe that mumbo-jumbo, do you? It's just a bit of fun." I didn't care, really. It's not as if I'm very religious and I didn't believe in ghosts. It was just a bit of fun.'

'And?'

'We started asking the board questions and we each put a finger on the glass. There were loads of jokes and wisecracks. Nobody took it too seriously, not even Wendy.'

Susan seemed to shudder.

'What happened?'

'All of a sudden it changed. We didn't ask the board a question, yet the glass started moving. It began spelling out the letters, Y..O..U A..R..E M..I..N..E. No-one said a word. Then the glass went sort of crazy – careering round the board, out of control, before it spun off and landed in my lap. I jumped and Wendy got scared. The lads were all laughing and saying things like "Ooh, I wonder how that happened?" I told them not to be so stupid.'

'Did it frighten you?'

'No, I was angry with them.'

The game had ended and Susan dismissed the 'prank'. She thought nothing more about it until in the weeks that followed she began to be woken at night by bad dreams. Most of them she couldn't remember in any precise detail, but they focused on her.

'That's when I began to see him . . . the man. I feel so stupid.'

'Who is he?'

'I don't know. He's older – I think maybe middle-aged – and he has a foul mouth; really nasty.'

'Is this something you're imagining?'

'I don't know.'

'What do you think is going on?'

'He says nasty things to me. I think he wants to hurt me; to push me out of my body; to take control . . .' She struggled to find the words, holding back from using terms like 'ghost' or 'phantom' because she was convinced that I'd bring out a straitjacket and have her committed.

At the same time she knew that her 'visitor' couldn't be real.

Eventually, she blurted, 'I think I might be possessed,' and looked up nervously.

'What do you think that means?' I asked, using my voice to reassure her.

She shook her head and tears gathered in her eyes. 'I'm cracking up. I don't know how to cope with this. Please, help me.'

I looked at the clock. The consultation had run out of time and another patient was waiting outside.

126

The story had come spilling out and Susan was dazed and distressed. I couldn't suddenly say, 'OK, I'll see you next week,' and let her walk away. What if she had a breakdown?

It had taken enormous courage for her to tell me these things. Now that she had opened the door and lowered her defences, I had to be sure she could deal with the trauma. I also had to be sure there were no hidden surprises still to come.

Sometimes when a patient realizes that I don't doubt what they're saying and I'm not going to ridicule them, it serves as a stimulus for them to release something more.

'Whatever is happening to you isn't normal,' I told Susan, trying to bring her down slowly from her crisis point. 'But at the moment we don't know exactly what that is. From your description this problem seems to be getting more difficult [I avoided saying 'worse'] and we need to help you get back in control of what is going on.'

'What do you think is happening?'

'Some people will tell you that you're imagining things . . .'

'That's what I thought you'd say.'

'No. You're not imagining this. And given what you've described, I don't think you are overreacting. But I'm going to be straightforward with you: I don't know whether this is something coming from a difficulty you have, or as a result of something that happened to you. Or it might be something entirely outside my competence and area of expertise.'

Susan had calmed down. She dabbed at her eyes with a handkerchief and then composed herself before leaving. I made an appointment to see her the following week. In the meantime, I would design an intervention that would help her regain control of her life.

During the next week, I spent some time thinking about Susan Fuller. She was a sensible woman who had no reason to be susceptible to seeing ghosts or phantoms. She wanted to be helped.

So what had happened?

I started to think in terms of hallucinations and psychotic processes, but decided there was no evidence of either. People who are not clinicians would talk about haunting, possession and split personality, but as a scientist I use the term 'dissociated state'.

The presence Susan described in her bedroom had a reality and a personality. This aggressive, foul-mouthed, middle-aged man had appeared several months after the Ouija-board game and had become 'more real' in the eight months since then, during which time Susan had finished university and started a job.

She had used the words, 'He wants to hurt me. He wants to control me. He wants to push me out of my body and take it over.'

This suggested a dissociation, yet if this were the case I would normally expect Susan to have a personality that wasn't as well integrated or as whole as the one she displayed. Similarly, some aspects of this *other* personality should have emerged from her history.

My first-floor office overlooked the entrance of the Mental Illness Unit at Leicester General Hospital. It had two chairs, a desk, a clock on the wall and an old examination table that adjusted up and down.

When Susan arrived she was much warmer towards

128

me and even managed a smile. From her point of view we had a more special relationship because I knew her secret.

I explained that I wanted to prepare her with relaxation skills that would hopefully increase her control over the physical symptoms she suffered. This is very important because a person may be intellectually aware of the way things are – with the intellect saying, 'This is stupid, it can't be real' – but as soon as the gut or heart kicks in, the intellect isn't worth buttons. Human emotions can easily swamp human intellect.

Another patient of mine, a man who had a phobia about needles, was entirely aware that unless he overcame this problem he risked dying from kidney disease because he couldn't tolerate dialysis and the various injections he needed. When I took his history I quickly established that this anxiety had begun in childhood.

'What a relief,' he said. 'I really thought I was going mad.'

Yet knowing the cause of the problem does nothing to change it. I'd been talking to his intellect, not his emotions. Unless I could help him control the latter, his phobia would be just as debilitating.

With Susan it was the same. I had to give her the tools to control her anxiety. This began by teaching her deep relaxation techniques. She lay down on the old examination table in the corner, which acted as my couch, and I slipped a cassette into a tape recorder. I recorded these tapes in a studio rather than reciting them to each patient. This avoided the possibility of outside noises interfering, such as car horns or voices in the corridor. It also meant that the patient could take the tape home.

'I want you to lie back and relax,' the tape began.

'Close your eyes and let your body go limp. What I'm going to ask will gradually become easy but I want you to concentrate only on what I'm saying. I want you to take a moment or two and let the rest of the world fade away. You might hear a car outside or a door closing, don't worry about that, just bring yourself back to what I'm saying . . .

'Close your eyes lightly, let your feet and legs go limp. Put your arms loosely by your sides with your hands open. Let them lie there. Just stay like that for a moment. Put your shoulders down. Now I am going to go to the different parts of your body and I'm going to ask you to do a series of exercises, tightening your muscles and relaxing them. Whenever I talk about a different part, I want you to bring your whole concentration to that place. Try to keep the rest of your body completely limp. You'll find it quite difficult at first, but don't get upset. It will come.

'Now concentrate on your right hand. When I tell you – not now – when I say, I want you to make a fist as tight as you can. I'll want you to hold it until I tell you to let go. When I tell you, I want you to release it suddenly, just letting the tension fall away. Now let's try that. OK, make a fist with your right hand . . . squeeze it tighter . . . tighter . . . tighter . . . much tighter . . . more . . . hold it. Now with your mind I want you to feel the tension, feel how tight it is, how hard. Now relax. Let go. Feel the tension just drift away. I want you to learn to feel the difference between the tension and the relaxation . . .'

I repeated this process for her left fist, her feet, ankles, calves . . . slowly moving up her body. Each new exercise had to be clearly described because I was teaching Susan a completely new skill. After about ten minutes we reached the lungs and I told her to take a deep breath. 'Deeper ... deeper ... more ... hold it! Feel the tension, feel the strain, don't let go ...'

Without warning, an angry laugh filled the room; a deep guttural sound that clearly came from a man. Susan's posture had stiffened and her chest swelled. Although she was still lying down, with her eyes shut, the muscles in her face began to change and become more masculine. An attractive twenty-two-year-old girl, with a light feminine voice, took on the features of a middle-aged man with a rumbling sinister laugh.

His lips curled into a sneer. 'She's mine, you bastard!'

A chill went through me. My mind became numb. What the hell was this? I'd never seen anything like it and couldn't recall anyone who had.

He laughed again, almost triumphantly. 'Don't think you can have her. You can't even imagine how powerful I am. I can crush you.'

What should I do? What could I say to him? A part of me wanted to yell down the corridor, 'Hey, come and listen to this!' Even stronger was the realization that I had to deal with it. Nobody else could help me.

All my training flooded through my mind. I could hear my old lecturers, John Annett, Steve Van Toller and Elizabeth Hitchfield, telling me that a psychologist in the field can't push the problem onto anyone else. 'Once you accept the responsibility, you've crossed the boundary – it's down to you.'

'You can't have her. She's mine.' He laughed, sounding supremely confident. 'Compared to me you're just a child.'

Having been brought up as a Roman Catholic, I knew all about the notions of devils and possession. It

131

was so easy to go in that direction. Here was a high-impact phenomenon. I had seen people in high-impact states before, but nothing as extraordinary as this. The physical and vocal changes were astonishing.

What are my options, I thought. Grab her and shake her awake? I couldn't be sure what that would do. It might damage her. Ignore the voice and carry on with the exercise? The relaxation tape was still running. If I kept giving her instructions she might move into a deeply relaxed state and disregard this phenomenon. Or maybe I could simply access her with my voice and bring her back.

None of these responses seemed right. Susan came to me with this problem; she told me something was taking her over and now I was confronted with it. It had to be an element of *her* personality. I had spent several hours interviewing and examining Susan. Now I had to start with this man. I knew I had to sound confident and cool, but I felt neither of these things.

I asked him, 'Who exactly are you?'

He laughed again. 'That's for me to know and for you to find out.'

'Well, it's easy for you to say that, but if I'm to help you . . .'

'You're not going to help me. Who do you think you are? You can't touch me. She's mine.'

It felt like I was arguing with a rival for a girl's affections. 'Why her? What's so special about her?'

'I chose her.'

'Why did you choose her?'

'Because she's mine.'

'She's come to me for help . . .'

'You can't help her. She's mine.'

'Why should I believe you?'

He laughed again. 'You stupid bastard. Do you think you can play word games with me? Do you know who I am?'

'No. Who are you?'

'That's for me to know and for you to find out.'

Anyone listening outside the door would have been convinced that two men were arguing. It had become an issue of control and a battle of wills, or maybe wits.

My mind was in overdrive. What did my training tell me? This sort of dissociation was normally manifested by a person with either some gross current stress in their life or a long history of environmental or family pressure that the victim felt could only be dealt with by splitting it off and letting a different part of their personality handle it.

Neither of these things was apparent in the history Susan had described. Even so, if this splitting is fundamentally complete, there isn't a crack or a wedge in the wall between the divided aspects of the personality. The division is so faultless that no-one viewing it from the outside will see the root cause.

Was this what had happened to Susan? Whatever the reason, I now had a unique opportunity to talk with another aspect of Susan's personality.

This is a natural phenomenon, I told myself. I have to understand it. I have to be able to bend it.

Susan had not moved. Her body was rigid and her chest full; her face that of a man. A string of obscenities filled the air.

'Why do you have to interfere with this helpless girl?' I said. 'What's wrong with you that you can't be what you want to be without her?'

'You stupid fucking cunt ... how can you be so

133

arrogant as to think that you can stop me. You're not having her, she's mine.'

'But she's not yours, is she? That's why she came to me.'

'Bastard . . . cunt . . . arsehole . . . fucker . . .'

I focused everything on that faceless voice. It was like negotiating with a kidnapper who had taken Susan. She had become a secondary victim because she was unconscious or disabled. The only way to hold an abductor such as this was to bend him with my words.

At the same time, I knew that in the rare instances of true multiple personality or dissociation, elements within the overall personality can change places for a while and my task might be to stop this fragmentation. To do this I had to deal with 'this' personality and face him down.

The abuse had continued.

'Words are cheap,' I told him. 'I hear what you say, but understand this – words are all you've got!'

His voice grew louder. 'BASTARD! . . . CUNT!'

'Yes, that's right. Keep shouting. It doesn't hurt me.'

'SHE'S MINE, YOU FUCKER!'

'I'm not going away. I'm not frightened of you and neither is she, now. She's had the courage to come here and to ask for help. She's with us now and you're not going to get her. You can try over and over and over again, but it won't make any difference. You're not having her. Do you hear me? She's not going to be yours.'

The invective came in a constant stream.

'She's going to be whole and complete. You may think she's vulnerable. You may not like how she is; you may think she's weak and passive, but you haven't got a prayer. Go now! Listen to me. Every time you try, I'll be there first. Remember that. I'm always going to be here. She only has to pick up the phone. You haven't been able to stop her doing that. Go now! While you still can. Go before I throw you out!'

There was no concluding riposte. No laughter, no anguished scream. I waited and watched the tension drain from Susan's body; watched as features softened and a frightened twenty-two-year-old woman returned. Her entire body seemed to shake. She hadn't opened her eyes and seemed to be in a slightly distant state.

Speaking very slowly, I began to reclaim her. 'Susan, listen to me. Just to me. Hear my voice. I'm going to count now, backwards from ten to one and as I count back you will become more and more wakeful. When I reach one you will be quite wide awake, and although you will be tired you will feel easy and relaxed. You will be able to talk to me. All right, I'm starting now: ten ... nine ... eight ... you're becoming more wakeful ... seven ... six ... five ... that's it, you're coming back to us ... four ... three ... two ... your eyes are opening ... one ... open your eyes.'

She lay still for two or three seconds, staring at the ceiling. Then she was consumed by an overwhelming bout of weeping. Tears tumbled down her cheeks until one shoulder of her blouse and part of her hair had become wet.

Slowly the sobs diminished. 'What happened?' she asked, all cried out.

'What do you remember?'

'Nothing.'

I told her in outline what seemed to have happened. She kept apologizing as though it had been her fault. I said it looked as though a part of herself had got out of hand but it wasn't clear exactly why.

'Usually when something like this happens, the person has had a particularly bad experience or is under some continuing difficulty but you haven't described anything like that. It might be something that's been blocked out so completely that we'll never discover the reason.'

'What happens now?'

'You'll keep coming to see me for a while, but having been through this experience you may find that it doesn't trouble you again.'

'It might be out of my system?'

'That's one way of putting it.'

I saw Susan perhaps another five times over the next few months. Her anxiety disappeared and she never again complained of having any sense of being 'visited' or troubled by anyone.

Interestingly, there were some subtle changes in her presentation. I had the impression of a young woman who had become more self-confident and assertive, not in an aggressive manner, but in terms of being more focused on what she wanted and determined to succeed. She had moved up the pecking order in the world and become less likely to give way to people if she disagreed with their decisions or opinions.

I think she had integrated the two elements of her personality. The woman I first met was lovely but not overly assertive. She wasn't inclined to put forward a strong opinion against someone else's or to set out confidently towards her goals. This all seemed to change following the watershed consultation. There had been a catharsis that had brought different elements of Susan's personality back into proper balance.

I don't regard what happened as being caused by the Ouija board. Whatever the underlying causal energy was that drove it, it was so well covered that I certainly didn't find it in the time I had available. Once Susan had recovered there was no need to keep searching – my job was done.

If I were a research psychologist, I might have felt it worth investigating further. However, having got over the consequences, I could see no reason. Sometimes fully unlocking the reasons behind a symptom can be more damaging than the patient's original problem.

Our mental defences serve a purpose. As long as Susan was able to function happily in the here and now, free of any symptoms, my role was complete. By investigating further and digging too deeply, I would risk taking down her natural defences and perhaps leaving her hopelessly exposed.

6

My working day usually began at nine thirty each morning and I had patients to see every hour. Each consultation lasted fifty minutes and I had ten minutes to write up the notes before my next session.

My case notes were almost a verbatim record of each consultation and I constantly tested and checked my work. I had become a painstaking history-taker, investigating every corner of a patient's life in the search for some small event, utterance or inconsistency that might unlock the reason for their difficulties.

Most of my patients had been damaged by unfortunate events in their lives – victims rather than perpetrators. However, by 1986 I found my clinical work had taken a more pronounced forensic turn.

My consulting room seemed to contain a growing number of patients who had committed crimes or were on the verge of doing so, as well as the victims of crime.

This had no link to my work with the police. It started off as the occasional referral growing out of my work in the sexual dysfunction clinic at Leicester General Hospital. There I had encountered people who hurt themselves sexually and others who had worrying urges and wanted help before they acted upon them.

For example, a young serviceman was referred to me with a phobic anxiety, yet I could not find sufficient evidence to support this. Eventually, he admitted that his real problem was that he'd been sexually molesting children he was babysitting. This hadn't been a cause of great shame until flashbacks of him abusing one particular child began intruding on his otherwise normal sex life with his wife.

Another patient, a nurse, couldn't stand anybody touching her neck. A colleague had made this mistake and she began screaming and raining down blows. Eventually it emerged that she had been attacked years earlier by a man who raped and tried to strangle her.

As well as these cases, I was also receiving an increasing number of court referrals, involving offenders facing charges such as indecent exposure, shoplifting or criminal damage. Psychologists are often consulted before sentencing. Sometimes the defence is looking to find something in mitigation for their client. At other times magistrates or judges are trying to understand what they are dealing with before passing sentence.

I didn't look for these cases and hadn't considered specializing in forensic psychology.

However, that summer I became aware that the post of head of the Regional Forensic Psychology Service had fallen vacant. For the first time I thought seriously about how far I wanted to go in this direction. It certainly meant a more highly graded post and a salary increase, but also a move away from the broad-ranging clinical work that I so enjoyed.

It meant providing a full-time in-patient service for people who had some of the most dangerous, depraved and damaged minds in the system. Did I want to spend all of my working life immersed in their dark worlds?

I thought about this for a long while and spent several nights at the kitchen table talking it over with Marilyn.

I couldn't deny that I was fascinated by the criminal mind. What made someone want to batter a woman or rape a young child? What were the triggers that caused one person to become violent and destructive and another to be a caring, conscientious member of the community?

These same questions had occurred to me in my twenties, when I was working as a night clerk for Automotive Products. One of the workers, Henry, was much older than I was. He stood out as having the ability to run the whole site as general manager, but he wouldn't change from his existing post which was more technical than man-management oriented.

Over breakfast in the canteen he occasionally commented on some overseas conflict that was in the news. However, he grew tense and silent if asked about his own wartime service. A few of the older men at the factory told me that Henry suffered from sleep disturbance and nightmares, and I thought this might explain why he chose to work nights.

Much later I discovered that he'd been a prisoner of war in Burma and suffered enormously at the hands of the Japanese guards. He'd been a commissioned officer or a senior NCO and he saw his men die from exhaustion, beatings and disease. I think he felt that he should have been able to protect them, but had let them down. This was wrong, of course. But even thirty years later a part of him was still back there in Burma, with his lost men. I have heard it said, and I agree, that the heart has reasons that reason itself knows nothing about.

The war emotionally scarred tens of thousands, but not all of them had Henry's nightmares. What made him different? Why did some old soldiers look back on those years as the most exciting and memorable years of their life? In the absence of war, everything seemed trivial – the politics, social changes and the people. Whereas for Henry, the war was something he desperately wanted to forget.

I couldn't have put it into words then, but incidents such as this and the questions they posed were part of the reason I became a psychologist. I was intrigued by people and the way their minds and bodies worked; why we do the things we do and become the people we are.

Years later, as a clinical psychologist, I met a man who suffered from a terrible stutter and the frustration this caused had led to angry outbursts and violence. As I began researching his history I discovered that his speech impediment hadn't emerged until he was seven years old. At about the same time his alcoholic father had begun sexually abusing him and his sister.

As he gave details of his family, I gradually realized that I'd once met his sister. It was on a school holiday in the late 1950s when I was about twelve and she must have been perhaps eight. The girl I remembered was hollow-eyed, in a hand-me-down dress. She sat watching most of our games, never joining in and rarely laughing.

She had the tell-tale signs of abuse but I didn't know it then. The memory left me with a sense of tremendous sadness. My childhood hadn't been perfect, but it suddenly felt strangely diminished and less happy. How many others were there, I wondered. Did they all suffer in silence?

Having talked it over with Marilyn, I applied for the regional forensic post. If I was successful, I knew that it wouldn't be easy to step back from forensic work. This area was not only emotionally challenging, it also carried one of the highest risks of clinical burn-out, although I didn't realize it then.

On 1 September 1986 I arrived at Arnold Lodge in Leicester to take up my position as the new head of the Regional Forensic Psychology Service. The squat two-storey tan-brick building was surrounded by a twelve-foot-high chain link fence and most of the windows seemed slightly tinted and couldn't be fully opened.

The regional secure unit housed about twenty-four patients, and had long-term plans for sixty beds. A control room at the main entrance was staffed by security officers, who controlled access to the complex through a series of airlocked doors that opened remotely, but never simultaneously.

Clearly, the residents were meant to stay inside, at least for the short term and theoretically for a maximum of two years. Some were to stay for very many more years than that.

The men and women at Arnold Lodge were mostly aged between eighteen and forty. Some of them had been responsible for or had the potential to do dreadful things – arsonists, paedophiles, rapists, sadists, killers . . . They were young, physically fit people and I could sense an energy in the unit, but it wasn't something exciting, rather something that had to be watched.

Among the patients were a woman in her mid-twenties who had set fire to a shopping centre and a man in his thirties who had cut out his daughter's eyes because he believed she was the devil's child. Another man had stabbed his father in the head while he slept; and a teenage poisoner had kept small, dismembered mammals in his bedroom.

Patients such as these had gone through the legal process, been convicted or detained under the Mental Health Act. Some of them had been sent to prison or a secure hospital such as Broadmoor or Rampton. Later they were transferred to Arnold Lodge for further specialist treatment on their way back into the community. It became our decision whether or not they still posed a risk to society, although some patients with particularly violent histories could be released only with the consent of the Home Secretary.

Among the other residents at Arnold Lodge were patients sent directly by the courts or from normal prisons. In each case they had to meet our risk management requirements and their psychological difficulties had to be viewed as treatable within the unit's timescale.

As head of the Trent Regional Forensic Psychology Service, my area of responsibility was the whole of Leicestershire, Nottinghamshire, Derbyshire, Lincolnshire and South Yorkshire. It was an area of roughly a thousand square miles and for the first few months, until I filled the posts around me, I *was* the forensic psychology service for a population of over five million.

My brief was to establish and develop a service that was appropriate for the region. One of the first things I recognized was that many outpatients were having to travel long distances to see me at Arnold Lodge. It took them hours to travel to Leicester and home again – all for a consultation that lasted fifty minutes.

It made perfect sense to me to set up clinics in the different geographical areas. Initially I travelled the region, meeting GPs and lawyers and explaining what I was doing. I set up the first clinic in Lincoln and soon after another in Barnsley. At first I did all the clinics myself, driving two hours each way and coming back to Arnold Lodge to do my in-patient work.

Soon I was able to appoint two very good psychologists to help me – Paul Cousins and a little later Steve Duffy. People who went into the forensic area in those days tended to be a little older and more experienced. Together we divided up the region. We all had Leicestershire, but I took Lincolnshire and part of Nottinghamshire for a while and then South Yorkshire.

Although there had been a forensic service in the region before, we were setting up a new system with fresh ideas and empty cupboards. Creativity and boldness were essential and we became adept at scavenging. If the service needed something, somehow we found it. Equipment appeared on our inventory lists at times when budgets or administrators were unhelpful.

Thankfully, these miraculous transfers of equipment didn't often raise eyebrows, although at one point a circular appeared asking budget-holders to be 'more in touch' with what was on their inventories. This led to some creative explanations about how our holdings exceeded our inventory.

In a very short time the new outpatient system proved to be so successful that we had more work than we could handle. People were referred by local doctors, often by solicitors and more rarely by clinical psychologists working in the NHS.

Nothing could have prepared me for how relentlessly grim it would be. Each day brought disbelief and sadness, particularly when I was dealing with the victims of crime or childhood abuse.

This is how Ray Knox first came to my notice – as an outpatient at one of the small regional clinics.

He was early for his second appointment. I noticed him sitting in his car in the car park. Perhaps he was settling himself to come inside. He still had his hands on the steering wheel. One of them was bandaged with gauze and strapping.

Five minutes later he came inside and sat down.

'What happened?' I asked, motioning to his hand.

'A work accident.' He didn't seem interested in elaborating.

'How has your week been?'

'OK.'

'Everything all right at home?'

'Yeah.'

He slid the cellophane wrapper from a packet of cigarettes and tapped a cigarette on the back of his hand.

'I'd prefer it if you didn't smoke.'

He shrugged. The cigarette stayed in his fingers, being twirled absent-mindedly. He fixed his eyes on mine.

'When you were being beaten as a child, where was your mother?'

'Out.' He spat the word.

'Did she know what was happening?'

'I couldn't hide the bruises.'

'Did she try to help?'

'When she was there.'

'Did your mother have to work?'

He shook his head. 'Maybe she did. She left him, you know. She left that fucking abuser.'

145

'When was that?'

'After I left home. She ran off with a bloke. I didn't find out until later that she'd been sleeping with him for ages.'

I could see Ray being torn up inside. He couldn't handle the possibility that his father might have been right about her. All of his faith and belief in this woman had been called into doubt.

'Where is your mother now?'

'She lives in Reading.'

'What about your dad?'

Ray flinched. He scratched at the scars on the back of his wrist. 'He disappeared when Mum left.'

'How old were you when that happened?'

'Sixteen.'

'How did you feel?'

'I was alive – that's something, I guess.' The words were laced with sarcasm.

'Did you see your dad after that?'

'Nobody knew what rock he crawled under. I hoped he was dead . . .'

I sensed he was about to add something, but he stopped.

'And then?'

Ray crushed the unlit cigarette between his fingers. 'He turned up again.'

'Where?'

'Not far from here. I saw him at a petrol station one day. He didn't see me. Do you know what happened?' He leaned towards me, as if sharing a secret. 'I was so scared I vomited. I sat in the car for an hour shaking like a leaf. Do you see what that bastard has done to me? You understand, don't you? He's got to be punished.'

146

I didn't answer. Ray had tried this already with me. He wanted his anger and violent thoughts towards his father to be legitimized. He wanted me to say, 'You poor man. You're absolutely right to feel this way.'

At the same time, he wanted to be helped. He had once been a polite, courteous, interesting and charming man. Yet now, in certain situations, he would become totally unrecognizable. There were bubbles of darkness within him that occasionally surfaced.

'I want to ask you about other areas of your life such as your schooling and work.'

'Why?'

'Because I need to know more about you.'

'But you know the problem. My fucking abuser is still alive. He's to blame. You can see that, can't you?'

'It looks as though he did some terrible things.'

'Terrible things! He *ruined* my life.'

'It's OK, Ray, I'm not brushing it aside. I understand why you feel this way, but I need to know how these things affected other areas of your life. For example, it must have been very difficult at school – hiding the bruises . . .'

'I wore long sleeves, or just didn't turn up.'

'Did you ever tell anybody?'

'No.'

'Why not?'

'How could I? I thought it was my fault, I was too ashamed.'

His eyes were no longer on me. The pace of his commentary had slightly changed. Ray's extraordinary sense of visualization had again taken him back nearly thirty years.

'How old are you?' I asked.

'Fourteen.'

'Is your father still abusing you?'

'Yes.'

'How do you spend your time?'

'School.'

'What about when you're not at school, when the bruises are too noticeable? What do you do then?'

'I go over the fields.'

'With friends or by yourself?'

'Sometimes with friends but mostly by myself.'

'What happens then?'

He paused. 'You're going to think I'm funny.'

'I doubt it. I won't laugh at you, if that's what you mean.'

'Well . . . I look for dead bodies.'

'What sort of dead bodies?'

'Well, I think that someone might have been killed and I will find their body.'

'How do you think you'll feel if you find a dead body?'

'I'm not sure. Good, I guess.'

'What would be good?'

He shrugged. 'I don't know. I can't explain. It would make me feel important.'

'What has happened? Have you heard something on the news? Does anything make you think there might be a body in the fields?'

'No, no. I know it sounds weird, but I just think I might find one.'

'What do you expect to find?'

'Perhaps a woman. She's on her back, with her arms out and her mouth open. Her clothes are rearranged.' He could describe how the woman was dressed and how she lay, but the details weren't as precise as a snapshot.

148

Here I was seeing the strong effects of chronic trauma. Even at an early age, in the solitary parts of Ray's life there had been a distortion. The damage had been done by events at home. Friendships hadn't developed; he had no sanctuary from brutality and instead had become emotionally isolated.

Why dead bodies? Because they offered something that he had never had in his life – a sense of control. Power over another living, or once-living, thing that couldn't threaten or hurt him at all.

Despite what Ray told me, nothing in my facial expressions or tone of voice could register any shock or disapproval. Instead I had to pretend to not even be there.

'Did you ever find a body?'

'Oh, yes.'

'How many?'

'Dozens of them.'

'What did you do?'

'I held them.'

'How did that make you feel?'

'Pretty good.'

A smile played on his lips. In his mind he was out there, walking in the fields. Such were his powers of visualization, he was able not just to remember past events but to create an entirely new world for himself. His own place – with all the detail that we'd expect in real life, right down to the grass and the trees and the breeze on his cheeks.

Some people are born with this heightened capacity for visualization. There seems to be a wide range of extreme sensory capacities. Many great chefs have the ability to 'taste' a combination of spices and foods simply by thinking about them. They can invent entire

149

dishes in their heads and know how each pinch of spice will subtly alter the flavour.

Similarly, there are musicians who have the ability to recognize and hear in their mind how any combination of instruments and notes will sound. Great vintners can taste a wine and know not just the grape, but what field the grapes were grown in and what time of year they were harvested.

Visualization was Ray's forte. In a child this shows as a heightened ability to fantasize and create imaginary worlds or games. When they daydream, they are truly in a different place. If he had grown up in an ordinary, nurturing family, Ray might have gone to art school or been a film director or painter.

Yet what would have been a gift for an artist was a curse for Ray. This sensitive child had been hurt and abused over and over again. A shutter in his mind had dropped. He didn't develop the same empathy and compassion that most children learn.

'Tell me about this place. Do you just walk through it?'

'No, I can do things there.'

'What sort of things?'

'Anything I want. It's my place. I can make it the way I want it to be.'

'How do you do that?'

'I just have to see it. I just live it.'

'Are you sitting down with your eyes closed, or are you walking along as you imagine these things?'

'No, no.' I could sense his frustration at not being able to find the words. His hands had become expressive. He leaned forward with his elbows on his knees. 'I'm in the fields and I'm walking. The path is muddy. I can smell the wet grass. But I can make it somewhere entirely new. I know it's imagining, but it's real. I'm there. I can see, hear and touch things. I can see round things. I can make things happen. I can make people do what I want.'

'The landscape changes?'

'If I want it to.'

'And what do you visualize?'

'Anything I want.'

'So what do you *want* to see?'

'That's when I find the bodies.'

'Did you always find bodies?'

'No. One day I found a rabbit caught in a snare . . .'

I didn't know if Ray was talking about the real world or his fantasy world.

'It was only just alive.'

'What did you do?'

'I held it.'

'How did that make you feel?'

'Good.'

'Why?'

'It was supple and warm. That's how bodies feel . . .'

'Did the rabbit die?'

'Yeah. I strangled it. It twitched a few times, but then it stopped. It stayed warm for a while.'

He spoke with a tremendous sense of peace. His eyes were closed and the lids fluttered slightly. His fingers were gently interlocked in his lap.

My voice didn't intrude on his calm. Meanwhile, in my own head, the alarm bells were ringing.

'What happened after that first time?' I asked him, already knowing the answer.

'I began looking for more. I started catching rabbits. We had some old snares in the garden shed. I set them up near the allotment. Rabbits were

151

always coming in to steal the carrots and beans.'

'What did you do with them?'

'I held them.' He hesitated.

'And?'

'I liked watching them die.'

He opened his eyes and glanced up at me, expecting me to recoil. I didn't show surprise or disgust. I understood that Ray's actions had arisen from his father's abuse and his mother's neglect and that ultimately this had poisoned almost every area of his life. He had low self-esteem, no friends and little social life.

The importance of physical closeness in a child's development is impossible to overstate. In the dying rabbits Ray had stumbled upon an opportunity to caress something that had mammalian characteristics.

Years ago, experimental psychologists conducted an experiment with baby monkeys which is quite dreadful when viewed today. The monkeys were starved until their body weight dropped and they were desperate for food. Then they were offered a choice between two substitute 'mothers' – one an open wire frame with a baby bottle of milk and teat attached and the other a wire frame covered in soft terry towelling but with no bottle of milk. Each time the baby monkeys chose the physical comfort of the cloth-covered 'mother' rather than the cold wire 'mother' with the sustenance. Despite their hunger, they chose something approaching mammalian warmth ahead of food.

I had to keep this in mind when considering Ray's actions. Caressing dead rabbits didn't make him a monster. Yet as he spoke, I heard familiar echoes. Quite recently I'd interviewed another man who described very similar actions. His name was Dennis Nilsen and he'd been convicted of killing six men in a five-year period during the late 1970s. His exact tally of victims is probably much higher.

A pale, thin man with a higher than average intelligence, Nilsen specialized in picking up homeless drifters and young men in London's gay bars and taking them home to his apartment in North London. Having cooked them a meal, he strangled them, cut up the bodies and tried to flush the human remains away into the sewers.

I interviewed Nilsen as a by-product of a Home Office 'Review of Offender Profiling'. In a companion study it was decided to develop a full library of pathological personalities on videotape. I would analyse and give a commentary on the interviews as a teaching tool for senior investigators.

For two days I sat opposite Nilsen at Albany Prison on the Isle of Wight. I took a history from him in exactly the same way as I do for any other patient. He described in detail how he picked up his victims, plied them with drink and some time during the night strangled them, usually with a garrotte made from string and a necktie. He would bathe the bodies, caress and often sleep with them for the first few days after death, and store them beneath the floor when not using them. One of the victims was brought out four times to sit in an armchair and keep Nilsen 'company' while he watched TV or listened to music.

As I talked to Nilsen about his childhood and adolescence, one of the features to emerge was his fascination with and the enormous emotional return he gained from caressing and interacting with dead animals. He spoke about the importance of being with death, caressing the lifeless body, 'the suppleness, warmth and control'.

From an external viewpoint this might seem to be a case of 'cruelty' to animals. But the word 'cruel' suggests a desire to cause distress and pain that isn't really correct. In the cases of both Nilsen and Ray Knox, the animal became a substitute human being.

Despite what might appear to be parallels, every case is different, and it's a mistake to put Nilsen's face on Ray Knox. We can never assume the outcome must be the same. Each individual is unique and complex. There are innumerable differences between all our lives.

The man sitting in front of me was a far more fragile human being psychologically than Nilsen ever was. The straight-line connection between what he suffered as a child and what he had become was also more apparent.

In comparison, Nilsen was more intelligent, articulate and egotistical. There was a much stronger sense of self-determination in the choices he made. He could so easily have chosen a different path from the one that led to Albany Prison.

Ray didn't have the same choices. And despite the similarities in their attitudes towards dead animals, it didn't mean that Ray was headed down the same path. Details such as this are not uncommon in people whose early years are traumatic. Mercifully, only a very small number go on to commit awful crimes.

Ray had fallen silent. He toyed with the gauze bandaging on his hand. He worried that he'd said too much. Could he trust me? For all his natural caution, Ray wanted to be helped. He was deeply ambivalent about acting on his violent urges. He wanted, even needed me to stop him.

I had travelled along this path before. Ray's amazing visual ability to create stories that were 'real' had started in childhood as a means of escape, but rather than waning as the years passed, it had grown stronger. He had added detail and richness to his imaginary world.

The 'finding of bodies' had been quickly left behind. Instead, his fantasies began featuring other forms of self-expression and self-control that were enhanced as he grew into adulthood.

The more Ray talked about his imaginary world, the clearer it became that it was now a most powerful and important influence in his life. He didn't try to hide the fact.

'Some folks who can visualize like this, Ray, eventually find that their ordinary, everyday life in the real world is quite dull and colourless compared to the richness of what goes on in their minds. How do you feel?'

He nodded slowly.

'Given the choice, where would you prefer to live?'

He gave an ambiguous shrug.

Ray knew that what I was suggesting made him sound quite mad. He also realized that if he told me the truth, it wouldn't be consistent with what he'd said earlier about how much he loved his wife and children.

I had no doubt that Ray preferred his alternative world. Given the choice – and with the exception of his family – he would rather live inside his head than in the here and now.

I wanted to know how he managed to keep his worlds separate. How did he divide his life?

'What about the external world, Ray? The here and now. What is going on there?'

'Well, I'm here with you.'

'Yes, but you've talked about how good it felt to be in control; to be calling the shots. A lot of people

155

would try to find some way of holding on to that feeling. What about you?'

'I suppose.'

'You spend a lot of time thinking about your father. You've already explained what a terrible impact he had on your life. When you think of him now, how does it come to you?'

'What do you mean?'

'When you relive events and hear things that were said, where are you?'

'In my place.' He tapped the side of his head.

'Is your father there?'

'Oh, yes.' His top lip curled in disdain.

'Do you wonder about all the things that have gone wrong?'

'Of course. Wouldn't you?'

'Do you talk to him?'

'Yeah.'

'In this place that you go to, are you still a child and he an adult?'

'No. I'm grown up.'

'And you find yourself saying things to him?'

Ray nodded. 'I could never talk to him before. He wouldn't listen. He just hit me. But now he's mine. He's in my place. I can say all those things I wanted to say.'

'What do you say to him?'

'I taunt him. I tell him what I think of him.'

'Does he answer?'

'He has to. That's the law. There's no right to silence in my courtroom.'

As soon as he mentioned the word 'courtroom' I knew it had tremendous significance to Ray's story. I asked him to explain what he meant.

'It's all there. I do things properly. There's a judge and a jury; the prosecution and the court bailiff.'

Ray had leaned forward in his chair. He began performing an elaborate play in which he took on all the roles. He had a different voice for each part.

'How do you plead? . . . Silence! Will the defendant stop snivelling! I'll now hear the prosecutor's opening statement . . .'

Ray half turned in his chair, as though addressing someone at the window. His eyes were closed. 'Why did you do this to me? Why weren't you like other fathers? Do you realize that you ruined my life?'

'What does your father say?'

'He denies it, of course. He's a liar and a bully.'

Ray opened his eyes and looked directly at me. 'I made him pay, you know. Just like I'll punish all of you.'

'What do you mean?'

'You can't get away with it. You're paying for it now.'

'Who is paying?'

'People like you.' He spat out the words.

'What have I done?'

'You're like the rest of them, aren't you?'

'Who?'

'You don't really care about me. I'm just your two o'clock appointment. What is it now? Twenty to three. Soon I'll be gone and someone else will be sitting here. You don't care about me.'

'Who have you punished, Ray?'

'Shut up! It's my turn. I'm the judge now. I do the sentencing.'

'But you haven't been to court. You didn't come from the courts.'

He smiled. 'You don't understand, do you?'

'No. Tell me.'

'It's not your court. It's my court.'

'Tell me about your court.'

'I put them on trial.'

'Who is being tried?'

'You all are. I am the judge. I am the jury. I decide what happens.'

'Where is this court?'

'At home. In the basement. With the chair.'

'What chair?'

His eyes bored through me. 'The electric chair.'

7

Ray blinked rapidly, as if something had caught his eye. Everything about his body seemed coiled to strike. He wanted to explode, to lash out at someone . . . anybody.

'Tell me about the electric chair?' I asked, keeping my voice unchanged.

I could almost see his mind coming back to me. It was like swimming up through dark water towards the surface. He looked at me as though he couldn't comprehend the world any more. What had he told me? Had the words stayed inside his head?

'Where did you get the electric chair?' I began again.

'I made it.'

'How did you do that?'

'I found the chair in a skip and it went from there.'

Was I dealing with something that was real, or a figment of his fantasy world?

'Where is the chair now?'

'In the basement at home. That's where I keep my tools. Stella doesn't go into the basement.'

'What did you do with the chair?'

'First I stripped off the paint. It had teddy bears stencilled on the seat. I sanded the wood until I could see the grain. I made the leather straps to hold the arms and legs and neck. I used the leather and buckles from an old saddle. The bands are wide. Then I bolted the chair into the concrete floor so it couldn't move or topple over . . .'

Ray didn't try to contain his excitement. He related the story with pride. Then he explained how he'd set up his 'courtroom'. The wood had to be cut, the joints made and glued together. He had carefully shaped, sanded and varnished each component. With such levels of detail this couldn't be a flight of fancy. This had to be real.

'How long did it take you?'

'Almost a year.'

'When did you find the time?'

'Weekends . . . holidays.'

'Why do you call it an electric chair?'

''Cause it's hooked up to a transformer and then the mains.'

'Why have you done that?'

'Why do you think? It's where I punish them. I put them on trial. I find them guilty. I sentence them to death.'

There was a long pause. I had to be very clear about what he was telling me. I couldn't put words in his mouth.

'I know this is important to you, Ray. I know it's taken up a lot of your time, but who exactly do you want to punish?'

'My fucking abuser. That's where I put him on trial. That's where he dies.'

My thoughts were swimming. I had so many questions. Ray's revelations had shocked me, but I couldn't let it show. How much of this was in the real world? Were these all fantasies?

160

'Do you know why they put leather masks on people before they go to the chair?' asked Ray.

I shook my head, not really wanting to hear the answer.

'Because their eyeballs pop out. And their bowels are supposed to open, but it doesn't always happen . . .'

'Ray,' I said, focusing his attention back on me. 'Who do you put in the chair?'

'My fucking abuser.'

'Your father.'

'Yeah.'

'Has he really been there?'

Ray suddenly looked disappointed.

'Who then?'

He paused. 'Well . . . you remember the rabbits?'

'The ones that you used to catch.'

'Yes.'

'Now I buy them at the markets and pet shops.'

'How do you get them home?'

'I've got a box in the boot of my car.'

'And what do you do with them?'

'I . . . I . . . put them on trial.'

It was important that I discovered all the details. How much thinking had gone on behind it? How much rehearsal? Once I had all this information, I could go back and investigate what went through his mind as he carried out his role-play.

I always question the veracity of any patient, but I could find no reason to doubt what Ray was telling me. His fantasies didn't need props like rabbits. He could punish his father over and over again in his imagination. That's why I knew the courtroom and chair had to be real.

To some people it might sound far-fetched that a

161

husband and father could turn his basement into an execution chamber and not attract suspicion. You might ask, 'Where was his wife all this time?'

In reality, a surprising number of people have their own special room or place. For men it might be a garden shed, a loft, a workshop or a basement. Women have studies, walk-in wardrobes or studios. It isn't an issue of doors being locked or 'Keep Out' signs posted. Instead, there is an understanding that each spouse accepts.

'And your wife never goes into the basement?' I asked.

'No. She used to – years ago – when I was working. She'd sit on the steps with a cup of tea and chat. I'd be repairing some piece of furniture or one of the girls' bikes. When the girls grew older, I started keeping it locked.'

The details of Ray's pathological fantasy had partly been determined by the facilities at his disposal. The basement was his private place. He had the key. He made the most of what he had available, turning the interior landscape into a real-world setting for his violent fantasies.

'So what happens in your basement?'

'That's where I put them on trial.'

'Rabbits?'

'Yeah.'

'What do you do?'

'I put each one in the dock. Then I read the charges.' Ray's eyes were fixed in a distant stare. '"You are accused of having abused and beaten an innocent child. You ruined his life. If I'm abnormal it's because of you. If I'm a failure it's because of you. The friends I never had. The fun times, the wishes and dreams that

162

never came true – these are your fault. You did this to me . . ." '

'What does your father say?'

'He pleads for mercy. He's snivelling and grovelling. I put a black cloth on my head and pass sentence.'

'What happens then?'

'I shave patches of hair on his head. That's so I can attach the electrodes. I made these metal discs with a rubber holder. I put a wet sponge in between the skin and metal plates to conduct the electricity better. I had to experiment a bit on the right voltage. Too much and it shocks them to death. Too little and the brain cooks. I've got it sussed now. Two charges are normally enough – a minute each, with a few seconds in between.'

Ray didn't revel in this description. This was an exercise in taking away pain rather than gaining satisfaction. This is a very important distinction. He knew it was abnormal to execute rabbits, but he could excuse himself because of what had been done to him. It was not his fault. It was his father's doing.

The session ended. I watched Ray walk down the path to his car with his head lowered and arms barely moving at his sides. He didn't make eye contact with a porter who held open the gate for him.

All I could think was, 'Where is he going now? What is he thinking?'

At home in his basement, this man had an electric chair. It wasn't designed just to kill rabbits. He'd spent hours preparing, symbolically at least, to execute his father.

There were two strands running alongside Ray's cruelty to animals. The first was a completely unyielding and undimmed anger and hatred for his

163

abuser. This was the engine driving him and its power couldn't be overemphasized. It might not have been visible when he walked down the street, but inside it fuelled him. It was the central reference point of his life.

The second strand – and the more dangerous – came as a consequence of his capacity to visualize. The boundary that existed between Ray's internal world and the ordinary external world had begun to fray.

He used to know what was imaginary and what was real. He could shut the door on his fantasy world and live quite normally in the real world, with his wife and family. Now aspects of his fantasies were leaking into his everyday existence.

Ray wasn't mad. He didn't hallucinate. Nor was he trapped in his fantasy world. He knew about his immense imaginative capacity. This was something he created and controlled. Until now the boundaries had been very well defined. But something had happened. A fuzziness now blurred the lines. He couldn't keep the two worlds separate any more.

Mercifully, so far the crossover appeared to have been mainly symbolic. But something had to have happened to trigger this change. What had caused the crossover? And if the boundaries were fraying, what else had moved from his fantasy world into the here and now?

I looked again at the time-line of Ray's history. He had built his electric chair two years earlier. His father had turned up five years ago. The gap between the events was too long for this to be the trigger. What had taken place in the meantime?

The following Thursday, Ray looked slightly dishevelled and tired. His hair hadn't been combed and it appeared as though he might have slept in his clothes.

'I've been driving around,' he told me.

'Any particular reason?'

He didn't answer.

'How long have you been driving around?'

'Since yesterday.'

'Where did you drive to?'

'I can't remember exactly.'

'Places you knew?'

'I don't know.'

He wanted me to change the subject. It wasn't avoidance as much as him not being ready to tackle the issue. He needed more time.

'Have you had many violent fantasies this week?' I asked.

He nodded and looked at me with a mixture of resignation and pleading. 'I tried not to go out. I didn't go to work for two days.'

'What did you do?'

'I stayed home. Stella was at work and the kids were at school.'

Ray scratched fretfully at the knees of his trousers, threatening to tear through the fabric. A splattering of mud had dried on his turn-ups. I could see where he'd tried to pick it off with his fingernails. At the same time his shoes were clean. He'd obviously changed them.

'But eventually you did go out?'

'Yes.'

'Where?'

'Nowhere.' His voice hardened and his eyelids began blinking rapidly. I'd noticed this happen in our early sessions, whenever a question put him under stress.

His voice softened. 'I tried, I really tried,' he said tearfully. He buried his face in his hands. 'What on earth is happening to me? When I'm on my own I lose touch with what's real and not real. Why shouldn't I be in my bright world all the time? But why do I always have to hurt them?'

'So where might you have gone?'

'I swear to God I don't know. I can't remember. When I do, it just goes hazy. I got dirty, but I haven't done anything. You know I don't lie to you, you've got to help me. I can't go on like this.'

'If it's hazy, Ray, how do you know you didn't do anything?'

'There's nothing, only mud. Just now I spoke to Stella on the phone. Everything's all right. I told her I was OK. She asked me where I'd been. I couldn't tell her. She wouldn't understand. You see, I couldn't get out ... I went inside my head and I couldn't get out. I know I haven't done anything – I haven't really been here.'

'The other day, when you hurt your hand, how did it happen?'

'I cut it with a wallpaper knife.'

'An accident?'

He shook his head. 'My mind started to slip. I had to stop myself. The pain helps. Whenever the urges get too bad, I try to change my thoughts. I used to pedal my exercise bike and build up a real sweat ... until that wasn't enough any more ...' The sentence trailed off.

'How long has it been like this?'

'Two years, I guess.'

'That's when you started buying the rabbits.'

He nodded. 'But it's not enough any more. I have to punish someone. I have these dreams, only they're not dreams. I ... I ...' He couldn't go on.

'Do you talk to Stella about them?'

'No!' He looked horrified.

'Tell me about her.'

'I've already told you.'

'Yes, but what's she like?'

'Wonderful. She dotes on me. You'd never find a better wife and mother.'

'That's really good to hear. You suffered so much at the hands of your father that it's great that you have something good in your life. How long have you been together?'

'Fifteen years.'

'How have you made it work?'

'What do you mean?'

'Well, you've talked about how you feel that you haven't had much going for you over the years. A lot has gone wrong. How does it feel having someone who is so wonderful, so lovely, sticking with you?'

'Well, good . . .'

'Tell me about her.'

Again the description was filled with words like beautiful, wonderful, lovely, kind-hearted and caring.

The woman doesn't exist who is this perfect. Neither does the man. I could almost see the wagons circling in Ray's mind, keeping everything inside safe and secure. What was he trying to protect?

'She sounds very special indeed,' I said.

'Yes, she is.'

'For a moment, let's set that alongside the way you describe yourself. How is it that such a wonderful person wasn't snapped up by somebody else? How did you manage to get her?'

I noticed a slight change in his breathing pattern.

'And how have you managed to keep her? She sounds like the sort of woman that other men might want to get close to.'

The change in his breathing had become more pronounced.

'It's a sad fact of our times, Ray, that some folks out there don't pay much attention to whether a person is married or not. Your wife works, doesn't she? How does she cope with the attentions of other men?'

'What do you mean?'

Because of his ability to visualize and hold things in different compartments, I knew that Ray was well practised at keeping things hidden. At the same time, he'd been struggling to get through the day-to-day act of living. Something wasn't quite right – there was a sensitive area that he didn't want exposed.

'So does she get attention from other chaps?'

'I don't want to talk about that.' The statement bordered on a threat. This wasn't the little boy talking. Here was a very decisive and dangerous adult male. He was letting me know that if I persisted, he couldn't be responsible for what happened next.

I had to carry on.

'You don't have to talk about it. There are a lot of reasons why some people try to block out particular things. Sometimes it's because they are too painful. Sometimes they feel it might embarrass them, or make them feel stupid. Sometimes they're afraid they might get into trouble. At other times, they simply haven't thought it through . . .'

I set out a continuum, starting with the most extreme things it could be. I had to reassure him that, whatever he said, I wouldn't be shocked or repelled.

'Problems come in all shapes and sizes. People find themselves attracted to somebody else and cheat on their wives or husbands. The marriage might break up or they could get back together again. Or it may be that a man who has been hurt terribly in childhood finds he is now doing similar things to his wife. He hates what he's doing, but he can't seem to stop ... What about you?'

'I *don't* want to talk about it.' The words were deliberate and laced with menace. Ray was half up out of his chair, making full use of his size to intimidate me. I had seen at first hand how explosive and dangerous he could be. The dents were still in the filing cabinet.

I backed off slightly, knowing that I'd bring him back to the subject. Instead I asked about his children – 'my girls', as he called them.

His face softened. 'They're great girls. Such sweethearts,' he whispered. Julie and Rita were 'daddy's girls', he said, forever crawling onto his lap and hugging him. He spoke of them in a way that suggested they were much younger than thirteen and ten.

'Julie will soon be a young woman,' I said.

He suddenly seemed deeply alarmed. 'She's just a little girl.'

'She's thirteen years old, you said. She's a teenager.'

'No, not really. She's just a wee thing.'

I could see problems ahead for Ray. Perhaps they had arrived already. His little girls were growing up. He wasn't sure if he had the capacity to nurture and guide them to mature, decent womanhood. That was his wife's role. He had always assumed that she would do this for his daughters, but something had shaken his belief – an uncertainty that he refused to tell me about.

'Does Julie have a boyfriend?' I asked.

Ray looked horrified.

'She's not ready for that. She's a child.'

'Are you ready for that day?'

He didn't answer. He didn't know.

I definitely needed to resolve his 'fairy tale' image of his wife and marriage. This took a long while and set the pattern for our immediate future sessions.

Each week I asked him about events at home. I tried to address any problems that were creating stress in his life. These small repair jobs were important because they were easing the pressures on him.

At one point he mentioned that Rita, his younger daughter, was being bullied at school. A part of Ray wanted to storm into the school and cause mayhem to all and sundry. I helped him deal with that. I gave him the psychological skills to rationalize what was happening and resolve the problem without aggression.

These might seem to be side issues, but our lives are like a complex web. All the threads are interlinked. You can't break one without it affecting the others.

Throughout that next month, I periodically steered Ray back to his marriage.

'I know this is painful, but we can't ignore it for ever. I know it might even be risky, but we can't leave it alone. I want to talk about your wife.'

He grew agitated.

'I don't want this to happen,' he said, flexing his fists.

'I know. Try to hold on.'

'Please don't do this.'

'I don't take any pleasure out of prying into what goes on in your bedroom. We have to do this. Even though your life is wrecked as far as you are concerned, the one thing you have managed to hold together is your marriage. Then, suddenly, two years ago, something happened to change that. I need to know what it was.'

Ray rhythmically rocked in his chair, backwards and forwards. His eyes had turned glassy.

'Let me do the talking, if that helps. But if I'm missing it, you might want to steer me in the right direction.'

He didn't respond.

'You have a wonderful marriage. Your wife is lovely, attractive, caring. But then something happened which you found difficult to cope with. You also say that everything is OK now. How has that come about?'

'It just did.' He sounded like an eight-year-old.

'All right . . . but when things weren't going so well, it must have been very difficult. I mean, this woman sounds as though she is the best thing ever to happen to you.'

The dam broke quite suddenly. Great tearless sobs rattled in Ray's chest. Slumping down in the chair, he struggled to speak. Broken sentences made him difficult to understand. Very painfully it emerged that two years earlier his 'perfect marriage' had faced a crisis. First, he had detected a change in Stella.

'How had she changed?'

'She was just different . . . more distant.'

'In what way?'

'Sort of mysterious, you know. She started going out more than before.'

'Where did she go?'

'Yoga classes, she said. But they were two and sometimes three evenings a week.'

'Was there some reason to doubt this?'

'Well . . . ah . . . maybe, I don't know. She just sounded a bit fuzzy when I asked her about it.'

'What did you do?'

Awkwardly, he replied, 'I followed her.'

171

Ray described how he parked outside the club and watched her go inside. She wore a leotard. He didn't like the idea of her in revealing clothes. He watched her through a window. There seemed to be one particular chap who spent a lot of time chatting to her before and after the class. They had a fruit juice together at the health bar.

Later, back at home, Ray had casually asked her about the yoga classes and whether she had made any friends at the gym.

'No, not really,' she replied.

'How many people are in the class?'

'About eighteen of us.'

'Men and women?'

'Mainly women.'

'So you haven't got to know any of them?'

'No.' She teased him. 'You sound very interested. Do you want to come next time?'

Ray told me that he'd believed her, but he didn't sound convincing.

'How did you feel about your marriage?' I asked.

The shutter dropped again.

'No, Paul, don't ask me. I can't talk about this. There's nothing . . . Don't make me. Please don't make me . . .'

This was eating away at him. He could not deal with the possibility that his wife and marriage might not be perfect. All that his father had ever said about women echoed down the years and reverberated through his head. All his bitter tirades about wives being sluts and telling lies.

It was several weeks before I could broach the subject again. Still Ray insisted the marriage was perfect. They had great sex. She was perfectly content with him.

'Did you stop following her?' I asked.

He lowered his eyes and shook his head slowly.

'Tell me what happened.'

The account he gave me sounded quite consistent with his fears. He had followed his wife and watched her. She had met the chap from the gym for coffee. Their rendezvous was in an out-of-the-way place and they arrived in separate cars.

Yet when Ray asked Stella, she described her ordinary day at work without mentioning anything else. It's quite possible this man was a perfectly innocent acquaintance, a friend. Yet Stella couldn't tell Ray because she knew how jealous and stressed it would make him.

Ray's distress was almost crippling. Everything his father had hammered into him about women was suddenly true. His cruel, dictatorial, sadistic abuser had been right. He tried to cope, but the doubts consumed him. Eventually he confronted Stella. Clearly frightened, she denied it outright, telling him that he'd misunderstood what he'd seen. She just happened to bump into the same chap a few times. Nothing more.

Although Ray knew in his heart that this was a very lame account, he insisted to himself that he believed her. This was because of his absolute need to sustain his perfect marriage and deny his father's assertions.

Soon, other stresses emerged. Husband and wife had slowly stopped having sexual intercourse. Another signal that her affections were elsewhere?

More immediately, it created great sexual frustration. Ray had an unusually high sex drive and needed to have intercourse at least once a day and often two or three times. He didn't regard this as being remarkable. Quite the opposite. His wife enjoyed sex just as much

173

as he did, he said. But now it had cooled, despite her assurances that nothing had happened in the marriage.

Unable to rid himself of his doubts, Ray found himself doing all the things that his father used to do – checking the bedding, looking for receipts in her purse, smelling her clothes. By any standards, let alone his own, he wasn't coping.

'Am I my father's son? Am I just like him?'

He began following her again. This time he found her car parked outside a quiet office block. The chap's car was parked nearby.

Ray waited until they left separately.

'What did you do?'

'I confronted him.'

'What did you say?'

'I didn't get a chance to say anything. He saw me and started running. He jumped in his car and tore off.' Ray laughed wryly.

'What did you say to your wife?'

'Nothing.'

Again I could see Ray closing down. He didn't want to say anything more. 'Everything is fine now,' he explained. 'We're really happy. She's wonderful.'

Whenever I tried to raise the subject again, he refused to answer. The curtains had been drawn on the issue. 'It's got nothing to do with my problems,' said Ray. 'So stop asking me about it.'

He was wrong. I had no doubt that these events had completely shattered the stable world that Ray had built around himself. He feared that his wife had been unfaithful. The one shining example of goodness and trust in his life had been called into question.

For Ray this was the final confirmation that he was a completely failed human being. He was such an inadequate specimen of humanity that this perfect wife had looked elsewhere. He didn't blame Stella. She was still on a pedestal. Instead he blamed his father.

Ray didn't use these words to me, but this is what came through when I looked at him and read between the lines.

'My life has been a mess,' he muttered. 'That bastard did this. Why can't I be normal?'

Ray believed that he hadn't achieved anything in his life. Everything had failed. Even the things that people take for granted, such as a loving marriage and children, had been spoiled. Why? Because of his 'fucking abuser'.

These were powerful energizing thoughts and feelings. They were the triggers for his violent urges. In childhood he had escaped his pain by going to his 'other world', where he controlled things. In those early days, the element of violence in his fantasies had been quite mild.

This had changed. Revenge now consumed him. He focused on little else. He planned it and revelled in the detail. He didn't have to tell me this directly, he said it through the rabbits and the electric chair.

Yet I needed to know the content of his main driving fantasy. How far had the boundaries frayed between his alternative world and reality? Several times already he had seemed to confuse events in his internal and outside worlds.

I began to talk to him about dissociation, trying to help him understand that he wasn't unique or mad.

'Sometimes terrible things happen to people and they have several options open to help them cope,' I told him. 'Some go under – by killing themselves or, occasionally, taking others with them. Some get carted

175

off to a special hospital and locked away. Alternatively, some people deal with it head on and try to put a new life together. This isn't easy. It's much easier to hide. I've met people who close great internal steel doors to the world and pretend that the problem has gone away. But it's still there, Ray. It hasn't been dealt with at all.'

He looked at me nervously.

'People try to hold it back. Sometimes they use their fantasies to release the pressure. But what happens if the line between fantasy and reality becomes blurred? What if they can't hold back their anger?

'Let me tell you what happens, Ray. A person will sometimes split off the part of their thinking and feeling that is hurting. Then they carry on as though everything is OK. The problem is that it's too strong. It pushes through when they're under great pressure. That's when they sometimes do things that are out of character. Often they're not properly aware of exactly what they've done. They tend to know they've changed or that they aren't their usual selves. But they can't quite put their finger on what's happening.'

Ray looked marooned in his misery. His brow had creased into deep hollows. I could see his carotid artery pumping in his neck.

'What are you going to do, Ray?' I asked. 'Are you going to press on, or try to put things right?'

He murmured, 'I want to put things right.'

'Let me tell you what I think. In the privacy of your head, you've developed ways of dealing with the pain. It worked when you were a little boy, and as an adolescent, and as a man until a little while ago. Now you're finding it hard to hold your life together. You can't do it any more.'

His shoulders sagged a little further. He looked up at me gently.

'Now, for the first time, somebody has offered you an explanation. I'm not justifying or condoning what happened to you, or how you feel. I'm simply telling you that I understand.'

'Is that why I feel like this?'

'Yes.'

He was about to ask another question, but I interrupted. I didn't want him taking us off on a tangent. I wanted him to focus on what I was saying.

What triggered his rich and deviant fantasy life was now evident, in the open as it were. This knowledge was like a key that would unlock his mind and let me inside.

I never assume that I have all the facts. On the contrary, I assume that patients are always holding something back. This normally means that I'm not surprised or taken off guard.

In Ray's case I knew there were things he hadn't told me, but I now had the chance to discover what really went on inside his head. What were the fantasies that frightened him so?

8

When I first set eyes on Broadmoor some fifteen years ago, I carried the baggage of its forbidding reputation. Like most people, I had grown up with the newspaper stories, TV reports and the myths that surround the criminally insane.

Of all the 'special' hospitals in England and Wales which treat men and women in a high security setting, Broadmoor has had the greatest impact on the national consciousness. The same could also be said for its immediate environment, where it dominates its surroundings. The red-brick walls are so high and so thick they reinforce the darkness of its image. No amount of tree planting or landscaping can soften the architecture.

In all my visits since then, I have never entirely shaken off the shiver of apprehension I felt that day. It isn't a pleasant place.

Now I was back there again. The drive from Leicester had been horrendous. A colleague from Arnold Lodge had offered to take his car and I unthinkingly agreed. His accounts of various road traffic accidents that had never been his fault were repeating in my head.

Driving down the M1 he stuck to the busy central lane, turning his whole head to talk to me. I stared directly out of the windscreen at the back of a lorry that we were closing on at frightening speed.

Should I say something, I wondered. At the very last second he swerved. I could count the rivets on the outside of the lorry.

'My God, did you see that clown pull out on us? Bloody maniac!'

Eventually we reached the back roads of rural Berkshire and turned left at a junction in the little village of Crowthorne. Climbing a long hill, I became aware of changes in the housing design. The mix of style, the clash of painting schemes, the jumble of new and older windows gave way to inherently sombre, institutionalized housing for hospital staff.

Of course impressions are influenced by expectations. No amount of effort by staff to individualize the homes could compensate for the silent presence of the walls towering above them.

We parked the car and climbed on foot up a long, sometimes stepped path through the pine trees to the main gate. In the old days the entrance resembled that of a Victorian prison more than a hospital, but a new entry section has been built since then, with reinforced glass above the counters and airlocks on the doors. The coffee machine is best ignored.

Through the main gate, across the neat new yard, I could still see the old multi-storey wings with narrow windows and doors with oversized locks. The business end of the hospital was much the same as it had been for a hundred years.

Broadmoor doesn't have the same odour as a prison. The cabbage smell is missing and some of the sweat.

179

Instead the air seems to contain a mixture of mustiness and floor polish.

Doors have to be knocked upon, keys turned and bolts slid open. Everything except the bedrooms and the nursing offices is on a large scale. The big solid doors have keys that could unlock a castle. I often wonder how the nurses can walk normally with so much weight on the keyrings dangling from their belts. Some of them looked more like archetypal prison warders than prison warders do.

Special hospitals like Broadmoor have long had a reputation for draconian and cruel regimes. Occasionally this reputation has been justified, as various reports and complaints have shown. Nurses and guards can be cruel. On my first visit, I began to understand the culture that can make some of these people swagger in their uniforms. The keys hanging on their belts are a very important symbol. It says, 'I am the keyholder. It is up to me to decide whether or not I open this door.'

Not everyone is like this, of course, but a fascinating experiment was carried out in the early 1970s at Stanford University in California. The Psychology Department recruited undergraduate volunteers to participate in a study of prison life. One group of subjects was randomly assigned to be prisoners and another assigned to be guards. The prisoners were picked up and taken to holding cells in the Psychology Department.

The plan was to simulate the prison environment – for both guard and inmate – and then study the psychological consequences.

Social psychologist Philip Zimbardo intended the experiment to last two weeks but had to abandon

180

the exercise after only five days. Some of those students assigned to guard roles had started to brutalize, torment and dehumanize the prisoners. Instead of commanding respect, they wanted total control and obedience.

Meanwhile, those who were called prisoners had become apathetic and psychologically disturbed. One of them had to be released after thirty-six hours, suffering from disorganized thinking and uncontrollable crying.

Zimbardo was interested in identifying the factors which led to prisons being violent and degrading places. He also wanted to gain an understanding of how people become socialized in their different roles. What are the forces that affect them?

The results of the experiment were quite frightening. The guards had internalized in their thinking a sadistic and punitive role for themselves. The ultimate stimulant is power. Meanwhile, the prisoners had become withdrawn and compliant, accepting their isolation and humiliation.

Not everybody succumbs to these expectations. Our prisons and special hospitals are now far better run and policed, but this has to be a dynamic process that is constantly monitored.

I've always had a tremendous admiration for the staff who work in places such as Broadmoor. It is a job I couldn't do. Every day of their working lives they are dealing with offenders for whom, in the main, society has thrown away the key. They are detained indefinitely. Somehow the nurses have to find some small progress in their charges and get professional fulfilment from this. It must be soul-destroying.

Each ward is nested in a unit that is nested in the hospital. The patients are dangerous people and the staff are always outnumbered. For this reason, there must be a relationship that is nurturing but also implicitly and explicitly controlling.

I had come to Broadmoor to interview a patient. Jimmy Fordham was in his early thirties and had spent nearly ten years there. Now the medical consultant and staff felt he was ready to be transferred to Arnold Lodge as a prelude to his structured return to the community.

Let me describe how the system works. When people are thought to be cured, or approaching being cured, they are considered for rehabilitation and release into the community. This is done gradually. An offender will be recommended for transfer to a regional secure unit (RSU) such as Arnold Lodge, so that further treatment can be provided very close to the community.

If all goes well then the patient may be tested with increasing amounts of leave; first in the grounds of Arnold Lodge, later in the local streets and finally back at home or deep in the city. Each stage begins with an escort and builds up until there is no escort and the patient takes full responsibility for him- or herself.

Occasionally there is a problem during the leave. A patient will fail to return, or will reoffend. The RSU takes responsibility for this, liaising with the police and media as necessary, but the local community takes the strain. It is their families in the front line.

When patients are assessed for transfer, their fate rests with visiting specialists and staff from the RSU, who must decide if they are ready for onward transition and preparation for final release. Are they better? What type and degree of danger do they present? With support and outpatient help, can they eventually live in the community?

This decision is normally made within two years, but some inmates are kept hanging on for much longer.

In Jimmy's case, he had a claim on Arnold Lodge geographically because he originally lived in our catchment area. If he moved on at all, it would be to us.

Jimmy wore a woven cotton short-sleeved shirt and a pair of worn black jeans. His shoes were brightly polished. He had washed, shaved and combed his hair. Although well past adolescence, he still bore the acne scars on his cheeks.

He was humming to himself as I walked in the door. We met in a day room off the main lounge where patients watched TV and played cards. Most of them were off on activities such as gardening and doing woodwork.

Jimmy had taken some effort to prepare himself. He knew how important these interviews were for his future. At the same time, he didn't quite have the neatness of presentation of a job applicant who knew the importance of looking his best. Small details were not quite right. A button was missing on his shirt. He'd left a smear of shaving foam under his ear.

Although not particularly bright, Jimmy came across as being polite and respectful. He was very tuned in to what I might want to hear, answering 'Yes, sir' and 'No, sir' very crisply.

Having entered his thirties, Jimmy very much wanted to be on his way. He knew that if I gave him the thumbs down, he would stay put in Broadmoor and nobody would review his case again for another couple of years.

Beforehand, in brief, I read the notes of his index offence. A seventeen-year-old girl had been brutally attacked and almost killed. She had been left in a wheelchair. Jimmy had been nineteen at the time of the offence. A court had decided that he had a psychopathic personality disorder and ordered that he be detained indefinitely in a special hospital.

Having made the introductions, I sat on the opposite side of a low table.

'I have looked at your notes, Jimmy, but I really want to hear from you. I want to know what you think about, what you've achieved here and why you came here in the first place.'

'Yes, Mr Britton.'

'First I need to go back to the very beginning. What happened that brought you here?'

'Well, Mr Britton, there was this girl. I beat her up.'

'Why?'

'She wound me up.'

'Why don't you start at the beginning.'

'Yes, Mr Britton . . .' He looked uncomfortable.

'Is there something wrong?'

'Well, Mr Britton, I've been over this ever so many times.' He slouched in his chair, one hand in the waistband of his jeans. Then he seemed to remind himself to sit up straight.

'Yes, I know. I've seen the file notes. I don't want to make up my mind based on what other people are saying about you, Jimmy. I want to get to know you a little bit. I want to know what you make of it all.'

'Yes, Mr Britton.'

'So tell me what happened.'

He chewed on the inside of his cheek, trying to compose the story. I could see him thinking, how much can I get away with telling him?

Finally he began: 'I was out at the pub. I stopped at

the chippie on my way home. Some girls started winding me up – asking me for money for chips. I said I didn't have any. They laughed and kept teasing me about having my chips. I wouldn't give them any. I was hungry . . .'

He ran out of steam and took another moment to compose his story.

'Then they went off. I started walking home, eating my chips. I sort of came across her – one of the girls. She started teasing me again. Winding me up. She must have heard somebody coming and got a fright 'cause she swung her handbag at me. It hit me right in the . . . in the . . . you know . . . the balls.'

'What happened then?'

'I just sort of lost it. I beat her up.'

'And then?'

'I ran back to my place. It was late, so I went to bed. I didn't wake up until the police arrived in the morning. I had to go to court and they sent me here.'

'And that's it?'

'Yes, Mr Britton.'

'There are a few things I'm having difficulties with. Here you are, all pleasant and courteous, and the staff are saying some very positive things about you. Have you always been like this?'

'Yeah, I think so.'

'And you've explained about getting into a fight and beating up a girl. I know that a lot of fights break out at weekends. People drink too much or beat each other up because they get angry or upset or jealous. Often it happens that a fellow hits a girl. Not many of them are sent to Broadmoor though, are they?'

'No.'

'What happens to them?'

'They get sent to prison.'

'So why were *you* sent here?'

'Well, I had a . . . a . . .' he mumbled a response.

'I'm sorry?'

'I had a personality disorder.'

'What sort?'

'A psych . . . psych . . . psych . . . a personality disorder.'

'OK. What do you think that means?'

'It means that it wasn't my fault. I wasn't responsible for what happened. I'm not mad. It's a personality disorder.'

'I see.'

It wasn't the right moment to explore the issue of responsibility. Instead I asked, 'How long have you been here now?'

'Ten years.'

'Is that a long or a short time?'

He didn't know the right answer and simply shrugged.

'What have you done while you've been at Broadmoor?'

Again he looked perplexed. He was thinking, what do you mean, what have I done?

'I've done my time, sir.'

'But you weren't given a specific sentence in terms of time.'

'No, sir.'

Jimmy showed clear signs of anxiety when put under pressure. This didn't take any special techniques or devices. My just being there was enough to make him feel stressed. As far as he was concerned, I was the Establishment.

We talked about the various programmes and

186

courses that Jimmy had followed over the years. They included social skills training, victim awareness training, anger control, occupational therapy and a host of general workshops and art classes.

Jimmy was right about not being mad. He was properly orientated in person, place and time. He knew exactly who he was, where we were talking and the day of the week. He showed no sign of psychosis or other mental illness. Yet he'd given me an account of his index offence which was very thin. I went over it again and again, unpacking things in many different ways, but his view of what had happened didn't change. The girl had teased and belittled him; she'd caused him to snap suddenly.

It was all too tidy. One of the absolute fundamentals of dealing with any forensic patient is having a clear formulation or diagnosis of precisely what it was about him that led him to commit a particular offence, at a particular time, in a particular way. Without this understanding of the forces that affected him, it isn't possible to design a treatment or intervention that will change him.

When this treatment is designed, you have to show that it has actually been put into place and implemented. Then you have to show that it has worked.

These are all separate requirements that are vital in determining whether a patient is still a danger. Once they are in place, any decision to release a patient or move them on tends to become a matter of policy rather than safety. It's important that these details are investigated. The care teams have to be hard-nosed about getting the right data. Otherwise mistakes can be made.

These were the details I now sought. Where was the

professional underpinning for Jimmy's case? What had happened to him?

Yes, he'd completed all the various courses. But why? What was he meant to have achieved from them?

The staff would answer that Jimmy had matured in the decade since his arrival. That he'd grown up and overcome the problems in his personality.

What problems are those? The ones arising from his inadequacies.

What does that mean? Where are they defined or explored? By what criteria?

If you didn't know exactly what it was about Jimmy that had led to him almost beating a poor girl to death, then how were the treatments going to be connected to what happened? How would they do any good? How would you know if they had worked?

It's very easy to sit on the outside and criticize prisons and special hospitals. I appreciate how difficult the work can be. I also understood why Jimmy was being offered to Arnold Lodge. In short, he hadn't been a management problem.

On the wards patients sometimes engineer terrible physical confrontations. Others, although quiet, secretly plan to abduct, rape and kill nursing staff. Amid all of these problem patients, Jimmy came across as polite, helpful and socially obedient.

'He's no trouble at all,' the nursing staff had told me.

My question was: 'Does that mean he's better?'

What if they hadn't cured him? What if they'd simply given him skills that covered over a problem in a way that convinced people that he was OK now?

In Jimmy's case, what had been done (and this gets to the heart of it) was that he'd been provided with an environment which was largely predictable, highly structured and safe. He had been looked after from the day he arrived.

'Jimmy, go and get your breakfast . . . Jimmy, put your bedlinen in the basket . . . Jimmy, here's your programme for the week.'

The ordered, secure environment of Broadmoor is entirely different from sitting in a cheap bedsit with no money, no job, no girlfriend and no self-esteem. And unless you're careful, the hospital environment will mask those issues that led to the index offence and you'll be lulled into believing that 'He's OK now. He's ready to move on.'

Jimmy had become a good little soldier. Yes, sir. No, sir. Where do I march now, sir?

The ward staff sold Jimmy strongly to us. On paper, he appeared to have been through many of the clinical hoops. There was no evidence of any violence in the previous ten years and he appeared to be more self-confident than when he arrived.

Although aware that nobody had dealt with Jimmy's pathology, I recognized that he was motivated enough to complete whatever treatment programme was still necessary. For this reason, Jimmy came to Arnold Lodge on a temporary transfer. He set out on the road back.

9

Ray Knox dumped two plastic carrier bags on my desk and wiped his hands on the back of his trousers.

'What are these?'

'I don't want them any more. I want you to have them.'

His eyes were bloodshot, with the skin pouched beneath them. He wore his familiar cotton shirt with double pockets. A Remembrance Day poppy was pinned just below the collar.

The bags contained books and magazines. One of the titles had spilled from a split in the plastic – *Madmen and Monsters*. Next to it was a magazine with a cover photograph of Ed Gein, who had abducted, murdered and mutilated so many young women. The headline read: 'The True American Psycho'.

Were they all about serial killers, I wondered, feeling uneasy. If so, what did it tell me about Ray? And why had he chosen to give them to *me*?

These questions needed thinking time, but that would have to wait. Ray had taken his seat, looking pleased with himself. Lifting the bags from my desk, I pondered where I could put them. Eventually I leaned them against the bookcase behind me, out of sight.

In the minutes before Ray's session, I'd been reviewing his case and developing a plan. I now had more than forty pages of salient points that I'd taken during previous consultations. As each session finished, I had completed the notes.

We had reached a stage, after eight months of talking, where Ray's natural caution and feelings of self-preservation had been reassured. He had started to put things on the table that he'd never revealed to anyone.

Bringing the books wasn't a dramatic cry for help, or a silent 'Please stop me'. It had more to do with the clinical relationship that had been built between us. Equally, Ray wasn't trying to show me how clever he had been. He did, however, need me to understand how seriously he should be taken.

A crossover had taken place between Ray's symbolic fantasies and the real world. This made him a very dangerous man. In his ordinary life, he had very little control or influence over others. He had rectified this in his private fantasy world – an alternative place where he was omnipotent and determined everything that happened, including how other people behaved.

But as this fantasy system developed, it required more and more of his energy for it to be as rewarding as it had been in the beginning. In particular he needed greater detail and colour. This is an escalating process and ultimately he had a set of images and sequences in his mind that were brilliantly and intensely clear.

When Ray punished his father, it wasn't a solitary, brief act of revenge. He wanted a punishment that had more substance and import. That's why he chose the courtroom setting. He held a trial where he became prosecutor, defence counsel, judge and jury. He passed sentence in the manner he had learned from TV, films and his books. 'I find you guilty as charged. You will be taken from this place to the electric chair. The execution will be at dusk.'

The execution had a sense of orderliness and it gave him a feeling of completeness and peace.

Ray realized that what he was saying might well move him into some predefined category from my point of view. But he didn't know what this meant. Was he a madman? Could I suddenly have him detained?

He knew that his thoughts and actions were wrong, or certainly not healthy. But where did it take him?

I sought to answer these unspoken questions by trying to define how people behave and what society regards as being normal.

'One of the things that sometimes holds people back from talking to a psychologist is they don't really know what is considered to be normal,' I said. 'Even if they do know, they're frightened that if they reveal their secrets I'm going to be shocked, or reject them. They think I might drag a straitjacket out of my top drawer and call the police . . .'

As I spoke, I carefully watched Ray's reactions.

'I can promise you that none of those things are going to happen. Nothing you say will shock me. For instance, I wouldn't be surprised if you told me that you've been following your father – watching his movements.'

Ray's eyes widened. He stared at me for several seconds. 'How did you know that?'

'I didn't know for sure.'

He mulled this over, uncertain of how far to go. Had he said too much?

I continued: 'And it also wouldn't surprise me to

discover that you carry various bits and pieces with you
– things like ropes or gags.'

His silence said enough.

'Where do you go looking for him?'

'He works at a freight transport company. I park outside and watch.'

'How do you know where he works?'

'I followed him.'

'When?'

'Remember the day I first saw him again?'

'At the garage.'

'Yes.'

'I went back there again, hoping he might show up.'

'The odds of that were quite small, I would think.'

'Yeah. It took a while.'

'How long?'

'A month.'

'Why did you wait for him? What were you going to do?'

'I don't know. Have it out with him, I guess . . .' His voice trailed off.

'You were going to confront him?'

'Yeah.'

'What did you hope to achieve?'

Ray shrugged ambivalently. It hid nothing. I knew what he thought. Perhaps not the exact details, but I knew he had rehearsed the scene countless times in his mind. It was like a film running through his head on a continuous loop.

'I wanted to punish him.'

'What actually happened?'

'Nothing. I followed him.'

'What did you imagine would happen, Ray? What did you see in your mind?'

His skin had turned grey and he fingered the scars

on his hands. I let the silence build. Ray's eyelids fluttered. I knew he was picturing the scene.

'He's got fat in his old age, but he's still wearing trainers – trying to look younger. I want to get close – I want to look into his eyes. He's just finished work. It's dark. He has to cross the car park to get to his Audi. Most of the street lights are broken.'

'Did you break them?'

'No. Kids.'

'Where are you?'

'In my car.'

'What do you have with you?'

'A ball-pin hammer, some rope, chains, a hessian sack. Normally I keep them in the boot, but I put them on the passenger seat so I can get to them quickly. He's got a rolling sort of walk. It's like he's drunk. He fumbles in his pockets for the car keys. Why don't people have their keys ready? They always wait until the last minute. It's like watching women at the supermarket checkout who never have their purses ready. They're always fumbling for them in handbags, holding up the rest of the queue . . .'

'Do you say anything?'

'He hears me at the last moment and tries to turn. It's too late. The sack slips over his head. I hit him once or twice with the hammer to keep him quiet. He goes down like a sack of shit. Then I bundle him onto the floor of the car.'

Ray was visualizing this scene in remarkable detail. He sat erect, looking ahead and past me, with his voice low but energized. He had incorporated real-world features into the fantasy. He could literally see the streetlights muted by the fog and hear the puddles splash beneath the car tyres.

The heater blasted warm air onto his feet. His father had gone to jelly. Ray kept up the verbal punishment, haranguing him mercilessly. Every so often he hit him with the hammer. Not on the head or hard enough for serious injury. He didn't want to kill him, yet.

Stella and the children were away for the weekend. He dragged his father into the basement and stood him in the dock. There was no explosion of rage or running amok. Ray's anger was cold and very calculated. It had frozen his life for a long time.

Everything about the trial and execution had been rehearsed. Nothing had been left to chance.

'He's squealing like a pig. I tell him to shut up or he'll be gagged. He keeps trying to interrupt, so I hit him again. "Silence in the court! All rise."

'"Has the jury reached its verdict?"

'"We have, your honour."

'"How say you – is the defendant guilty or not guilty?"

'"Guilty."'

A smile of triumph creased Ray's face. He savoured the word, as though tasting a wine. His chest filled and he seemed to grow in stature as he delivered the death sentence. There could be no other result.

Working methodically, Ray strapped his father into the electric chair, tightening the leather noose at his neck and the belts that secured his forearms and legs. He attached the metal plates and sponges.

'Then I flipped the switch.'

Playing this scene against his now closed eyelids, Ray could almost see the body twitching. After a minute or so, the twitching stopped.

'What happened then?' I asked.

Ray looked disappointed for a moment, but suddenly bucked up as though an idea had just occurred to him.

I didn't interrupt his monologue, but I soon noticed a sharp divergence after the execution. Death, Ray decided, hadn't been enough for his abuser. He added another punishment – humiliation.

He stripped his father naked, wrapped the body in a blanket and bundled it into the boot of the car. Then he drove until he found a quiet woodland glade.

'That's where I left him – sitting in a deckchair.' He laughed.

'Why a deckchair?'

'I remember him on our picnics at Stratford-upon-Avon. He'd sit in his deckchair and demand that everything be done for him. "Get me a beer!" "Give me another sandwich!"'

'The place you chose to leave him. Had you been there before?'

'I found it.'

'When?'

'I went looking. I'd go out in the car, or on long walks.'

'Why did you choose this particular place?'

'It had to be public but private as well. Somewhere I could leave a body without being seen, but where people would find him sitting there, fat and bloated, with everything hanging out.'

Ray didn't revel in the atmospheric details of his father's death. This wasn't a fantasy where pleasure came from spilling blood or breaking bones. It was far more sophisticated. Afterwards he'd sat on a tree stump and marvelled at his handiwork.

'I told you so,' he said to the body. 'This is payment,

you fucking abuser! You monster! You had no right. You broke my bones. You blackened my eyes. You ruined my life . . .'

I let him talk. Not just to vent his spleen, but because I needed to capture the details. There was no sense of triumph in Ray's voice. Justice is less passionate than revenge.

Some people kill impulsively, in the heat of the moment, and are immediately horrified by what they have done. The image haunts them. They haven't expected there to be so much blood, perhaps, or that a dead person will look as they do. Ray, however, was already familiar with the images. His imagination made them vivid and the focus razor sharp.

I'd witnessed a chilling account – a murder fantasy so vivid that I could see Ray's skin prickling and the hair rising on the back of his neck. Clearly, parts of this fantasy had already crossed over into the real world. But how far had Ray gone?

I remembered how he'd talked of his mind 'slipping' and how he'd cut himself to hold on to reality. And there was also the time when he'd driven around all night but couldn't remember anywhere that he'd been.

'You told me that you knew where your father works.'

'Yes.'

'Do you know where he lives?'

He nodded. 'I've followed him home.'

'Have you spoken to him?'

'No.'

'How close have you been?'

He shrugged and opened his hands. I could see his eyes dancing with possibilities. For a moment he

197

contemplated holding back, but he'd come too far and said too much already.

'I waited for him one night.'

'When was this?'

'I don't know. Eight months ago, maybe. I waited in the car park.'

'What were you going to do?'

'Exactly what I always do. Wait till he got to his car and then hit him with the hammer.'

'Just like the fantasy you described to me.'

'Yeah.'

Ray paused suddenly. A shadow flitted across his face and his body seemed to deflate. His eyes filled with tears.

'What happened?'

He couldn't answer me for a long time. When he did speak, his voice seemed rusty and half-choked.

'Remember I told you about seeing him again for the first time?'

'Yes. At the petrol station.'

'Do you know how that made me feel? Frightened. I've never been so shit-scared. It wasn't because of what he did to me. I've been over that too many times to have nightmares any more.'

'So what frightened you?'

Ray swallowed a lump in his throat and squeezed his eyes shut. 'It was because . . . because . . .' He started to sob. 'Because I looked just like him. Like that monster; that fucking abuser! Can you imagine what that feels like? Can you? The man who abused and made fun of me. The man I hate most in the world. I look like him.'

We sat in silence, with Ray immersed in his misery.

Finally, I asked, 'What happened on that night that you waited for him?'

'He didn't show up.'

'How did you feel?'

'Disappointed.'

'How often have you been back since then?'

'I haven't.'

'Why is that?'

'I started coming here.'

I could only assume that Ray was telling me the truth. He'd been honest about so many other things – risking the consequences. Yet despite his sincerity, I knew the story wasn't finished.

His trawling for locations to place the body concerned me greatly. Here was an element of real-world rehearsal. It was concrete behaviour – no longer symbolic. He had physically driven to places in his car and identified them. This same car contained chains, ropes, a hammer and a deckchair.

Our session had ended and Ray stood up to leave. He didn't say goodbye. His mind was elsewhere. I walked with him along the corridor and out of the front door. Although it was spring, a chilly wind was blowing.

I paused at the gate. Here in the small outpatient clinic many miles from Arnold Lodge, there were no padlocks or high security fences. Even so, I wondered for a moment, do I open the gate? Should I stop him from leaving?

I didn't want him to go. I worried about him. Just as importantly, I worried about his father.

Regardless of what I felt, I had no professional or legal capacity that could stop Ray walking out of my consulting room. People often imagine that psychologists have wide-ranging powers to have people committed to special hospitals or psychiatric wards with immediate effect. The reality is quite different.

All psychologists begin their professional training in the study of the normal nature and functioning of the human mind. This covers most of what we know of people as individuals and members of groups. It includes reasoning, emotion, intellect, learning, memory, consciousness, social behaviour, persuasion, criminal and deviant behaviour, sexuality, aggression and conflict, error, love and attraction – all that makes us human, even creativity.

From this starting point, psychologists go on to specialize. The clinical psychologist becomes immersed in the abnormalities of the mind, ranging from anxiety-based conditions that spoil so many lives through to the complex, difficult cases where the personality structure itself is damaged or where the trauma has been so severe as to lead to defensive dissociation between the damaged areas and other aspects of the patient's mind. The clinical psychologist will use a broad range of psychological treatments based on an understanding of how external factors lead to mental change.

Some psychologists work with psychiatrists in treating patients suffering from mental illnesses with a clear physical base and who require drug treatment. The psychiatrist initially trains in medicine and later specializes in the pharmacological treatment of this smaller group of patients whose physiological imbalance so disturbs their functioning that the expert application of powerful neuroleptic medication is needed to keep them in normal mental health.

Clinical forensic psychology was not established as an autonomous profession in the NHS when the 1959

Mental Health Act came into effect in 1960. In those days nursing, psychiatry, general practice and social welfare were the main groups working with the mentally ill or abnormal. Psychiatrists took formal responsibility for these patients and this arrangement has remained unchanged ever since.

In practical terms it means that beds in secure units and special hospitals are attached to individual forensic psychiatrists. It is their formal responsibility to admit and discharge individual patients.

Clinical psychologists are independent of this. I can accept, treat and discharge patients, but I don't control beds and therefore can't formally admit somebody. Instead, I have to start a referral process.

The Mental Health Act has two main thrusts – to protect the community and to protect the rights of the individual. Both are equally important. In the past unscrupulous relatives and the authorities have had people committed for spurious reasons. Elderly aunts got locked away because they became a financial burden or an annoyance. Others were silenced when their political views were deemed unacceptable.

At the beginning of my clinical career, in the late 1970s, I learned of an elderly lady who had been a psychiatric in-patient for sixty years. Over time people had forgotten why she was there in the first place. The paperwork had been misplaced and the staff had constantly changed. Ultimately it was discovered that she had been declared a 'moral imbecile' at the age of seventeen because she became pregnant and had an illegitimate baby. Her family had her committed to a mental hospital where she spent the rest of her life. This is a sobering story but such abuses are now extremely uncommon.

* * *

Ray had reached his car. His keys were in his hand. What other options did I have to stop him? I could go to the police, perhaps. This would mean breaking the privilege of confidentiality that a patient entrusts in me. What would I tell the police? As far as I knew, Ray hadn't committed an actual crime – except perhaps cruelty to animals.

There is an American precedent for disclosure. Some years ago a patient set out to kill a specific, named person and told his clinician, who believed that the murder would be committed. The clinician felt unable to report the situation on the grounds of confidentiality. The killing took place and the legal system took the view that in such circumstances it is appropriate for disclosure to be made.

How confident was I that Ray would kill his father? The police can't detain someone for very long on suspicion alone. And if they interviewed Ray, he'd know immediately that I had betrayed his trust. He wouldn't come back to see me. Nor would he ever trust a health professional again.

Instead his anger would escalate. His sense of hopelessness would be vindicated. He had reached out for help and not only would I have given up on him, I would also have betrayed him. This was the worst outcome imaginable. Ray would slip away and nobody would know where his fantasies were taking him. Nobody would be there to stop him.

What should or could I do?

For the time being, I had a clinical hold on Ray. He didn't have to come and see me. Nobody had compelled him. The fact that he kept coming back was vital and it gave me reassurance. Equally important was his claim that he hadn't stalked his father since first coming to see me.

If I could keep this clinical hold on Ray, he was no immediate risk to his father. This was a big 'if'. Should I lose that grip then Ray would become much more dangerous. I would then have little choice but to involve other agencies, even at the risk of increasing the level of threat Ray posed.

I had already considered the possibility of persuading him to admit himself as a voluntary patient. The chances were small. He had a wife and children he adored. He wouldn't easily be separated from them.

Another difficulty surrounded the beds in secure units, which weren't usually available to voluntary patients. At the earliest sign of pressure, Ray would probably discharge himself. He'd leave in a state of heightened agitation and disappear into the landscape.

In any event, I knew he'd ultimately say no to being admitted.

I couldn't afford to lose contact with him. Our consultations seemed to be the main anchor holding him in the real world. Regardless of what happened, I had to stay with him.

I loaded the carrier bags into the boot of my car and took them home. In my study, most of the floor is taken up with boxes and books that are stacked around my desk. It might not be pretty but it's my space, my clutter.

Over the years, I've always tried to keep many aspects of my work away from Marilyn. She possesses an enormous capacity to empathize with people in crisis or distress, particularly when it involves the victims of appalling abuse and violence. It hurts her, and I find that hard.

Forensic clinical casework places a heavy emotional load on those who work in the field. The same is true of psychologically analysing serious crime. Going to the scene of a new murder or to an outpatient clinic is similar to sponge-diving. You have to take a deep breath and learn to hold it long enough to stay down until the job is finished. If I can, I try to keep it separate from my family life because that's where I come up for air.

I began sorting through Ray's books and magazines. Most seemed to glorify serial killers or psychopathic offenders. I normally take a deep pleasure in books, but not this sort of material. I'm also quite careful about looking after books. I don't like to see notes in margins, or corners folded over to mark a page.

I noticed that Ray had folded some of the corners. At other times the book fell open where it had been pressed flat at a page. Each marked page or section referred crudely to multiple personality disorders and, by implication, clinical dissociation. There were brief explanations and case studies, as well as lists of symptoms.

These pages hadn't been marked by chance. Either Ray was trying to point me at something – or he was trying to misdirect me. He had never asked about so-called multiple personalities. He had shown no awareness of the clinical process, although he was very alert when we discussed dissociated states. In fact, he'd reacted with surprise that such conditions could exist.

He'd asked me, 'Do you think that could be me, Paul?'

Yet here were books with whole sections on forensic psychology, albeit in lay terms. Clearly Ray knew far more about this particular subject than he had ever let on. Why had he put these in front of me?

Had he a glimmering, perhaps, of some sort of recognition of dissociation? It isn't always the case that different 'personalities' are completely hidden from each other. A sufferer may have an 'executive personality' who knows that all is not well.

Occasionally, at times of stress or in particular circumstances, a new alter ego such as a 'mischievous personality' will emerge. This can cause resentment between alter egos and lead to a battle of wills for the driving seat.

The 'mischievous personality' may deliberately leave clues behind – by moving materials around or putting messages on tape – in the hope of embarrassing the 'executive personality'.

In Ray's case this was extremely speculative. He'd shown definite signs of dissociation, but I didn't believe that he had a multiple personality disorder.

Why had he shown me these things?

There was another possible motive and it brought a cold empty feeling to the pit of my stomach. What if Ray was preparing a defence in advance? What if he was trying to set me up? Get the psychologist on side first; establish that I have a severe mental problem; then I can kill my father and avoid going to jail. A stint in a special hospital, a remarkable recovery and then I'm free.

This would be an enormously high-risk strategy. And surely he'd shown his hand by giving me the books. What on earth was he up to?

I put the books away and began reviewing the case again. None of our sessions had ever been stereotyped. Ray was too bright for me just to hammer the same theme, or try to mislead him. He was easily frustrated and very wary.

As I read the most recent notes and drained my coffee, I couldn't rid myself of a nagging question. Who was really running these sessions – Ray or me? Or did he have a 'mischievous alter ego' running both of us?

10

The Trent Regional Forensic Psychology Service was only one small part of the much larger forensic service that covered the region. Other specialities included psychiatry, occupational therapy, social work, nursing and non-clinical administrative forensic services.

All these specialities came under the umbrella of the Trent Regional Forensic Service, which in turn was run by the Leicestershire Mental Health Services Unit.

In 1989 I was appointed general manager of the Regional Forensic Service. This surprised me as much as it did everybody else. It meant that I was responsible, in managerial terms, for all areas of the forensic service, not just psychology.

From a practical viewpoint, it meant spending less time at outpatient clinics. Three half-day sessions a week were given over to my responsibilities as general manager. I kept the same office at Arnold Lodge, only the badge on the door had changed.

During my first week in the new post, I was approached by a delegation of nurses, complaining about all sorts of irregularities at Arnold Lodge. Certain members of the night staff, I was told, were bringing alcohol into the unit and using the offices for romantic purposes. Goods were not properly accounted for.

I was compelled to launch an inquiry. The 'system' required action, but I had to look for a way to deal with the problems without giving up a scapegoat. I knew that the real culprit was the institution itself. Working at Arnold Lodge is like living in the TV sitcom *M.A.S.H.*, but you need a much blacker sense of humour. The staff have a very difficult job. They are dealing every day with patients who could kill them if they turned their backs.

In this sort of environment it's vital to have outlets for stress, but in those days there were very few of these at Arnold Lodge. For this reason, it was wrong to be too strict in enforcing rules and regulations, particularly those drawn from a theoretical version of a perfect world.

That's why the staff in such a place tend to be buccaneers. They are assertive, boisterous, funny, fully rounded people, rather than shrinking violets or wallflowers. They have to be like this to survive emotionally.

Yet when it comes to patient care and public safety, very rarely do these front-line staff make mistakes. They know that people's lives depend upon them – not just fellow workers, but patients and the public at large.

I saw Jimmy once or twice a week at Arnold Lodge. He took a while to settle in because he'd become accustomed to the routines at Broadmoor. Now he faced closer supervision and initially fewer freedoms.

His world had shrunk to a ward of fewer than fifteen patients, most from the courts or prisons or other special hospitals.

He was very compliant in those first few weeks on the intake ward. Afterwards he joined our 'therapeutic community' (TC) of people with personality disorders. The TC was designed to teach people how to live and work together normally, and was based on the notion that most people with personality disorders haven't been able to learn the rules of living because of their earlier life experience or temperament.

The TC operates like a big shared house, the difference being that in most shared houses the housemates haven't raped, killed, taken hostages or maimed themselves. Day-to-day decisions concerning the running of the TC are made democratically after everyone has talked them through.

Particular clinical staff were normally dedicated to the TC and didn't usually work on other wards. They had the paradoxical task of leading and guiding while at the same time – as the numerically smallest group – accepting the decisions of the majority.

This theoretical model rarely holds for very long in practice – particularly when the community members are drawn from the forensic pool.

Several times a day the community came together to discuss different issues. Some were housekeeping groups, deciding on washing rosters and menus. Other groups solved conflicts and worked through their feelings on issues and in particular the problems that brought them to Arnold Lodge.

This is the classic group therapy session you often see portrayed in films. The residents sit in a circle and over several weeks take turns to give their story. Then the group takes it to pieces, using their own experiences to help that person find a way first of understanding and then of resolving their life.

So if someone said, 'I can't cope with rejection ...
Hey, could that be why I set fires?' others would reply,
'I've been there. I can hear what you're saying, but
you're putting it on the wrong people. Have you ever
really thought about ...?' As part of this process
they set one another goals and tasks for the coming
week.

Most of the residents were quite young, in their early
twenties to mid-thirties. Ideally there is an even mix of
men and women, but in the forensic setting there tend
to be more men. Inevitably, sexual tensions become
part of the group dynamic because these are factors in
any normal community.

Personality disorders can be very different in nature
and effect. Sometimes not enough care is taken about
which people are put together. I think of one man in a
TC who walked away from a rape, didn't feel sated, so
went back and raped the woman again. A young
woman joined the TC who had committed arson as a
direct consequence of having been brutally raped.
These two people were living alongside each other,
daily fighting their own histories and sometimes each
other; the young woman fared badly.

Having coped reasonably well in the intake ward,
Jimmy didn't adapt well to the TC. Staff couldn't
understand why; he'd been making such good progress
at Broadmoor. What had happened?

I sat in on some of the groups and began to see that
while Jimmy talked well enough at a superficial level,
nobody was getting underneath this to do any deeper
work. Similarly, when he had to consider or comment
on someone else's problem, he simply couldn't do
it.

When emotions are running high, some groups can

be savage rather than nurturing. They get frustrated and aren't equipped to know why. In such an environment, Jimmy began to feel marginalized and persecuted.

I could see a man who fell apart intellectually under the very slightest of genuine interpersonal pressure. It seemed that he had a hole in the middle of his cognitive functioning that wasn't always apparent. When pressure kicked in, he seemed capable of only a very primitive way of operating.

Apart from the group sessions, I spent time with Jimmy one-on-one. I still wasn't convinced that we knew enough about his history and his index offence.

During one interview, I noticed something about his behaviour that struck me as unusual. He always studied my face intently, as if trying to read something in my eyes. When I first met him at Broadmoor I had put this down to his desire to make a good impression. Now I wasn't so sure.

'Tell me, Jimmy,' I said, turning my head to face the window. 'Do you think it's going to rain today?'

He suddenly appeared not to be listening – hoping I'd ask the question again.

'We've had a lot of rain this month. Don't you agree?'

I turned to Jimmy as the question ended. He looked at me blankly.

'You didn't hear me, did you?'

'No.'

'How long have you had hearing problems?'

Jimmy lowered his eyes. 'Since I was a kid.'

'Why didn't you say anything?'

He didn't answer, but a lot of things became clearer. It turned out that Jimmy was profoundly deaf in one ear and hard of hearing in the other. This was one reason why he'd struggled in the group sessions. With so many people around him, he couldn't tune in to one person and read their lips and facial signals.

Why hadn't we known? Why hadn't anyone known? It was potentially very important and yet I could find no mention of it in any of the files from Broadmoor or earlier.

There is a well-documented correlation between deafness and paranoid thinking. It stems from the suspicion that if we can't hear what people are saying, they might be talking about us.

Questions arise. 'Are they laughing at me? Are they putting me down?'

It's very easy for the hard of hearing to get into situations where they are ridiculed or the source of jibes. Someone says something to them and they're too embarrassed to say, 'I'm sorry, I can't hear you. Will you say that again?'

Instead they respond to what they think they hear, or look rather vague. If they misjudge and give an inappropriate answer or reaction, then people think them dim-witted. Others start behaving differently towards them and everything they silently fear about people making fun of them steadily becomes true.

I knew that Jimmy must have suffered all of these developmental insults.

Armed with this new information, I began to go back over parts of his history. He had struggled at school because of his hearing. After leaving at sixteen, he started working in a fabricating plant, cleaning the machines. He wasn't a good time-keeper, but didn't shirk hard work.

Two years later he found himself his first girlfriend, Amy, who was fifteen and still at school.

'I loved her, Mr Britton. I'd never met anyone like that before. And she loved me. We were gonna be together for ever.'

'How did you meet?'

'At the pictures. I walked her home 'cause it was raining. I lent her my coat so she wouldn't get wet.'

'You were quite a bit older?'

'Only three years.'

'How long were you together?'

'Six months.'

'Some couples go out together for quite a time before they feel comfortable enough to kiss each other, or to move on to a deeper sexual relationship. What happened with Amy and you?'

Jimmy bristled a little. 'Nothing smutty. No groping or quick pokes. We made love, if that's what you mean.'

The romance had a classical Doris Day feel, according to Jimmy's descriptions. It was flowers, valentines, hand-holding and lovemaking.

'What happened?'

'Her bitch of a mother stuck her nose in.' He spat out the words. 'She broke us up. She took Amy away.'

'Why?'

'She didn't like me, did she? Amy could do better, she said. Why waste herself on me? But this was love, Mr Britton. You don't break up people who love each other, do you?'

According to Jimmy's account, Amy's mother went to great lengths to break them up – forging notes and spreading poison about him. She succeeded in ending the relationship, leaving Jimmy desolate and disconsolate. All his attempts to rekindle the romance failed and Amy moved away from the town.

I had no way of checking Jimmy's story. Based on his account he was either amazingly unlucky in love or there was something else.

Buried in the notes, I had come across a brief reference to an assault twelve months before Jimmy's index offence. There was no explanation, it was simply listed as a previous conviction. Apparently Jimmy had assaulted a shop assistant.

I began to probe gently and discovered that he had walked into a newsagent's, taken out a knife and stabbed the woman behind the counter in the chest. He was arrested later that day by the police who came to his work and interviewed him. They found the knife in his locker. The magistrates' court had given him a year's probation.

Nothing in the history or notes made anything of this. It wasn't flagged or highlighted as being particularly important. This astonished me. Here were the hallmarks of a very serious offender in the making and nothing had been done about it. If things had been dealt with differently, Jimmy might not have gone on to commit the second offence. A young girl wouldn't have been paralysed.

When I asked him, Jimmy said, 'I can't remember. It was a long time ago.' He wasn't dismissive. Instead, he minimized. As always, he concentrated on my face and lips, looking very focused and locked in. He wore jeans and a sweatshirt with a hood. I'd often seen him in the TC wearing the hood up and listening to a personal stereo. His deafness wasn't an issue when he listened to music. He had an excuse for not hearing people's questions.

'How did you come to stab her?' I asked.

'She just wound me up. I thought she was laughing at me.'

'What made you think that?'

'I said something. I couldn't see her face.'

'Does that mean you didn't hear her?'

He nodded. 'I thought she was making fun of me.'

'So you stabbed her.'

'Yeah.'

I knew this didn't make sense. What was he doing with the knife in the first place? Why was it in his hand? There were too many holes in the story.

It took me a month, seeing Jimmy twice a week, to get to the heart of what happened. Each time I broached the subject, his answers were the same. He grew frustrated at my persistence. He complained that I kept asking him the same things.

'Tell me about the newsagent's. Why did you go in there?'

'Like I said, I went there every day on my way to work. I bought some chewing gum and a packet of cigarettes.'

'So it's on your way to work?'

'Yeah.'

I knew the town where the attack took place. I held an outpatient clinic there a couple of times a month. Although I couldn't name the streets, I could picture a lot of the shops and businesses in the High Street.

'Isn't there a newsagent closer than the one you went to?'

Jimmy pretended not to hear the question, using his deafness to give himself extra time. This had become a new tactic since his hearing difficulties had become

215

apparent. We'd arranged for him to have a hearing aid, but he rarely wore it. He preferred to wander through the clouds of his own thought, as he always had.

I asked the question again. 'Isn't there a closer newsagent to your work?'

'I don't know. Maybe.'

'When you went to this shop every morning to buy chewing gum and cigarettes, how long did you spend outside looking in through the window?'

His face changed. A tiny smile played on his lips. 'Only a few minutes.'

'What were you looking at?'

'Just in the window.'

'What were you looking at in particular?'

He knew that I knew.

'I was looking at her.'

'Was she nice?'

He nodded.

'What did you like about her?'

'She was really pretty. She used to smile at me.'

'Tell me about her.'

'She wore bright clothes. Even her lipstick was bright. And whenever I walked in, she had my order ready. She called me darling and gave me a special smile.'

It had taken me weeks to get this far with Jimmy. He had stalled and stonewalled for most of that time, claiming not to remember.

I had a fair idea that Jimmy had been running a set of romantic masturbatory fantasies involving the shop assistant. I knew he would find it difficult to acknowledge this, so eventually I asked him directly, using a leading question that he could either accept or deny.

'Tell me, Jimmy, do you still think about her when you're wanking, or was that just back then?'

'No, just then.'

'Had you ever seen her outside of the newsagent's?'

'No.'

'When people have sexual thoughts about someone else, there is a whole range of things that they might be thinking about. They might imagine the girl taking a fancy to them and inviting them upstairs for sex. Or they might imagine taking her out for a drink and then back to their place. Sometimes it's seducing her on the way home and having sex wherever they can. Sometimes she has to be encouraged. Where do you fit into all this?'

'I just wanted to have sex with her. You know, go out with her . . . for us to be together.'

'When you were thinking about being with her, what did she do?'

'Well, first up she doesn't take much notice of me. But then I win her over. She really likes me.'

Poor Jimmy, I thought. With his hearing problem, low intellect and lack of interpersonal insight, not many girls were going to swoon over him. Yet he dreamed and daydreamed of heroic achievements. In his imagination he was forever rescuing fair maidens and winning their hearts. These are ordinary fantasies for a young man with nothing in any way wicked or sinister about them.

'What did she normally wear, this shop assistant?'

'Overalls. She had them in lots of colours.'

'What did she wear them over?'

'I used to think she had on a bra and knickers underneath.'

'Why did you think that?'

217

'I dunno. She used to leave the top button undone. She liked showing a bit of tit.'

'How did that make you feel?'

'Pretty good. I thought, maybe she was doing it for me.'

'Why?'

'She was always so nice to me . . . the way she smiled and called me darling. I thought maybe, you know, she liked me . . .'

'Did you ever say anything to her?'

'I wanted to. There were always people coming in and out. I tried to talk to her . . .'

Jimmy had rehearsed what he was going to say. He just wanted to make conversation, he said. 'To get to know her better.'

On this particular day, he bought his chewing gum and cigarettes as usual. Then he waited until the shop emptied of other customers and went back inside.

'Do you remember what you said to her?' I asked.

He shook his head.

'What happened?'

'She laughed at me. She wound me up.'

'How?'

He couldn't remember exactly what she'd said to him, but he used the word humiliated. That's when he stabbed her.

I went over the scene many times. Each time I unpacked the actual stabbing, Jimmy stonewalled me. Eventually I let the story move on, knowing that I'd bring him back later.

'Why did the police come and arrest you at your work?'

'Because I did it.'

'What were they looking for?'

'The knife.'

'Was it a sheath knife or a folding knife?'

'A pocket knife.'

'Why did you carry a pocket knife with you?'

'I used it for work – cutting string and stuff.'

'When you went into the newsagent's, was the knife in your hand?'

'In my pocket.'

'When did you take it out?'

'I don't know.'

'When did you open the blade?'

He shrugged. 'I didn't really mean to stab her. I just had the knife in my hand. It wasn't a long blade. It didn't go in very far.'

Although I had discovered a lot more about the attack, I still wasn't happy. When somebody finally builds up the courage to talk to a woman they fancy, they don't normally have a knife in their hand. Not unless they're running an abduction fantasy, perhaps, where the knife is meant to control the victim.

No matter how many times I probed the offence, Jimmy would never go any further. I couldn't prompt him by saying, 'Here is a fantasy. That's you, isn't it?' There are so many fantasy scenarios that the chance of me just guessing the right one, in all its detail, was remote. If I were to get it wrong, he'd think, 'What's he talking about?' and I'd lose him.

One of the clinical holds that I had on Jimmy was his belief that I knew things about him that, up to then, only he knew. This could very easily have been undone by making rash guesses and propositions.

As I looked at the details of the knife attack, I knew that something didn't add up. The same was true of the index offence. The forces that drove Jimmy still weren't understood.

When I'm not satisfied, I go back and back and back. It is repetitive, but it's during this process that new material reveals itself.

11

During my brief stint as a police cadet I had to escort a young lad, who must have been about ten years old, to a children's home south of Birmingham. I was only seventeen, much closer in age to the boy than the PC who came with us.

Our civilian driver, Reg, drove the Black Maria van with a constable alongside him. I sat in the back on the slatted bench seats opposite Jonathon, who wore short trousers and scuffed but polished shoes.

I didn't know the circumstances of Jonathon's transfer. For the police to be involved meant it was probably court-ordered and I imagined it was something to do with being beyond parental control.

Not surprisingly, the lad was quite subdued about being taken away from home. For the first half-hour he sat in silence, pulling at his cheek. Between his knees he had a small brown case with a broken catch.

'If I'm good I'm going to get a bike when I get back,' he said.

'That's great.'

'Yeah, Mum promised. Have you got a bike?'

'Yes, I have.'

'What sort is it?'

'I'm not sure. It's just an old second-hand one.'

'What colour is it?'

'I think it used to be green.'

'I want a red one with gears.'

Jonathon had no doubts that he'd be home before long. Then he'd get his bicycle.

He was obviously nervous about going to the home. The constable had reassured him, 'It's not that bad. You'll be all right.'

Jonathon looked at me for confirmation, but I didn't know what to say. I had never been to this children's home, but I doubted if the reality would match his expectations.

An hour after leaving Leamington we pulled up outside a large Georgian double-fronted building, with plaster rendering and a polished wooden door with narrow glass panels on either side. It looked like an old vicarage and was surrounded by a lovely garden.

A matron met us at the front door and took us into a room off the hall. It was the principal's study, with wooden bookshelves rising to the ceiling and a big desk with a leather inset. A photograph of the Queen hung on the wall.

Jonathon looked very small and nervous as we handed him over. He clutched his brown case in his right hand.

The principal was a man in his fifties with a neatly trimmed moustache and thinning hair. He addressed the lad sternly. 'Well, you are here with us now, Jonathon. It may well be that you haven't had proper discipline before, but we don't tolerate misbehaviour.

'When you leave here you'll be a different person. I

can promise you that. You won't be running off the rails any more. I want to show what happens if you don't do as you are supposed to.'

He walked to the corner, just inside the door, where a brass umbrella stand held eight or nine bamboo canes of different thickness and length.

'Put your hand out.'

Jonathon looked totally lost, but raised his hand. Three times the cane whistled through the air.

Crack!

Crack!

Crack!

Jonathon stood there, absolutely numbed by the shock and the pain. He began crying and then stopped himself. He stood there, holding his hand, and he looked at me as if to say, 'You let me down.'

My last view of him was as he was led down the corridor, with his nose running and his stinging hand pressed beneath his armpit.

I found myself shaking. 'How could you do that?' I asked. 'The boy had done nothing wrong.'

'It's none of our business,' said the PC.

'But it's not right.'

'There are things you don't understand. You'll learn them as you grow older.'

I continued protesting all the way to the van. Finally, the constable told me, 'If you want to make a success of this career, you keep your mouth shut and your nose clean.'

The drive back to Leamington Spa was very bleak. I chose to sit in the back instead of riding up front between Reg and the constable. Up until then I had tended to assume that I was on the right side, but suddenly things had become much greyer. I wasn't so sure. When people do things that are wrong, they deserve to be punished, but what had this lad done?

I've thought about this incident a lot in the years since then, particularly when I have to make decisions that affect whether children stay with their families or go into the loneliness of a children's home.

In one particular case, I recall standing in the witness box, facing the court and being asked to show why a very young girl should not be left with her mother. The clinical examination clearly demonstrated the risk to the child from the woman's delusion-like beliefs, intellect and personality.

As I answered counsel's questions, I noticed the mother slip into the back of the courtroom. She listened as I gave my evidence and the case mounted against her. She loved her daughter – I had no doubt of that – but the child couldn't stay in her care and control.

The way the courtroom was arranged, there were only two people who could see her clearly – the judge and myself in the witness box. As I gave my answers she became racked with silent, suffocating sobs. She couldn't close her ears. She listened to all those reasons why her child would be taken away from her. Finally, she slid off the seat and was lost between the benches, lying unconscious on the floor.

I have never forgotten her agony. Nor should I. There are often far-reaching consequences of clinical decisions and it's important, albeit difficult, that we anticipate what these might be.

I first met Malcolm Harris in a probation service waiting room, where he sat on a plastic chair, picking at his fingernails. His hair had been neatly combed and he had on a soft well-worn blue shirt and a deeper blue tie. Occasionally he glanced at the door.

I checked my notes. He looked much younger than his twenty-four years. And although he presented well, he seemed sullen and withdrawn.

'Thank you very much for coming, Mr Britton.'

A young probation officer handed me the file. She wore a simple sleeveless linen dress down to her knees and sensible shoes. Her shoulders in the dress were slim, almost thin, but the muscles in her left arm were bunched where she carried a briefcase. She looked young, perhaps in her mid-twenties, and spoke with an intensity that creased her forehead.

'I've told Malcolm you were coming,' she said. 'He's a little nervous. He hasn't talked to a psychologist before. And I've prepared this for you.' She pointed to a briefing document at the front of the file.

I smiled reassuringly at Malcolm and read her report. Malcolm seemed to stare at the door out of habit. His fluffed-up red hair made his face even more pallid and his eyes greener. The young probation officer had gone and he seemed to be listening for her footsteps in the hall.

Malcolm's index offence related to stealing ladies' underwear from a washing line and watching a woman showering in her bathroom. There was also a reference to 'absconding', when he failed to appear for a court hearing. Following a guilty plea, he was put on parole for a year.

I could see no prerequisite or condition of his sentence that he had to see someone like me. Then I recalled what the probation officer had said: 'It's this business with the women's underwear. That's not really our field. I thought it might be something for you.'

The notes on Malcolm were reasonably comprehensive. He lived with his mother, who was in her fifties, in a council house. Of six children, he was the only one still at home. He and his mother apparently had a close relationship – even more so since the death of his father.

He had a history of truancy from school and had once been assessed as being on the borderline of educational subnormality. I put a question mark next to this conclusion. *'Who says so and when? Where is the data?'*

He was described as being 'highly disturbed' at home where his parents were unable to control him or keep him within limits.

He had been in the Social Services' 'concern' system for a long time, although he remained at home with his mother. A social work report said, 'He seems to be reacting with anger and frustration to an unsatisfactory home situation. This is markedly different from his behaviour at school where the main problem seems to be that he is extremely withdrawn.'

His truancy continued and attempts were made to place him in voluntary care for a period of time before his sixteenth birthday. These failed because of his determination to stay with his mother.

Overall, the picture that emerged from the paperwork was of a rather lonely, isolated young man, lacking self-confidence and the social skills to make friends or contacts among his peers. Instead he became tongue-tied and opted out of conversations.

He wanted to be a painter and decorator. He also wanted a girlfriend, but didn't know how to go about getting one. I checked his age again: twenty-four.

'I'm sorry to keep you waiting,' I said. Malcolm

shrugged and said nothing. He wore a pair of baggy jeans and trainers that were only half-laced.

'Do you know why you are here?'

''Cause they told me to.'

'Who?'

'Them from the court.'

'Why were you in court?'

He mumbled something unintelligible and appeared incapacitated by his awkwardness.

'Most people find it a bit difficult to just sit down in front of a stranger and have to talk about very personal information, even if someone's told them it's OK. Would it be easier if I went over what the notes say?'

'Mmm.'

'Well, it says here that you took some clothes from a woman's clothes line.' He didn't speak or look up. 'Is that about right?'

He nodded but kept his eyes on a point several feet in front of him on the floor.

'They say you were seen in her garden . . . and that you were looking at her in her bathroom.'

'Yeah.'

'You played with yourself?'

'I told 'em that I had a wank,' he said defensively.

'It does say that in the notes, but they don't always get things quite right. I need you to help me to understand how it all really happened.'

'Well, that's it.'

'Yes,' I said very gently. 'What were the clothes you took?'

'What?'

'Did you take her blouse, her skirt, her knickers, her bra . . .?'

Now I waited. I had started in a soft empathic style;

he would have closed like an oyster if I'd been overly authoritarian. Instead, I'd made sure that he joined the conversation. Now the implicit social rules put him under pressure to carry on.

'Her knickers.'

'Why them?'

'They're nice.'

I probed gently, using questions that carried no hint of censure or criticism. Malcolm revealed that he stroked his face with the underwear and rubbed his erection. He stood in the back garden, watching her and masturbating. Afterwards he used her knickers to wipe himself clean.

At one point during the questioning, Malcolm grew angry and confrontational. 'You don't have to keep asking me. You know, don't you?'

This anger disappeared quickly as he nodded miserably in answer to his own question. It wasn't that he regretted his actions; he simply didn't like the idea that he was so transparent.

'How many times had you been into her garden and taken her underwear?'

He shrugged and shuffled uncomfortably in his chair.

'It didn't happen just once, did it? The lady reported things going missing for weeks. I'm not the police, Malcolm. I can't lay charges or lengthen your sentence. I'm just trying to understand what happened.'

I framed the question differently. 'Do you know her garden well? Is it a short cut you use? How long has she lived there? When did you first notice her?'

'About a month ago,' he said.

I made a note: '*Probably not true.*'

Already it had become clear to me that this wasn't a

young man who'd been cruising the back streets and seen a pair of knickers that he fancied on the clothes line. He knew more about the young woman than he'd let on.

'Where did you see her?'

'Through the window. She was watching TV.'

'Does she live alone?'

He shrugged.

'Tell me about her. What does she look like?'

He didn't want to talk about this. I had to prompt him using closed and leading questions. His answers were single words or short phrases.

Eventually I discovered that she was in her early twenties, with long, straight dark-brown hair and brown eyes. She was average height, with full breasts, a small waist, good legs and a bottom that 'wasn't bad'. She normally wore tight jeans or dresses that were sometimes short. She preferred knickers that were black and very small. Occasionally she wore stockings and suspenders.

'How do you know?' I asked him.

'I've seen her a few times – shopping at Tesco's and down the local butcher's.'

'What is her name?'

He didn't expect me to ask this. He pondered what to say. Everything in my demeanour told him that I expected him to know the answer.

'Jill.'

'How did you get to know her name?'

'I read the charge sheet upside down when she complained about me.'

This statement triggered something in Malcolm. His muscles tightened and his eyes narrowed. 'She's plain,' he said suddenly, with a harsh edge to his voice. 'She's not so fucking special. None of them are.'

He wanted to belittle her. She had betrayed him.

Up until then, most people had assumed that Malcolm had a romantic fixation with the girl and had wanted to get close to her. I had my doubts. His anger at what he perceived as her betrayal might flag his more general attitude towards women.

'Have you ever talked to Jill?' I asked him.

He shook his head.

'Why not?'

'She told the cops about me.'

'Yes, but before that, when you saw her down the shops?'

'No.'

'Why not?'

'I wouldn't know what to say. I go sort of red, you know. I don't . . .' His answer trailed off.

Malcolm lacked the social skills and confidence to talk to women in normal conversation, let alone to woo one. It's quite likely that his earliest attempts had failed or been greeted with amusement or ridicule.

In such cases, young men often find themselves drifting towards pornography and masturbation to satisfy their sexual needs. This in itself is not dangerous. Most young men grow out of it and eventually mature emotionally, albeit a little late. When this happens, they begin to be able to talk to women for themselves.

I began talking to Malcolm about masturbation in general terms. Why do we do it? What purpose does it serve? How does it happen?

When people masturbate they normally have mental pictures that drive or fuel them. I had to find out what pictures Malcolm used. It took a little while because he had never learned that having sexual

230

fantasies was quite normal. The only time it becomes dangerous is when the fantasy themes become spring-boards to violence for a small, predisposed group of people who haven't had the compensating or offsetting experiences that most of us enjoy. Another, quite separate group is socialized into sexual violence by having been victims themselves.

This distinction between whether sexual fantasies are normal or deviant is central to assessing someone as a future danger.

Malcolm had been talking to me for less than an hour, but it was enough for me to build up some rapport between us. The office had very little that could distract him. This meant that he had to focus much more on my voice, which I used to reassure him. At the same time, I had to try almost to disappear and cease to be there in a judgemental capacity. He had to feel that I knew him and understood how he felt.

'How often do you think about Jill when you masturbate at home?' I asked.

'Sometimes.'

'More or less than half of the times?'

'Depends . . . about half.'

'Take me through what you see and think about. When you start to feel excited, where are you?'

'In her bedroom.'

'What time is it?'

'Night.'

'How do you get there?'

'I climb through a ground-floor window.'

'Is it open?'

'No, I have to smash it. She's upstairs undressing.'

'Does she hear you?'

'Yeah, but I'm too quick. I race up the stairs and

yank her onto the bed. She's wearing a see-through nightdress.'

'What does she do?'

'She's screaming. Her mouth is flappin' up and down. I start touching her up.'

'How do you touch her up?'

'I fondle her tits through her nightdress. She has great breasts. Then I rip her clothes off.'

'What does she do?'

'She fights, but I give her a fist in the face to keep her quiet. Then I do it.'

'What do you do?'

'You know. I make love to her.'

Malcolm had no conception of consensual sex. Any form of penile penetration and ejaculation into her body was 'making love', as far as he was concerned. In his fantasy he hit her four or five times when she continued to resist him. Then she fell limply onto the bed and he ran off.

Throughout this exchange, I had to be very careful not to suggest things to Malcolm or introduce content. It is very easy for someone like him to adopt ideas rather than give me the pure fantasy images that he created and masturbated over. For this reason, all my prompts had been neutral: 'And then what?' and 'What happens next?'

'Where do you run to?'

'Downstairs.'

'And then what?'

'I look for a knife.'

'Why?'

'So I can kill her. That way she can't identify me.'

I noticed an increase in his arousal. This wasn't a flat, matter-of-fact response, as though killing would be

232

like a housekeeping chore. There were possibly other reasons. I wrote in my notes: '*What else?*'

'What happens after you get the knife?'

'I stab her in the chest.'

'How often?'

'Four or five times – until she stops screaming.'

Malcolm's eyes now shone with an intensity that I hadn't seen before. He felt good about this fantasy. He liked the idea of killing her. His fingertips drummed on his knees, keeping time to a rhythm that I couldn't hear.

At no stage did I recoil from him or rebuke him. Throughout his account of the rape–murder fantasy, my voice and posture had remained unchanged. At the same time I was rapidly assessing all the information.

The young man in front of me displayed a potentially dangerous deviant sexuality, yet he wasn't in custody or under any obligation to seek treatment. Instead he was on twelve months' probation for what the police and probation service had regarded as a minor sexual offence.

To assess the level of risk he posed I needed to go back and unpack his imagery even further. Just as with Ray Knox, I needed to find out how much, if any, of the fantasy had been taken into the real world. Had there been a crossover?

Malcolm had been expecting massive censure from me when he told me his innermost thoughts and desires. When this didn't happen, he had begun to relax. He had never spoken about these things before to anyone. They were *his* secrets. Now he discovered how liberating and exciting it could be to share them. His eyes were still bright and alert.

'When you first saw Jill, you said she was watching TV. How is it that you could see her?'

233

'Well, there's a window.'

'Where exactly?'

'Downstairs. They're French doors really. And she has lots of plants in pots sitting outside. I used to sit in there among the bushes and watch her.'

'How long for?'

'Until she went to bed. I'd see her turning all the lights off before going upstairs.'

'What did you do?'

'From a dark corner of the garden I could see her bedroom window. I watched her shadow against the curtains. She'd get undressed. Fully naked, she'd be.'

'How do you know?'

'I could tell.'

'What did you do?'

'I had her knickers from the line. I used to imagine her rolling those little black knickers down her long legs. She liked black knickers. I used to imagine that last moment when the panties pulled away from her crotch. It's a shame they'd been washed. They smelt of soap.'

'Is that when you imagined having her?'

'Yeah.'

'And what did you do with the knickers?'

'Like I told you. I wanked in them.'

'What happened then?'

'I went home.'

According to Malcolm's account, this was the point where reality and his rape–murder fantasy diverged. I had to be sure.

'When you imagine having her, when you picture it in your mind, what are the pictures like?'

'They're not just videos or books, it's like they're real. They make me feel dead sexy.'

'And while you're masturbating in the dark, and you're picturing her in your mind, what else are you doing?'

'What do you mean?'

'Well, you're watching her shadow on the curtains. She's undressing. You have her knickers. You imagine having her. Do you do anything else?'

'Yeah, I guess. Sometimes.'

'What?'

'I wonder about the windows.'

'What about them?'

'Whether they're locked or not. I sort of hope she might have left one of them open.'

'Most people close their windows.'

'I know.'

'How did you find out?'

'I tested a couple of them. I couldn't get them open.'

'How hard did you try?'

He shrugged. 'One time I brought a Stanley knife. I thought I could flip the latch.'

'Is that the only reason you took the knife?'

'I could stab her with it – instead of having to go looking for something.'

I sensed he had a problem with this notion. 'Is something wrong?' I asked.

'Well, a Stanley knife isn't really for stabbing. It's more for slashing.'

'How do you know?'

'I sort of ripped up her knickers.'

'What were you thinking about when you did this?'

'About her.'

'What do you think would have happened if you had got into the house?'

He shrugged and tried to change the subject.

'Nuthin'. I wouldn't have really gone in. I like Jill. She's a good looker.'

'So why kill her?'

'Because she'd tell the police.'

'If you did stab her, how do you think you'd feel?'

'I haven't touched her,' he said warily. 'I done nothing wrong.'

'I know that. But when you think about her and have pictures in your mind, how do you feel when you are stabbing her in the chest?'

'Good, I guess.'

'Why?'

''Cause I'm the man. She has to do what I want.'

I needed to discover how Malcolm came to have these fantasies. When did they start? Although his probation service reports included a history, I had to make my own exploration, particularly into the darker areas he'd only just revealed.

I started by taking him back through his early childhood, family life, school years and employment history – up to the present day. When I began asking him about relationships with girls and if he'd had any past girlfriends, he shook his head.

'Have you asked them out to the pictures or the disco?'

'Yeah. But they always turned me down.'

'How did you feel?'

'Pissed off. Some of 'em were laughing at me.'

'What makes you say that?'

'I just know they were.'

'So what did you do?'

'Nuthin'.'

Malcolm's masturbatory history had started a little late – around the age of fifteen. His fantasies contained

236

fairly ordinary images for a teenage boy. He pictured what he deemed to be consensual romantic sex, with no force or coercion involved.

Clearly, however, he didn't have any model to work from. He had no internal pictures of foreplay or mutual consenting sex. He didn't understand the mechanism by which women become sexually aroused.

Usually, this sort of knowledge comes to growing boys over time; from their first kisses in the dark and games of kiss-chase.The girls teach them about girls and other boys swap information about wooing and gaining consent from girls. Some of this is to show off or to reassure oneself, but it all adds to a boy's knowledge. For this reason, most fifteen-year-olds come to sex with a caring rather than a selfish attitude.

Malcolm, however, began taking his cues from pornographic videos and magazines – particularly those containing rape-related images. This probably began with softer material from the top shelves of corner shops. Eventually he moved on to material involving sadism, sexual murder and rape. Such violent and exploitative magazines and videos are illegal, but can still be found through mail order catalogues and sex shops. There is also a trade between like-minded men.

This motif became established early on and Malcolm began to favour pornography that focused on exploitation and coercion. 'They turned me on,' he said.

I asked him what features of the videos and magazines especially turned him on.

'I like it when they're wearing a uniform – you know, like a policewoman – and when they're wearing black knickers and bras underneath.'

This interest in pornography had increased and became more specialized as he grew older. This is where

237

all his ideas about sex had come from; he had no first-hand experience to draw upon.

On a Friday and Saturday, the same nights that he went prowling, he would rent videos in town. These weren't standard X-rated pornographic films but rape and slash videos, probably passed from under the counter. And there was a direct link between the videos and his offending because he talked about watching them and then going straight to Jill's house.

Malcolm couldn't or wouldn't tell me the names of his favourite videos, but he could describe in detail what they were about. He watched them in his bedroom, while he caressed women's underwear that he'd taken from lingerie counters or clothes lines. Jill's knickers were special, he said, and he kept them in a shoebox under his bed.

Just like the carrying of the Stanley knife, here was another real-world crossover. There were more. As I pressed him further, Malcolm talked of sometimes choosing women and following them home. He hoped they would walk down quiet alleyways or across playing fields. At other times he waited in bushes and in lonely places, watching young women walk their dogs. Each time he had an erection.

'What were you thinking about?'

'Doing it to her.'

It had been a long session – nearly two-and-a-half hours – but I still needed one more piece of information before I could be sure about Malcolm. According to the briefing notes from the probation officer, he'd been given a real scare by his court appearance. He had learned his lesson and mended his ways. If only justice were this simple.

'You're living at home?'

'Yeah.'

'How have things been?'

'OK, I guess. Mum's pretty dirty on me getting into trouble.'

'How often do you watch the videos?'

I could have asked, 'Are you still watching the videos?' but that would have suggested that I was uncertain about his progress. It would also make it easy for him simply to deny it.

'Mostly on the weekend.'

'Where do you go afterwards?'

'Different places.'

Whatever natural caution Malcolm had initially felt towards me had now been fully allayed. He didn't see me as a threat or a source of potential punishment like the police or probation service. He also, in his naivety, didn't realize the ramifications of his words. As far as he knew, our session would soon be over, then he'd get up and leave.

'When was the last time that you saw Jill?'

He blinked a few times and I could almost see the wheels grinding into place. 'It were last weekend,' he said.

'Were you in her garden?'

He grinned shyly. 'Yeah.'

I quickly calculated the date. Less than twenty-four hours after being dealt with in court, he had gone straight out prowling again. Only this time I knew that he had a new emotion – anger. She had betrayed him. She had reported him to the police. She had caused him a lot of grief with his mum.

Malcolm might have been too scared to talk to her, but he wasn't too scared to rape and kill her. I had no

239

doubt that if he could have gained entry to the house without making too much noise or alerting someone else, he would have tried to do so.

I was familiar with the pathway he was on. For him it was like an irresistible urge, an itch that had to be scratched. I also knew that he'd have other women in his fantasies.

Glancing at the probation notes, I looked at the signature of the young officer who had given me the file. Kelly Doncaster had come across as an attractive, confident and committed young woman. Clearly, she took her job very seriously.

Malcolm had stretched his legs out and slid down until his head rested on the back of his chair. He was tired of talking. He wanted to go home.

'Just a few more questions,' I said, encouraging him. 'You've been very honest and open with me. I really appreciate that. Let me ask you for a moment about Jill.'

'What about her?'

'Well, you've talked about her underwear and how she looks. She's an attractive woman.'

'So what?'

'You've not talked to a woman like that before, have you?'

He went very quiet. 'I dunno what you mean.'

'Well, let me go back over what you've told me. You said that you'd seen her in the shops and in the street, but never spoken to her. You've also seen other girls. You've followed them home or watched them walking their dogs.'

'Yeah.'

'This made you feel excited. You wanted to have them. But you never talked to these girls. You've never had anything to do with them.'

240

He shrugged.

'What about Kelly?'

'What about her?'

'She's your probation officer. You see her all the time. She's an attractive woman. You talk to her and tell her things that are worrying you, or on your mind.'

'Yeah.'

'How do you fit her into your fantasies, Malcolm?'

He smiled as if sharing a secret.

'When you picture her in your mind, what's happening?'

'We're making love.'

I already knew Malcolm's definition of this was different to that of most of us.

'Where are you?'

'Here, in the office. She takes her clothes off. She's wearing black underwear. We do it on top of her desk.'

Malcolm's voice had become strangely distant. He had forgotten me. I was no longer in the room. 'I don't want to force her because she'll start crying. The buttons on her blouse are undone. I fondle her tits. They're quite nice. She's got nice legs too. She's lying naked across the desk, with her legs draped over the side. Her hair is sort of half across her forehead. She pushes it behind her ear. She's wearing pink lipstick . . .'

Malcolm was describing part fantasy and part reality. He knew exactly how Kelly tied her hair and did her make-up. The way her blouse fell over her breasts and how the light sometimes caught the tiny, almost invisible scar on her forehead. He had asked her about it. 'A childhood accident,' Kelly told him. 'I fell off a swing.'

241

Malcolm had used each of his probation appointments to gather details about Kelly. He collected every detail of her dress, make-up and mannerisms so that he could add these to his rape fantasy and make it more vivid and real.

After each of these weekly meetings, Malcolm would go straight to a nearby toilet and masturbate. He claimed that there was no force in his fantasy. He was too worried about getting caught.

'She wants me to do it,' he said. 'I lock the door so we're not disturbed. Then I give it to her doggy-style. She likes it that way.'

Many of the people sent to me by the courts or the prison service are not particularly bright, or blessed with pleasant personalities. These are often thought of as the dregs of society – people for whom nothing has gone right.

Most of them are not irredeemably bad or evil. Some *want* to be helped. Others can't recognize that they have a problem.

My greatest compassion has always been for the victims of crime and their families. Even so, I can't escape feeling compassion for the casualties of abuse and neglect like Ray Knox and Jimmy Fordham. These men were so damaged by their environmental experiences that they went on to commit crimes, or become a risk. Malcolm fell into the same category.

I watched Malcolm leave. He still had a teenager's loping walk, as though he hadn't got used to growing eight inches in adolescence. He couldn't quite make his limbs operate in tandem, so he looked gangly and uncoordinated.

Kelly intercepted me in the corridor.

'How did it go?'

Just as Malcolm had described, she wore pink lipstick and pushed her hair behind her ears. I took her to one side and asked her to sit down.

'What's wrong?' she asked. Her brow furrowed in consternation.

'Malcolm was very honest and open with me. Unfortunately, what he said to me may come as a profound shock to you.'

'Why?'

'He has very violent sexual fantasies that he uses when he masturbates. One of the women he fantasizes about is you.'

The colour drained from her cheeks.

'When he leaves this office after seeing you, he masturbates in the toilet at the end of the corridor . . .'

'No! No!' She looked at me wide-eyed.

'His fantasies are dominated by images of rape and coercion. I'm telling you this because you are at risk.'

Her hands were shaking. She tried to still them in her lap. Taking a deep breath, she pushed her hair back again and fixed her eyes on mine. 'I'm always very careful,' she said. 'I follow procedure.'

'I'm sure you do. I just wanted you to be aware of the situation.'

'Thank you,' she said, getting to her feet. She fought any unsteadiness and smoothed down her dress.

It never ceases to amaze me how people working in these very sensitive and potentially dangerous situations deal with risk by pretending to themselves that it is not there. Even very bright professional people fail to understand the nature of the threat.

Young women like Kelly are especially vulnerable because in a shifting culture they are taking on many

243

jobs that were previously denied them. They can be assertive, confident and wonderfully qualified, but this won't be worth tuppence when a man like Malcolm pulls a knife and starts stabbing.

That afternoon I wrote a letter to the probation service:

> *Following your urgent request, I saw Malcolm Harris for a preliminary consultation. It does seem important to make an interim report on his current condition before completing my assessment and producing a more comprehensive report.*
>
> *He has described a series of sexual fantasies that accompany his masturbation which suggest quite strongly that he is an immediate danger to the woman named Jill, who I believe initiated the current charge against him.*
>
> *His fantasies are sufficiently developed for him to have started to act them out in part. Unfortunately, the fantasies include both rape and murder of the lady named.*
>
> *He has already attempted to enter her house armed with a knife with the intention of killing her. I am reasonably sure at this stage that he would be better served and the woman properly protected if he were remanded in custody until my assessment is finished.*

In the following days I had lengthy meetings with the probation service, the police and various lawyers. Each time I expressed my considerable concerns about Malcolm. However, he couldn't be arrested again without new charges being laid. And the only evidence of his having reoffended was his admissions to me.

To make matters worse, I knew he wouldn't come back to see me. Once he knew of my attempts to have him taken into custody, he would refuse to talk as openly again to anyone about his fantasies and actions. Therefore the only way to get our clinical hooks into him and do the work was to have him detained.

I kept agitating for the police to act, but there were problems. 'His admissions aren't strong enough evidence to arrest him,' said a senior policeman who had worked on the original case.

'But he acknowledged going back to the woman's house,' I argued. 'He has acknowledged attempting to break in, with a knife, with the intention of killing her.'

'Yes, but now he's denying it. He says he told you nothing of the sort.'

'So it's my word against his?'

'That's right.'

I couldn't hide my frustration. They only had to charge him, not convict him. Once charged, he could be remanded in custody awaiting trial. Then we'd have the opportunity to assess him fully and argue for detention and treatment under the Mental Health Act at any court hearing.

'Look. This is the situation,' I said to the police officer. 'This man is a grave risk to women. Sooner or later he is going to act out his fantasies. And that means he's going to rape and kill somebody.'

'I hear what you're saying, Mr Britton, but you can't be certain of that. Malcolm has been around for twenty-four years and hasn't killed anyone. He's a knicker-sniffer. He's not a killer.'

'Then the very least you can do is alert the woman. You might also arrange some counselling for her. It's a traumatic thing to know there is somebody out there who is targeting you.'

'We can protect her.'

'I'm pleased to hear that, but she's not your only problem. He doesn't have the determination and skill to wait until you lose interest, or she makes a mistake.'

'So he'll give up.'

'No. On the contrary, he'll focus on someone else. He will disappear into the woodwork, but the next time you hear from him – and you *will* hear from him – he will have done something to fulfil his fantasy. There is going to be a break-in and an attack on a woman.'

'That may be your opinion, Mr Britton, but I can't act without something more concrete than your theories.'

I disagreed bitterly with the decision, but I understood how the system worked. It's not only designed to protect the public, but also as a filter. If you look at the barrage of potential offences, remands and detentions that the police and courts face each day, then you come to understand why they develop some sort of informal, discretionary cut-off criteria.

The obvious cases are the simplest – an offence has occurred, the evidence is presented and action is taken. In Malcolm's case the offence had been minor. He'd stolen some knickers and watched a woman in the shower.

Unfortunately, those around him didn't understand the potency of fantasy as a driving force for real-world sexual aggression. That's why I had so many people saying to me, 'He doesn't look very dangerous. He's quite pathetic really. He could do with some nice girl to bring him on.'

Others argued, 'You're asking us to convict someone on his fantasies. We all daydream.'

I kept thinking back to one of the early police investigations I worked upon – the Narborough murders in Leicestershire. Two schoolgirls were killed less than a mile apart, but the crimes were separated by three years.

During that investigation I told David Baker, the senior investigating officer, that the man they were looking for would have come to the attention of the police before, perhaps for minor indecency offences, such as sexually exposing himself.

Baker struggled with this. The conceptual leap between a man flashing his erect penis at a woman and someone raping and killing a schoolgirl was too great. However, predatory rapists don't simply arrive out of the blue. They have to start somewhere.

Usually there is some history of sexual deviancy that escalates slowly. If you were to draw it on a graph, with time and sexual aggression as the two axes, there would be a steady rise in aggression over time rather than a sudden leap from flashing to murder. I had seen this over and over in the histories of serious sexual offenders.

More than a year after I gave David Baker this advice, the killer Colin Pitchfork was caught and confessed to the murders. It emerged that he had indeed been arrested previously and was in the record system for flashing. Baker apologized to me afterwards for not having heeded my advice.

Now, confronted with Malcolm, I thought that if I hadn't been able to convince a senior and highly skilled detective, what hope did I have of convincing the uniformed branch at a small district police station that had rarely worked on such cases?

After weeks of meetings and many letters going back and forth, I had to admit defeat. I couldn't have Malcolm detained and I felt as though I was letting him down, as well as seeing innocent women put at risk.

At that moment, he had a relatively minor tariff sheet (conviction sheet) and there was still the chance to turn him round. But the next time he offended, the system would come down hard on Malcolm. His life would be wrecked, along with that of some young woman.

12

When I was first appointed as General Manager of the
forensic service two wards at Arnold Lodge were fully
open and planning for a much-needed third was in
progress. Unfortunately, strategic approval for the new
ward to begin operating was constantly being post-
poned. Each time we removed one obstacle another
seemed to appear.

The Department of Health had already allocated the
funding, but it was up to the 'Region' to earmark the
monies for the forensic service. This couldn't happen
until 'District' had finalized a 'case of need'. 'District'
couldn't do this without 'Region' releasing the funds.
All this reminded me of the children's song, 'There's A
Hole In My Bucket'.

Meanwhile, the core clinical team of nursing, psychiatric and psychological staff had been appointed for
the new ward, but we didn't have the money to pay
for them or to open the beds.

A long waiting list of patients with personality disorders who were to be assessed for admission was
building up across the region.

I shared my frustration with a young woman
from the Regional Health Authority in Sheffield.

'It's a pity that nobody goes straight to the top,' she said.

'What do you mean?'

'The Department of Health.'

'Who would they go to?'

She smiled and handed me the name and number of the most senior civil servant at the department.

I rang his secretary and asked if I could make an appointment. After a few minutes she came back. 'Yes, he'd be delighted to see you. Would you like to come along on Thursday morning at ten thirty?'

Over the next few days I put together a briefing paper and all the documentation showing what had happened. The ward was ready and so were the staff. There were now only the small matters of the money and the final approval.

I went by train to London and by Underground to the Department of Health. Soon afterwards I was ushered into the under-secretary's presidential-style office.

An immaculately suited man of early middle years stood to shake my hand, but seemed perplexed as we met. He admitted his error immediately. He was expecting somebody else. My name was very similar to that of a GP in the Midlands whom he knew very well.

'It's a small mistake, but let's see if we can make it a fortuitous one,' he said. 'Do tell me why you're here.'

I spent about an hour and a half with him, going over the problem.

'Well, it does seem to be a nonsense, doesn't it?' he said. 'Would it help if I dropped a note to the chairman of the Regional Health Authority confirming that the money has been made available?'

'I would be very grateful,' I said.

Confirmation of the release of the funds reached Leicester before I did.

Unfortunately, this simultaneously signalled the end of my short career as general manager of the forensic service.

'If everyone did this, the service would dissolve into chaos,' I was told. 'There wouldn't be any structure . . . no line of management.'

Now regarded as a maverick, I knew my strained relationship with the bureaucrats wouldn't help the service or my clinical effectiveness. As a result, I resigned as general manager, electing to return to my primary role as head of the Forensic Psychology Service.

The ructions that I caused didn't change my attitude. I would do exactly the same thing if I was given my time over again. People like Jimmy Fordham needed treatment and now they were going to get it.

Ray Knox failed to keep his next appointment. I sat for an hour in the clinic, occasionally glancing out of the window. Where was he? Was he trawling for locations again, or stalking his father?

For the next two days, I heard nothing. I contemplated calling his telephone number, or asking my secretary to call.

While Ray continued to see me I had a clinical hold on him and his dangerous urges had an outlet. But if I lost my grip, I knew the danger he posed increased immeasurably.

I never assume that my forensic patients are telling the truth. My one certainty with Ray was that he wanted my approval. He needed this from me in the same way that most children seek it from a parent

– unconditional acceptance, of him as a person.

This was why he had continued to talk. I hadn't chiselled information from him; I had created the conditions where he could volunteer it because he wanted me to understand him.

This need in Ray for acceptance and friendship was one of the things that I relied upon as I waited to hear from him. The rapport between us had reached a point where he had a need to get his hooks into me.

He would ask, 'Am I a good patient, Paul? You know I'd never let you down. What about when people let *you* down, it must make you fucking fed up. But you can't show it, I guess. If I was you, I'd sort the fuckers out! I'll do it for you if you like.'

Ray would often try to do this – reach past my professional role and elicit personal feelings that he could commiserate with. He asked questions about my family, to set against his own experiences. When this happened I gently steered him back to his own situation.

I knew there were things that Ray hadn't yet disclosed. Some of the clues were revealed unintentionally in things he said, and other things he didn't say. One phrase in particular had come up repeatedly: 'They're all going to pay.'

Who did he mean?

At other times the phrase altered slightly. 'You're all going to pay,' he said, full of hate and looking directly at me.

Clearly, I represented the sort of person whom he blamed for all of the world's problems, not just his own. I was a father – a figure of authority. In Ray's mind we were somehow all to blame. That's why he'd wanted to lash out at the café owner for 'throwing his weight around' in front of the teenage lads. He, too, was probably a father, or had the same sense of authority. Yet Ray couldn't escape the fact that he, too, had children. This preyed on his mind and he couldn't trust himself.

Two days after missing his appointment, Ray left a message with my secretary apologizing for his failure to attend. 'Tell Mr Britton I'll be there on Thursday,' he said, without giving an explanation. 'Tell him I'm sorry.'

The following Thursday he arrived very late. I had already written once more 'Did Not Attend' in the notes when the receptionist rang to say he was waiting. In the past Ray had normally been early for consultations. If anybody was prone to being late it was me – delayed at the previous clinic, or caught in traffic.

Something else had changed. Usually Ray and my secretary got on well. She thought him quite shy and handsome and they often swapped greetings. This time she whispered down the phone: 'Please take him in quickly, something's wrong.'

Ray came in awkwardly. Every muscle and fibre seemed tense, so much so that his shoulders curved forward. He wore a crumpled beige jacket with sleeves that were too short for his arms. There were heavy plasters on his hands and newly scabbed cuts on his forearms that the jacket failed to hide. One of them had been bandaged and blood leaked through the gauze.

I was about to say something when his face twisted in grief. He howled, 'It's no good! IT'S NO FUCKING GOOD! It just can't go on!'

I could hear distant doors opening as people looked out into the hall, wondering what had happened.

Meanwhile Ray held out his hands, then lifted his shirt front. There were bruises and what looked like small burn marks. They were too big to be cigarette burns and too numerous to be accidental.

'Ray, what's happened? Have you seen a doctor?'

'Don't you see, it was me. I did this. I had to stop. It was the only way . . .' His voice trailed off and he wept into his bandaged hands.

Once you have seen self-mutilation you rarely mistake it for something else. The directions of the wounds and their locations made it immediately clear. I'd seen these sorts of injuries on young women and much more rarely on men, especially of Ray's age.

'Why this?' I asked, trying to hide my disappointment.

'It's been a bad week,' he answered, unaware of the obvious understatement. He held his arms above his thighs, attempting to avoid the pain of putting pressure on the wounds.

'I tried to stop myself,' he blurted. 'See? See what I did? I couldn't get them out of my head. I had to punish them . . .'

'What happened?'

'I didn't want to do it. You know I'm trying.'

'Yes.'

'That's why I locked myself in the basement – to stop myself going out. I called in sick. I stayed down there. But I couldn't get the thoughts to go away. I got trapped . . . inside my head. I couldn't get back to Stella. I could hear her calling me and knocking on the basement door. But I couldn't get back to her . . .

'I thought I must be an evil bastard. If I don't come back, I'll be just like him. But someone's got to be punished. So I hit myself with a chisel. It didn't really seem to hurt, but I felt better, sort of closer to home. So I hit myself again and again.'

'What about the burns?'

254

'Soldering iron.'

'And the cuts?'

'Wallpaper knife.'

'Have you seen a doctor?'

'No. It hurts, but it's OK. The pain helps. I don't want to go back there again. I don't want to leave Stella. I can't let this happen again. What if the girls saw it?'

He shook his head and sniffled. With his damaged hands, he couldn't even pull a handkerchief from his pocket. I gave him tissues. How on earth had he managed to drive? The pain must have been terrible.

'You should have called me,' I said. 'You can always call me. Any time. Someone will page me. I'll get the message. You don't have to do this on your own.'

Although physically exhausted, Ray seemed more at ease after his outburst than I'd ever seen him before. The pain had somehow cleansed him and made him feel better.

At the same time, I knew that he really couldn't go on like this. The mental battle to control his violent urges was torturing him. My clinical hold over him alone wouldn't be enough. He had tried to isolate himself by not going to work or leaving the house. But when his fantasies took over and the urges grew too strong, he had to find ways to bring himself back and ease the stress. Pain could do that for him.

We had come a long way, but I had more to learn about Ray and the journey promised to be mostly uphill. At least he hadn't directed his trauma outwards.

It was important that I pressed onwards, trying to fill the gaps. I took Ray back to the time when he'd been waiting for his father in the car park.

'You said you were disappointed when he didn't show up.'

'Yes.'

'What else did you feel?'

'Cheated.'

'Anything else?'

He fidgeted, picking nervously at the scabs on his forearms. His breathing had altered slightly. He didn't like being uncomfortable.

'I guess I felt relieved,' he said.

'Why is that?'

Ray couldn't hide his self-loathing. 'Because ... because I didn't have to confront him.'

This answer didn't surprise me. Despite all the elaborate plans he'd made, I knew that Ray still faced a major hurdle in his bid for revenge. He had to overcome his fear of the man who had abused him.

He wouldn't acknowledge this to me – it was too painful. Through all of his young life this monster had belittled him. That bowel-loosening fear had never gone away. I could see it whenever Ray spoke of the man. He almost trembled.

It must have been a gut-wrenching disappointment to discover that he didn't have the courage or confidence to confront and deal with his father on an interpersonal basis. His own weakness disgusted him. His father was too powerful. It wasn't going to happen.

Another factor, I think, was the realization that even if he did succeed in taking revenge it wouldn't take the police very long to point the finger at him. Ray could rationalize all of this. He didn't want to get caught.

At the same time, his desire for revenge didn't dissipate. If anything, with another failure to add to his list, his anger grew more intense. If he couldn't get back at his father – what then?

One option was to end his misery by taking his own life. However, I suspected something else. Ray had invested too much in revenge to surrender now. It had become the centre of his existence. If he couldn't punish his father, then the years of fear still had to be paid for. But by whom?

'Did you go out driving in the past week?'

He nodded.

'Were you looking for locations?'

'Yes.'

'What else were you looking for?'

Ray didn't answer.

'Who else have you followed?'

He turned away from me. I could see his anxiety rising. His face had coloured and he no longer worried about his bandaged hands. His fists curled and uncurled.

'Tell me about them?'

He didn't answer.

'Do you know them? How old are they?'

'Middle-aged.'

'Are they married?'

'I suppose so.'

'You assume so?'

'Yes.'

'And perhaps they're fathers.'

'Yes.'

'Have you followed anybody in particular?'

'Once or twice.'

'Where?'

'I see them walking their dogs.'

'What have you been thinking?'

257

'About how I can get them without being seen.'

'Do you know their names?'

'Nah. It doesn't matter.'

'When do you think about looking?'

'All the time. I can't help it. I try to stop.'

'Are these the people who "have to pay"?'

An explosion detonated. 'THEY'RE ALL FUCK-ING ABUSERS! People like you!' He stabbed his finger towards me. 'You all ruin your children's lives! You play God!'

The muscles on his forearms bulged and the scars threatened to reopen. His fists were closed tight and his face had twisted in hatred. At that moment, I knew he wanted to wipe me from the face of the world.

The telephone rang. It was the duty co-ordinator at Arnold Lodge. One of the patients had barricaded herself into a room. She had a broken bottle and was threatening to kill herself.

As leader of the crisis management team at the lodge, I had to be called whenever such a problem arose.

'It's Angela Franklin,' said the duty co-ordinator. 'She's cut herself already, but it's not serious.'

'When did it happen?'

'About ten minutes ago. The ward manager has labelled it a critical incident.'

'Is anyone talking to her?'

'Bill Carpenter. He was on shift. She's threatened to kill him if he tries to come in.'

'OK. Make sure there's someone in Bill's line of vision at all times, but not hers. If he signals for something I want an instant response.' I looked at my watch. 'I'll be there as soon as I can.'

It could have been worse; it often had been. A certain amount of internal strife is unavoidable in a place like Arnold Lodge where the patients are often very damaged and volatile. Angela had come to us having lit a string of fires, one of which almost killed her grandparents. She had seemed to be making good progress but clearly something had upset her.

A lot could still go wrong, but I felt easier with Bill Carpenter outside her door. He was one of the most talented but underutilized nurses I'd ever come across and put tremendous energy into taking care of the patients, particularly when organizing their leisure and social activities.

Bill had taken one of the earliest hostage negotiator courses that I'd run at the lodge. He'd shown a wonderful ability to work through the most dangerous and demanding situations, functioning at a very high level in a crisis. He could also remain focused for extraordinary periods of time. If I were taken hostage, I'd want Bill on the other side of the door.

As I drove back to Leicester, I ran through the critical incident drill in my head. By now the ward would be a sterile area, with a clear perimeter and no-one wandering about.

I had also asked for a room to be requisitioned for the crisis management team, close to the scene but not interfering with the rest of the unit. We would need tables, chairs, flipcharts, situation logs and the clinical files, as well as some coffee.

Angela had been barricaded inside the room for an hour by the time I arrived. I needed to know exactly what had happened.

'There was a ruck on the ward,' said the duty co-ordinator. 'Roger Henderson [another patient] completely lost it. He went for Alice, the new nurse.'

'Why?'

'He said that she was putting Angela down.'

I'd met Alice once or twice on the wards. Compared to Roger Henderson she was a slip of a thing. He could have hurt her badly.

'Is Alice OK?'

'Yes. Just a bit shaken. She can thank Jimmy Fordham for that.'

'Why?'

'He saved her. He came out of nowhere. Roger had cornered Alice and was about to attack her when Jimmy took him down. He held him until the rest of us could get there.'

Well done, Jimmy, I thought. He'd never struck me as being particularly powerful. Now he'd rescued a fair maiden in real life and not just in his fantasies. For his long-term recovery, it represented something of a problem: it wouldn't make him popular with the rest of the patients because he'd sided with the staff, and it was therefore likely to accentuate his isolation from the rest of the therapeutic community.

The crisis management team met in a room near Cairngorm Ward (each ward is named after a UK mountain range). The team members included a psychologist, a medic, a nurse and a senior manager.

Their backgrounds were relevant, but more important was their crucial role within the crisis management team. I had run a five-day training course setting up the system. Runners began taking instructions and questions to Bill Carpenter, who was still outside Angela's room.

She had blocked the door with her bed, wardrobe and other furniture. It was very securely wedged and nobody would be charging through there in a hurry. Bill had to speak to her through a small fanlight over the door.

Angela's arm was bleeding but it wasn't serious. Even so, she was building up to a full-scale suicide attempt. Now she was highly agitated, her perception of those around her was deeply distorted. The nurse had been 'cruel' and 'hateful' to her. Roger had been her champion. He had come to save her. As a result, she was convinced that he was now 'drugged up' and in seclusion.

As far as she was concerned there was no way forward. If she surrendered the broken bottle and came out, she'd be punished. The night staff would take revenge on her for what had happened to Alice.

Bill, of course, was gently showing the reality – that none of this would happen.

Angela replied, 'How can you say that? You don't know what goes on at night.'

The incident with Alice had been just the catalyst. Angela didn't want to go on. Things weren't working out for her at Arnold Lodge, she said. She was determined to die.

'My fucking parents will have the last laugh. They didn't want me at home so they got me in here. Now they'll see me leave in a box.'

Managing any hostage situation is delicate even when dealing with a single suicide threat. Rather than a macho hard-bargaining attitude, a negotiating approach is vital, with a focus on 'needs' instead of 'positions' and a long view instead of a dangerous rush at the door.

This way we usually win control of the field. It also means we preserve a calm atmosphere on the wards and clinical work can be maintained.

Negotiating alone doesn't always succeed. That was why we had two C & R (control and restraint) teams ready, with jackets and helmets but no shields. Shields were too big to give any chance of getting into the room before Angela cut herself.

The police and fire service had also been alerted. If necessary, they could take out the window frame to give us another means of entry. The worry, however, was that any approach could be seen from her window.

Even if they managed to get this far, Angela would attack herself, or them, at the first sound of the jack-hammer and the wrench. These were clearly last resort measures.

The C & R teams in the NHS are made up of men and women (almost always nurses) who receive additional training in techniques for holding violent patients until they can be either calmed or subdued, with or without sedatives. Normally each team is at least three strong.

If the unit has a wider disturbance, the crisis management team can authorize the C & R teams to use protective clothing and shields. The aim is to protect themselves and the patients from serious harm.

However, the sight of a paramilitary-style force in full riot gear can create long-term damage to the clinical ethos of a ward, which is why the use of this option is almost unheard of.

Although Angela was bleeding, she was in no immediate danger. Bill had kept her mind open and I was hopeful we could resolve the problem through negotiation. Only if Bill signalled that things were going pear-shaped would the C & R commander be given the green light.

The crisis had now been running for three hours and

I knew that Bill had to be rested. If he lost concentration he risked losing control of the situation. A new negotiator was introduced, but the situation deteriorated rapidly. Angela cut herself again and said that she'd only speak to Bill.

Rumours were rife among the patients about what was being done to Angela as punishment. They were angry, emotional and hostile. They also knew the C & R teams were in the ward.

This caused growing pressure from outside the crisis management team for a C & R solution. Tension increased within the teams, who had been waiting in protective clothing for hours with their adrenaline pumping.

Trying to calm them down, I explained that we were reviewing the situation constantly. 'We haven't lost Angela yet. Nobody else has been injured.'

'Yes, but surely you can feel the strain in here,' said one of the team members.

'I know the unit is affected, but it's being held. The situation is under control.'

As the siege entered its fifth hour, I asked senior nurses to give regular updates to patients and staff to calm anxieties and correct the rumours. These had to focus on the caring attitude being shown towards Angela, but give no information about what she was saying or threatening to do. In particular they had to set the potential for physical intervention in a reasonable context.

Angela was still refusing to talk to the new negotiator. Several times she'd screamed abuse and hurled things against the walls. As she was unwilling to talk to staff, it was suggested that I try to reach her. This went against the normal procedure of the crisis management team, but I agreed to hold the fort until Bill returned.

Angela's room opened into a corridor, which had been cleared of personnel. To speak to her, I had to stand on a chair and put my head near the fanlight above the door.

She sat on the floor, holding a broken bottle in her hand. She was a slight young woman wearing jeans and a light pullover; her feet were bare. Usually she made me think of a prickly garden fairy; now her face was dull, ashen and tear-marked.

There were blood tracks along her wrists and low on her neck. She was tired, but continued to watch the door, the fanlight and the window. A young woman in a bombed-out cellar waiting for the occupying soldiers to break in wouldn't have looked more desperate.

'Hello, Angela.'

'Oh, it's you now,' she said, at the sound of my voice. 'Is Kate Adie outside?' The words were laced with scepticism and irony.

'It looks as though we've missed something pretty badly if you've had to lock yourself in like this.'

'It's a bit late now, isn't it?'

She took the bottle and cut the palm of her hand, not deeply, but enough to spread blood onto the front of her pullover. She gave no sign of feeling any pain.

'You're better than that, Angela. I can't stop you cutting up, but I know you've got through a few real lows since you started here.'

'Yeah, well, I can't any more. I'm going to finish it now.'

'It's been very hard for you locked in here, but you've managed to stay together for quite a few hours so far. You said Bill was all right – that at least he listened to you instead of just writing you off.'

'And for what? He's pissed off now, hasn't he?'

'No, he's frightened that if he doesn't keep his head together, he'll let you down. He wants to make sure he knows what the situation is outside so that he can see how you and he might work something out. I've come to make sure you know that. No-one's trying to pull the wool. Bill's coming back in a bit. You know I don't tell lies on the unit, even if it means having to say hard things to people. You're working it out with Bill, he won't let you down. I'm just staying with you till he gets back.'

'Can you get me a drink . . . ?'

'Sure.'

Bill returned within twenty-five minutes, having rested and been briefed. He immediately re-established a rapport with Angela.

They spent time talking and agreeing about how sometimes families really foul kids up, but they didn't always know it. They then worked on ways that she could perhaps show her family how she felt.

As the hours ticked by, Angela's trust continued to build. She paced up and down her room, talking to Bill and coming up with ideas.

Ten hours after the crisis began, she gave up the broken bottle. Bill had promised her that nobody would come charging in. She could stay in the room until she wanted to come out.

He also reassured her that she wouldn't be jumped or made to walk a jeering gauntlet when she emerged.

Her injuries were treated with sutures and she spent the night in seclusion under close observation.

Both she and Roger were returned to the ward, but underwent continual 'specialing' (observing) for several days while their emotions and beliefs about the incident were explored.

As unwanted as these situations are, they can often be the source of a wealth of new clinical data about a patient. In Angela's case this related to her catastrophic belief that she had been 'abandoned' by her family.

The front-line staff and particularly Bill Carpenter were congratulated on their efforts. The 'retrieval' had hinged on Bill's skill and endurance, which went above and beyond the call of duty.

Meanwhile, a critical incident report had to be completed. At the debriefing afterwards, I helped staff work through the emotional impact of the incident. All those involved had an opportunity to say how they viewed what had happened, how it had affected them and if they felt anybody was to blame.

These debriefings were among the most difficult activities I had to undertake at Arnold Lodge. Members of staff were encouraged to react as people rather than to maintain professional objectivity. This meant they were extremely honest about their feelings and it led to tears, anger, fear, shock, blame and shame.

It is important to have outlets such as this because they help remove the emotional burden from people who do a very difficult job. This enables them to carry on working with patients who pose a risk to them and to one another.

In all the commotion, I didn't have time to think about Ray until I drove home that evening. His words of abuse still echoed in my mind. There had been angry outbursts from him before, but never directed so clearly towards me and what I represented. I had no doubt that at that moment he had wanted to kill me.

If I'd called for help there was nobody nearby who could have stopped him losing control. I'd simply have endangered other people. And if I had chosen to run he would have followed me.

Ray had pushed me, tested me and tried to frighten me. At the same time he needed to know that I could withstand him. If he thought he recognized fear, then I knew that he'd lose respect for me. This wasn't some sort of macho game where men try to stare each other out. I simply had to show Ray that I wasn't going to flinch or turn away, no matter how tense and uncertain I felt.

As I drove through Leicester city centre, I found myself thinking about what Ray had said. 'Somebody has to be punished!' He couldn't rely on his father being at the right place at the right time. Nor could he trust his own ability to stand up to his tormentor. So what did he do? He looked for someone else – a substitute for his father – just as the rabbits had once been surrogates. Only this time he chose real fathers.

Outside on the streets, people were heading off to the cinemas or out to dinner. Among the crowds there were men who were about my age. Some were no doubt married and had children. They were heading home to their families; hoping to be there before their youngsters were in bed.

Any one of these men fitted Ray's criteria for a victim. It might not seem logical to anybody else, but to him it made perfect sense. Even if he knew nothing about these men, as far as Ray was concerned, they were bound to have abused their own children. Therefore, they deserved to die.

This mutation in the real-world crossover created an

even greater problem for me. I no longer had any idea of who his victim might be. I had no way of warning a person, nothing I could usefully tell the police. All I had was a 'type', a very weak outline of a middle-aged man with children. It had been easier when he'd planned to kill his father.

This touched upon one of the most difficult aspects of clinical work in the forensic field. When a patient was detained in a hospital there were always risks, but at least when they walked out of my consulting room every day they went back to a secure ward. I had no such comfort with Ray.

Quite the opposite: I had the added complication of knowing that I, too, was a perfect fit for his victim. How much did I know about him? More importantly, how much did he know about me? Did he know my address? Could he have followed *me* home?

For a brief moment, I found myself looking in the rear mirror and studying the drivers around me.

On one superficial level, I was probably the worst person to be treating somebody like Ray. Then again, nobody had understood the nature of his problem before now. I couldn't back out.

Perhaps there was even a benefit in my being a middle-aged father of two. I could demonstrate normality. This wasn't something I could show in five minutes, but over a period of months I could develop a decent, ordinary working relationship with Ray that would show him that not every man was an abuser.

This had risks, of course. At that moment, in the boot of his car, he had the hammer, chains and ropes. Each week I had one therapeutic hour in which to manage his stress, diffuse his anger, and try to construct a healthy man from the ruins of a terrified child.

As he left each session, I knew that he was always at his least dangerous. But it wouldn't be long before the pressure started to build. By the weekend he'd have to fight the urge. And when it got too strong, he'd get in his car and go cruising.

He would look for a victim to match the picture in his mind. And he'd keep going out – day after day – until he found one. It was just a matter of time.

13

'We have a man who is killing homosexual men in London,' said Detective Chief Superintendent Ken John. 'He's promising to kill one a week until we catch him.'

'What's the count so far?'

'We think it's five.'

It was Thursday 17 June 1993 and I was speaking from my office in Arnold Lodge. I had never met Ken John but I could sense the urgency in his voice.

He had several pressing questions, including whether the five murders were in fact linked. Were they dealing with just one offender?

'More importantly, I need to know if we can stop him killing again,' he said.

I looked at the dates. The most recent victim had been discovered two days earlier (a Tuesday) but had probably died the previous Saturday. If the killer kept to his promised timetable, we had two days before he struck again.

I confirmed that I had no clinical commitment the following morning and arranged to travel to London. As it turned out, it dovetailed perfectly with an existing undertaking to review a tricky pharmaceutical investigation where a disgruntled ex-employee had made threats to kill the board.

I had assessed the threat as being very serious and warned the company that the blackmailer had both the emotional drive and the technical capacity to carry out his threats. An added complication was that the Queen was scheduled to visit the company. This couldn't go ahead if the risk remained.

Lawyers had warned that charges wouldn't hold and in my view an attempt to charge him would make the ex-employee even angrier. Instead, a covert operation had been set up using police officers posing as arms dealers. This would give the suspect the chance to volunteer information about his intentions if he chose to buy weapons.

In an unrelated case, I'd spent the previous afternoon and evening with a young rape victim in the West Midlands, who had been abducted in broad daylight and terrorized. She was so traumatized by her ordeal that she'd been unable to give police much help in describing her assailant and what had happened.

Using techniques to protect her from the trauma and to take her back cognitively, I managed to draw out a more detailed statement. She described his smell, his accent, his right-handedness, his local knowledge and his attempt to confuse her about his past. This process took hours because I had to be sure that I didn't further emotionally damage the girl by having her relive the attack.

The following morning I drove to London. The city is divided up into different operational areas in terms of policing, with each area having a specialist rapid response team for major incidents. In a serial murder investigation each crime has a separate investigating officer, with an officer in overall command. In this instance, that was Ken John.

Similarly, each of the murders had its own incident room, with one of them acting as a co-ordination centre. The headquarters in Kensington looked like an old school, with sandstone foundations and red-brick walls.

A reception hall and narrow corridors gave way to a larger room with desks and computer terminals. Many of the detectives were out, no doubt following up leads. Others, their shirtsleeves rolled up, were manning the telephones and processing statements.

Along the walls there were white boards with photographs of each of the victims. Arrows radiated out linking details such as places and contacts. Some of the lines were solid, indicating the information was fact. A dotted line meant the link hadn't been verified.

There is always a sense of urgency with any murder investigation, even in the reinvestigation of an old or 'cold' murder. This is normally driven by public expectations, the media and the professionalism of the police. However, serial killings create an even greater pressure because of the fear they generate in communities.

Most 'simple' homicides are motivated by avarice, anger, jealousy, lust or revenge. The murderer tends to have links with the victim and is usually caught within hours or days. These one-off killers are often filled with remorse and guilt, even if they had intended to kill. This means they're more likely to flee the scene in haste leaving clues and witnesses.

Serial killers, however, are more difficult to pin down, physically and psychologically. Their motives aren't as transparent or linear. They may kill from a need that could make anyone fitting their picture a victim; or they may be motivated by a force that they don't understand themselves.

Highly evolved serial killers rarely commit 'simple' homicides. They often torture and take delight in their victim's agonies and cries of pain. They plan their escape route, leaving few clues behind. And afterwards, they camouflage themselves in normality or sometimes dance just beyond the police's reach, taunting them.

In a small room upstairs from the incident room Ken John motioned me to a chair and sat opposite. He took a sip of coffee and then flinched. It had gone cold. 'I'll get us some more,' he said and then seemed to forget about it. There were more important things on his mind.

A plain-spoken man who didn't waste words, he began the briefing. 'This man seems to be responding to the media coverage of his crimes. We had two telephone calls from him yesterday. The first came to Kensington. That's when he boasted, "If you can't stop me I'll kill one a week."

'The second call came later in the day to Battersea Police.' Ken John picked up an information sheet. 'This time he said: "I will keep going until I am caught. I'll do another one. Do I qualify as a serial killer yet?"'

'And you're quite sure these aren't hoax calls?'

'As sure as we can be. The voice is the same. He didn't come through the switchboard. I don't know how he managed to get the numbers.'

I nodded. 'Tell me how I can help.'

'For a start I need some answers. I've got the media crawling all over me and the gay community running scared. Is it possible to stop this guy, or at least slow him down?'

273

'Yes, it may be possible to influence his behaviour and perhaps stop him killing.'

'How?'

'It means managing everything you say and don't say. The entire media strategy and release of information have to be carefully scripted and controlled. When is your next media conference?'

'This evening.'

This gave us a matter of hours to come up with a strategy. I gave Ken John a list of what I needed – the chronology, crime scene photographs and everything that had been learned about the victims. I also needed any transcripts or tapes of telephone conversations.

'Is there somewhere quiet I can work?'

'We'll find you an office.'

Fifteen minutes later I was shown to a small room off the main corridor downstairs. The office looked rarely used and people had turned it into a makeshift storeroom for miscellaneous office furniture. It was stiflingly hot and poorly ventilated. The window had been painted shut and the sun beat down through the dirty glass. Waiting for me on the desk were five sets of photographs, statements, intelligence materials, interviews and pathology reports.

I had only a few hours to discover everything I could about an unknown killer. If I could understand him, then perhaps I could communicate with him via Ken John through newspapers, radio and television. By pulling the right psychological levers, we could shape the killer's emotional responses and stop him striking again, at least in the short term.

I opened the first folder.

Peter Walker, aged forty-five, was a theatre director and choreographer who had worked on a string of

West End musicals. He was found dead in his Battersea flat on 12 March 1993, having failed to appear for rehearsals.

The crime scene photographs began with general interior shots of a bright and relaxed flat that was designed to be lived in rather than just looked at. The pictures on the walls were in different styles and frames. The chairs were comfortable and the shelves contained dozens of books. There were no signs of a disturbance and nothing seemed to be amiss.

Only the bedroom showed signs of disarray. Clothing lay untidily on the floor and crumpled bedding had been strewn on top of the duvet. A plastic linen bin stood near the end of the bed.

The next photographs revealed what the bedclothes had been arranged to conceal. Peter Walker lay beneath the duvet, naked except for a pair of thick grey ankle socks. Deep burn marks were visible on his wrists where a rope had been used to secure him. He had been suffocated, with condoms forced into his mouth and over his nose.

The lividity marks, from where gravity had settled his blood, showed that he had died on the bed. A soft furry toy rabbit lay on his stomach; he had one hand wrapped over it, much as a child would cuddle a comforter in sleep.

The post-mortem photographs indicated that Walker had been caned and beaten before he died.

Six hours after the body was discovered but before the killing had been made public, a man rang a national newspaper saying he wanted someone to free two dogs locked in Mr Walker's flat. He then confessed to killing the former dancer, who was HIV positive, adding: 'It was my New Year's resolution to murder a human being.'

From the original reports, it appeared the police had treated the case as an isolated sex killing. Focus had immediately centred on Walker's lifestyle.

He was a shopkeeper's son from Liverpool, who had made his mark in the West End as an assistant director and choreographer. He had worked on the hit musical *Chess* and Gilbert and Sullivan shows including *Pirates of Penzance* with Bonnie Langford and Paul Nicholas. His latest show was the musical *City of Angels*.

Walker dedicated a lot of his spare time to AIDS benefits, but was also known to spend his evenings cruising the gay bars around Soho, looking for sexual encounters.

I read the statements. A colleague had become concerned when Walker uncharacteristically failed to turn up to rehearsals two days running. He called at the flat but couldn't get an answer. Finally he phoned the police.

Initially, detectives suggested that Walker had died in a sex game that had gone wrong – something involving asphyxiation to heighten sexual pleasure. Little effort was made to link his death with other unsolved cases.

I picked up the next set of photographs. Christopher Dunn, aged thirty-seven, was listed as a librarian from North London, but such a description could give a very misleading impression of his lifestyle.

Although he wore a suit to work each day at Harlesden Library, back home in Byron Road, Wealdstone, Dunn transformed himself. He put in his earring, donned black leathers and a studded dog collar and went cruising the gay bars of central London. Well liked, intelligent and articulate, he almost seemed to lead a double life, with two separate sets of friends and acquaintances.

His body was discovered on 30 May in his flat. He was naked and buckled into a riveted leather and metal ring harness. He wore other intimate sexual equipment associated with masochistic activity and appeared to have been caned. A bondage video lay in the video recorder.

This time the somewhat crowded bedroom showed no signs of disturbance or disorder. However, at least four large mirrors had been arranged around the bed or propped around the edges of the walls. This had the effect of ensuring that wherever anyone stood in the room, the bed and its contents were reflected back at them.

As with Peter Walker's death, the police initially thought that Dunn had died accidentally during a sado-masochistic sex session. They didn't regard the death as suspicious until weeks later when they were telephoned anonymously by a man who asked why the murder hadn't been reported in the newspapers. No connection was made between the two murders.

Following the telephone call, the police looked more closely at the case. They discovered that Dunn's cash card had been used after his death at an ATM. It seemed likely that his killer had tortured him into revealing the access number before strangling him.

By then, 7 June 1993, another body had been found – American businessman Perry Bradley III.

Friends and family insisted that the thirty-five-year-old Texan wasn't gay. He was certainly well connected. According to the media, his father was a prominent American politician and political fund-raiser.

Bradley was the international sales director for an American adhesives firm and had arrived in Britain three years earlier. A tall, good-looking bachelor, he travelled extensively for work. His spare time was spent playing golf, water-skiing and visiting stately homes.

His luxury Kensington flat showed no obvious signs of his sexuality. There were no mirrors for display and none of the masochistic paraphernalia that had been present in the other victims' homes. Painted in pale colours and lightly furnished, it indicated a slightly austere man who was more interested in ideas than adornment.

This poor man had not died easily. The post mortem indicated that he'd been whipped and tortured before being garrotted. The ligature had been tightened with such force that it broke the skin of his neck.

His naked body was positioned on the large blue bottom sheet of a double bed. His ankles were crossed, indicating that he had been rolled onto his face after death. There were deep rope cuts on his wrists and ankles. His cash card was missing, along with £100 in cash.

This killer didn't flee the scene, or worry about over-staying his welcome. Instead, he calmly cooked himself a meal in the kitchen while his victim lay dead. It takes a rather unusual human being to sit calmly and eat just after killing. The same is true of someone who carefully packs up the dirty plates and utensils and takes them with him, ensuring that no clues are left behind. This man had a forensic awareness beyond that of most murderers, either opportunistic or planful.

Two days later he struck again. The naked body of Andrew Collier, aged thirty-three, was found in his flat at a residential home in Dalston Lane, North-east London. Collier was a warden at the home, looking after the elderly residents. His parents, from Bourne-mouth, weren't aware that their son was a homosexual.

As I glanced through the photographs it was clear that Collier had been safety conscious. Apart from a standard Yale-type lock on the front door, he also had a fish-eye viewing lens and a mortice or deadbolt lock.

Again the flat was essentially intact; the killer had focused on the bed and his victim. Collier had been tied up and tortured. A ligature had been used to strangle him and then removed, as were the other bindings.

Some of his personal possessions had been searched and papers rifled. A letter found near the body confirmed that he was HIV positive.

As with Bradley, Collier's ankles were crossed indicating that he had been turned after death. In addition, parts of his body had been burned. In a bizarre display of theatre, the killer had broken the neck of Collier's pet cat, Millie, and draped it obscenely over his naked body. The cat's tail had been placed in a condom and then put inside Collier's mouth and his penis had been pushed into the cat's mouth.

The final folders contained the most recently discovered murder. Emanuel Spiteri, a forty-two-year-old Maltese chef, had been found in his Catford bedsit on 15 June. Spiteri made no secret of his homosexuality. With his short-cropped hair and penchant for designer clothes, he was well known in the West End gay clubs and pubs.

The first photographs revealed a room that seemed to be completely burned out. The killer had piled up chairs and other furnishings at one end of the room. The blaze had burned intensely and coated everything – the walls, furniture, ornaments, curtains, floor and bed – in a film of soot.

The body of Emanuel Spiteri was almost invisible against the blackness. He lay face down and naked on top of the bed, wearing a masochistic chain body harness. He, too, had been garrotted. Peering through the sooty layer that covered him, I could see that his body had been arranged with his arms loosely resting at his sides.

I looked at my watch: I had less than three hours before I had to brief Ken John. I sat back and tried to understand how this murderer and his victims came together. What did each of them bring to the encounter? They each had a past and personalities that collided at a particular moment and helped create and shape the tragedy.

These murders were premeditated and meticulously planned in broad detail. They were also carried out effectively and with considerable self-control in settings previously unknown to the killer.

He had been extremely thorough in sterilizing the scenes of clues and making sure that he hadn't drawn attention to himself. He hadn't left any victim gagged or bound. The ropes and ligatures were removed and taken with him, along with everything else he had brought.

This man had a deviant sense of theatre and showmanship. This was obvious at all of the crime scenes. With Peter Walker, he had purposely arranged the bedclothes so that whoever arrived would begin tidying the room and then come across the body. There was perhaps a subtle irony about the victim being a theatre director. This time it was the killer who set the scene and staged the play. He knew people would find the body. He wanted them to.

This sense of theatre was even more pronounced at some of the other scenes and, in each case, the killer emphasized his mastery of these people, his ability to command them with his presence; and his disdain for them.

At the same time his audience was as important as the actors. He was doing this for the police and anyone else who stumbled upon the bodies. He wanted to shock them.

Going over the case materials, it was quite clear that this man was responding to media reporting of the murders. When he failed to read anything about Christopher Dunn's murder in the newspaper, he telephoned the police.

Earlier, he'd rung a national newspaper saying he wanted someone to free two dogs locked in Peter Walker's flat. Afterwards, the press labelled him as an animal lover. In response, the killer included Collier's cat in the next murder. He telephoned detectives and explained, 'I killed the cat to prove I'm no pet lover.'

This was an important clue as to how this man functioned. He intended to make it very clear that the newspapers had no idea how he behaved or what he thought. At the same time he was scouring the press for any mention of his crimes and revelling in his growing notoriety.

Three days after the murder of Emanuel Spiteri, he called the Samaritans and the *Sun* newspaper admitting the killings. He didn't want somebody else claiming the 'credit' or to have his handiwork ignored.

What else did I know about this man? The media had already labelled him the 'gay slayer'. It was the sort of nomenclature that would have appealed to his sense of theatre.

Did he hate gays?

Maybe he thought so. Yet behind his arrogant

281

showmanship and the theatrical eroticism there was a strong suggestion of sexual ambiguity. He had managed to lure five men to their deaths. In each case they must have believed that he had similar desires to their own.

It would not have been difficult to find victims. The make-up and character of the gay scene provided a ready supply of young men looking for casual sex. Nobody had paid particular attention to him leaving a club or pub with his next victim. Alarm bells hadn't sounded or suspicions been raised. This indicated that he must have been able to blend in reasonably well. It didn't mean that he looked or acted particularly gay. It told me more about his psychological comfort in these settings than his physical appearance.

This 'comfort' factor wasn't the only explanation for how he'd managed to attract so little attention as he trawled for his victims. There was a very real possibility that people had seen him pick up these men. Perhaps they themselves had been propositioned but turned him down or side-stepped the issue. The reason they hadn't come forward to the police might be their fear of exposure.

Although most of us deny being anti-gay, the fact is that homosexuals in our society often still report discrimination and abuse, so much so that many go to elaborate lengths to conceal their sexuality. Some keep this secret from their families and their spouses. They covertly seek gay lovers and lead almost double lives.

The fear of discovery could very easily prevent someone from coming forward – even if they had spoken to the killer or seen him leaving with one of the victims.

My first priority was to develop a strategy that would allow the police to communicate with the perpetrator via the media and stop him striking again. The media coverage of the murders had demonized this man and portrayed him essentially as a depraved monster. With the exception of his alleged care for animals, the picture was brutal, negative and demeaning.

I knew this wouldn't fit with the strong anti-hero image the killer had of himself. He wanted the police to regard him as a worthy opponent; a criminal master-mind who deserved their professional respect. In the years to come, when young detectives were taught about famous crimes and clever criminals, this man wanted his name to be there.

Although he showed great forensic awareness, he didn't fear being caught, as long as he felt it was on his own terms and that he was in control.

This was an arrogant man. He wanted to be admired. By seeming to do just that and engaging him properly, I knew we could bring him closer to being caught. More importantly, in the short term, we could stop him killing. First the police had to make him feel that he had their complete respect and attention. If so, he wouldn't have to prove himself by killing someone else. Once he felt this, he would come in more easily, hoping to celebrate his superiority over them and revel in his cleverness.

I drew these conclusions from everything I had learned about this man from the psychological mind trace he left behind at the scenes. I also drew upon my understanding of the relationship between human emotion and behaviour. There was no room for guess-ing or intuition.

In many ways this was like negotiating over a hostage. I had done this in clinical settings at Arnold Lodge and also in crime-related situations for the police. If this killer had been holed up in a house, threatening to kill his next victim, the tactics I adopted would have been very similar.

In some ways that would have been easier because at least I'd have known his name and more details about him that could have been used in the strategy. As it was, I had only a psychological picture of this man and had to 'negotiate' via the police and the media.

Later that afternoon I sat down with Ken John to discuss the strategy. Every minute weighed heavily upon him, but I couldn't afford to rush. If I began jumping to conclusions, I could end up reflecting things that he wanted to hear instead of basing my advice on the evidence.

'Every comment attributed to the police is important,' I told him. 'By structuring what you say and the tone of it, you can pull particular psychological levers in the person who is committing these offences.'

'How do we start?'

'To begin with you should be looking to establish a relationship with him. The media will search for different angles every day, but the message from the police should be clear, simple and consistent. That's why it's important for a single person to be associated with all public statements. Someone who can build a rapport and speak to the killer on a one-to-one basis. That person should be you.'

Ken John had already fronted daily news conferences and made earlier statements. In my judgement he had a good mix of authority and strength. At the same time, he didn't have the sort of personality that would demean or antagonize the killer. Most importantly, he didn't come across as being arrogant, but had a sensitivity and intelligence that would appeal to the killer's ego.

'What do I say?'

'We don't have time to write a word-perfect script and have you rehearse it. Instead you'll have to remember the broad themes. The first should be, "Can you help me to understand why you are doing this?" This will appeal to his sense of being cunning and astute. It shows clearly that you respect him.

'Follow this up by saying, "Although I'm aware of the extent of your activities, I am not yet near to knowing who you are or anything about you. I want to know what's making you do this. What has put you in a position where you have no choice but to follow this course of action? What did these men do that forced you to do what you did to them?

'"You put a soft toy on Peter Walker. A rabbit. What was it about him that made you do that?"'

Ken John looked puzzled. 'Why do I want to know about cuddly toys?'

'Because you're playing his game with him. This man set up the scene for you to find. The rabbit was important. You're telling him that you're intelligent and emphasizing that you really want to understand him. This is flattering. It makes him feel good. He wants you to think of him as a powerful and worthy contender.'

Negative and unflattering images simply fed the murderer's pathology. He wanted to correct misunderstandings and demonstrate his courage and ingenuity, which he felt had been unrecognized. That's why he made the phone calls.

'The media might be correct in the way they are describing this man, but operationally it's unhelpful.

The last thing we can afford to do is to goad him. He wants respect, not vilification.'

This strategy had to extend beyond the public statements of the police. The same attitude had to apply if he contacted them again directly. If possible, Ken John had to take these calls and continue to foster a relationship. If he wasn't available, then whoever took the call had to respond within the strategy.

'Where is this going to lead us?' asked Ken John.

'Gradually, over the course of these contacts, the aim is to move you into the leading position, so that you can begin dictating events. For example, if he calls and the conversation begins drifting, you have to say, "You've given me a lot to think about. Why don't you let me give it some thought and phone back later?"

'You can even suggest a particular time. If this succeeds then straight away the balance has swung back slightly towards you. *You* have started managing events.'

'What if he wants assurances that his calls won't be recorded or traced?'

'Give them, even if such promises aren't kept. But remember it's vitally important that you don't break a promise that can be found out. If he discovers that you're lying to him, he will kill someone else as a punishment.'

As I left the police station, I pictured Ken John fronting the media conference at Metropolitan Police headquarters. Had he absorbed everything I said? Had it been coherent and logical enough? So much depended on his performance.

I was confident that the strategy could prevent another immediate killing, but I couldn't be sure that the murderer would make early contact with the police, or for how long the killings could be contained. I could only base my strategy on his behaviour so far and my understanding of sexual predators and psychopaths.

I was also painfully aware of the consequences of getting it wrong. If I had made a mistake or misdirected investigators, then someone else might die.

That night I watched the TV news with a growing sense of relief. Ken John spoke about the investigation, at times looking directly at the cameras as if delivering a personal message. The tone was right. He didn't challenge, demonize or disparage. Instead he wanted to understand the crimes and, particularly, the killer. He seemed to be saying, 'Talk to me. Help me to understand. I'm listening.'

14

At home over the next two nights, I immersed myself in the details of the murders. I closed the study door, so that Marilyn would knock first and wouldn't accidentally see the photographs. I chose a location shot of each crime scene and propped them on the desk in front of me. These wide-angle pictures showed the victims' bodies lying on their beds, as well as details of the rooms.

People sometimes talk about 'reading between the lines' as a way of explaining the abstract processes used in inference and deduction. In my work the analysis has to leave the page and go into the mind of the killer. To know him, I have to be able to see the world through his eyes.

This means putting aside my own moral values and compassion for the victims. I step away from the vocational impetus of my clinical career and sink fully into the killer's sense of climactic achievement. At the same time, I see the shock, pain and final terror of his victims.

In this case, as always, I asked myself four questions: what has happened; how did it happen; who did it happen to, and why? Only when I had answers to these questions could I address the fifth: who is responsible?

These same questions apply to my clinical work, particularly when dealing with victims, but in a slightly different way. In my consulting room I see someone who is damaged or in pain and I have to find out who they are psychologically and how they got there. In this instance I didn't have a victim across the table from me and had to rely on others to tell me about the men who died.

In a series of theme-related crimes like this, the victims can often fulfil an increasingly symbolic role in the drama being enacted by the killer. As the offences progress, each individual victim becomes less than a fully rounded person. They are much closer to being toys moved through a doll's house to someone's script. For the killer the crucial element is the scenario running through his head and the incomparable pleasure he gets from slotting each victim into their role in his mind and then making them into what he wants them to become.

For me, as an investigator, the victims aren't bit-part actors. They are my collaborators in understanding and, if we are fortunate, unmasking the offender. By knowing them, I move a step closer to knowing him.

I began reading the statements again and looking at the photographs. I studied the common aspects of how the dead men had been arranged, the lividity marks on the bodies and the precision with which the victims had been chosen and controlled.

What did I know about him?

This man didn't panic. He got excited, but stayed in command of himself and his victims. He spent a long time in the flats and apartments. He took great care not to leave clues behind, wiping surfaces clean and taking things away with him.

He had immense physical confidence. This didn't mean that he overpowered his victims. The lack of defence injuries on the murdered men suggested they were either willingly tied up or controlled so effectively that they couldn't resist. They may have thought it was sadomasochistic sex play.

The binding of the hands and feet exhibited considerable force and physical strength. To the killer it was like closing the snare – a perfect way to immobilize a victim.

I went from photograph to photograph. Each scene was distinctly theatrical. They weren't bloodbaths. These were tableaux that had been arranged for visual impact.

Some people work with paint, others are film directors; this man designed with death.

I looked at the fluffy rabbit cradled in Peter Walker's hand and at how mirrors had been positioned around Christopher Dunn; the ostentatious preparation of the meal at Perry Bradley's flat and the symbolic arrangement of Andrew Collier's cat. Finally, there was the dramatic use of fire after the killing of Emanuel Spiteri.

These were deliberate, relaxed, almost euphoric actions. Here was an artist at work. He wanted to intrigue and puzzle. More importantly, he didn't want anybody ever to forget what they saw when they first walked into these bedrooms.

'I am not a butcher – I'm an artist,' he is saying. 'I am in control.'

It wasn't bloodlust. He hadn't fallen out with someone, or been consumed by sexual anger or desire. He had done this purely because he wanted to kill.

There was no direct evidence of sex with any of the victims. No bodily fluids were found. This man was far too forensically aware to leave behind semen traces.

My eye was drawn to the final murder in the known series – Emanuel Spiteri. The use of fire intrigued me. In the police's view the killer had set the fire to conceal evidence while he made his escape.

Quite often a killer's signature will change across a series of murders. Feelings that are primary at one point slowly give way to new behaviour or a 'creative' motif as the mental pictures which drive his fantasy evolve.

Fire had been a factor in some of the other killings, clearly as a form of torture. But in the fifth murder, part of the room had been deliberately set alight.

Why?

Perhaps he hadn't been careful enough and bodily fluid had been spilled onto the chair beside the bed. That would explain why he started a localized fire – to destroy the biological evidence.

I doubted this. This man didn't make obviously elementary mistakes.

I looked through the folder of photographs again. The first shots showed the front door of the bedsit and gave no indication of a blaze. There were no traces of soot or scorching. The door opened to reveal an unexpected scene, with the room seemingly burned out.

The visual impact of the fire was striking. Only when I looked closely did I see that the blaze damage was isolated. Furnishings had been carefully piled up away from the walls, so the flames didn't spread. The blaze had burned very intensely, but in an area that covered only a few square feet.

At the same time the smoke had turned the room into a shadowland with black, oily soot covering every surface and ornament. Amid all of this, lying on the bed was the body of Emanuel Spiteri, almost invisible.

The fire wasn't intended to destroy the scene; it was designed to enhance the visual impact. The killer was showing his skill as a 'director' – using fire as part of his deviant theatre.

Towards the end of the series of photographs, I came to a close-up of Spiteri's body lying on the bed. I remembered the image well because in London it had prompted me to ask Ken John how accurate the photographs were as an original record of the scenes.

'They're completely accurate,' he told me.

'So the scenes and the bodies are exactly as they were found. Nothing has been moved or taken away or added?'

'Of course not,' he said, getting slightly irritated.

I had to ask. A tiny detail altered at a crime scene might make no difference to the evidence from the police viewpoint, but it could change everything in the psychological analysis.

Such was the case here. One small detail had been overlooked in the photographs, yet it told me an enormous amount about the killer's personal history and his motivation.

Emanuel Spiteri had worn no neckband of any type, yet around his neck there was a thin skin-coloured stripe distinctly visible in the film of black soot that covered his body. This was where the ligature had been tightened to strangle him and then removed – just as in the other murders.

This raised the question: why wasn't the stripe covered by the soot from the fire?

And the answer: because the ligature must have been removed *after* the blaze.

This meant the killer had stayed in the room while

the fire burned and until it went out. If he had left after setting the blaze and returned later there would be some evidence of smoke or soot markings outside the bedsit. There were none. He would also have risked being seen, particularly if a neighbour or passer-by had smelled smoke and reported the blaze.

It takes someone with a very special relationship with fire to stay in a room while it burns, lying on the floor beneath the smoke and riding the fear that would overcome most of us. It takes someone who knows the nature of the beast; how to control it and harness it.

How does a person gain that type of skill and experience? By being trained in fire-fighting.

Meanwhile, Ken John and his team were following up every lead, desperate to make a breakthrough. In particular they were tracing the last known movements of each victim.

Emanuel Spiteri was believed to have met the killer at the Coleherne pub in Brompton Road, London. It had been a Saturday night and the bars were crowded. At some point they had made their way to Spiteri's bedsit in Catford.

Spiteri didn't normally drive when he went out. This left three options. Either the killer had a car, or they caught a cab, or they took public transport.

The police had been looking at all of these possibilities, interviewing taxi drivers, bouncers, barmen and British Rail staff on duty late on Saturday night. As part of these inquiries, detectives began studying videos from security cameras mounted above the concourse at Charing Cross station. Several frames showed Mr Spiteri walking through a doorway as he entered the station. A man followed him and they seemed to be together. The images were grainy and of poor quality, but it was still possible to get a description. He was aged between thirty and forty, six feet tall, heavily built, with close-cropped brown hair. He wore jeans and a dark bomber jacket.

This description closely matched the one given by several patrons at the Coleherne pub, who also reported him to be clean-shaven, with discoloured teeth.

On 1 July the police released the security video, along with still photographs taken from it. They appealed for anyone travelling on any of the lines going through Charing Cross station between 10.15 p.m. and 10.45 p.m. on the night of the murder to contact them. In particular, they were seeking a woman shown on the video walking towards the two men. She might have had a much better look at the suspect.

Within twenty-four hours the appeal brought twenty-two calls from the public, all from people claiming to know the man.

The London *Evening Standard* published the video stills and later received a letter from serial murderer Dennis Nilsen. Under the pretext, I suppose, of 'it takes one to know one', the newspaper gave Nilsen another moment to savour the spotlight as he described the killings as the work of a 'ritual strangler seeking potency, power and control'.

Despite rumours that he might be consulted about the killings, Nilsen wrote that he had 'not heard a peep from any police ... nor have they expressed any interest in my *expert* experience through other parties'.

'These are not homosexual murders but crimes of personal psychological inadequacy where the victims just happen to be homosexual along with the perpetrator,' he wrote. 'They were enacted as a temporary [but] necessary expedient for the growing inner pressures of lack of achievement and self-esteem.'

Nilsen's rambling letter was more an attempt to turn the spotlight on himself than to shed light on any new 'gay slayer'. Perhaps Dennis was feeling a little put out that someone else had captured the headlines.

For the next few weeks, I heard little from Ken John. Nor did I take particular interest in the media coverage. I rarely have the time to read newspapers or watch TV.

Even so, I was well aware of how the public had reacted to the crimes. London's gay community had felt the brunt of the paralysis. There were calls for greater vigilance and a bigger police task force. Gay pubs and nightclubs were virtually deserted.

In the meantime I had my own patients to deal with – some of whom were potentially just as dangerous as the so-called 'gay slayer'.

At his next appointment, Ray Knox looked happier and less weighed down by the pressures of his world. There was a calmness about him which might have been a good sign.

The keys and money in his pockets exaggerated the width of his hips as he sat down. He raised his left hand in greeting. The plasters had been removed.

He reached into his jacket and pulled out a battered brown wallet that had moulded itself tightly around the cards and cash crammed inside. He opened it and took out two ragged photographs.

'This is a picture of my girls,' he said proudly. 'They're older now. Julie's in high school and Rita has longer hair. I don't like it cut short.'

The photograph showed the sisters sitting one behind the other on top of a water slide. They were laughing at the camera, about to launch themselves down towards the pool.

The second picture was of a woman in her late thirties, sitting on a sunlounger and wearing a large straw hat and sunglasses. She had a sarong wrapped around her waist and was reading a book.

'That's my Stella,' said Ray, running his thumb over the photograph. 'We were on holiday in Majorca.'

'When was that?'

'Four years ago. She loves the sun.'

He brought out a third photograph, showing the whole family.

'It looks as though they're talking to you, not posing for a picture.'

'I said it wouldn't look like a proper photo if we weren't all in it, and they were telling me to focus it and put the delay timer on the button and run round to get in the picture.'

'They're nice photographs.'

'I got whole albums at home. I'll bring them, if you like. Sometimes I sit and go over the pictures for ages.'

'It looks as though you had a nice holiday.'

'I had a bad time at the end. Rita went missing from the market. She'd only gone to the pool with some kids she'd met, but I couldn't find her. My heart was in my throat . . . I thought . . . you know . . .'

'What happened?'

'It was OK. She'd asked someone to give us a message but they didn't see us. I was beside myself. I had to go off to our room. I kept thinking that if I'd gone missing like that when I was a kid, my fucking abuser would have killed me. He'd have said I was running messages for my mum. Christ! It took me right back. I was bad for the whole day.'

I began going over what Ray had done in the previous week. He had taken sick leave, so what time had he woken up? When did his wife leave for her work? What did he do next? When did he have lunch?

I tried to pin down the specific details of each day and what it contained because it could give me some idea of how much time his deviant fantasies and role-plays were taking up.

How much of his day did he spend in the basement with the rabbits and his electric chair? How often did he go trawling for victims, or locations to dump their bodies?

Since the earlier incident when Ray had gone out driving all night and couldn't remember where, I had identified at least three more 'absences' that he couldn't account for. These were of great concern. So much so that in my worst moments I wondered if he had killed already. Were there victims that I didn't know about?

For example, he remembered being at a shopping centre, following a man who had carried a case of wine to his car. Next, Ray remembered being in the country-side hours later, with no recollection of how he got there.

I began pressing him further, but each time he wouldn't accept that these 'gaps' existed. He thought I was going to accuse him of something dreadful or have him locked up.

'I'm only trying to find out what happened,' I explained. 'That's why we have to explore the absences.'

'No, no. You've got it wrong. They don't exist.'

'But you said yourself . . .'

'No, I didn't. You're the one who calls them

297

"absences". So what if I can't remember what I did last Wednesday afternoon? A lot of people don't remember stuff like that.'

As I'd done before, I tried to explain about dissociation and the idea of the fraying between his fantasies and the real world. This is how some people protect themselves.

'For years they've given you a place to go; a place where you call all the shots. In that place you can destroy people who've hurt you in the outside world . . . the real world. But now, from what you've told me, you feel a pressure building inside you. You've said that Stella and the girls are about the only good things in your life. If it wasn't for them you'd prefer to be in your other world all the time.'

'Paul, I'm a good father.'

'I know you are.'

'I love Stella and my girls.'

'Yes, I know, but you're losing track of things. Sometimes you're not sure which world is which. You've said so yourself. The edges are fraying and the fantasies are leaking into the ordinary world.'

'I know. I know. But you're going to help me, right? You're going to stop me.' His voice was tinged with desperation.

'This is what we have to consider,' I said, trying to reassure him. 'You – the Ray Knox sitting there – you know how bad some of these thoughts and feelings are. You also know where they'll take you if you act them out. The problem is, you can't stop them. You're already starting to put them into action.'

He shook his head, not wanting to hear any more.

I continued, 'It's likely that your own mental defence mechanisms – we all have them – are protecting you from knowing quite what's going on. The urges can't be hidden, but it's as if your mind is dropping huge steel shutters around some of your unacceptable activities and making them inaccessible to normal memory.

'But this has an emotional cost, Ray. Keeping the shutters in place is only partly successful. That's why you're distressed and even more frightened. You fear what you *may* be doing, or have done already.'

I could almost hear the shutters drop. 'You're trying to say that I did something, just because I can't remember.'

'I'm not saying that.'

'You're trying to put words in my mouth. You want to get me locked up.'

'I can't do that, Ray. Even if I wanted to.'

'Then leave me alone.'

He retreated into silence, trying to shut out my voice, but I knew I could still reach him. I explained that his 'absences' were important for a variety of reasons. To a degree we all have them. We might be driving our regular route to work and suddenly become aware that we can't remember the last five miles. How many traffic lights were red or green? Did I cross the bridge? I must have done. This doesn't mean we're driving danger-ously or running signals. Instead it means that the journey has become so routine that we operate on a kind of autopilot. Using examples like this, I helped Ray acknowledge the gaps in his memory.

'When you suddenly "came to" in the countryside, did you recognize where you were?'

'No.'

'What time of day was it?'

'Evening. It was dark.'

'Were you in the car?'

'Yeah. I was parked in a lay-by.'

'How did you find your way home?'

'I drove until I recognized some signs.'

'How long did that take?'

'About an hour.'

'What else did you notice?'

'My shoes were muddy.'

'Why?'

He shook his head.

'What do you think might have happened?'

'I must have gone for a walk.'

He looked at me very directly. 'Do you think I could have done something?' he whispered. 'Is that what you think might have happened?'

'We can't really say that, Ray. We have to find a way to remember.'

'I don't know any more. I don't know what's real and not real.'

Ray's distress seemed genuine. The fact that he couldn't remember blocks of time worried him. I didn't have answers for him. At the same time, I couldn't rid myself of the nagging doubt that he knew more than he let on and might be setting up a defence. Assuming the absences were genuine, I still didn't know if they were just a symptom of his being unable to cope with the stress in his life. Maybe a door had closed in his mind.

I had seen a clinical case where a factory boss had left work one lunch hour to go to a newsagent's and disappeared for three days. His wife and family were beside themselves with worry.

When this chap eventually turned up, he was two hundred miles from home. Dirty and dishevelled, he'd clearly been sleeping rough. He had no idea what had happened to him or where he'd been, but he carried a camera. When the film was developed it contained photographs of his grandparents' grave, a house his grandparents had lived in and a tree he used to climb as a child.

I can't explain completely why his fugue state (absence) took him on this precise journey. Nor why he had no recollection afterwards. I suspect that it had something to do with the stress created by his struggling family business.

He was a proud man who was used to making things happen his way. The possibility of being humbled by bankruptcy or external events set off a self-doubt that he'd never experienced before. Behind a calm façade he was suffering extreme emotional pain and perhaps the fugue was a defence against this. He had visited sites associated with his grandparents because they represented a time when he felt warm and settled, without the worries of adult life.

As you can see, absences don't have to be indicators of great horror. In Ray's case, however, the way he dealt with his stresses was by living in his constructed reality – a construct that involved killing people and one that had started to leak into the real world.

I had discovered his trawling before I discovered the absences. And the gaps he described were far more profound than occasional lapses of memory; they took up more and more of his time.

Three weeks after the security video from Charing Cross station was shown on national TV a man walked into a solicitor's office in Southend-on-Sea. Colin John Ireland admitted to being the man with Emanuel Spiteri.

In a written affidavit provided by his solicitor he denied murder. He claimed to have gone back to Spiteri's flat on that Saturday night and discovered another man there. He left because he wasn't interested in a threesome.

Having provided this explanation, Ireland's solicitor said that his client would refuse to answer any further police questions.

I knew nothing about this when Ken John contacted me again. He made no reference to a witness coming forward or the fact that he had refused to be interviewed. Instead he asked me for a full psychological profile of the person responsible for the murders.

I understood completely the need for operational secrecy. Similarly, Ken John didn't want the emergence of a suspect to influence anything I might say at the briefing.

The cramped conference room was typical of so many I'd seen at police stations up and down the country. The furnishings were standard, along with the grey carpet squares and strip lights on the ceiling. A dozen detectives, among them the SIOs for each of the murders, had taken up chairs around the table. Most had shrugged off their suit jackets and loosened collars in the heat. The air-conditioning system struggled to stir the air.

Ken John made the introductions and then turned to me. I had written the profile in bullet point form, but explained each of my conclusions.

'The suspect will be male and in the same age range as the victims, i.e. mid-thirties to mid-forties,' I said, glancing at my notes. 'The methodology, degree of planning and confidence strongly indicate a certain amount of maturity.

'The literature on offenders of this type also suggests they tend to take people of more or less the same age as themselves. We also have to remember that these victims went voluntarily with this man – expecting a sexual encounter. Serial killers are more likely to select victims of roughly the same age.'

I paused to make sure this had been understood.

'The killer is capable of planning well and executing his plans well. He is not likely to lose control in the course of events. I'd say he has at least an average IQ, probably not more than one standard deviation above.

'He will be able to hold down a job if he chooses to, but will have a chequered employment history.

'He has reasonable social skills and a deceptive ability. Andrew Collier was very cautious and had a strong sense of personal security. Even so, the killer managed to get close to him.

'From his telephone calls, we know that he has a south-east accent. He is also likely to have a broad knowledge of London and south-east England. He was able to go home with these victims late at night and disappear in the morning without being noticed. He knew his way around.

'His telephone conversations also suggest he is of a socio-economic ranking below that of his preferred victim group which is established at group 2/3.'

I knew this was quite unusual. Normally this type of offender tended to choose his victims from the same socio-economic pool. The one variation to this pattern was Emanuel Spiteri, who had a more humble and less intellectual life than the other known victims.

Perhaps this indicated the killer had been feeling the pressure of his own declared goal to 'kill one a week'.

Maybe he had to broaden his specifications for a preferred victim in order to find someone in time.

'He will not be exclusively homosexual. He may well have been married and been involved in heterosexual relationships, but these won't have been stable.'

Ken John interrupted. 'So you're saying he's bisexual?'

'I think he's sexually ambivalent. If he had been extremely anti-homosexual the victims would have suffered even more and most likely been disfigured. Instead he showed disdain for them. He didn't like what he saw.

'At the same time, the victims must have seen something in him. Unless they were convinced he was a homosexual, they wouldn't have invited him home or allowed themselves to be tied up.

'He won't like the fact that they regard him as one of their own. He won't be comfortable with being labelled a homosexual. He'll most likely resist it, even though he probably had sex with some of them.

'This is why I talk of his sexual ambivalence. He has sexual inclinations that he's not altogether happy with, but in this case they made him comfortable in homosexual settings. He was able to gain the trust and intimacy of his victims.

'He is ruthless, confident and able to effect the tactical elements of a plan with precision. I cannot tell how exactly he follows these plans in the strategic sense because we don't have the absolute detail of his overall strategy.

'There are several strong pointers towards him having militaristic training or an interest in survivalist techniques. Look at the precision of each killing: the use of ligatures, bindings and pain. All were understated but absolutely effective. He also caused minimal disturbance – particularly to the first four flats.

'Added to this, you have the "command and control" style of communication with the police and the media. This tends to confirm that he's approaching the killing campaign very much as a military-style operation.'

Although I didn't voice my concern, I knew this made our killer more difficult to catch. He could think on his feet and react quickly.

I doubted if his long-term strategy was as well defined as the precision he showed at each crime scene. Nevertheless this man could adapt tactically along the way and it made him harder to wrong-foot.

'The timing of his murders is not entirely driven by a long-term plan. It is driven by an internal clock. This is why the period between each murder has grown shorter. His inner need is not primarily sexual. He's not a sex killer in the normal sense of the term. As I mentioned earlier, he is sexually ambivalent. His satisfaction came from seeing the tableau he created – imagining the effect it had on you, the finders. Quite possibly he took photographs as a keepsake.

'There are remarkable similarities in posturing between some of the scenes. The killer knew exactly what effect he was trying to achieve in the arrangements of the bodies. He seemed to be working to some clear mental picture. This composition had a dual purpose. One, it gave him pleasure. And two, it set you a puzzle.'

With each murder, he had tried to recreate a scene from inside his mind that would have been refined and rehearsed, developing over a long time. Just as Ray Knox had fantasies that leaked into the real world, so did our killer. And in just the same way, elements of the fantasy had shifted over time and new motifs emerged or changed in intensity. The use of fire was the best example.

'He is not working to a static picture,' I told the detectives. 'That's why I'm quite confident that it didn't start off here.'

'What do you mean?' asked Ken John.

'There are more than five murders.'

'How can you be sure?'

I drew a graph on a blank sheet of paper. 'Look at the characteristics of the known killings – fire, for example. Let's plot each of them from one to five. Notice the escalation. It started with rope burns and burns to the pubic region and then moved on and up to the larger fire.'

I pointed to the start of the graph. 'This may be "murder one" as far as you are concerned, but it's not the killer's first murder. There are things that have happened way off, before the start of this graph – older deaths that you don't yet know about.

'This man has practised and refined his theatre. These are things that develop over time. Peter Walker wasn't a clumsy first attempt at killing somebody. It was too sophisticated – the degree of control was too great. Our man has been here before.'

I knew this was a difficult notion for the SIOs to accept. Despite the nature of their work, these policemen had rarely confronted someone like this killer. To begin with, they found it difficult to understand how a person could live in the ordinary world, as a married man with a job and neighbours, yet at the same time – in parallel – exist in a dimension that very few people could conceive of as being real at all.

This is what prevents people from understanding.

They can't readily grasp the intense pleasure, joy and exhilaration that this man gained from using the bodies of young men as the props and punctuation marks in his statement to the world.

'What did you mean when you said he was setting us a puzzle?' asked another of the detectives.

'He's been reading about himself in the newspapers and listening to what's said on TV. Right from the first known murder he's been seeking to engage you – the investigators. That's why he phoned a newspaper two days after killing Peter Walker. He feared that nobody had found his handiwork. He couldn't wait for your reaction. He's looking for your respect.'

'Respect? He's a friggin' nutter.'

'You say that, but there are no signs of mental illness. This man has a personality disorder, but that's not the same. With a personality disorder, you won't necessarily have any casually observable signs. He's not going to be walking down the street talking to himself, or head-butting lamp-posts.'

This, again, is something that people often struggle to understand. They assume that anyone who kills so ruthlessly and then boasts about it must be mentally ill. It's not so.

Mental illness is a name we use for conditions that tend to separate the sufferer from ordinary reality. In schizophrenia, for example, sufferers may hear voices or see delusional images. They sometimes believe people are trying to hurt them, or that celebrities are in love with them. A schizophrenic's personality will be fragmented, which means they can't hold themselves together to live in an ordinary, straightforward way.

Mental illnesses, including affective disorders such as depression, can be severe enough to have a profound

307

effect on the biochemistry of the body and the mood of the sufferer. These conditions are usually treated pharmacologically, using medications.

Personality disorders, like the offences they give rise to, are quite different. Jimmy, for example, was broadly able to share the same general reality as the rest of us, but had a mixed personality disorder, featuring poor sexual impulse control, narcissism and over-dependency on authority figures.

Most personality disorders are associated with abnormal intensities of various thought patterns and reactions that most of us have. A person with a psychopathic condition – with what is nowadays generally known as an anti-social personality – may well have normal intelligence and normal abilities to be in the world, but they cannot properly empathize with other people. They have a low capacity to feel guilt or remorse but a high capacity for egocentric feelings and behaviour. They can see the world only from their point of view and other people exist essentially for their benefit and pleasure.

Returning to the profile, I took out a folder of photographs. 'This man is a risk taker and a risk assessor,' I said. 'Witness the fire at scene number five.'

I pointed to the thin band of skin visible around Emanuel Spiteri's neck. 'Why isn't this ligature mark covered in soot like everything else?'

The policemen leaned forward to get a closer look.

'There is only one explanation. He took the ligature off after the fire. Which means either he went and came back afterwards or he stayed there while it burned. I think he stayed there while it burned.

'This man knows fire,' I said, stressing the point. 'At

some time in his life I think he's worked as a fireman or was trained by fire-fighting specialists.'

Having delivered the profile, I asked if there were any questions.

'Why did he choose gays?' asked a heavy-set veteran detective, who looked a fit man for his age.

'Because they're easy targets, apart from anything else.'

It was almost the same reason why so many prostitutes get murdered, although most prostitutes have some realization of the risks they face. I had no wish to pass any moral judgements on their lifestyles, but I had to point out that the evidence showed most of this man's victims were openly promiscuous, although sometimes discreet. Some of them enjoyed mild sado-masochistic sex games.

I doubted if any of them appreciated the risks they ran – not with someone they believed to be one of their own. They were more likely to be concerned about HIV or anti-homosexual violence than about a lover they brought home.

'This man chose his target group very carefully,' I told the detectives. 'He didn't have to break in. They invited him inside. He could make mild sadomasochistic suggestions and not ring any warning bells. His victims may well have allowed him to tie them up on the first date. What other group of people would have done this?

'What they didn't expect was to bring home a fully fledged sadist, with an agenda that they knew nothing about. He wanted their bodies – not for sex, but to make him famous.'

As the briefing ended, Ken John raised the subject of an interview strategy. He still made no mention of having a new witness and possible suspect.

On my first trip to London I had strongly urged him to select his interview teams in advance and begin training them. The police had a rare opportunity to choose the best people and give them intense preparation.

My advice hadn't altered. 'If you're interviewing the man that I've profiled, then you're going to face serious difficulties. He's looking forward to this. It's part of his challenge. He's going to match his wits against yours and he thinks he can win.'

Ken John chose that moment to reveal the existence of a suspect.

'You've left it very late,' I told him. 'If this man is the killer, he'll refuse to answer any questions in a police interview. He'll stonewall you completely. That's why I suggested you start preparing sooner.'

At Ken John's request, I agreed to brief the interview teams. In the meantime it was vital that the police discover all they could about Colin Ireland.

Under the terms of the Police and Criminal Evidence Act, they had a limited time to interview him before either charging him or setting him free. A clock had been set running and he was watching it tick down.

15

Born in Dartford in 1954, Colin John Ireland was the illegitimate son of a shop assistant who worked for a local newsagent. Patricia raised her son as a Mormon but never revealed the name of his father. For most of his childhood Colin lived in a three-bedroom semi-detached council house with his mother, his stepfather and his grandparents.

He left school at fifteen and began a life of petty crime. He didn't hide the fact that he'd been in and out of Borstal and prison. 'He said the worst thing he did was tie up a cinema manager and rob him,' said one friend. 'The rest was petty stuff.'

According to police records, Ireland had been arrested as many as thirty times and had nineteen convictions in all – the first at the age of sixteen. His tariff included theft, burglary, robbery, deception, blackmail and possession of an offensive weapon. He had also been acquitted on charges of domestic violence.

Eighteen of the convictions had occurred between 1970 and 1985. There had been only one since then. He had two names on file and six aliases. Among the occupations he'd listed were security officer and industrial fireman.

At the age of twenty-seven, Ireland had been working as a restaurant chef when he married his first wife, Ginny – Virginia Zammit, who had been paralysed from the waist down by a hit-and-run driver. They met in Islington at a workshop on survival. Ginny was nine years his senior.

When interviewed by police she described Ireland as having a 'disturbed personality' – he could be violent one minute and gentle the next. Yet she also revealed how he doted upon her epileptic daughter, Laura Ann, as if she was his own.

'One side of him was really lovely to me but he was like a schizophrenic. The other side of him was the complete opposite.'

The four-year marriage broke down in 1985, shortly after the family moved to Houghton Regis in Bedfordshire. Ginny and Colin divorced a year later.

Ireland then began a whirlwind romance with Jan Young, seven years his senior. When he first met her, she was running the Glove pub in Buckfastleigh, Devon. Ireland had arrived there one day during one of his 'survival weekends' on rainswept Dartmoor.

He wore combat fatigues and was fascinated by survival techniques. He boasted to friends how he could make soup from tree bark, cook snakes and watch birds to tell which berries were good and bad.

The clothing he wore and magazines he read all emphasized the importance he placed on self-testing and challenging himself. He gave the impression of being an accomplished soldier and claimed to have served in the French Foreign Legion. However, no records could be found of any official military training. The most likely explanation is that he failed to gain admission to a military elite and picked up his knowledge from SAS manuals and military biographies.

A year after his divorce came through, Ireland married Jan Young and moved into the pub. The marriage failed within months and Ireland took off in her car, which she reported stolen.

By 1987 he was unemployed and homeless in Southend-on-Sea. After moving between a succession of DSS lodgings, he eventually volunteered to work in a night shelter set up in the town. Soon he found himself promoted to deputy manager and was described by his boss as being polite, hard-working and reliable.

Another volunteer at the night shelter, Joanne Loh, knew Ireland as Colin Williams when they met in 1992.

'He could be very charming and nice and then boom! He could turn nasty,' she told police. She also claimed that he 'classified' people in the night shelter as being gay or straight. He didn't like gays and she assumed this stemmed from something that must have happened in his youth.

Ireland eventually settled in DSS accommodation at the Palace Hotel in Southend. He rarely invited anyone into his room and even his closest friends knew very little about him because his stories changed so often.

Something happened early in 1993 that caused Ireland to resign from his job at the night shelter. 'Unproven allegations were made against him,' according to the manager, Richard Higgs. 'Colin was devastated. He lived for the place.'

Mr Higgs and his wife Debra saw Ireland on the day before he approached a solicitor in Southend and asked to meet police hunting the gay killer. He had been in good spirits and as he left he told them, 'I hate queers.' Perhaps he'd been trying to forewarn them and explain.

* * *

313

All of these details were given to me when I arrived at Islington Police Station on 19 July 1993. Twenty-four hours had passed since I delivered my psychological profile. Now I came prepared with an interrogation strategy.

'It's definitely him,' said Ken John, far more certain than the previous day. His face told a story of elation and relief.

'How can you be sure?' I asked.

'We can now link him to two murder scenes. He's admitted being with Spiteri and we've found a fingerprint at one of the other scenes.'

'Which one?'

'Andrew Collier. It was on a window.'

Ireland hadn't emerged as an acquaintance of either man in the background checks. What were the chances of him knowing both men? It was more than just coincidence.

In addition, police had unearthed an interview with Ireland from 1991 when he'd been charged with domestic violence. An officer had recognized the voice as being the same man who'd called police threatening to 'kill one a week'.

'What does he have to say?'

'Nothing. Not a word.'

Everything I knew about the psychology of the killer had told me that he wouldn't surrender information easily, or readily incriminate himself. For him, the 'interrogation' would be the last stage of his quest for immortality.

During Ken John's briefing I had been jotting down points in a notebook.

He has knowledge of homosexual settings.
He is bisexual with sexual ambivalence.

He comes from a Mormon background, a minority religion, and his mother remarried while he was a child. He never knew the identity of his natural father.

He has two failed marriages with indications of at least one other failed relationship.

He has one GCE O-level.

There are signs of impulsive criminal and socially unacceptable behaviour up to 1985 – seemingly more controlled thereafter.

He is very planful – more recently shown by his tactical approach to a solicitor in the expectation of his arrest for these offences.

He has had many jobs and no stable career.

Past claims of work are as an industrial fireman, security officer and French Foreign Legion trainee.

He has a very strong interest in survivalism. This is important to his self-image.

This last point was perhaps the most crucial. It signalled what lay ahead. This man was determined to survive.

Summer had made a bold start. The police station was stifling in the heat. Electric fans stirred the air and lifted the corners of papers bundled on desks. Notices pinned on cork boards fluttered like trapped birds.

Ken John gathered the interview teams in a conference room at the station. The sense of elation seemed universal – they had got their man, it was only a matter of time before they wrapped up the case.

I was about to disabuse them.

'If this man is responsible for the murders, you can expect that he will sit there and say nothing. He has come prepared to sit out three days of questioning in absolute silence.'

A murmur of discontent greeted this statement. As professional interrogators and investigators they didn't want to believe this.

'This man has a strong interest in survivalism and the military. Every soldier knows to give nothing away under interrogation. They're taught to stare at a spot on the wall, lock onto it, close their mind. That's what he'll try to do.

'You have one thing in your favour – he isn't truly a trained soldier. He doesn't have the personal resources to sustain himself indefinitely. It is extremely difficult to maintain a silence, and he doesn't yet know just how difficult. He's going to learn.'

Already the sense of elation had disappeared along with feelings of complacency, of having finished the job. At the same time, I got the impression that some of those present thought I was giving Colin Ireland too much credit.

'This man thinks he's mentally and physically stronger than you are,' I said. 'At one level, he sees this whole exercise as a game or a contest.

'How do you counter that? Well, to begin with, you never let your frustration show. You have to be confident, relaxed and relentless, but not oppressive. You must be able to keep on talking coherently for as long as it takes. It will feel like a one-sided interview, but that doesn't matter. He *is* listening.'

I began by discussing attitude and demeanour. The interviewing officers had to show Ireland that he was dealing with professionals who knew the truth and in the fullness of time that truth would be established.

I suggested they take a bundle of relevant papers into the interview room. 'Make the bundle larger than you need. This means that Ireland can't watch you working your way down a list of questions and anticipate relief as you near the end.

'But if you do this, you must be aware of what you are carrying. You can't fumble. Any sign of flagging or faltering will give him heart. The same is true if you give him any indication that you are just going through the motions. This will help to sustain him and give him encouragement.

'You need to understand and believe in your strengths. If this man is the killer, he's learned to distinguish true inner strength from a charade. This is one of the elements that contributed to his mastery of his victims.'

Having outlined the strategy in general, I began to give specifics. I suggested playing Ireland a tape of his interviews with the police in 1991. He'd been charged with actual bodily harm after a domestic dispute, but the case ended in acquittal.

'Tell him you understand why he hasn't been speaking. Obviously, he doesn't want his voice compared to the anonymous caller who claimed responsibility for the killings. But now that you have earlier tapes of him to use as a comparison, he doesn't have to worry. He no longer has any reason to be silent. On the contrary, you want to provide him with every opportunity to give an account of himself so there is no chance of a mistake being made, or of him being wrongly accused of something.'

If after this Ireland still failed to co-operate, the interviewers could quite rightly tell him that they had no alternative but to look more seriously at him.

'Say to him, "You have put us in this position, Colin. We have no choice. You appreciate that, don't you? Now if we look at you, what do we see?"

317

'You must then paint a very subtle but unflattering picture of him. If this man is the killer he is very particular about his public image. He's gone out of his way to correct what he sees as inaccuracies in the media. He wants to be respected. If you paint him in a poor light, he will feel a powerful urge to correct you.

'You cannot do this crudely,' I warned. 'Otherwise he'll see through it as a ploy. In reality, it doesn't need to be a ploy at all. You can objectively list things that we know about him that he won't like.'

I suggested the interviewers start with areas that didn't relate to the offences. This might allow Ireland to comment because he knew he wasn't likely to incriminate himself.

'Say something like, "Looking at your history, Colin, you haven't been very successful in your relationships with either men or women, have you?"'

Ireland had walked out on his disabled first wife and stolen a car from his second wife. Another relationship had ended in charges of actual bodily harm.

'Don't accuse him, but linger on certain points. "Why did your marriages fail, Colin?" Watch for his reactions. If he grows uncomfortable, you need to maximize this pressure by focusing on the particular point.

'You mustn't harangue or demean him; don't push it down his throat. Be able to leave questions hanging in the air and let him work out for himself what a poor view you have of him.

'By the same token, if he grows too comfortable with a line of questioning, move on to something else.

'You have to give him the idea that when you look at his life, you find it somewhat unimpressive. It's the very opposite of the kind of legend he's been trying to establish.

'Ask him when he first started to think he might be bisexual. He must have been confused by it. Perhaps he still is.

'Why couldn't he manage to hold down a job?

'Why did he say he spent only three months in the French Foreign Legion? Is it true? Couldn't he survive as a legionnaire? Was it too hard? How did he get away?

'Why did he change his name to "Ireland"? Apparently he had done so by deed poll in 1990. Was it because his parents went to Ireland? Why didn't he see his parents any more? Is it because he had let them down?

'Why didn't he do well at school? He only had one O-level.

'Why did he claim to be a survival trainer? Who does he train? Where did he get his qualifications?

'Why has he got six aliases?'

All of these questions had the potential for immediate impact. They would put enormous pressure on a personality like the killer's. He'd want to set the record straight and defend himself. The urge to correct things would build and build.

All we needed was that first comment. Even a simple 'yes' or 'no' would be a breakthrough – a chink in his defences.

'Don't challenge or confront him. That's what he expects. That's what he's steeling himself for. Instead, ask reasonable questions in a reasonable way. This is your only chance of getting even a limited response from him. It's also your best chance of slowly building the pressure within him.'

The briefing took over an hour. Not everyone embraced my analysis. One of the officers claimed I was over-complicating matters. 'We've got the bastard now. We'll break him.'

Another echoed his sentiments. 'We're just wasting good interviewing time.'

I could only give them my advice – I couldn't make them use it.

Sitting in the conference room, I drank bottles of Orangina and waited for the first interview session to end. Forty-five minutes later the team came back.

'We'd like a moment to have a word with Sir,' they said, indicating Ken John.

I waited in the corridor until summoned back into the room.

'What happened?'

'He said nothing,' answered the older of the two detectives.

'How did he react?'

'Like it was a kid's party game,' said the other. 'He leaned back in his chair, folded his arms and gave us this smug half-smile.'

'He's a cocky bastard,' echoed his partner.

This time when I explained the strategy I sensed a greater willingness to take it on board. I also tried to reassure the interviewers that although Ireland might not be saying anything, he *was* listening. 'Everything you say is going drip, drip, drip into his mind. He has to see two people in front of him who are very confident and self-assured. He's watching your body language. You are calmly presenting him with an overwhelming body of evidence. This is going to stay with him.'

'And if we do this, he'll cough?' they asked.

'No, not right away.' I hated to disappoint them.

'So we're just going through the motions?'

'No. You're doing much more than that. Don't go looking for a confession. Go for his account of what happened and how.'

'Isn't that the same thing?'

'No, not necessarily. Even if you do everything perfectly, the chance of this man confessing to you now is very slim. But after you've finished – in a couple of weeks – he'll make a statement.'

This idea of a time lag between pressing the psychological buttons and getting a response is difficult to get across. The police had to understand that this man might well sit there for three days in silence. He might show all the external signs of surviving the interrogation in silence. But if he killed these men, then he would confess. And when it happened, it would come in a rush.

'What makes you so sure?' asked Ken John.

'It's what I said earlier. This man wants to be seen to be in control. That's why he gave himself up. He knew it was only a matter of time before somebody recognized him from the security video. This way, by giving himself up, he's in control.

'And even though he regards himself as a survivalist, he didn't head for the bush and brew up berries and live off the land. Instead he chose to pit himself against you. This is a different test. It's like the interrogation phase that he's read about in books about SAS selection. He knows that he must say nothing. Even a simple "yes" is a first concession – an acknowledgement that he's losing control.

'But at the same time, he's someone who has been very particular about what is thought of him. He's gone out of his way to contact newspapers and correct them when he didn't like the way he was being portrayed.

'Although he's saying nothing, he's listening to what you say about him. All the negative opinion will eat away at him. He wants your respect. He wants you to view him as a worthy adversary. That's why he will have a powerful urge to correct you.

'He can't let you see him as a failure. He wants to be admired. He wants to be seen as a successful serial killer. He can't let you have these "misconceptions" about him. He has to correct them. If he's the killer that's why he'll confess.'

The interviews recommenced. Upstairs we waited. Empty coffee cups built up on the desks, along with the bottles of Orangina. With more time we could have set up a direct monitoring system and I could have at least listened to the sessions.

Periodically the detectives emerged and interview teams were changed. They no longer seemed disheartened, even though Ireland still hadn't said a word.

There were six or eight officers assigned to the interviews, working in pairs, but it soon became apparent that two or three of the policemen had adapted more quickly to the strategy. They were able to master the material and keep up the constant flow of questions. More importantly, they could maintain the gentle commentary on the possible reasons for Ireland's silence.

My task was to sustain them. Just as it's very difficult for anyone to maintain a silence for three days, it is also incredibly draining to carry out a one-sided interview for that long.

As the interviewers grew in confidence, they were able to interpret the tiny fluctuations in Ireland's behaviour. He seemed surprised that they had learned so much about him in such a short space of time. This unnerved him and he began wondering what they'd spring on him next.

The clock ticked down and the second day began.

To help them understand what they were dealing with, I tried to explain what went on inside the killer's head. How did he become a sadist and what motivated him?

First it meant explaining the very nature of sadism. It is the attainment of pleasure (often sexual pleasure) through the pain, fear, distress and ultimately the destruction of a victim. Even more important, however, is the desire for complete control. The pleasure comes not just from inflicting pain, but actually seeing its effect on the victim.

In this case, four aspects of this killer's behaviour were particularly significant: the emphasis on theatre in the arrangement of the bodies and the scenes; the pleasure that he took in his work; the vital need for external recognition; and his preoccupation with control.

This last point was apparent in his obsession with survival training and self-discipline. He regarded himself as being better than the lesser specimens he saw around him. It made him special. In the ultimate battle of existence – survival of the fittest – he would prevail.

The truth, however, was very different.

This man was likely to be sexually incompetent in a variety of important ways. I don't mean that he couldn't sustain an erection or have proper sex. He was incompetent because he couldn't deliver what most partners wish for in a consenting sexual relationship. Everything focused on his personal satisfaction and need for control.

If he couldn't 'perform' or his partner didn't seem interested, he perceived this as rejection. Similarly, if she wanted more sex than he could manage, this threatened his perception of himself as a virile survivalist with a highly trained body.

This incompetence cut to the very heart of his identity. He couldn't always rely on others seeing the same image as he did, particularly if a person got close to him. Therefore it was much better for him to push them away and become emotionally independent, because somewhere deep inside he knew that he was inadequate. But he would do whatever was necessary to have the world think otherwise.

How did these factors develop into motivation for murder?

In the case of Colin Ireland, I had only half the pieces of the jigsaw. Even so, I knew the pattern. For most ordinary men sexuality is profoundly important. Often it's at the very centre of their existence and they're acutely aware of how their sexuality is perceived by those close to them.

Colin Ireland suffered problems with his sexuality. These can be very distressing but most ordinary men find acceptable ways of dealing with them – by seeing a doctor, perhaps, or a sex therapist.

In Ireland's case his problems were coupled with his emerging sadistic feelings and needs. There are numerous theories about where such urges come from, but they don't necessarily evolve through choice. At some point, however, Ireland chose to submit to these feelings and develop them.

This man had failed in most areas of his life. All of his important relationships were disasters. He never knew his father and felt let down by his mother and stepfather. He turned his back on their way of life and took to crime.

His two marriages failed. So, it seems, did other relationships with women. He failed in his education (his intelligence warranted more). He failed in crime (continually getting caught and apparently not learning by his criminal experiences). He failed in his occupation (never managing to hold down a steady job). Some would say he had 'loser' written all over him.

How did he respond?

He began to develop a militaristic, survivalist persona based on macho self-discipline and self-sufficiency. This increased his isolation, but at the same time began to compensate for all his failures. Finally he had found one area of his life where he had total control – or so he believed.

Nobody could spoil this for him because personal survival against the elements didn't require co-operation with others. He could rely entirely on himself. He could prove that he could control his mind and body in ways that few others can. This made him special.

He was kidding himself, of course. His action-man image was full of flaws. He failed to gain recognition or employment as a survivalist. Apparently, colleagues on training weekends had nicknamed him 'Chicken' Colin because he used to slip into the nearest town for some fried chicken and shelter.

Having been caught out, he tried to compensate by putting to one side even basic comforts allowed on survival weekends. He separated from the group, sleeping alone in only a survival suit. He shunned tents or rations, trying to prove he was harder than the rest of them. It infuriated him that others did not see him as he saw himself.

Ultimately he couldn't ignore the sad truth. He had failed yet again.

This man resented how his life had turned out. He was angry and frustrated. He wanted to show the world that it was wrong about him. He wanted respect . . . so he chose to kill.

All his survivalist training hadn't been a complete waste of time. He could use some of it now in designing and implementing his plans. The signs were there in the selection, entrapment, physical torture, execution and finally the arrangement of the bodies to a preconceived pattern. Afterwards he had sterilized the scenes and made his escape.

The psychological characteristics were equally clear. He had displayed courage, risk assessment, ruthlessness and detachment from others' pain (except in so far as it gave him pleasure). He had also used torture to extract information.

These skills and psychological characteristics were brought together in each of the killings. They served his resentment. With each new murder he would show people how clever and creative he could be.

Look how he responded to the security video at Charing Cross station. There was no evidence of panic. He selected a strategy of making a statement to a solicitor and then remaining silent.

Yet at other times he'd displayed his weakness. He didn't need to phone the police, the Samaritans and the *Sun*. Why did he take the risk? Because he couldn't resist the desire to have his work acknowledged and to observe its impact.

He knew there would be a public outcry and he enjoyed watching the clamour for answers to his puzzles. Yet these would go nowhere unless he chose to offer more clues. This was an extension of his power.

The same was true of his boasting to friends about having done something 'special' and 'notorious'. Vanity and self-importance were fundamentally more meaningful than anonymity. This is a perfect illustration of how ultimately he lacked the discipline to be truly 'a man alone'.

His phone calls to the police served two more aims. First he wanted to satisfy some of his resentment towards them. They had banged him up enough times. Jealousy also played a part. I'm quite sure Colin would have liked to be part of a disciplined organization like the police force or the military. In his view he would have excelled in such a setting, if only he hadn't been barred from joining by his juvenile offending.

Secondly, his calls to the police allowed him to boast about his handiwork to the only people who knew exactly what he was talking about. They had seen his deviant displays of theatre; his audacity and expertise could genuinely impress them.

When he gave himself up to the police, he didn't know about the fingerprint at Andrew Collier's flat. At that stage he thought the video at Charing Cross station was the strongest evidence against him. If so, then he stood a good chance of getting off.

He had succeeded before by sticking to a pre-conceived strategy – this was how he killed – but he'd never had to maintain a strategy for more than a few hours. And never before had the stakes been this high.

As the deadline approached for either charging Colin Ireland or letting him go, I tried to reassure the interview teams that they had done all they could.

'The most crucial time is when the clock ticks over

327

on the last minute on the third day,' I said. 'That's when you take him away and have him remanded. When he doesn't get up and walk out through the door a free man, he's going to realize that this is a much bigger game than he ever dreamed.

'And in the small hours of tonight and tomorrow night and the night after, he will still be hearing the questions you ask him. Even when remanded and moved to prison, he will remember what you say.

'It won't be a question of using survivalist skills any more. It will be the day in, day out routine of slops, sharing a cell and the numbing succession of meals and exercise – all the things that he has grown to hate. He will be back, cheek by jowl, with all the people from his criminal past. He has been through all of this. Worse still, this is where you think he belongs. You don't understand him.

'This is when the realization will dawn on him that all of his grand thoughts, expectations and schemes have come to nothing. If he is to survive in any way, he has to put this right. He has to set the record straight. That's when he'll confess.'

Three weeks later, as Colin Ireland was being driven to a hearing before magistrates, he asked to speak to the police, 'but not those bastards who interviewed me. They really got under my skin.' He confessed to all five murders, giving officers information that only the murderer could have known.

'I just wanted to be a serial killer,' he said. 'I read the books and thought, "I could do that."'

Describing his feelings after the fourth murder in the series, Ireland said, 'I was reaching the point where it was just accelerating. It was speeding up and getting far worse. It wasn't just him making me angry, it was like a roller-coaster effect.'

Of his choice of victims, he said, 'I had gone with the idea that if someone approached me then something would happen – it would be a trigger – sort of stepping over the line, in a way.'

Ireland revealed the meticulous care he took not to leave clues behind. He carried a different pair of gloves on each murder expedition so as not to leave fingerprints. The cord he used to tie up his victims had been chosen as a type so common that police would be unable to trace it.

He took handcuffs to immobilize the men, having taken care to buy them at different shops. And before setting out he emptied his pockets of everything except money so there was no risk of him leaving personal belongings at the murder scenes.

After each killing he spent time wiping surfaces clean and packing up everything he had taken with him to secure his victims. He also collected cups and plates he had used and any food he had left uneaten. Usually he stayed at the homes until morning when he could slip out and join the peak-hour crowds on their way to work. Then he made his way via Fenchurch Street station to Southend.

Of theatre director Peter Walker, he said, 'I put a plastic bag over his face. As he suffocated and began to panic, I told him, "That's how easy it is." '

He and librarian Christopher Dunn had watched a sadomasochistic video together before Ireland bound and gagged him. He then tortured him with a lighter flame until he revealed his cash card number.

American businessman Perry Bradley III was also tortured into giving his bank account PIN before being throttled.

Of Maltese chef Emanuel Spiteri, Ireland said, 'He was an extremely brave man. He wouldn't give me the number. But I couldn't allow him to stick around and recognize me.'

Ireland told the police that he'd been bullied as a youngster and said, 'In some moods I would be happy to burn the world down.'

At the Old Bailey in December 1993, Colin Ireland pleased guilty to all five murders. Evidence emerged that he had studied books on crime and serial killers, reading up on Peter Sutcliffe (the Yorkshire Ripper) and Dennis Nilson. He had also rented the film *Silence of the Lambs*.

Part of his reading was an FBI handbook on serial killers written by Robert Ressler, who classified a serial killer as someone who had murdered 'one over four'. In one of his calls to the police, Ireland had said, 'I've got the book. I know how many more I have to do.' And when he reached five, he telephoned again and boasted: 'I've done another one.'

In sentencing him, Mr Justice Sachs said, 'By any standards you are an exceptionally frightening and dangerous man. In cold blood and with great deliberation you have killed five of your fellow human beings. You killed them in a grotesque and cruel fashion. The fear, brutality and indignity to which you subjected your victims are almost unspeakable.

'To take one human life is outrageous. To take five is carnage. You expressed the desire to be regarded as a serial killer. That must be matched by your detention for life.'

Only days beforehand, Colin Ireland had sent Christmas cards to his friends saying, 'Watch the news on 20 December.' He knew he would be sentenced on that day. He wanted them all to know.

My Christmas that year was typically joyous and heart-warming. As a youngster I didn't enjoy Christmas quite so much. Marilyn and the children have made the difference and now it's probably the highlight of my year.

I usually dropped in to Arnold Lodge on Christmas Day to spend a few minutes with the patients and staff. It was wonderful to see the hard façades drop for a while and the joy on people's faces.

Back in those days the departmental Christmas parties were legendary. The various clinical groups in the psychiatric hospitals, wards and departments would each host a gathering. Invitations began to arrive at the end of November. Meanwhile decorations were bought, provisions arranged and drink of all sorts put into store.

The parties were witty, awesome, merry, riotous, relaxing and sentimental. They were hardly ever drunken or unseemly and rarely did anybody face embarrassment in the New Year.

The stress of working in the forensic field is enormous and, as I've explained, any outlet for this is vital. That's why the parties were so important. The goodwill and camaraderie that flowed from them did more for the morale and motivation of the service than any number of presentations by management gurus. It was the same right across the NHS.

Inside the clinical perimeter of Arnold Lodge, Christmas wasn't quite the same. Bill Carpenter and the other staff performed wonders every year to make the festivities memorable. They staged a pantomime and revue for the patients. Many of them took part in the show, or spent hours helping build and paint the huge cardboard stage props.

On Christmas Day the staff, acting as waiters, would serve a traditional lunch of roast turkey with all the trimmings. The cutlery was plastic for safety, but everyone was allowed two glasses of beer.

The laughter and the smiles couldn't hide the sadness and silent tears. For many of those detained at Arnold Lodge, the tinsel and the tree were simply reminders of what was missing in their lives. They knew that if the gates were suddenly opened to them on Christmas morning they would have nowhere to go.

Although the 'gay slayer' was now behind bars, I had recommended that the search for other victims should continue. Ireland was an extremely dangerous man with a history of sexual deviancy.

The only way to get at the truth was to go back and look at Ireland's life point by point, tracing his movements and whereabouts. Key witnesses had to be interviewed, including his ex-wives and ex-partners, both male and female.

In particular, I wanted to know what happened in his life in 1985. Up until then he had been convicted nineteen times in fifteen years. But in the following eight years, he was charged only once and found not guilty of causing actual bodily harm.

Why the change in his criminal behaviour? Either he had stopped committing crimes or he had stopped getting caught.

In 1985 his first marriage had just broken up and he was heavily involved in survival courses and training. This could explain why he stopped getting caught, but I suspected a more sinister reason for the silence. It could flag a new strand of offending.

He worked in a night shelter as a volunteer and was

soon promoted to deputy manager. This is the sort of place where people quite easily fall through the cracks. They may be vagrants and loners who have lost touch with their families. How many disappeared while Colin Ireland was around?

One detail that emerged later had great resonance in my clinical work. As a teenager, Ireland had had a history of torturing and destroying cats. Later, as part of his survival training, he snared and killed wild rabbits. He doubtless tortured them while they were alive.

These things were part of his sadistic development, but didn't necessarily lead seamlessly into killing humans. They formed part of a rehearsal process. In the real world he learned how much pressure it took to garrotte an animal. He taught himself how to deal with a struggling body and how to clean himself afterwards.

Later he will have practised enticing men into situations where they were isolated and under his control. These practice runs may have included binding potential victims, who never realized how close their sadomasochistic lover came to killing them.

Colin Ireland didn't emerge as a fully fledged sadist all at once. He became one over a period of years. That's why it was important to look for other crimes with elements of the same motifs, such as sadism, bondage, fire, theatre and refined torture. This might seem obvious, but in reality the police had linked none of the first four murders until Colin Ireland had called the Samaritans and the *Sun* and admitted he was the killer.

I don't know if the police took my advice. Perhaps they took the view that Ireland would have confessed if he'd committed other murders. This isn't true. A man such as this will only ever draw attention to the murders that he is proudest of. He's unlikely to talk about a crime scene that he failed to control, or a killing that he botched.

I have a feeling we'll hear from Colin Ireland again. As he languishes in prison and his public notoriety fades, he'll want to talk about his *other* successful crimes. He'll want to stand in the spotlight again and show how clever he is. Such is the nature of the beast.

16

During my year as a police cadet, I had occasionally helped escort remand prisoners to Winson Green Prison in Birmingham. In those days, in the early 1960s, these transfers were much more leisurely than they are now.

Rather than big armoured trucks with armed guards, we had 'Agnes', the Black Maria van, with Reg driving. As the escort, I had to sit in the back with whatever hooligan or miscreant was being transferred to prison. Normally, but not always, I had a PC with me because at sixteen I was considered too young to go alone.

When we arrived at Winson Green, Reg drove through the big wooden gates hinged with metal. He waved to the various guards he knew from his regular run. We pulled up and took the prisoners to the processing office, handing over their personal effects to be bagged and logged.

What I remember most is the noise. Imagine five hundred people living inside a big saucepan. That's the sort of noise – a constant buzz, clank and clatter. I loathed the smell. It was a mixture of sweat, boiled cabbage and fear.

Many of the prison officers were ex-military and

would banter among themselves while keeping watch over the yard of the dispersal prison. Among their charges I could see both the sad and the predatory.

Although the officers seemed complacent, there was an edge to their work. Prisons are places where violence and aggression are never far beneath the surface. Someone bumps into someone and suddenly they're squaring up to each other.

I've been inside a lot of high-security prisons since those days. The smell hasn't changed, but there is now a greater atmosphere of fear and a need for constant vigilance. It takes only a very small spark to ignite a conflict.

The prison population is also a lot younger nowadays and there are more sexual offenders identified and convicted. There is a greater onus on prisoners' rights and the prison service has faced a great deal of criticism in the past four decades.

Nowadays there are mission statements on the walls that make bold declarations: 'Our job is to contain and to rehabilitate . . .' I always find this ironic when I look at the officer standing beside the statement and I know he isn't going to rehabilitate a soul.

I am destined always to remember my last visit to Winson Green as a police cadet. Something had changed in the atmosphere. As I came through the gate there were no friendly waves or nods of recognition. People's faces were different. They didn't make eye contact. Elsewhere, the landing had gone quiet and the clatter had become muffled.

'What's going on?' I whispered to Reg.

'Hanging.'

That's all he said. Not another word was exchanged between us. I could see it in the eyes of the guards and the prisoners – none of these men had the stomach for this. They might go through the motions and believe in the system, but none of them enjoyed the task.

I felt sick then, just as I feel sick today at the memory. The notion that people, as part of their daily job, will ritualistically kill fellow human beings is something I find extraordinary. And this is supposed to be a deterrent to others?

People have often asked me how I feel about capital punishment. They assume that because of my work I must have strong views. It's true – I do. My psychological profiling work has given me first-hand experience of the terrible crimes that people commit. I've spent hours looking at the remains of dreadfully defiled young men, women and children. I've been at the crime scenes and read the autopsy reports.

These sometimes overwhelm me with horror, yet even more abhorrent is the idea of a civilized society having a policy of ritualized, judicial execution.

I can understand that random, spur-of-the-moment executions sometimes happen during wars or coups. These fill me with nausea, but at least they are an instant response at a personal or very local level. However, the notion of waiting a few weeks, then taking someone from a prison cell to the place of lawful execution, having someone put a noose around their neck and pull a lever, is positively barbaric.

Nevertheless, when I look into the eyes of someone who has committed a terrible crime, or is excited by the prospect, it's not easy to put my flesh and blood memories of real crimes to one side. I can't forget the victims.

At the same time, I cannot just write off a person I'm trying to help as an evil creature. Instead I have to engage each patient on a human level – regardless of what they've done or what they're capable of. I have to accept unconditionally that each patient is a potentially valuable human being. Otherwise, how can I hope to work with them?

Some are more difficult to accept than most. I have prejudices just like most people. I have no time for men or women who for business reasons prey on, degrade and corrupt innocent lives. These include pimps, non-addicted drug dealers, pornographers and corrupt police officers. I can find nothing but contempt for them.

Tony Doherty might be perceived to be part of the above group, but in truth he was little more than an adjunct to them. From the moment he first arrived in my consulting room, he brought with him an air of menace and aggression. Yet at the same time he seemed almost embarrassed by his size and strength.

The fact that he turned up at all surprised me. Tony had missed his first two appointments without calling to apologize or explain. Now he stood in my office doorway, seeming to fill the space with ease.

In his late twenties, he wore a neatly tailored suit. He struck me as being physically very crisp and strong, but psychologically off at a tangent. It was like watching a much more sinister version of Lenny from John Steinbeck's *Of Mice and Men*.

He spun his chair slightly so he could keep one eye on the door and his back to the corner of the room. This seemed to happen automatically, as if it was a natural response.

'Why did you want to see me?' I asked.

'Ah, well, it's like this, you see . . . ah, uumm . . .' He had a heavy Scottish accent and struggled to

338

find the right words. I could smell alcohol on his breath.

In a rambling, roundabout way Tony explained that he normally worked in Glasgow but came down to Leicester every few weeks to visit his mum.

'I'm worried about upsetting her,' he said.

'How?'

'Well, you know, I seem to get into a lot of scrapes.'

'Scrapes?'

'Fights.'

'Oh, I see.'

'And I don't want to hurt anyone – not here.'

'Why "not here", in particular?'

'Because of Mum, of course. I don't want to embarrass her. She's a good woman.'

Tony seemed genuinely concerned – not about hurting somebody, but about upsetting his mum. It still puzzled me why he had missed his first two appointments. I needed to understand his motivation before deciding how serious he was about getting help.

'What do you do in Glasgow, Tony?'

'Normally I work in the restaurant trade,' he said, quite proud of the fact. 'All the best places – five-star joints. I've worked in London and Manchester. Now I'm in Glasgow.'

'Is that what you do now?'

'Sometimes.'

'Have you another job?'

'Not really. I just give my boss a hand from time to time.'

'In the restaurant business?'

'Oh, no.' There was a long silence and Tony tugged at the sleeves of his jacket. 'Sometimes he needs a job done and I give him a hand.'

'At what?'

Tony seemed concerned for my sensibilities – as if I'd be shocked. 'Well, you know, it might be somebody has upset him by not paying their bills.'

'So you collect the money?'

'No, never. I don't deal with the money.'

'What do you do?'

'I sort them out.'

'What does that mean?'

He rolled his eyes, as if wondering how I could be so stupid. 'I give 'em a smack.'

'Oh, I see.' By this stage I'd have been happier if Tony was five hundred miles away and had never heard my name. Steeling myself, I pressed onwards. 'Just so I'm clear on this, Tony, can you give me an example of what actually happens?'

'Well, that depends on how serious the boss says it is. It might be that a couple of us go there, knock on the door and break his legs.'

'Mmm . . . And how do you do this?'

'With a pickaxe handle.'

'Do you carry that with you?'

'Yeah.'

'So you break legs.'

'Yeah, that's what I said.'

'Do you have to do this very often?'

'I don't count, do I? I go, I do it and that's it.'

He still looked at me incredulously. I felt like an elderly judge on the bench asking, 'Exactly who are the Spice Girls?'

'And what happens if it's more serious?' I asked, keeping the same matter-of-fact manner.

'We make the message a bit clearer.'

'What with? Iron bars? Knives?'

'No, I don't use knives. I don't like 'em. Messy things.'

'Firearms?'

He went quiet and looked at me carefully. 'I don't really like 'em. You haven't got the same control, have you? With a pickaxe handle I know what I'm doing, but with a gun . . .' He paused and grew slightly irritated because we were wasting time. 'That's not why I'm here. I want you to help me.'

'Exactly how can I do that?'

'Well, I'm down here to see Mum and I'm worried about getting myself into trouble. When I go to the pub, I have a few pints and it really does my head in. I hear people jabbering – saying this and that. My head starts buzzing. All I want to do is flatten somebody.'

'Why?'

'Because that takes the buzz away. I'm worried that I'm gonna really hurt some geezer.'

'But that's what you do for a living.'

'Yeah, but that's *work*. This is home. This is where Mum lives.'

The complete inconsistency of this made perfect sense to Tony. He had a peculiar but very precise moral system, not unlike that of the Mafia in how it related to family, business and religion. He doted on his mum, he didn't 'go out with tarts'; and whacking people was 'work'.

I had met institutionalized gangsters before but never one with Tony's problem. First I had to be clear about exactly what I was treating. Most people would think that I should cure Tony of being a hit man and some-how change his vocation, but that is not what I do.

The fact that he was a gangster made no difference. I've had professional boxers come to me with very similar problems – they keep getting into fights outside the ring – and my approach is the same. I had to concentrate on the episodes of uncontrolled violence and help Tony deal with them.

I had to understand the relationship between the 'day job', so to speak, and the episodes of unpredictable aggression. This meant spending a long time going over the history and trying to understand his moral system.

To an outsider, somebody like Tony might seem to have no morals at all, but this is not true. Criminal codes of conduct are often as strong as religious strictures to some people.

Moral systems are quite interesting. Take a successful businessman who believes strongly in his family and supporting the local community. He is an expert at buying companies and stripping their assets, closing them down and making people redundant – practices that impact upon hundreds of families and whole communities. But if you were to ask the businessman how he felt about doing this to all those families, he might well say, 'Well, that's business.'

Morally he has made a distinction between what he does at work and outside work. Tony does the same. Of course, it's not illegal to close down a company and sack a workforce, but it is illegal to whack people.

How did Tony's moral structure develop in this way?

His history wasn't out of the ordinary. He had a stable and nurturing childhood growing up in Leicester with his mum and dad. Mum sounded like an upright, honest member of the community. His dad had been a factory foreman and a good provider. He had died of a heart attack eight years earlier, soon after retiring.

Although not a bright student, Tony managed to

find work easily enough after leaving school at sixteen. He had stints as a bouncer and security guard before becoming the maître d' at various restaurants.

Since then the structure of his life had fallen away, although his mum still believed that he worked in the restaurant trade. Tony was quite proud of his employment record. In a matter-of-fact way, he announced, 'I've worked in all the best restaurants. I can pick up the phone or walk in the door and they'll happily give me a job.'

This seemed, at first, a little discordant with the man in front of me. Tony looked like he'd frighten most patrons. Although not enormous, he was very solid, with huge hands. His nose had clearly been broken a few times and he had a scar across his neck, just visible when he loosened his tie and began to relax.

Tony glanced occasionally at the door when he heard a sound from the corridor outside. He kept his hands available and carried himself in such a way as to make maximum use of his size. It could make him look very frightening, but I wasn't sure whether this had grown out of the work he did or whether perhaps he had some mild neurological problem. This might also explain the 'buzzing' in his head and some 'blank spots' in his memory.

'These other jobs you do, what do you think about them?' I asked, starting to explore his moral structure.

'It's good honest work,' he said, without a hint of guile or deception.

'In what sense is it honest?'

'Well, I earn my money. My boss has things he needs done and I do them and I get well paid.'

'But you hurt people.'

'Yes.'

343

Clearly, this was purely a commercial enterprise to Tony, no different from a farmer taking cows off to market.

'Do you know these people whose legs you break?'

'No. Not usually.'

'Do they say anything to you?'

'Oh, yeah. I get all the excuses and the promises. They start begging and bawling.'

'But you're not interested?'

'It's none of my business. The boss makes the decisions. If there's something to be put right, I do it. It's nothing personal.'

There was no bravado in this statement. He didn't look at me to gauge the impact. From the tone of his voice he might just as easily have been talking about organizing a trip for the local boys' club.

I began to see a man who had a very curious idea of human beings and his relationships with them. He had a wealth of knowledge and empathy towards those people who were significant to him, such as his mother and his boss. Yet he could completely disregard or simply not see the richness of personality and value of other human beings.

He didn't care about those people whose legs he broke. He didn't know them. He wasn't interested.

Tony didn't turn up for his next appointment and arrived a week later. When I asked him what had happened, he apologized and explained that he'd been busy.

'I was looking after some girls.'

'What girls?'

'We've been having some labour problems. A few of the girls wanted to freelance. Some geezer has been bending their ears about giving them a better deal.'

344

'A pimp?'

'Yeah.'

'So what did you have to do?'

'I had to mind the girls – see they were OK.'

'Is that all?'

'I didn't hurt 'em, if that's what you're asking. The boss didn't want them marked.'

'Would you have any qualms about hitting a woman?'

'No.'

Despite his unusual occupation, nothing out of the ordinary had emerged from Tony's history. The only factor that I flagged as being salient was his ability to lead almost parallel lives, incorporating his day job and his regular trips home to see his mum.

In one life he was a fearsome, extremely brutal enforcer. In the other he was a loving son who doted on his mum and wanted her to think him a success. This meant that one day he'd be breaking someone's legs and the next day he'd be home again, crying with his poor mum because she'd accidentally dropped her favourite vase.

Although I wasn't looking at a multiple personality, there were interesting parallels. People behave differently in different situations, of course, but Tony's life had a radical division.

Imagine a car engine with a manual gearbox. When the engine is idling, it is simply waiting for someone to select a gear – either forward or reverse. Tony was like that engine. He could switch direction as smoothly as changing gears.

From doting on his mum and helping her wash the dishes, he'd suddenly wake one morning and say, 'I've got to go to work today.' Then he'd get himself dressed,

345

catch the train to Glasgow and go to his boss's office.

'So you're back then?' his boss would say.

'Yeah.'

'Ready for work?'

'Yeah.'

Having slipped into gear, Tony would be everything expected of him as an enforcer. He had no misgivings about breaking bones or spilling blood.

A fortnight later, Tony would tell his boss that he needed to get away. The 'engine' was slipping back towards neutral. Maybe there was some heat from the police, or another reason to lay low. More likely, however, I think Tony sensed that all was not well in that side of him. He couldn't articulate his disquiet, yet these feelings were possibly the beginnings of an emotional crisis.

He went home to his mum's, where he said he 'slept for a couple of days'. Of course, nobody really sleeps for that long – but he was obviously very tired. Then he started going out in the evenings, visiting pubs and nightclubs.

Tony had difficulty describing what happened next.

'People are just chatting, you know. The place is packed. I got somebody saying this, somebody saying that . . . and it is just buzz, buzz, buzz in my head. All I want to do is flatten somebody because that takes the buzz away. I don't like what I've done. Afterwards, I think, oh, you poor bastard, but really you should have given me some space. You should have known . . .

'That's what scares me. If I seriously hurt somebody, I'll finish up in court. Mum won't be able to hold her head up any more. She'll be ashamed of me.'

Tony's mum sounded like a stalwart of her local church and community. There was no evidence that she knew about his day job. On the contrary, he had kept it from her as he tried to live up to her expectations.

Understanding this, I now had to decide what to do about Tony's problem. Was it neurological?

Perhaps, but he wasn't keen on this suggestion.

'No thanks, I don't want some geezer taking snaps of me brain.'

'It's only a scan.'

'I don't care. Anyway, I'm claustrophobic.'

I couldn't persuade him. Instead we began to look at ways he could deal with uncontrolled anger and arousal.

'I never get angry normally,' he said. 'I'm calm. I've got this friend, Frank. He's a little fucking pain. I don't know why I call him a friend but I've known him for yonks. You can't rely on Frank. We were due to go to Manchester the other morning and he said he'd drive me. You see I don't drive. He told me he'd be around to pick me up at eleven o'clock. There I was, waiting for him. He still wasn't there by twelve. I finished up getting a taxi. I was late and I felt bad.'

'I see. What happened then?'

'Well, I got to give him a smack.'

'Who?'

'Frank.'

'When you say a smack, what do you mean?'

'Well, he's got to learn. He can't do that. Not to me. He knows what I'm like. He knows he's got to have a smack.'

'What does a smack mean?'

'I'll work him over.'

'What with?'

'Oh, don't worry, just my hands.'

'When is this going to happen?'

347

'When I find him. He's not stupid, Frank. He knows what's coming. That's why he's making himself scarce.'

'Does that make you angry?'

'No, no. That's just something I've got to do. No, that's what I mean about not getting angry. It doesn't normally happen to me.'

'Well, what happened the other night when you hit somebody?'

He turned up his hands in puzzlement. 'Fucked if I know, Mr Britton. I'm out on the town, minding my own business and it just sort of happened.'

'Where were you?'

'In a pub near the clock tower. There are three or four young guys throwing their weight around a bit.'

'What were they doing?'

'Mainly teasing the barmaid, being cheeky. I don't like that. Maybe I've had a drink or two. I like a drink. I have a drink most days. Just a couple, mind you. I had a drink before I came here, but I'm not drunk. Mum doesn't like me drinking too much.'

'You were saying?'

'Oh, yeah, these young guys were getting a bit cocky. I don't know what it is – maybe it's something about me – but guys just seem to pick me out and have to say something.'

'What did they say?'

'I can't remember now. That's what I mean about my head going muzzy. The buzzing won't stop. Next minute they're lying on the floor. People are running about, shouting for the police and the ambulance . . .'

'What did you do?'

'I laid 'em out! There were two of them on the ground, unconscious. One of 'em had a busted jaw.'

Tony described the scene without any sense of regret

348

or concern for the victims. At the same time, I knew he didn't really have a handle on what had happened. It is almost unheard of for somebody to experience a true explosion of rage or arousal without any escalation or warning signs. Unfortunately, Tony didn't have the ability to perceive this escalation. He couldn't read the signs.

My task was to teach him how to win control of the situation, by enhancing his perception of his body and his thinking.

'When these young lads were talking to the barmaid and being cocky, how did your stomach feel?'

'Like it always does,' he said, shrugging.

'What about when the fight was over and you saw them lying on the ground?'

'Oh, then it was like a knot.'

'How does it get from being OK to being like a knot?'

'Well, maybe there was a little bit of churning.'

'When exactly?'

'They were telling the barmaid she'd short-changed them. They said they gave her a twenty instead of a tenner. Bollocks!'

'Your stomach started churning.'

'Yeah.'

'What about your head?'

He looked at me blankly.

I tried a different tack. 'When it was over and you realized what had happened, what can you remember feeling?'

'It felt like someone had turned the lights up.'

'Had they?'

'No.'

Slowly Tony began discovering there was a whole

349

range of physical changes that preceded the attack. His vision had narrowed and the light seemed to grow darker. His muscles had tensed and his stomach churned.

An internal monologue accompanied this escalation. Tony told himself, 'Cocky bastards! Leave her alone! Who do you think you are? Don't turn round . . . Don't think you can face me down . . . He's right-handed . . . The guy next to him is left-handed . . . He's holding a glass . . .'

Eventually, a small thought loop took over and played repeatedly in his head: 'This is trouble – I've got to drop the bastards. This is trouble – I've got to drop the bastards . . .'

At some point in the thought loop, Tony said, 'It's got to be now.'

'How often has this happened to you?' I asked.

'I'm getting a reputation. That's why I try to stay in – I keep out of trouble. I haven't had a fuck in months.'

Here was another stream, which had to be explored. 'Do you have a girlfriend?'

'Nah. I mean, what girl can really put up with that? It's not right. Nice girls don't want their fella getting into fights when they go out for a drink.'

'What about in Glasgow?'

'I'm not going out with tarts, if that's what you mean. I'm not interested in that. I want a proper girl. A good lass. That's why you gotta help me.'

Somehow I had to intervene in the cognitive loop that preceded and accompanied Tony's explosive outbursts. This meant teaching him to recognize the changes in his heart rate, stomach, muscles and vision.

He had to listen to his internal monologue. Up until then, he hadn't known that his own unspoken words were turning the situation into a dangerous one. Nor could he recognize that his body was sending him alarm signals. Once he could identify the warning signs and hear the dangerous thought loop, it would be possible to give him behavioural strategies that would interrupt his arousal and anger.

The most dangerous times seemed to emerge when he went out drinking. Someone like Tony is a beacon to certain types of young men who go out looking for trouble, trying to pick the toughest guys in the bar, or someone they can bully into a confrontation.

The idea of 'backing off' had never been an option for Tony. He'd lose face. People would think him a coward and his reputation was important to him.

To counter this, I provided strategies to help deal with the consequences of withdrawing. He had to remind himself that if the young men had really known who they were dealing with, they'd never have started it. By holding back he was being manly. It would have been unfair for him to take advantage of their ignorance. If he turned the other cheek, so to speak, and they still initiated physical aggression, then his experience and prowess would bring the proceedings to a close in very short order.

Tony had to understand that the way he looked at other people could also be a catalyst for trouble. I taught him how to monitor his own facial expression, to smile warmly and to make eye contact in a way that wasn't challenging or menacing.

You can't just tell someone to 'look friendlier'. In Tony's case, he didn't know how. Part of his business 'dress' was a granite-like expression with the eyes fixed, as though staring someone out. As he watched a person, he looked at the rest of the room with his peripheral vision, which made his gaze seem even more rigid. He was never the first to look away.

For Tony to learn how to work his face, first he needed to see it. I didn't have a mirror in my room, so we headed down the corridor to the men's toilet which was full of polished metal. Before leaving my office, I spent time getting Tony to practise smiling in a relatively neutral way. I didn't want him grinning like an idiot or beaming like a lottery winner. Instead he practised a smile that might accompany an introduction or gentle opening remarks.

The bathroom was empty. Tony stood in front of the handbasins and gazed into the mirror, trying to give a soft, friendly smile. It quickly became apparent that he couldn't smile and talk at the same time.

'OK, let's try it one more time,' I suggested. 'Relax. Loosen up your face muscles. You're not visiting a dentist, you're smiling at a barman.'

Tony gave a good impersonation of Jack Nicholson in *The Shining*. This was obviously going to take some time.

Unexpectedly, the bathroom door opened and a man of about Tony's age walked in, obviously in need. I didn't know him – he must be a visitor, I thought. He stopped, looking at us uncertainly.

'Ah, hello, mate, come on in,' declared Tony, in a rumbling voice. He pushed his face forward and turned it slightly to one side. The smile was a combination of a grimace and a sneer. 'What do you think about this then . . . not bad?'

The visitor's mouth dropped open. He was already backing out, mumbling to himself, 'Er . . . er . . . er.'

'Something wrong, mate?' asked Tony.

'No ... no ... no ... no.' The swing door had opened and I could almost hear this poor chap sprinting down the corridor. There was no other men's toilet in the building but I don't think he cared.

'I haven't quite got the hang of this yet,' said Tony, with classic understatement. 'Maybe I should practise at home?'

Within a few weeks, he'd mastered a smile that didn't immediately have women clutching their children's hands and shooing them indoors. I still had to help Tony deal with his anger. First he had to understand where the anger came from.

Tony had been an enforcer for years. He had always prided himself on his self-control. What had changed?

Ultimately he had to understand that it arose out of his violent career. He had tried to keep his day job in a box – entirely split off from the rest of his life. Unfortunately, the box was beginning to splinter.

Each time he came home, his mother became his conscience. She viewed him as the perfect son – a wonderfully thoughtful and sweet-natured boy who looked after her. This was nowhere near the truth and Tony knew it. He whacked people for a living, he did it well, he did it for money and he did it because there was some part of him, which he couldn't explain, that actually needed it.

This created in him what psychologists refer to as cognitive dissonance. It is an important feature of human beings, particularly when people are faced with conflicting realities and conflicting desires or needs.

The example most often used in the literature involves smoking. A person will talk about cigarettes being enjoyable and relaxing. They will also accept that smoking is harmful and slowly killing them. These discordant concepts set up a dissonance or conflict within them.

Normally this is resolved by people choosing sides. They will accept one concept, usually the one they like best, and simply discount the other. When this happens, the person who continues to smoke will either say, 'I don't care about dying,' or, 'No, it's not true. It's all propaganda.'

Sometimes when a smoker gets annoyed, the dissonance kicks in and he says, 'This is not my problem. It's yours.'

Tony's dissonance revolved around his acceptance of violence as a natural and necessary part of his job. This was set against his need to be the man his mother thought he was, particularly when he visited her.

One way of dealing with this would have been for Tony to close his mum out completely and ignore her feelings. He couldn't do that. He loved her. Instead he spent his time at home constantly churned up and unhappy. He didn't have enough intellectual equipment to deal with the dissonance. Instead of embracing one and pseudo-reasoning away the other he had, quite unusually, remained caught in between mutually exclusive alternatives. He was being squeezed by his own dissonant views of the world.

Pressure had begun to build during his stints in Glasgow until eventually he had to get away. By coming home he made the problem even worse because his mum was there, lavishing love and approval on him. If she really knew what he did in Glasgow she'd be heartbroken and full of reproach.

Deep down Tony knew that he had a deficit. He

didn't understand it exactly, but clearly his mum was a model of what was right and proper. He could also remember as a lad being taught these things. She had aspirations for him.

These memories were a burden to him and whenever he went home he was constantly reminded of them. There were family photographs on the walls and his old sporting trophies on the mantelpiece. His bedroom was painted in the same colours as when he grew up.

Tony might never be able to articulate his pain and anxiety, but eventually I would expect it to begin spilling over into his day job. He might well gain control of his aggression, but this wouldn't tackle the primary cause of his confusion.

As I've said earlier, one way of dealing with it would be simply not to come home any more. He couldn't do that. He needed somewhere to escape to when the pressures of whacking people became too much. As he grows older, I'd expect these breaks to become more and more necessary.

I had a real soft spot for Tony. He was a very matter-of-fact chap, with a pragmatic view of life. I think he had to develop this perspective, reinventing the people he hunted as 'straw people'; trying to block out their pain, denying to himself the reality of what he was actually doing. He lacked the pleasure gained from pursuing people so evident in the true psychopath, therefore I knew he wasn't driven by his career.

Even so, I wasn't willing to desensitize him from the pain and disquiet created by his day job because although he might then feel better, it wouldn't exactly benefit the community or his potential victims.

My natural inclination was to help Tony understand how he could undo the pain and disquiet by changing what he did for a living. If he failed to do so I knew his effectiveness as a hitman would diminish as his problem grew worse. It might even prompt him to leave.

Resigning from his sort of job would be far more complicated than simply handing in his notice.

He admired his boss. 'He's been good to me,' said Tony. 'There's always a roll of notes, whether there's work or not.'

'What would happen if you left?'

'I don't want to disappoint him.'

'I appreciate that, but what would happen?'

'I don't know. He might not be happy. He appreciates loyalty.'

'But he'd understand?'

'Maybe. I think so. If my mum wasn't well and my mind wasn't on the job.' Tony mulled this over, trying to convince himself. 'Guys like me don't normally retire.'

'What do they do?'

'Some just disappear. Others leg it and spend the rest of their days looking over their shoulder.' I could see his mind pondering these scenarios. 'I suppose I could make it clear to the boss that if I had an inkling he meant me harm, I'd come and sort him out on my own account.'

Oh, my God! I thought.

'I think he'd understand. He's a good boss. He says I'm like a son to him.'

'Even sons have to make their own way in the world.'

'Yeah, I guess so.'

I didn't see Tony again, but I've thought about him often since then. By breaking things down in his complex life and dealing with small parts, he'd slowly become able to deal with the pressures he faced.

This didn't make him a better hitman – perhaps it made him a worse one. I like to think that he changed his career. Then again, I'm also relieved not to know.

17

Throughout the early 1990s I saw the effect of various reorganizations and money-saving exercises at Arnold Lodge, but most of the cracks they created were papered over by hard work.

The forensic service is not a prison. It works with the most difficult patients from the community, which has provided the mandate, saying, 'We are not locking them up and throwing away the key. We want you to treat them, turn them round and rehabilitate them.' That's what we attempt to do.

It will never be the case in a hospital designed to treat and discharge forensic patients that all clinical judgements will be 100 per cent right. There will always be something that goes slightly wrong. This doesn't mean we can be complacent – on the contrary.

If we could press a button and have the answer come out correctly every time, you wouldn't need forensic psychologists and psychiatrists. This is a clinical process. We are not farming cabbages. We are dealing with sentient, pathological, abnormal human beings, who are detained because they represent a danger to the community. It may be tomorrow or five years from now, but there will always be critical incidents. The service will do everything it can, but there will be a next time. And that next time may see somebody hurt, or perhaps die.

Four years had passed since Jimmy arrived at Arnold Lodge – twice as long as most residents stay.

During that time we had looked at the whole range of his intellectual and emotional functioning. It was a mess. Yet throughout it all, he remained a polite, well-mannered man; the same good little soldier whom I'd met in Broadmoor.

Jimmy had refused to acknowledge there was something else that lay behind his attack on the teenage girl whom he had left paralysed. Each time we unpacked what had happened, the result was the same.

When I asked Jimmy if he thought it was the first time that a fellow had been ribbed by a couple of girls on a night out, he said no.

'How often do you think it happens?'

'All the time.'

'How often do you think that fellow kicks the girl until she's almost dead?'

'I dunno.'

'Why did *you* do it?'

'I dunno. I was stressed up. I'd broken up with Amy.'

This didn't wash with me. Just as the attack on the shop assistant had a deeper motive, so did this one.

In my view, Jimmy wasn't stable enough to function in the community at large because nobody had yet discovered what lay behind his index offence. If you don't know what's broken, how can you say it's fixed?

Given a choice, I would have sent him back to Broadmoor, but many of my colleagues weren't happy with this. In a sense they were right. What was the point of sending him back? He'd been there for ten years and no-one had flagged the problem. How could we expect them to treat it?

But what did we do with him at Arnold Lodge?

This is where the pressure on the regional secure units to process people shows. When you have a problem like Jimmy it jars. What do you do?

Internally he still wasn't coping with the therapeutic community. Staff remained reasonably constant but other patients came and went. I no longer worked in that area but dealt with individual patients on other wards and at outpatient clinics.

In the ebb and flow of the therapeutic community, people fell in love, fell in hate, lusted, envied and laid blame. Jimmy tried to be part of all this, but he struggled. In particular, he couldn't deal with women.

He had developed a very simplistic John Wayne approach towards the opposite sex, as was made evident by his behaviour during the hostage crisis a couple of years earlier. At a surface level he wanted and expected to protect them. He had a romantic ideal of the 'fairer sex' being soft and vulnerable.

However, the same view saw Jimmy cut to pieces if a woman made a caustic remark to him. If his old-fashioned romantic overtures were slapped down, he would blame the woman for not being good enough.

Rarely, however, did Jimmy get angry at individuals or the system. Instead he tended to become very quiet and withdrawn as the banter and discussion went on around him.

It was clear to me that he was falling further and further behind the intellectual and emotional movement of the community. He couldn't keep up while around him other patients had progressed.

Jimmy wasn't a bad person. He was damaged. He had grown up isolated because he couldn't hear what people said to him. He had no close friends to take him along and show him the ropes.

Masturbation was a bad thing and probably a sin to Jimmy. It was not something people talked about. Sex was clean and wholesome like in Doris Day movies and 1960s TV sitcoms.

In the early days, Jimmy had tried to start soft, gentle friendships with girls but they had always rebuffed him. He just didn't attract them. When he found a girl, Amy, who did want him, it was the absolute pinnacle of his dreams; all his wishes come true.

Sadly, it didn't last. Increasingly, Jimmy began living in his head. Unfortunately, there wasn't very much in his head to live with. He had all these partial emotions and partial conclusions. He wasn't formally mentally handicapped but he couldn't process and integrate the subtle variables of relationships and emotions. Instead his intellectual deficit was like a black hole in his head that was exacerbated whenever he was put under stress.

On top of this I had a growing conviction that Jimmy had a major psychosexual problem – some deviance that hadn't been flagged and treated, but was connected with his original offences.

It had been several years since I last talked to Jimmy when I was asked to see him again. His case had been nominated for assessment by a tribunal and quite a few health professionals were promoting the idea of his release. Collectively they were arguing, 'What is the probability of him doing it again?'

My answer remained that it all depended on the circumstances.

I could predict their response: 'Oh, come on, he's been in the system for nearly fifteen years. Nothing's happened. There has been no indication of a sexual risk. He's been around women in the therapeutic community. He hasn't attacked them. Don't you think you are being over-cautious?'

The answer remained no. It didn't matter how many years had passed. When the attack happened, it was the most important and profound thing in Jimmy's life, after Amy. Purely through good luck, a young girl survived – otherwise we'd be dealing with a murderer.

My appointment with Jimmy was on Monday morning and I took the case notes home for the weekend to reread them. I had been over this material so many times it came back to me very easily – the story of the chip shop, the ribald exchange with the teenage girls and then going their separate ways.

It was a Saturday evening at about this time of year, I thought as I glanced at the deepening shadows in the late summer garden. I could hear Marilyn packing the dishwasher. Soon she'd ask if I wanted a coffee.

I knew the places Jimmy described in his statement. I'd been to the fish and chip shop. It had a good reputation. Occasionally, if passing through the town, I'd buy lunch there, eating a bag of chips in the car and drinking tea from a polystyrene cup.

What more could I do for Jimmy? Unless I knew exactly what motivated him to attack the girl, I could never put a precise shape to his personality functioning. Without that, I could never sign him off as having been successfully treated.

'Where are you off to?' asked Marilyn, as I put on my shoes and coat.

'I'm going out for a while.'

362

'Don't you want a coffee?' She knew it was work.
'Maybe later.'

After forty-five minutes, I drove into a pub car park.
Jimmy had told me a lot about that evening. I had a
clear picture of so many things but I didn't have
a proper sense of place. What did he see and when did
he see it?

I couldn't rely on street maps. They don't reveal the
light levels or the undulations in the footpaths or
the line of sight. At what point does someone disappear
from view as they walk down this road? Is the path a
regular short cut between obvious locations? How well
lit are the garages where the attack took place?

The only way to get answers to these questions was
to do exactly as I would if asked to investigate an
unsolved crime. I had to walk through the mind of the
man responsible and see the world through his eyes.

I started at the pub where Jimmy had first come
across the teenage girls. A fug of cigarette smoke and
noise spilled out as I opened the door. There were
people two deep at the bar and a jukebox playing.
Places go in and out of fashion on a Saturday night,
but even all this time later it was still a young person's
pub.

Jimmy had arrived at about 8.30 p.m. He had five
pounds in his pocket – enough for a few beers and a
feast of chips on his way home. The girls asked him to
buy them a drink.

He didn't hear them properly at first.

'Are you gonna buy us a drink then?' the dark-haired
girl shouted, nudging her friend.

'I got no money.'

'Oh, come on. You have. You're holdin' out.'

363

Again he couldn't quite hear her, but they were giggling to each other. Both were dressed for a night out in jeans and tight-fitting tops. They wore make-up and had glitter dusting their hair. The music thumped and seemed to shake the floorboards.

I finished my drink and walked outside. Insects danced in the glow of the streetlights. The air smelled cool and damp. In the distance, a dark outline of trees marked the banks of the river.

I turned left and the road curved gently as it skirted behind the main retail strip and headed up towards the church. How much had changed in fifteen years, I wondered? Some of the offices were clearly quite recent additions. The one-way street system had probably been here, although some of the mini-roundabouts might have been added later.

As this was an old market town, there were plenty of pubs to choose from. Jimmy dropped into a few more as he made his way home. He didn't strike up any conversations or bump into friends – he didn't have many.

The fish and chip shop had plastic flags draped from the awning and a blackboard propped on the light pole outside. The smell of frying fish was unmistakable from half a street away. Half a dozen customers waited at the counter. Earlier in the evening a lot would have been picking up dinner for the family. Later, as the pubs shut, another wave would arrive.

I bought a bag of chips – vinegar but no salt. A noisy group of teenagers were chatting to others in a car that had pulled up outside. The stereo was loud.

Remembering Jimmy's account, I pictured the young girls bumping into him again. I have only his description of this. For all I know, he may have followed them from the pub.

'Hey, look who it is! You said you had no money,' they scold him.

'I . . . ah . . . didn't.'

'Get us some chips, then?'

'I'm skint. I just spent the last of it.'

'We'll have yours then,' teases the dark-haired girl.

Jimmy becomes tongue-tied and stressed. His discomfort amuses the girls. They're only playing, no harm intended. Jimmy's cheeks flush and his voice stammers.

The dark-haired girl is slim and tall in her heels. She's pretty and she knows it. There is nothing gawky or ungainly about her. Already she has developed a confidence that young men take much longer to achieve.

According to Jimmy, he left the girls and started walking home. I followed the footpath along the main road, past an estate agent's and a church.

At the next intersection he turned right. He was taking a short cut home across the playing fields. I stopped and I felt that old, cold emptiness. It didn't make sense. Turning right couldn't be a short cut – it took him further away.

I carried straight on for a few minutes. Eventually I stood outside Jimmy's home of fifteen years ago. Then I retraced my steps and turned right on his 'short cut'. The street ran down to playing fields and a playground. I could just make out the swings and the brightly coloured climbing frames reflecting from the lampposts behind me. Otherwise it was bleak and very quiet.

A footpath branched off the road and gently curved across the fields, between the touchline of what looked like a soccer pitch and a tall wooden fence. The path looped around until it rejoined the main road further on. Just before then, it crossed a rough single-lane driveway leading to the rear of a set of garages. This is where the attack had taken place. The young girl's body had been pressed up against one of the roller doors as Jimmy kicked her repeatedly in the head.

According to Jimmy, he'd been taking this short cut home when he came upon the dark-haired teenager. Something had spooked her and she lashed out at him, at which point he 'snapped' and lost his temper.

This was a lie. There was no short cut for him this way. What had really happened here?

Cleaning my glasses, I went back to that night, as the pubs emptied and revellers made their way home. Taking his history and the records of the assault, I ran the scenario in my mind.

Rather than 'coming upon' the girl, Jimmy had followed her. At some point she and her girlfriend had gone their separate ways and he chose to follow the dark-haired girl, who had done most of the teasing.

What did he feel?

Anger. He wanted to confront her. He wanted to tell her what he thought of her and to bring her down a peg or two. But then something else took over . . . arousal.

He pictures her laughing face and her tight jeans. He can still see her outline ahead of him in the darkness. She's confident and pretty. Everything that he'll never have in a woman.

It's dark as she crosses the playing fields. She can't see him. Perhaps she hears a footstep and turns, but there is nothing except blackness and shadows. She knows this area intimately, which is why she isn't scared of walking home at night. But Jimmy knows it, too. It's his patch.

As he follows her, keeping his distance, he remembers how she'd treated him. She's going to pay for putting him down. She has made him feel foolish. She's showed him up. This might not be so to anybody else, but it is true in his mind.

Jimmy doesn't normally feel angry. He avoids anger because he can't cope with where it gets him. As a result, he hasn't developed the means that most people have of regulating themselves. Normally people talk themselves down, or go somewhere quiet until they can get a grip on their emotions. Others cry themselves to sleep or throw crockery at the walls.

Jimmy doesn't have these coping routines. Instead he watches the girl's silhouette ahead of him and thinks, she's not going to get away with this.

As his anger rises, so does his sexual arousal. It's a powerful cocktail of emotions. He didn't start out planning to rape her, but now the idea excites him.

I'm going to have her, he decides. I'm going to make her pay.

He scans the darkness, keeping watch on her on the path. He has to be careful. It's very public. The rec is deserted, but still open. People often walk their dogs late at night or teenage couples find a quiet place to snuggle up.

She turns down the single-lane driveway towards the garages. Here is the place. It has to be now!

Jimmy closes the gap and seizes her. Lust and rage overwhelm him. He tears at her clothes, wanting to rip them away. He's hard. He wants her.

Panic-stricken, she fights back. She can't believe it's him. Her handbag strikes him in the testicles.

Jimmy reacts, lashing out. Her head snaps back and she crumples to the concrete. Barely conscious and trapped against the garage door, she is kicked repeatedly in the face. Her head is bouncing off the door.

Hearing the noise, an elderly couple hurry down the pathway to investigate. Jimmy sees them coming and stops kicking. He's emptied of anger, his arousal is gone. The garage entrances are isolated but well lit. He can't let them see him.

It's only a few minutes to home. He washes and goes to bed, already fearful of what he's done. There is no masturbation or triumphant memory. This time he's gone too far. How long will it be before they come?

Jimmy had put on a little weight since I last saw him and had his hair cut shorter. He still had a boyish face and eager-to-please expression. He had put a pen in his top pocket, perhaps hoping it would make him seem more businesslike.

'Well, Jimmy, here we are again.'

'Yes, Mr Britton.'

'I believe you have a hearing coming up.'

'Yes, Mr Britton.'

'Do you think that they'll send you out?'

'Oh yes, Mr Britton. I've learned a lot in here. I've matured.'

'Jimmy, I want to go back over what happened fifteen years ago.'

His shoulders slumped a little. His eyes were almost pleading with me to let it go.

'I've told you before that I'm not happy. I still don't think we understand what it is that's behind these events. All along you've maintained that you were taking a short cut home when you came across the girl you attacked.'

He nodded.

'But it wasn't a short cut, was it?'

'Yes, it was.'

'When you left the fish and chip shop, why didn't you go directly along the High Street and home?'

'I did go straight home.'

'No, you didn't. You turned off. You went down through the rec. That's not a short cut. It's at least twice as long a walk to get home. I know. I've been there.'

Jimmy said nothing. I could see his stress level rising.

'Why did you go that way?'

He looked down at his hands.

'You went that way because that's where she went. You followed her.'

He didn't look at me.

'Jimmy, when we talked about you stabbing the shop assistant, eventually you told me what happened, that you fancied her and it went wrong. There is a sexual element here as well. I know it and you know it. I can't force you to tell me, but I'm not going to give up.'

His mind was in turmoil. He was angry and disappointed. He hated the fact that I demanded things of him. Silence and good behaviour had always been enough for everybody else.

'Listen, Jimmy.' I leaned closer towards him and made sure he could hear every word. 'I won't ever feel comfortable saying, "I think you're ready to leave here," until we get to the truth of this. I'm not trying to trap you or pin you down. You've already spent fifteen years in the hospital system. To some degree you've been let down because we haven't found a way of helping you to tell us what really happened. What I do know, without any doubt, is that if we let you go home today or tomorrow you are just as big a danger as the day you came in.'

Jimmy looked stunned. He chewed at his bottom lip and refused to look directly at me. Shifting in his seat, he stared out of the narrow window. The clouds had started closing in after a sunny morning.

'You've done a lot for me, Mr Britton. You've put in a lot of time. I can talk to you.'

I waited as he chose his words.

'I suppose I might as well tell you the truth. You seem to understand.'

What he really meant was that I hadn't believed him. I wouldn't let it go.

'I was going to rape her,' he said.

'What happened?'

He took me back to the very beginning and described how he had followed the girls from the fish and chip shop. The scenario was very close to the one I had played out in my mind when I visited the scene. Jimmy trailed the dark-haired teenager, wanting to punish her, but these feelings had been overtaken by sexual arousal.

Having unburdened himself, Jimmy found it much easier to talk about a whole range of feelings and thoughts. As with so many secrets, it's often far easier to let them go than to spend enormous psychological energy trying to hold them back.

In particular I was able to explore Jimmy's masturbatory fantasies. I discovered a series of scenarios, some of which included coercion and control. Yet unlike in the case of Ray Knox, it wasn't the pathology of the fantasy system that drove him. Instead this young man had a strong need for sexual expression but not the social skills and knowledge to satisfy it.

370

He had grown up as a loner, with poor hearing and verbal skills. As a result he became very sensitive to being hurt and sexually frustrated at not being able to develop good, ordinary relationships.

As he matured into adolescence and beyond, Jimmy's sexual fantasies became increasingly aggressive. They weren't highly sophisticated abduction and torture scenarios. Instead they focused on sexual conquest rather than degradation. He wanted to get his own back. 'Take this, you bitch! I'm the man.'

In many ways his fantasies came to mirror his predicament; he didn't value others because they didn't value him. Eventually, the anger, bitterness and resentment consumed him and his sexuality and aggression became inextricably linked.

I don't know exactly what triggered his explosive rage when he attacked the dark-haired girl. Perhaps he lost his erection or maybe, as Jimmy claimed, the girl did hit him in the testicles as she fought back. Regardless of how she responded the outcome would most likely have been the same. He was far too enraged to have listened to her pleadings, even if he had been able to hear her.

Having discovered how Jimmy functioned and what drove him, I now had a new challenge. Recognition is one thing, effective treatment quite another.

Jimmy had overcome a major hurdle by finally admitting the sexual motive behind his index offence. This meant, however, that he wasn't going back to the community. A treatment programme now had to be devised that addressed the true issues.

No system, however, is perfect. There are always pressures for beds, to move people on. Regional secure units are at the sharp end of decision-making. In a special hospital you don't have to worry about parole beyond the perimeter – the person is detained indefinitely and, in difficult cases, will go through an RSU rather than to the community. At Arnold Lodge the decision to release somebody always has immediate real-world consequences.

With somebody as apparently docile and ordinary as Jimmy, it was very easy to believe the job was almost done. That's why his treatment had tended to focus on his social and reasoning deficits rather than sexual aggression. The therapeutic machine had rolled on for years and, like a snowball down a hill, it couldn't easily change direction.

I didn't hear of Jimmy for another year. The news when it arrived almost defied belief. There had to be some mistake. How could he be in prison? How could he have been let out without supervision, to attempt another rape?

The ramifications were being felt everywhere. Questions had been asked in Parliament. Explanations were being sought.

The story that emerged is a classic lesson in the dangers of believing that time cures all ills.

Jimmy hadn't been sent back to Broadmoor. Nor had the therapeutic machine focused on the true problem behind his index offence. In reality, very little work had been done on Jimmy's sexual problems; his assurances that all of that was in the past had been accepted.

The emphasis of his treatment remained on insight and problem solving. And because he was well behaved he entered the next stage on the road to freedom – escorted walks in the grounds of the hospital. Soon he progressed to unescorted walks in the grounds and then accompanied trips to the local shops with a member of staff.

As always, Jimmy didn't prove to be a problem. Eventually he reached the stage of going out on his own – normally down to the shops or the cinema. He caught a bus into town and back again.

However, on the day in question, Jimmy chose another activity. He visited a local massage parlour and tried to rape a young woman who worked there. He denied this, of course. He went hoping to pay for sex, he said, and she just started screaming.

Soon afterwards, Jimmy was committed to a special hospital to be detained indefinitely. He's still there now, as far as I'm aware.

An interesting postscript to this story emerged a year or so later when I was asked to examine Jimmy once more, at his specific request. I drove north to Rampton Special Hospital, located in remote countryside in Nottinghamshire, some six miles outside Retford. Spread over a wide campus, the wards are surrounded by perimeter walls and fences. Unlike Broadmoor, the hospital fits into the landscape rather than oppresses it.

As I walked into the interview room, Jimmy looked up from his chair and recoiled as though struck with a cattle prod. Until then, I don't think he realized what his request meant.

His face still had a youthful roundness, but his hair had started to thin. He had put on weight, although he was still obviously a fit man. His light grey trousers rode up over his black socks and slip-on shoes.

I sat down, pressed my fingers together and looked at him intently.

'Do you think I should be here?'

'Yes, it is your job to be here.'

'Do you know why I am here? I have to give an opinion on whether you are ready to go into the community.'

He nodded glumly.

'I will be honest and straightforward with you, Jimmy. I'm not here to fit you up, but I'm not going to hide anything either. I have no choice but to look at everything that has happened and what treatments you have and haven't had. We have been down this road before. You know that I can't let it go.'

He nodded.

'Are you really sure that you want me to do this?'

'Ah . . . um . . . I don't really know.'

'Why did you ask me to come here then?'

'Well, I didn't like to say no. I thought you might be offended if I didn't ask you. We go back, you and me.'

I smiled, but I could have wept. The man in front of me was a violent, narcissistic sex offender, but at the same time he was still the confused, deferential, polite young man whom I had first met in Broadmoor six years earlier.

Jimmy hadn't changed . . . and that was the problem.

18

'Mr Britton, I think you better take this from me.'

Ray pulled a hammer from beneath his jacket. He clutched the handle, with the heavy end pointed at me. The silver head was pitted and scarred.

I stared at the implement, painfully aware of my vulnerability. The door was closed. The nearest help was down the corridor. How long would it take them to reach me? Far too long, I decided. Best to go with it.

Patients have handed me all sorts of things – knives, clubs, guns, bars ... That first moment when the weapon is pulled into view is guaranteed to make the heart pound. It's also a telling reminder to be vigilant.

'Why are you giving me this?' I asked, feeling the coldness of the hammer against my palm.

'It's best that you have it.'

'Why?'

'Because I might hurt someone with it.'

He drew a heavy chain from his overcoat pocket.

'You better take this as well.'

I put the hammer and chain in my desk drawer. The metal echoed against the wood.

Ray sat down and looked relieved. He was also waiting for some sort of commendation from me, like a schoolboy who'd handed over a catapult and confessed to breaking the canteen window.

Although this was a very positive development, it wasn't a dramatic turning point or breakthrough. Cases like Ray's rarely have them. The process is long and drawn out with each step won at a cost.

When I first met Ray, I had told him that I needed to answer two questions. 'Who are you? And how did you come to be who you are?'

It had taken months to get the answers. Sometimes I had a child in front of me; at other times an adult who raged against me. I could also, if I created the right circumstances, see the predator.

Knowing these things about Ray, though, wasn't enough. Neither was it enough simply to hold him in check and stop him acting on his deviant urges. Unless I could pick up the pieces of his life, he remained a grave risk.

Unfortunately, it was not something a cup of tea and a biscuit could make better. Nor could I say, 'Relax, Ray, that's all in the past. Forget about it.'

Not every child who is abused is psychologically scarred. Even if they are haunted by the memories, many victims manage to lead reasonably normal lives.

In every case of abuse there is an interaction between the abused and the abuser. All children are not the same. They are not all uniquely pure and potentially perfect white canvases. Nor are they lumps of formless clay that can be moulded to fit any shape.

Ray had been a very sensitive boy, with a tendency to be introspective and even introverted. If he had been different, his father's violence might not have had the same impact upon his life. He might not have been so badly affected by such a legacy.

I'm not making excuses for his father. What he did was unforgivable. I'm simply stating the fact that Ray, quite innocently, had characteristics that magnified the effects of the abuse.

As with all of us, a range of circumstances had come together to create the person sitting in front of me. Ray had very few older male role models in his life. He had no uncles or teachers who might have shown him that not all men were the same. His father had been such a strong personality that for Ray it was like having a great searchlight shining in his eyes. He didn't see the less powerful torches held by others. Even his mother had abandoned him to save herself.

For all his thoughts and fantasies of murder, Ray wanted to be stopped. At the same time he wanted to succeed. This was his ambivalence.

What he most wanted to hear me say was, 'You poor thing, this is all your father's fault.'

I wouldn't give him this. I couldn't justify his murderous feelings, no matter how terribly his father had treated him. Doing so would have given him an excuse for his behaviour. He could say to himself, 'I am helpless in the grip of these forces. If I kill somebody, it won't really be my fault. I'm a victim.'

Ray's entire rationale was to blame his father for everything negative in his life and not look any further. My task was to get him to look at himself and to redefine how he labelled his pain.

First I had to help him understand and accept his father. This was a terrible task.

'Let me ask you a question, Ray. Do you think your father is unique?'

'What do you mean?'

'Well, you've described what he did to you. It certainly wasn't loving or nurturing. He denied you so many of the things a child needs. Does that make him unique?'

Ray knew what I was asking, but wouldn't have it. The muscles in his neck tensed. I could see the tell-tale tracks of veins beneath his skin. He had expected me to side with him unconditionally. He wanted me to legitimize his anger. He didn't want me to turn the spotlight on anything else.

'What are you saying? That fucking bastard! How can you say that? You're taking his side.'

'I'm simply asking you if you think your father is unique.'

'I told you what he did.'

'Yes. But does that make him unique?'

'He's a fucking monster.'

I spoke very softly, as though talking to an angry child. I knew it hurt, but I needed Ray to look at things in a slightly different way.

'Are you unique?' I asked him.

'What do you mean?' His voice had a menacing edge.

'Every individual is different – even identical twins are never totally the same. What do you think?'

'I suppose.'

'Looking at the terrible things that happened to you at your father's hands, do you think they make you unique? Are there other children who have had similar experiences?'

'I only know about me.'

'What if I were to tell you that a lot of people suffer terrible childhoods, full of violence and abuse. It shouldn't happen. There are no excuses. But, sadly, it goes on every day of the week. Is that something you would accept?'

'Yeah.'

'Now how many of those children do you think will grow up and come to see someone like me?'

'I don't know.'

'Some do. You did. Some will see other psychologists who work in different areas of speciality. Most don't see anyone at all. Why is that, do you think?'

'What is this, twenty questions? You're supposed to be helping me. Why are you asking me all this stuff? I don't know the answers. You trying to be funny?'

Ray had become tense and agitated. There were the beginnings of hostility. If I were a radio, he would have switched me off. Of course, he could have simply stood up and walked out, but we had reached a point in our relationship where he found it hard to escape. The rapport between us had led to expectations.

This is similar in many ways to the expectations that politicians and political interviewers have when they sit down in front of the cameras. It is a very controversial event to see a minister stand up, brush aside a microphone and walk off. This is because there is a strong social pressure to stay and enact the implicitly agreed role.

Slowly, I tried to have Ray look more closely at himself. Until then he had automatically blamed his father and looked no further. Now I wanted him to consider the possibility that there were other factors involved.

I took him back to the original question, 'Is your father unique?'

'No.'

'And what about you? When you look at the damage done and the failed ambitions, are you unique?'

'I guess not.'

'So, why is it that the great majority of people who suffer as you did don't end up seeing me? What happens to them?'

'How should I know?'

'Let me tell you about some of them. Many of them have very sad lives. They don't fulfil their potential or achieve their goals. But at the same time, they don't become risks to themselves or to others. A goodly number actually get past it, in spite of all the difficulties.'

I expanded on this, giving Ray examples. Then I turned the conversation back to him.

'OK. Why is it that *you* are here now, with me, discussing these things?'

'Well, because of my father.'

'Yes, we know that your father is a contributor. We know he had a terrible effect. But we also know that this isn't the whole story. What is it about *you*?'

'Why are you being such a bastard to me?'

'I don't think I am, Ray. I'm simply trying to look at things from a different perspective.'

'You're trying to blame me. How can it be my fault?'

'I'm not blaming you. No man should have done to them what your father did. But you've already accepted that not everyone who suffers the way you did finishes up sitting in front of a psychologist. Your father isn't the whole story. What is it about *you* that brings you to me?'

A long silence followed. Tears welled in his eyes. He vainly tried to hold them back. With a long, deep, racking sob, all the anger and tension spilled away like the tears that ran down his cheeks.

I kept talking to him gently. 'I am not a judge, Ray. I don't judge people in the way that you judge your father and the rabbits. That's not my job. Nor am I here to hurt you. My role is to try to understand what is going on. I'm trying to help you.'

As the tears continued falling, I recognized within the adult body elements of the little boy who needed his hurt to be taken away. At that moment I suspect Ray finally realized that I was never going to validate his plans of revenge.

A part of him wanted to walk out. He didn't because I was now important to him. I knew his worst secrets and had never rebuked or criticized him.

Because I couldn't change what his father had done, I had to help Ray to change. I had to get inside his head, extremely carefully, and help him to know how important it was to try to undo the damage that he had suffered. We had to make it safe for *him*, as well as everybody else.

Many strands had to be considered. Although I might take one and analyse it and work it through, I had to be constantly aware that, as in my analogy of the fishing net, the human mind is made up of millions of knots. Some you have to open and untie. Some you have to cut out and let fall away, then build a new knot to replace it. All the knots connect to one another. If some are retied in the wrong positions, or incorrectly, the whole net is awry. This weakness might not be obvious until later when the net breaks, or doesn't work as well.

For Ray, this next stage of the process would span years. After helping him see the world through the eyes of others, I had to introduce him to the real man that his father was – the damaged individual, not just the monster.

Among the details that emerged was that his father's first marriage had failed because he felt his wife played fast and loose. Ray didn't readily volunteer this information. He didn't want to give his father any excuses, so he had pushed this knowledge out of his thinking.

'That must have been difficult for him,' I said.

'I'm not here to talk about him. You're trying to defend him.'

'No, I'm trying to discover more about him.'

Ray exploded. 'Well, he wasn't special. You can't pretend he was some perfect person. He spent five weeks in a mental hospital . . .'

'How did that come about?'

'It doesn't matter.'

'I'm interested.'

'He couldn't cope with losing his wife. He cracked up.'

'How long was this before he met your mother?'

'I don't know – I wasn't there obviously.'

Ray fought against me. He accused me of twisting his words. He was bright enough to see where I was taking him.

'You're just like him, aren't you? You're criticizing me. You're all the same. I should kill you all.'

Many times Ray wanted to close the door on me or turn me off, but he had too much invested in me to walk away. He hated me, but nevertheless still wanted my approval.

Often I had to approach my line of reasoning obliquely so that Ray didn't anticipate and blindly turn away from where I was taking him.

'What is the job of a judge?' I asked him during one session.

'He is there to send people down.'

'Is that all that judges do?'

'What do you mean?'

'OK, let's leave that for a moment. When you hold your trials you take the role of the judge and also the prosecutor. What other parts are there to a trial?'

'There's a jury.'

'Yes?'

'And the bloke being tried.'

'Does he have anyone?'

'Yeah, the defence lawyer.'

'What is the job of the defence?'

'To get the bastard off!'

'In all my experiences of the legal system I've never seen a case as black and white as you describe.'

'What do you mean?'

'Well, I've been an expert witness at quite a few trials. Sometimes I've been commissioned by the defence and at other times by the prosecution. In your courtroom everything is painted black or white. There are no shades of grey. There are no mitigating circumstances.'

'That's just a fancy phrase used to get people off.'

'You're right about that – up to a point. Defence lawyers do occasionally get people off who are guilty. But let me tell you what normally happens. Far more often the defence is simply helping a person give his or her side of the story. That's a basic right that all accused people have.'

I let this sink in and then continued: 'As a judge, part of your absolute duty is to make sure you hear from both sides of the case and give everyone a fair crack.'

The penny dropped. Ray covered his ears. 'You can't

make excuses for him. Look at me! Look at what he did! My whole life is ruined . . .'

The two driving forces in Ray's life were his desire for revenge and his love for his wife and children. I had to use the more positive of these – his family – as a way of keeping him in check.

Despite all the dreadful traumas of his childhood a part of him had risen above it. Look at his marriage. Look at his children.

'I know what your father did to you, but have you ever even slightly done that to your children?'

'No.'

'Why not?'

'I wouldn't do that.'

'Why do you think that? Why haven't you passed on the same sort of violence to your children?'

'I just wouldn't. I love them.'

'So clearly a part of you has managed to stay secure and intact after all that has happened to you. You have created a little island – your family. All marriages have their difficulties, but you and Stella are still together.'

'Yes.'

'You didn't punish her. You didn't beat her up. You didn't turn on her.'

'No.'

'And that's because you, Ray Knox, despite all that's happened, are essentially a good human being. That is what we have to build from.'

Ray had always imagined that if he killed his father there would be a sort of metamorphosis in him. All of his pain would be wiped clean and he'd suddenly be a complete human being. This wasn't just about vengeance, it was about rebirth, he thought.

I had to change this thinking. I had to show him what the real outcome would be.

'What happens when you get dragged away and sent to prison for life?'

'I wouldn't be caught,' he said.

'Oh, come on, Ray. We both know they'll find you. They'll lock the door and throw the key away. How will your children feel if their father is sent to jail for murder?'

'I won't let them take me. I'll shoot it out. They won't take me alive.'

Because of his visualization capacity, I knew Ray could picture outcomes very clearly. He could see the police cars arriving, the mêlée of shots as he went down fighting, almost heroically.

As this scene played out in his head he relaxed back into his chair. The ending was still OK.

I countered this image with another.

'So you're willing to die for what your father did to you?'

'Too right.'

'What about Julie and Rita?'

'What about them?'

'Are they going to see you being gunned down? Will they see you lying there in a pool of blood? And then there's Stella. What words is she going to use to explain to them where Daddy is?'

Ray became very agitated. Again I had questioned his plans. First it had been his courtroom and now it was his vision of a heroic death. I hadn't often confronted a patient so aggressively, but in this instance it was necessary.

'Julie and Rita won't know the background. All

385

they'll see is a perverted monster – their father – who has gone out and killed. Your face will be splashed over the newspapers and TV. They'll probably label it a homosexual crime because you stripped a man naked and left him in the woods. What will your girls think then?'

Ray blustered, 'Well, that's not what I'm . . . I don't . . . they wouldn't . . . I'll write them a letter. I'll explain things.'

'What good will that do? If you had a letter tomorrow from your father explaining why he abused you and apologizing, what good would that do? Would it make up for it?'

'No.'

He leaped to his feet, screaming at me to shut up. He covered his ears with his hands. For a moment I feared for the filing cabinet again. I could still see the repair job where the new paint didn't quite cover the dent.

When we read about somebody being arrested, tried and convicted of child abuse, we often think the case is closed. But it's never closed for the victim – not even when he or she is grown up. What you often see, as with Ray, is that five, ten or twenty years later you have an adult whose whole life has been distorted and damaged by what happened to them in childhood.

All the rich possibilities and potential have gone. The only thing to do is to help repair whatever is left. In his case, it was not until eighteen months after meeting him that I could watch Ray leave my consulting room without some anxiety that he might hurt somebody.

This is where my police work affects my clinical work. Sitting at the back of my mind is a thought that shouldn't really be there: the notion that one day I may be called to a crime scene and find a naked middle-aged man sitting in a deckchair.

This is what I dread.

Ray had come a long way, but had a lot further to go. His entire existence had been focused on his deviant fantasies and desire for revenge. If I managed to take this away, what would replace it?

Ray also realized this. During one session, he asked me, 'What am I going to have left? I'm not going to be me any more. I won't exist.'

He had come to rely upon his deviant, negative, narcissistic self-being. Now he was frightened that if I took these characteristics away, he wouldn't be able to cope with the result. All his life he had regarded himself as a victim. This gave him self-respect and a certain dignity; it wasn't his fault.

I could understand this fear. Ray didn't know anything else. The terrible pain had become almost all of him. Without it, he'd cease to exist.

'We're going to find things to replace the pain,' I told him. 'We're going to look again for the things that were available to the young boy you once were; the things that filled your dreams, wishes and hopes. Hopefully, you'll be able to do some of those things you always wanted.'

He looked at me as if I was suggesting the impossible.

I had two new questions for Ray and they were almost the opposite of those I had first asked him: 'Who *can* you be? And how do we get you there?'

If I helped him recognize the strengths and assets that he possessed, these would begin to offset the deficits and self-pity.

It can be a luxurious feeling to blame somebody or something for all your problems. There are no demands or responsibilities. 'I am defective and it is not my fault.'

Very occasionally I have seen this with people who have been disabled and make no effort to rehabilitate themselves. It is as though they say, 'I have my ticket. From now on I'll be looked after.'

Ray had these feelings of self-pity. He could legitimize his hatred and immerse himself in thoughts of failure. To counter this, I gave him coping strategies that allowed him to say, 'Hang on. Look at what's good in your life. You don't have to focus on him any more. If you hurt him you give him more power. Focus on the good life you will give to your children. You can shake off the damage he did.'

I built thought loops with him that would act as brakes for his behaviour. One of these was to think of the consequences – the risk of losing his wife and children. A secondary thought loop allowed him to see his father as a defective and damaged human being, deserving of pity.

There were some bloody-minded battles during these weekly and fortnightly sessions. At times Ray grew frustrated at my asking the same questions or probing him about his movements.

'You're still trying to hide from this,' I told him. 'I know you've been out cruising. I'm not going to criticize you. I understand the pressures you feel. But it does no earthly good lying to me, or simply saying, "Sorry, you're right. I couldn't remember."'

Ray looked downcast. He didn't want to disappoint me.

'So, where did you go?'

'To my father's house.'

'Why? What were you thinking about?'

'I wanted to go. I sat outside the house.'

'Look at the risks you are taking. What about Stella and the girls?'

He shook his head.

'What about the alternative thought loops? Why weren't you able to use them? What was the problem?'

He shrugged.

Another time I discovered that Ray had been writing letters to his father – hateful diatribes that detailed what he wanted to do to him. Thankfully, the letters hadn't been posted. Ray brought them to me instead.

'Every day you continue to allow your life to be closed down by what your father did to you, you increase the power of the man that he was. How many years ago was it?'

'Thirty-odd.'

'If you met him now and he took you back inside your old house, what would happen?'

'I'd rip him to pieces.'

'Why?'

'Because he's an old man.'

'That's right. Yes, you could do that, you're certainly strong enough – but then what? You rip him to bits and what happens tomorrow? Nothing! You don't have to allow this man's hold on you to continue. You can stop this.'

'How?' He looked at me, almost pleading.

'You know the answer. Yes, he damaged your life, but it's not your problem – it's his. Don't let him keep doing this to you.'

'It's easy for you to say that.'

'If this man had broken your legs so badly they had to be amputated, I couldn't say, "Forget all about it, just walk away." But the damage he did to you is psychological. It *is* possible to repair that. Nothing that we do here is going to change the past. Nothing we do will take away all the pain. But we can draw a line and start from a new place.

'Look at what you've achieved. Others who have suffered like you have lost everything – their wives, children, jobs, home. Many commit suicide or become alcoholics. They finish up in prisons and special hospitals. But you, Ray, in spite of everything, have managed to hold on. That really sets you apart.'

In the months that followed, I helped Ray improve his social skills and confidence. It had been years since he'd popped down to the local pub and had a pint with the lads. He didn't think people were interested in him because he was such a failed human being. In truth, they didn't even know him. Ray had locked himself away.

'What are you going to do with the next forty years?' I asked.

'What do you mean?'

'Well, you don't want to kill your father or anyone else. We know that. So what is the point of your life going to be? What is the aim?'

'I'll watch my children grow up.'

'Good.'

'And I'm back at work.'

'Great. What else do you like doing?'

He shrugged.

'Between now and our next meeting, I want you to go to your local library and get a list of what's happening in town. I'm not saying you should join a club or take up a hobby, that's probably asking too much at this stage. But at least we can talk about activities which might interest you.'

The following week he arrived with a brochure about a rock-climbing weekend for beginners. It took him another fortnight to phone the number. On the Thursday before the course, he was like a nervous schoolboy – excited and anxious all at once.

I didn't know if he'd make it, or cry off at the last minute. If he didn't do it on this occasion, then maybe next time. The process was like learning to walk again after a stroke. You start with small steps, not all of them in the right direction.

Ray was learning to focus on positive thoughts and push away the deviant drives. The aim wasn't to create some unattainable flawless core state. Nobody's life can be made perfect. Treatment had finally allowed Ray to come to terms with his abuse in childhood and to be freed from the burning need to kill his father. More than that, the best Ray could hope for was ordinary existence, just like the rest of us.

19

At home one evening I had a call from a Scottish journalist working in Glasgow. He wanted me to comment on the murder of several prostitutes north of the border.

'They're saying it might be another ripper,' he said, with obvious excitement. 'How would other prostitutes be feeling?'

It was a silly question. He spoke as though prostitutes belonged to a different class of humanity from the rest of us – as though they didn't share the same hopes, dreams and fears.

Prostitutes are ordinary women who have many different reasons for selling their bodies. Society perceives prostitution as a career that attracts girls from the gutter or the wrong side of the tracks, but it's not only the daughters of troubled or deprived families who are destined to become prostitutes. It can be the well-bred and educated daughters of perfectly ordinary, stable families.

Prostitutes hurt too. I have seen them dead. I've seen them alive. I've kept them out of prison and treated them when they've come from prison. And yet they remain fundamentally misunderstood.

Several years ago I gave a presentation to the Association of Chief Police Officers (ACPO) crime committee at the headquarters of Hampshire constabulary. Another speaker at the meeting was a senior woman detective who, afterwards over a drink at the local pub, was keen to talk about psychological profiling generally, and in particular about the murder of a young prostitute in London, who had been disembowelled. The inquiry team had recently been stood down after the prime suspect was acquitted of the killing.

So as not to influence my opinions, she presented the case to me as if it was a new offence – concealing any details of the suspect. Because I couldn't visit the crime scene, I warned that my advice had to be limited.

Jenny had been what you might call a classic prostitute. She had done many of the right things in terms of protecting herself. She had an agency and a telephone that would filter clients. She was on the first floor, which is safer than being at ground level. The entry mechanism had an intercom and closed-circuit TV link.

She had taken all these precautions, yet she lay naked on her bed with her entrails beside her. Her upper body and genitalia had not been damaged.

After studying the photographs and statements, I took the view that the killer had a very particular and deviant interest in his victim's reproductive system – her breasts, womb, Fallopian tubes, etc.

This man's urge wasn't to dominate, humiliate or punish a woman for being sexually threatening. Nor did he focus on her pain for his intense sexual release. His interest had nothing to do with the sexual coupling between a man and a woman. He was entranced and coldly angry at the mother (his mother) who, he would say, had seduced him into wanting her. This, he believed, had then contaminated all his future relationships with women.

I went on to describe the psychological, demographic and other background elements that I could attribute to the murderer. This both excited and saddened the detective because the offender profile proved to be an exact match for the acquitted man.

'The killer will strike again,' I said. 'He's not going away.'

This case cropped up again a few weeks later, when another inquiry team approached me. The man acquitted for the earlier murder had started to spy on women again, particularly those who were similar in appearance to the first victim.

After being questioned on the suspect's likely future behaviour, I was asked to design and monitor a covert operation that would divert his attention towards a woman who would act as a decoy for the police. If the man chose to attack her, the police could then arrest him.

Financial factors delayed the operation and the suspect became aware the police were shadowing him. He went underground. If this man had killed Jenny, then he'd be back again.

The ethics of the covert operation intrigued me, not just at the time but also much later when Colin Stagg's acquittal for the murder of Rachel Nickell caused a furore over the use of such practices. I couldn't see why it was acceptable to create a crime opportunity for a serious suspect and charge him if he enacted it, but it was unacceptable to explore, by covert means, what a suspect might already have done or not done.

* * *

People very quickly jump to conclusions when they see a murder such as Jenny's. There is an expectation that it *must* involve a 'slayer' or a 'ripper'.

I remember another crime I had to look at where a prostitute was found in an old garage forecourt in Leicester, with her throat cut and her body completely drained of blood. Oh God, what have we got here, the detectives thought, this has to be some weird vampire slaying. This is just the sort of notion that starts the hare running, particularly if the media gets wind of it.

The rational explanation was that the poor woman had been killed elsewhere. Her throat had been cut and she'd been left where she fell with her feet higher than her head on a flight of stairs, where gravity pulled the blood from her. Later, her killer had put her in a bath and washed her because the sight of blood put him off.

This was a much simpler and more plausible scenario than having a vampire slayer on the loose.

It is a sad fact that people don't treat the murder of a prostitute in the same way as they treat the murder of some other poor unfortunate woman. Even the police approach the scene with a different attitude. I'm not saying that they take their eyes off the ball. They are simply not seeing the same quality of human being.

There is a stereotypical view that degrades prostitutes. They are deemed to be all the same, so therefore they are all killed for the same reason, regardless of where or how they are found.

Prostitutes are individual people and so are the men who kill them. Jack the Ripper chose his particular victims, in part, because they were available and he could get close to them. He could also get away with indolent ease.

In more recent times, when Michael Sams wanted to

practise his elaborate abduction and ransom plan, he chose Julie Dart as his first victim because she suited his wider criminal purpose. As a part-time prostitute, she was inexperienced so easier to acquire and more anonymous than most women. Her disappearance wouldn't create the same headlines as abducting, say, a schoolgirl on her way home.

Michael Sams didn't want to have sex with Julie Dart. Nor did he expect her family to be rich enough to pay a ransom demand. He was only interested in the teenager because he needed a manageable woman to kill, so he could convince the police that he was to be regarded as a serious adversary.

Although Julie was fairly similar to many girls who drift into prostitution, each of them is unique. She was an attractive girl, five foot nine inches tall with brown eyes and shoulder-length curly brown hair, normally tied back. She had a distinctive chipped front top tooth.

At school she'd been a promising athlete, winning dozens of medals and trophies. She carried on running after she left at the age of sixteen and got a job at a High Street chain store. According to friends, she enjoyed karaoke nights and going out for a drink.

She hadn't been a prostitute very long and only worked part-time when her life collided with that of Michael Sams. He crushed the back of her head with a blunt instrument and dumped her body in a muddy field eighty miles south of Leeds. He later went on to kidnap the estate agent Stephanie Slater before being caught.

When I think of Julie, I think of another case – a wisp of a girl, barely eighteen years old, who had been charged and convicted of stabbing a man with a knife. I first saw her in Holloway Prison – one of the most repellent of all the prisons I've seen.

Mandy came from Leicestershire and had a fairly ordinary childhood in a stable family and a comfortable middle-class home. Although not a particularly bright student at school, she was always the apple of her parents' eye – particularly her father's.

As she grew into a teenager, she became more independent and slightly unruly. She showed signs of wanting to be her own person, but this didn't please her father. She no longer fitted his model of the perfect daughter. He called her a tart – which she wasn't – and berated her for not being good enough. Nothing she did was right.

Eventually Mandy moved out of the family home because of the friction. It was all downhill from there. She fell in with a crowd who introduced her to drugs – not hard drugs, but they were moving in that direction.

She found herself a little bedsit and wanted to be a beautician. Unintentionally she became pregnant by her long-term boyfriend. He didn't stick around for the birth and left her to cope alone.

Mandy swallowed her pride and went back home with her child. She tried not to listen to her father deriding her as a 'worthless slut'. But the final straw came when he put her baby in the dustbin.

She left the house and found a flat. She couldn't work and look after the baby so the debts began to mount. Before long she fell under the influence of a man who was, in fact, a pimp. These men tend to prey on certain types of vulnerable women. They can smell the desperation and the poverty.

He began by becoming Mandy's lover and helping to support her. Then he gradually introduced other men and asked her to help out with the money.

'He's a mate of mine and he fancies you. Just this once.'

When Mandy refused, he grew angry. He accused her of being ungrateful. 'Do you think I'm made of money? Why can't you do your bit?'

Just the once turned into twice and three times. Before she knew it, Mandy was on the game.

Different clients look for different things in different girls. Mandy looked particularly young and childlike. She attracted the sort of men who enacted child abuse scenarios in their minds. As a result, she was grossly violated and brutalized.

At one point she was imprisoned in a flat for an entire weekend and used sexually. The man refused to pay. Mandy complained to her pimp, but he blamed her. He claimed she'd got the money and was holding out on him. He began to beat her with a broom handle.

Finally something snapped inside her. She picked up a pair of scissors and stabbed him in the abdomen. That's how she finished up in Holloway Prison.

In the course of my work, I've come across girls who become prostitutes to service a drug habit and others who use the money to work their way through college. Some are well educated and sophisticated, with lovely houses in nice areas and their children at private schools. They work the high-class hotels, or for agencies that rent them out for thousands of pounds a night as escorts. Most are very good at what they do and they enjoy the trappings of their success.

They say things like: 'I have an attractive body. I like nice things. Why shouldn't I let one pay for the other?' or, 'It's no different to a rugby player taking money because he's good at kicking and passing a ball,' or, 'I can certainly fake an orgasm and I meet some very rich people.'

Some finish up married to these rich men. Others lead almost double lives, working a few nights a week and spending the rest of their time as homemakers and mothers.

Among these women, there are those who enjoy the work. It's exciting to mingle with people who have power and influence. And they love the sense of control they feel in those last few seconds before a man ejaculates. They can look into his eyes and believe they truly rule the world.

Such women are very different from the young girls on the streets. They normally invest their money wisely and get out before they lose their looks. Very rarely do you find an ageing high-class courtesan working the streets.

Life is very different at the bottom end of the scale. Even so, I can understand how people like Mandy, Tracy Turner and Julie Dart fall through the net. The prostitutes I have seen in my consulting room have been there for all sorts of reasons. Some were crime victims, or criminals, or had been damaged psychologically. Others suffered anxiety problems, phobias and difficulty in coping. I even had one who complained of her increasing difficulty in having sex.

This was the experience I called upon when I helped identify the naked body of Tracy Turner in March 1993. It was there in the back of my mind when I drew up a psychological profile of her killer. I delivered this to David Cox several days before Tracy was identified.

The murder squad assembled at Leicester police headquarters for the briefing.

'This man will be in his mid-twenties to mid-thirties,'

I said. 'He is not going to have a stable career and will have worked at a fair few manual jobs.

'He is a traveller, it's his job. Look at where he left the body. Bitteswell and Woodby Lane are hard to find, even when you're looking. For this reason I think he has some knowledge of the immediate area.'

I asked them to look at the scene against the bigger picture. If Woodby Lane were not a dead end it would almost run into the A5. Less than five minutes away is Junction 20 of the M1. Traffic moves between the M6 and the M1 at Lutterworth – Junction 20 again. The M69 crosses the A5 a few miles away and a side road off the A5 brings you almost straight to the western end of Bitteswell where the body was dumped.

'This man knows the Midlands – not just the macro-geography, but the micro-geography as well. He knows it as a driver.'

'That hardly narrows it down,' said a young detective with short-cropped hair.

'Yes, but I'm talking about someone who has driven or drives for a living. Also someone who uses common street prostitutes and kills them for a particular reason.

'There are two main factors behind this woman's death – anger and expediency. He didn't carefully plan this murder. Nor did he act out a sexual fantasy. He had chosen an unremarkable victim and made no dramatic statement at the scene when he dumped her body. He hadn't bound her or played with her for some refined sadistic purpose. Nor does he seem interested in boasting about his crime on a big scale.

'It's a farmyard murder, brutal, brief, one animal goring what it sees as another, just because it's expedient. There's no real reflection, no particular pleasure,' I said. 'He's not really a planner – he reacts. That's why he left behind his DNA.

'He's arrogant. He needs to be in command of situations with women. If he gets anxious about his sexual performance, or feels sexually threatened or scorned, his anger boils over and he kills them.

'This man is a rape risk. If he can't afford a prostitute, or if something happens to trigger his anger, he'll find some other poor woman to take it out on. This isn't because he fantasizes about rape – he simply needs to release his anger.'

I explained that the killer would have a poor record in heterosexual relationships. No woman would stay with him for very long. His life would be unstable – much as his childhood had been – and I doubted if there was anybody at home to cover up for him.

'He is almost certainly already in your system – probably for violence or sexual assault,' I said. 'They'll be offences serious enough for him to be flagged as a future risk, or sent for treatment.

'He is physically confident and will try to face people down. But he's also the sort who likes to impress the lads, either by boasting or teasing. He tells lies and, depending on what he thinks will impress people the most, he'll make all sorts of claims about his achievements. This could be his undoing.

'His social skills and personal presentation are good enough not to frighten off a working girl. Mind you, they do accept some rough trade.

'He'll be a regular user of prostitutes, but not well liked by them. He'll have different girls in different places and they'll be important to him, as a group – a sexual facility – rather than as individuals. They fascinate him and he won't be able to stay away from them. That's why he'll turn up again.'

Soon after Tracy Turner was formally identified, I was asked to consider another murder that was being investigated by a separate force.

On New Year's Eve 1992, three months before Tracy's death, the decomposing body of a woman was found in a ditch in Stanford Road, Swinford, a tiny village on the back road between Rugby and Market Harborough.

A horsewoman had made the grim discovery as she rode past the five-foot ditch that ran alongside a hedge bordering a field. The victim was aged between eighteen and thirty-two and wore a short black evening dress. She'd been strangled and hit on the throat.

It took three days for her to be identified. Samo Paul, aged twenty, was a prostitute from West Bromwich in the West Midlands. She had an eight-month-old baby daughter.

The last known sighting of Samo had been on Friday 3 December, when a taxi driver dropped her in the Balsall Heath area of Birmingham.

The investigation, led by Detective Superintendent David Unwin from West Midlands Police, had centred on interviewing her clients and fellow prostitutes. Detectives had appealed for information from vice girls in the Birmingham and Leicester area. It was thought that Samo might have worked increasingly in Leicester after having been arrested several times in her own city.

An unmarked police car drove me to the scene. Samo had lain undiscovered for almost a month. In that time, exposure, decomposition and water flowing through the ditch had removed much of the forensic evidence.

Her body had been dumped a short distance to the south-east of Swinford. I knew the area reasonably well and thought that the last violence it had seen was probably at the Battle of Naseby during the English Civil War. Although I'd been driving through Swinford for seventeen years, I had never travelled along this particular stretch of road before. Approaching from the West Midlands the right turn into Stanford Road was sudden and tight, halfway through a sharp left-hand bend in the village. As we took the turn, the village immediately gave way to the remote agricultural land-scape of the Leicestershire/Northamptonshire borders. Passing traffic was minimal.

The psychological contours of where Samo Paul was left were identical to those for Tracy Turner. Both scenes were close to a small village, on a roadside verge, with a hedge giving way to fields. The farm gateways were used by tractors during the day and as cover for courting couples at night. Apart from that there was little if any nocturnal traffic.

An array of underwear and intimate articles had been thrown up by the fingertip search. This isn't unusual in manual searches around rural scenes of crime. Normally the items are quickly eliminated from the inquiry and cast a baleful light on what goes on, unnoticed, around us.

The wider macro-geography of the location interested me. Although only three-quarters of an hour from where Samo Paul lived, Swinford was very close to the same M6, M1 and A5 trunk roads – and the same net-work of lanes and minor roads – as the Tracy Turner site. As the crow flies, the scenes were only a few miles apart. In rural terms it amounted to being next-door neighbours.

I asked for a day to get my thoughts together and then found myself back in the same small room at Leicester police headquarters. Apart from the residue of tobacco smoke, it had the dark-stained wood, strip lighting and nylon carpets that typified modern office design. A flipchart made one end of the room the front.

'The fresh condition of Tracy's body and the fact that it was found exactly as it had been dumped were key elements in building the profile,' I told the assembled officers.

'Neither of these points hold for Samo Paul. The water, decomposition and animals have all nudged her into the position you found her in, so it's hard to be absolutely sure about how she was originally dumped.

'The question you asked me at the very beginning was if you were looking for two killers. The answer is no. The same man killed both women.'

Nothing I had seen suggested an elaborate fantasy-based murder. Nor had Samo Paul been abducted, held over time and played with for sadistic pleasure.

Like Tracy, her body didn't appear to have been arranged to make a dramatic impact on whoever found her. If this had been the aim, he'd have left her on the verge rather than in the ditch.

Police inquiries had revealed that Samo was perhaps a little more streetwise than Tracy. It hadn't saved her. She was used and strangled, probably in the same farmyard manner as Tracy.

'The same man murdered and dumped both women. I'm satisfied that he worked alone. I suspect that he may have cut things a bit fine with Samo. He couldn't undress her in time and had to dump her more or less as she was. Perhaps he was lucky to have found such a deep ditch. It's also possible that he knew exactly where he was.'

I outlined again the psychological profile of the killer, pointing out his use of micro- and macro-geography.

'There is a connection between the motorways and trunk roads. He picked up both women in the West Midlands and transported them forty to forty-five miles. He knows this area well.

'He's a driver and these aren't his first outings. He may be farmyard in style, but he is also practised, slick and comfortable. He's locked into prostitutes and he will attack again.'

My analyses of the crimes left the room divided. Neither inquiry team particularly welcomed the linking. This wasn't just because of concerns about an active serial killer. It could mean a joint investigation, with additional costs and organizational demands.

'Don't the clothes make a difference?' asked one detective. 'Samo Paul wore a dress.'

One of his colleagues echoed, 'And it isn't a dead-end lane at Swinford like it is at Bitteswell.'

David Cox was one of the few present whom I was able totally to convince that the killings were linked. He also accepted my analysis that the killer would continue to assault women and kill them if they triggered his anger or sense of inadequacy.

As I packed up my notes and prepared to leave the station, I had another thought to offer, which had been exercising my memory. I had seen more dead prostitutes than most, if not all, of these detectives. I'd seen them lying in bedsits, beneath hedges, dead in doorways or dropped beside anonymous docks. That's

405

always the most difficult part of getting away with murder – disposing of the remains.

Taking David to one side, I told him that having looked at both murders I realized that I had seen something very similar before. I mentioned the murders of Janine Downes, whose body was found at Shifnal near Stafford, and Carol Clark, discovered near Dursley in Gloucestershire. David knew of neither case, but suddenly the tiredness in his voice had gone.

Janine Downes had been found in a lay-by about fifteen miles from where she was last seen. The site was uncannily similar to where Tracy Turner was found, right down to the quiet rural road, grass verge and the nearby hedge. She, too, had been stripped naked and dumped at night. Externally she was in very good condition, but had suffered a lot of internal damage. Her killer had displayed real anger.

Carol Clark, another prostitute, worked at the lower end of the market. She was taken at night from the red-light area in Bristol. Her semi-naked body was found over twenty-five miles away the following day.

She had been left in a dock used by seagoing ships passing along the River Severn. The body was just off the motorway, down a small slope, lying partially in the water. She, too, had died of a neck injury, but was otherwise unmarked.

In the light of what I knew about Tracy Turner and Samo Paul, I could see psychological similarities between all four murders. All the victims were near naked or naked. Carol Clark had cowboy boots on and underwear around her lower legs. Samo Paul wore a short black evening dress.

All were disposed of in a similar way and, symbolically at least, in the same sort of place – roadside verges, a ditch at the edge of the road or a sea dock beside a road. They were all prostitutes. They were all acquired in a similar fashion. They were all strangled. The nature of the injuries in each case didn't show very much external damage.

'As far as I'm aware, none of these cases has been solved,' I told David. 'There have been other women as well, a lot of them prostitutes. Looking at the perimeter area, it's bordered by Bristol, Telford, Sheffield, Nottingham and Northampton/Luton.'

'Birmingham sits somewhere in the middle of all that,' he said.

'I think it's worth having a look at them all. You might find some interesting links.'

'You don't know what you're starting,' he said, not wanting to hear an answer.

The moment you have two or more prostitutes killed close together in time or geographical space, the idea that there is another 'ripper' out there takes on a very strong energy. The victims are no longer the story – it is the 'monster' who is killing them. The prostitutes are just straw women, or grist to the mill.

From a police viewpoint, most officers would prefer such crimes not to be linked. There are two reasons for this. One is the shadow still thrown by the Whitechapel murders across the killing of any prostitute in Britain. The second reason is the terrible realization that somewhere out there is a man who will keep killing unless *they* catch him. The pressure builds with each new victim.

A series of murders has a colossal impact on the public and police psyche that is exponentially far greater than the sum of the crimes. It normally means a media hue and cry that distorts the investigative priorities. The headlines are relentless: 'What are the police doing?' 'Why haven't they got him yet?'

For this reason senior police administrators are reluctant to risk over-interpreting and jumping to unwarranted conclusions about possible serial offences. Joint investigations are also more problematic.

After my conversation with David Cox, a number of unsolved murders were compared and contrasted. David took this very seriously and argued strongly for an overarching investigation into all of these cases. This became known as Operation Enigma.

Officers from the original investigating forces linked up with computer database specialists and representatives from what is now called the National Crime Faculty. Overseas specialists were also called in. Ultimately the aim was to produce matrices of the murders, featuring the details of each victim and her death. By sifting for similarities and relationships, the researchers hoped to recognize patterns and groupings that had previously been missed.

I wasn't directly involved in the operation, but it took on the principles that I'd described to David Cox. The difficulty, however, with such a process is that it's very easy for the parameters of the search to get wider and wider. It begins by looking at the murders of prostitutes and then someone suggests, 'Why don't we look at all outstanding murders of women?'

This adds enormously to the data that is thrown up, but can create problems of focus in how it should be interpreted.

The starting position should always be that none of the murders are linked. Then, taking a baseline murder – such as Tracy Turner's – all the other killings should be compared and contrasted in terms of geography, methodology and victimology. What are the similarities and dissimilarities? Which ones are significant?

Objectivity is vital. You mustn't force the information to fit the hypothesis. Unless you find yourself in a position where the similarities are so great they push you inexorably in one direction, then you have no choice but to assume the crimes are not connected.

I don't know the outcome of Enigma. From my understanding various separate groupings were proposed, but the number of criteria used for comparison was quite small. For this reason, I fear it might not have been precise enough to capture the subtleties of each crime.

The sort of questions that I would have chosen go far beyond the mere physicality of the crime scene, the victim and her injuries. I'm referring to things that you *don't* see:

> *What was the victim's temperament?*
> *How practised was she in what she did?*
> *Is she a common prostitute or more of a courtesan?*
> *How attractive is she?*
> *Where did she work – in flats, or on street corners, or in hotels?*
> *Did she work in a group?*
> *Did she and her working-girl friends look out for each other?*
> *How sophisticated was she as a prostitute?*
> *What was her speciality?*
> *What did she normally wear?*
> *What sort of men did she attract?*
> *Was she normally aggressive or passive?*
> *Did she engage in various forms of bondage?*

If so, did she assume the role of either sadist or
masochist?
How mobile was she?
Did she carry a weapon?
Did she have any knowledge of self-defence?
Is she the sort of prostitute who mothers her clients,
or treats them with undisguised disdain?
How bright was she?

All of these things influence the degree of risk that a
prostitute faces. Crucially, they also say something
about the sort of person who kills her.

The Behavioural Science Unit of the FBI at
Quantico, Virginia, has a very useful computer program called VICAP. It doesn't produce psychological
profiles, but it is very good at comparing offences and
ranking them by the strength of the links between them.
A local version of VICAP would be helpful in the UK.
If it was properly designed and run, I would expect it
to link a significant number of cases and lead to
prosecutions.

Operation Enigma was a worthy exercise, but
information is only as good as its validated source.
Then – to be of maximum operational value – this
information has to be transformed into intelligence.

I had no doubt that a serial murderer was operating
in the Midlands. Definitely one and probably another,
with a slightly different motivation and victim specifi-
cation. I also had no doubt that unless these men were
caught, there would be more victims – and once again
they were likely to be prostitutes.

When this happened, it would be important for the
police and public to see these women as something
more than just grist to the mill of a serial killer. In a

sense the more we talk about the victims, the more we tear down the mystique that we build up around the 'monster' who killed them.

We also have to treat the scenes and the victims in exactly the same way as we would treat the murder of the local beauty queen, or an elderly pensioner. If investigators were to apply the same level of intensity and sharp focus, then even the naked body of a prostitute on a grass verge beside a lonely rural lane would tell them something about the killer.

20

On 5 June 1995, I had a telephone call from the
Thames Valley Police.

I wrote in my diary:

> *Janet Brown. Age 51. Murdered by an intruder during
> the night of 10/11 April. Remote house. Lying down-
> stairs. Face down. Bound and gagged. Ten blows to
> the head ...*
>
> *Det Supt Michael Short: 'We can't make head nor
> tail of it!'*

Five days later, having juggled my appointments, I
arrived at a modest two-storey police station in Thame.
The modern tan-coloured brick building had a small
public car park to one side and a cramped inquiry
area.

Michael Short and his second in command, Detective
Inspector John Bradley, met me at the front desk and
took me through double wooden doors and upstairs to
an office. The incident room was the smallest I had ever
seen, with barely enough room for half a dozen desks.
I guess nobody ever expected to investigate a long-
running murder case in the sleepy market town. The

rest of the investigation team had finished for the day and we had the place to ourselves.

Pinned on a noticeboard was a yellowing newspaper cutting from the *Oxford Mail*. It was dated 12 April.

> *MURDER OF CARING MOTHER*
>
> *A full scale murder hunt was under way today for a bloodstained killer who battered an Oxford nurse to death in her home.*
>
> *Mother of three Janet Brown, 51, was found naked, handcuffed and face down with severe head injuries at the family's luxury isolated farmhouse in Spriggs Holly Lane, near Chinnor, yesterday.*
>
> *Detectives believe the murder was committed by a burglar who beat elaborate security precautions to get into the £350,000 house.*
>
> *They say there were signs of forced entry. They believe Mrs Brown went to bed and was disturbed by the sound of breaking glass.*

Michael Short was a solid man with close-cropped hair, who looked like he might have played rugby in his youth. He'd loosened his tie at the end of a hard day and undone the top button of his shirt.

'In two months we have come up with very little,' he said, unable to hide his frustration. 'This is the sort of case that you feel ought to have been solved quickly – there seemed to be so many obvious places to begin looking. The problem is, we've now looked at every one of these; we've followed up every hint of a lead.'

The SIO had a quiet confidence and he struck me as the Mark 1 version of the modern policeman. He was part of the first generation to begin thinking in terms of scientific profiling. As the briefing began, there was

413

no mention made of needing a psychological profile of the killer. The initial aim was for a fresh eye to look at the case. Perhaps I'd see something new.

Short began by outlining the details of the crime. Occasionally Bradley chipped in with additional points. The two worked well together. It was like watching two men plastering a wall, with one applying the mix while the other used a fine trowel to add the surface pattern.

The body of Janet Brown had been found in the family home by a tradesman who arrived early one morning to start work. The mother of three grown-up children shared the house with her youngest daughter, Roxanne, aged seventeen.

The eldest girl, Zara, twenty-two, was a languages graduate who worked in London. Ben, twenty-one, was at university in Exeter and Roxanne was studying for her A-levels at nearby Wycombe High School.

'What about the husband?' I asked.

'Dr Grahaem Brown is a medical man who lives and works in Switzerland,' said Short. 'He comes home once or twice a month for a day or so. According to him, he and his wife haven't been particularly close for ten years.'

Bradley picked up the thread: 'He seems to be quite a high flier. He works for Ciba Geigy, a pharmaceutical company in Basle, Switzerland. His last trip home was on the weekend before the murder. They were selling the farmhouse and were packing up ready to move.'

'Where were they moving to?'

'Canada.'

'What are your impressions of Dr Brown?'

'Well, I don't think he killed his wife, if that's what you mean. He's been helpful from day one – providing all his records and details of his movements. He was in

414

Switzerland on the night of the murder. Interpol has confirmed his alibi.'

'The marriage was pretty distant,' added Michael Short, 'but they seemed to have come to a mutual understanding. They led their own lives.'

Mrs Brown had gone back to work about two-and-a-half years earlier. She had a job as a researcher for Oxford University's Department of Public Health and Primary Care. Since then her life had revolved around work and home. She rarely went out and often ate dinner alone, while sitting on her bed. At night she studied and went to sleep early. She was a woman known for her probity.

As the detectives talked I took notes, underlining certain details and putting question marks next to others.

On Monday 10 April Janet Brown had gone to work as usual. She drove home that evening and parked in the driveway, alongside Roxanne's car. Soon afterwards her daughter phoned from a friend's house in nearby Beaconsfield to say that she wouldn't be coming home that night. Her friend had just passed her driving test and they were going out for a meal to celebrate. Janet said she was tired and looking forward to an early night.

One of Roxanne's schoolfriends telephoned Hall Farm at 8.10 p.m. and became the last known person to speak to Janet. When Grahaem called from Switzerland at approximately 8.30 p.m. he received no reply. A local builder, Nick Marshall, rang at 9 p.m. to discuss some work he'd been doing at the farm and also got no answer.

At 10.20 p.m. a motorist driving past the house heard the external alarm sounding. Later that night, as he passed again, the alarm was silent.

415

Several albums of crime scene photographs were placed on a desk in front of me and the detectives flicked through them, explaining the floor plan of the house and outlining their theory on the probable sequence of events.

One series of images showed the patio doors that led from the sitting room into a small walled courtyard at the side of the house. A full-height door pane in the middle of the three doors had been smashed. Glass fragments lay inside the room and outside. Looking closer I could see all-weather tape hanging from sections of the broken glass.

'He tried the old-fashioned way,' explained Bradley. 'A glass-cutter scored a hole in the door and he put the all-weather tape over the markings . . .'

'Isn't that a double-glazed door?' I asked, studying the pictures.

'Yeah. It proved a problem. Looks as though he got frustrated and decided to smash his way inside. That's probably what woke her up.'

Short explained that Janet Brown normally slept naked, but I put a question mark beside my notes: how did they know? Her daughter wouldn't necessarily be aware of such a detail and her husband claimed that he hadn't been intimate with his wife for ten years.

'She probably came downstairs to investigate the noise,' continued Short, 'but there is evidence that the initial confrontation took place in the bedroom. We found a small piece of packing tape on the floor. He wrapped the tape around her head as a gag and hand-cuffed her, with her arms behind her.'

'How was she found?'

Short opened another album of crime scene photographs. Janet Brown's body lay at the bottom of the

416

stairs, face down in a pool of blood. The back of her head had been beaten to a bloody pulp by the force of at least ten blows with a blunt instrument. Her hands were behind her back, still cuffed.

'We found the keys underneath the body,' said Bradley.

'Were there any defence injuries?'

'Nothing to speak of.'

'What about the murder weapon?'

'It hasn't been found. The pathologist says it could have been an iron bar. There's no physical evidence of any sexual assault.'

Short added, 'We pulled sixty good fingerprints from the house and have eliminated all but four of them. There's no other forensic evidence of any significance.'

'Was anything taken?' I asked.

'No,' they answered in unison. Short continued: 'We found traces of diluted blood on four or five light switches upstairs.'

'Were there signs of a search?'

'A few cupboard doors ajar, but not enough to be certain.'

Bradley's voice grew bitter. 'She couldn't go anywhere. She was helpless. That's why I reckon she may have recognized him. Why else would he kill her?'

I didn't answer. It was too early to make any call.

Janet Brown had lain undiscovered until shortly after eight the next morning when the builder Nick Marshall arrived with his fifteen-year-old son. As they entered the drive and parked their vehicle they heard an internal alarm ringing. Lights were on throughout the house and curtains were open. When nobody answered the door, they looked through the front window and saw Mrs Brown lying naked at the bottom of the stairs.

417

The implications of almost everything described to me pointed to a burglary gone wrong – a woman asleep, disturbed by the sound of breaking glass, confronted by an intruder who panicked and killed her. Yet already I had question marks dotted through my notebook.

I looked again at the photographs. Janet Brown was wearing jewellery – large hoop earrings, a watch, a bracelet, several rings and a weighty single-hoop, solid metal necklace. It didn't make sense.

Many women will take off an earring to answer the phone. They certainly don't wear this much jewellery to bed. The solid metal necklace would have been particularly uncomfortable.

And what woman, sleeping naked, would go to confront an intruder without putting something on? There were two dressing gowns in the bedroom. If Janet had been woken by the sound of breaking glass, surely she would have put one of them on.

I mentioned none of this to the detectives. I didn't want to close them down psychologically by questioning something they had or hadn't done. Instead I kept soaking up the details.

'Can we visit the crime scene?' I asked.

'Of course. There's a car waiting.'

'And I'll need copies of all the statements, crime scene photographs, maps of the area and the layout of the house.'

Michael Short had anticipated this and arranged a full set of the materials.

We left the station in an unmarked police car and very quickly the quiet streets of Thame gave way to rolling fields, splashes of thick woodland and scattered farmhouses. Many of the houses had been carefully renovated, by those who had made a lifestyle choice to live in the countryside. The hedgerows were thick with summer growth and that spring's lambs were now walking on steady legs in the fields.

'What a lovely patch you have,' I said, thinking how much it reminded me of the deeper Cotswolds I had known even before my own early days as a police cadet in Warwickshire. The murder of Janet Brown would have been particularly hard felt in an area such as this. Even surrounded by such beauty we are all, ultimately, only a hand's touch away from violence.

We parked in the lane a short distance from the scene and began walking. I could still see scraps of blue and white police tape hanging in a hedge. The driveway opened up quite suddenly with small brick-wall-mounted entrance gates on our left. A sign announced 'Hall Farm'.

Immediately the eighteenth-century farmhouse filled my view. An old wisteria, now in flower, twisted and climbed up the walls. Two things stood out. Here was a house that should have had a long sweeping drive; all the proportions suggested it. At some point it must have been extended because I couldn't imagine it being built on this scale so close to the road.

Secondly, the openness to view meant that anyone approaching the house that evening in April would have seen lights on and curtains opened.

To the left of the main house stood a stable block, now converted into a garage. Neat piles of orange tiles were stacked against a stone wall. Nick Marshall, the tradesman who found Mrs Brown, had been reroofing the building.

'There were two alarm systems in the house,' said Short, crunching gravel underfoot as we walked up the driveway. 'The external alarm rings for twenty minutes before cutting out.' He pointed to the signal box on the exterior wall. 'The internal alarm will keep sounding as long as the power supply is connected or until someone punches the code into the control box.'

'How is it triggered?'

'There are two panic buttons – one by the front door and the other in the main bedroom, beside the bed.'

I turned and looked back at the lane. What good is an alarm system if nobody can hear it? A passer-by might hear the external alarm ringing, but they were unlikely to detect any internal alarm unless they walked onto the property. The nearest neighbours were two or three hundred yards away.

Hall Farm had been built on a wooded ridge with views over rolling countryside. As we walked around the main building, this view opened up across the back garden that dropped away on a gentle slope. The garden consisted mainly of a large rectangular lawn, with only a few shrubs and flower beds. A rail fence was at the horizon where the land fell away to undulating fields.

I took note of places from where someone might have watched the house, or approached it without being seen. The trees were now in full leaf but in April there would have been less screening.

'It has eleven acres,' said Bradley admiringly. 'The family had agreed a sale for £345,000.'

I looked closely at the wooden-framed sash windows. These are a gift to burglars – one screwdriver and you're in. The Brown family had obviously spent quite a bit of money on alarm systems for the house, but any local crime prevention officer could have told them this was worthless unless other changes were made.

There were several obvious ways to break into the house.

We came to an arch with a heavy wooden door. It led into a small, enclosed courtyard at the side of the house. The door opened awkwardly and we had to squeeze through. On one side of the courtyard was the entrance to a storeroom that contained various garden tools, sun chairs and a barbecue. On the other side were the patio doors I had seen in the crime scene photographs.

Here again something didn't make sense. The courtyard was completely concealed from the road and the rear of the house, which might make it appear like the perfect place to break in.

But the patio doors were modern and metal-framed. The twin layers of glass sandwiched together wouldn't give way easily. Why didn't the burglar choose one of the sash windows at the rear of the house? These were out of sight of the lane. If someone had approached he could have quietly blended into the shadows.

The courtyard had only one means of escape – the heavy wooden door. If someone had blocked it suddenly, a thief would have nowhere to go. Most burglars give themselves more than one escape route.

I still puzzled over the photographs of the smashed patio door. When using a glass-cutting wheel, most thieves score a small circle or triangle on a single pane of glass. Tape is put over the score marks, then a sharp tap causes the glass to break. The tape prevents the piece from fragmenting or falling down. The burglar then puts a hand inside and flips the latch or turns the handle.

In this case, someone had tried to cut a man-sized hole in a double-glazed patio door. He'd managed to get through the first layer of glass, but had risked having it fall on him. One large piece had been found in the courtyard garden.

The burglar had another layer of glass to get through but grew frustrated, according to the police. He had abandoned the silent approach and smashed his way inside. Why? Quite apart from the noise this made, he stood a good chance of hurting himself. And he must have known there was someone in the house.

I wasn't happy with any of this. From the first moment I saw the photographs I questioned why there was more broken glass outside the door than inside on the lounge carpet. It suggested that the door had been broken from inside rather than out. But why would that be? It didn't make sense.

Bradley opened the patio doors and I stepped inside. As I walked through the extended sitting room, the crime scene photographs began to take on a more concrete familiarity. I looked at the open fireplace and the tasteful furnishings. There were so many things that could have been easily disturbed – cushions on the sofas, books in the shelves, plants in pots – but this was a house characterized by orderliness and lack of use. The Browns had been in the process of moving out, but even so, it seemed that many of the rooms were rarely used.

'The TV and video recorder were unplugged,' said Short, motioning to the corner.

Up several steps and through another sitting or dining area, we passed the front door and reached the stairs. Beyond were the rear lobby and back door. The foot of these stairs was a narrow, bottleneck area; it was here that Janet Brown had died. Given the lack of space, her killer didn't have much room to swing the object that bludgeoned her to death.

'Where was she when the blows were delivered?' I asked.

'On the floor,' said Short.

'For all of them?'

'Yes.'

Silently I flagged this with a question mark. It was an inconsistency. How did she get to the floor? Did she fall down the stairs? Did he push her? Did he order her onto her knees? Or did he hit her from behind as she tried to run?

'There were no signs of a struggle elsewhere,' offered Bradley.

'What do you mean?'

'No blood spots or signs of a fight.'

The lack of blood didn't necessarily mean there were no blows.

The front door and back door were both chained internally. The alarm could have been triggered by either panic button, but there was slight evidence of a half-turned key that favoured the one by the front door. There was no way of being certain.

The kitchen and dining area were generally very tidy, but there was some evidence of occupation, with a cup and knife on the draining board. A slide-out bin with a black plastic liner contained an empty packet of a chocolate ice-cream dessert.

The downstairs office was cluttered but tidy. Husband and wife both had a desk. Books and files were balanced in piles. Anyone searching for valuables would have found it difficult not to knock something over. There were framed photographs of children and cables snaking from computers. Nothing appeared to have been upset or interfered with.

Climbing the very narrow staircase, I paused at a

tiny alcove with potted plants and a shelf that contained copies of *National Geographic* magazine. Again, nothing had been disturbed. Everything looked as though the cleaner had just left.

On the landing we turned towards the main bedroom. The curtains were open and late afternoon light spilled inside. The forensic teams had been through and I couldn't be sure if the room still looked as it had done on that night two months earlier.

The same was true of the other rooms. Bloodstains on light switches had been wiped away. Carpets had been replaced. Michael Short had promised me a video taken on the morning after the murder. I hoped it would give me a clearer picture of what had happened.

I wandered through the upstairs bedrooms and bathrooms. Most of the windows had blinds or curtains but none of them was closed. I paused to look at a handful of books on photography.

'Mrs Brown had an interest,' explained Short.

'Was she a member of a camera club? Did she have a darkroom?'

'I don't think so.'

Roxanne's room was easy to recognize from the photographs of her and her horse. Her A-level textbooks were on her desk, surrounded by family snapshots. Again the curtains were open.

In the third bedroom, a wicker blanket box containing flippers and scuba-diving gear had been found with the lid open. Janet Brown had apparently done some diving a year previously. This struck me as being totally out of character with the bland, almost anonymous woman who had been described to me. It also confirmed how little the police had discovered about Janet Brown.

She had about £40,000 in her account; her life insurance had been cancelled some years previously and she had died intestate, unbeknown to her husband. Her pension entitlements would go to her children.

Police had interviewed friends, neighbours and colleagues, who described her as 'quiet', 'pleasant', 'safety-conscious' and 'private'. She was 'a lovely woman', 'polite and generous', who 'always had time for a chat'. These are what I call 'empty descriptions'. They tell us nothing. In reality, they show that people thought they knew Janet and it wasn't until they were asked that they realized this wasn't the case at all.

Very rarely had I come across a person as two-dimensional as this – someone with no apparent social life, excitement or interests. How did this marry up with someone who had an interest in photography and a rattan chest full of diving gear?

It was also quite interesting that the chest had been one of the few things interfered with by her attacker.

There were other irregularities flagged in my notebook:

> The toilet seat is propped open in the en suite.
> A man's dressing gown is on the bathroom floor. Who does it belong to? The husband? What is it doing there?
> The shower head is adjusted for someone quite tall. Janet Brown was 5' 4".
> A burglary gone wrong? PROBLEMS.

This last point was potentially the most contentious. One of the reasons I take so much care when coming to my conclusions is that I know the likely impact of getting it wrong. If I make a mistake and guide the police in the wrong direction, the entire investigation can be compromised. At best, resources will be wasted. At worst, someone else could die before the killer is caught.

This was why I had to be so sure before I began questioning their assumptions. Already there were too many anomalies. The burglary scenario didn't explain the motivation or fit many of the facts. For one thing, the entry made no sense. Would a halfway decent burglar have made such a hash of it?

Only a handful of people knew that Roxanne wasn't at home that night. There were two cars in the driveway. The lights were on. All of which begs the question, how many people did the killer expect to find?

Why would a burglar bring two types of tape – the all-weather tape found on the patio door and the brown packing tape that he wrapped nine times around Janet Brown's head?

Did he bring the handcuffs or find them there?

Would a burglar have stayed in the house afterwards with an alarm ringing in his ears? Would he have washed his hands, stepped over the body and gone looking through the rooms, leaving diluted blood on the light switches?

From a psychological perspective there is an enormous difference between someone who kills in the panic of discovery and flees a scene and a person who calmly washes his hands and makes further use of the house.

All of these questions intrigued and disturbed me as we drove back to Thame police station in the fading light. I needed answers.

Michael Short helped me carry copies of statements and photographs to my car.

'So what do you think?' he asked, hoping for some early insight or theory.

'It's too soon to say.'

'But you do have some ideas?'

I felt for the car keys in my pocket. 'Have you ever wondered why he stayed in the house for so long afterwards?'

'A little, I suppose. Why?'

'Perhaps he was waiting for Roxanne.'

21

That evening I didn't get home until late and I didn't feel like eating. That's often the way after I've visited a murder scene.

Turning on my desk lamp in the study, I spread the statements, photographs, post-mortem report and maps across the desk and on the floor.

I took the crime scene video into the lounge and slid it into the video player. After a few seconds of scrambled images, a tree-lined lane appeared. The date was stamped in the top left-hand corner – 11 April 1995. I could hear the morning chorus of birds on the video and the sun shone brightly, creating a dappled shade on the roadway.

The cameraman walked along the lane and turned to face Hall Farm. Blue and white police tape was strung across the driveway and along the hedges. Half a dozen police cars were parked outside.

At this stage the police weren't quite sure what anything meant, so the cameraman was filming everything. One of the traps this creates is that whenever he zoomed in on something, you could be misled into thinking it had some specific relevance. At one point he focused closely on a pair of scissors found lying in the

428

grass near the farm gate. All sorts of explanations emerged, but most of them were harmless. The scissors have never been linked to the murder.

The camera swept across the front of the farmhouse. Two cars were in the driveway: Janet Brown's Volvo estate and Roxanne's red Metro with 'L' plates attached.

The main door of the house was at the side of a small porch that jutted from the front wall and was covered in wisteria. Janet Brown's bedroom was on the first floor at the front, overlooking the driveway. The lights were still on. If she hadn't closed her curtains it could certainly have been seen from the lane.

As the camera approached I could hear the internal burglar alarm ringing. The constant squeal grew louder. It gave me some idea of how close you had to be to pick up the sound. It wasn't audible from the lane.

The cameraman circled the house, filming the exterior and the grounds. Neighbourhood Watch stickers were attached to several windows, along with a sticker warning of a guard dog.

The camera entered through the back door. The alarm grew louder. Square duckboards crossed the floor like a series of stepping stones to prevent the police contaminating the crime scene.

I now had the chance to see the patio doors as they were found – with shattered glass and tape hanging from the edges. The video confirmed how much glass lay outside the door and how little was inside on the carpet. If the door had been shattered from outside, I would have expected the majority of the shards to be inside. Similarly, small slivers of glass should have been spread through the house by the intruder's feet.

I wrote a question for the police: '*Was any crushed*

or splintered glass found elsewhere in the house? If the doors had been broken from outside, the killer must have walked through the debris.'

The camera panned slowly to reveal the house to me again. As it looked back at the patio windows from within the lounge, everything in the room seemed to be immaculate and in place. A single cushion lay on the floor amid fragments of shattered glass.

If this man had shattered the door, he must have known it would alert anybody inside. He would then have had to move very quickly to silence Mrs Brown before she could trigger an alarm. Yet there were no signs of panic. In a fully furnished family home, nothing, apart from the cushion, had been knocked over or disturbed.

This was true of all the areas downstairs. Coats were hanging on pegs by the back door, beside a bicycle and wellington boots. Nothing had been knocked down or displaced.

From the kitchen the camera entered the narrow point beneath the stairs where the naked body of Janet Brown lay in a pool of blood. The force of the blows had caved in the back of her skull. Brown packing tape concealed most of her face.

I noticed where blood had dripped onto her back, most likely from the weapon as her attacker wound up for each blow. The brickwork and fire-grate were also splattered with blood, as well as a nearby settee. Her head faced towards the bottom of the stairs. She had spun to ward off the blows. A spray pattern of blood speckled the wall and ceiling.

The handcuffs had to be cut off in order to roll the body. That's when they discovered the keys lying beneath her.

The camera passed the body and moved up the stairs. The little alcove was undisturbed. Turning left at the top, the camera entered the main bedroom, where a dressing gown lay crumpled on the floor.

A small piece of brown packing tape seemed out of place on the floor next to a pine chest or blanket box. On top of the box sat a portable TV, with its handle raised. The bed had obviously been occupied, with the duvet thrown back over it.

Perhaps Janet Brown had been getting ready for bed. She couldn't have been wearing the dressing gown when the handcuffs were put on her wrists.

A bedside lamp had been knocked slightly and a rug on the floor was fractionally askew. In the corner beneath the window sill I noticed a small delicate table. This was a complex little area. A mandolin was propped upright against the wall and a lamp with a trailing flex rested on the windowsill. Whoever had lowered the blind had done so carefully, so as not to knock anything off the sill.

According to the police, Mrs Brown didn't normally shut her curtains or lower her blinds. This made it more likely that her killer had done so. If so, he showed no signs of panic or haste.

A dressing room adjoined the bedroom. It was here that Grahaem Brown last remembered seeing a pair of handcuffs several years earlier. He couldn't remember how they came to be there.

The camera panned slowly around the en-suite bathroom. A man's dressing gown lay on the floor. The positions of the toilet seat and shower head, as I had noted before, suggested recent use by a man.

Someone would have had to be very careful in washing himself not to leave some hint of blood. Yet the police had dismantled the waste pipes and checked the S-bends without finding a trace.

There was no blood on the stairs or in the downstairs bathroom, toilet or kitchen. This puzzled me because the killer must surely have been heavily splashed after battering Mrs Brown so savagely. On the other hand, he had left watery blood on some of the light switches. He *had* washed his hands somewhere.

I needed a house plan, as well as an aerial view that located Hall Farm in its surroundings. I still didn't have a strong enough sense of place. What happened here, I asked myself. Why doesn't this tell me the same story as the police? Am I missing something?

The photograph of Janet Brown used by most of the newspapers had been taken on her last foreign holiday in Kenya with her husband. She was a pretty if not physically striking woman, who kept fit by 'whizzing about on a bicycle' according to locals. Glancing at more pictures, I got the impression that Janet wore clothes that might mislead people about her age. She dressed younger than fifty-one and was fond of chunky jewellery and gold earrings.

Janet Brown met her future husband while they were both training at St George's Hospital in Tooting, South-west London. On graduation Grahaem Brown became an army doctor and was eventually posted to Hong Kong. After this he took a job with Glaxo in Britain and was later sent to Canada. He had moved to Ciba Geigy three years earlier. The Browns had lived at Hall Farm for a decade and had been trying to sell the house for more than a year.

Several years earlier Janet had helped to set up a Neighbourhood Watch scheme in the area because of a burglar preying on homes around the village. The

432

first meetings were held in the front room of Hall Farm. She also bought a Great Dane as a watchdog but it had died eighteen months previously.

On 10 April Janet went to work as usual. She was employed as a research nurse at the Regional Health Authority HQ in Old Road, Headington, Oxford. For the past two and a half years she had worked on a project looking into the long-term health of women who had undergone fertility treatment. The three-year grant was due to run out in October. Detectives had interviewed her colleagues who talked glowingly about Janet's work.

We are all conditioned not to speak ill of the dead – particularly when someone has died tragically. Friends and relatives invariably paint a picture that is so angelic and blemish-free that it cannot be real. I understand this, which is why I had to look past the hollow descriptions and platitudes to discover what Janet Brown was really like.

Grahaem Brown had been quite frank and straight-forward about his life. I had a reasonably clear mental picture of him and a similar knowledge of the children. With Janet, I had the photographs of her but little context.

She had received a telephone call at work that morning which police hadn't managed to trace. Later in the day Roxanne called to pass on her plans for the evening. These incidents appeared on various time-lines prepared by the police to help locate Janet and Roxanne Brown in the weeks leading up to the murder.

There was also a time-line for Hall Farm, indicating who had come and gone. Another dealt with the Triangle – an area nearby where a car could have been parked without attracting too much attention. A

433

separate time-line for Spriggs Holly Lane showed the sightings and movements of people and cars in the week prior to the murder.

The police had already made two appeals for public help on *Crimewatch UK*. The second was a re-enactment filmed at the farmhouse and broadcast on 18 May. Afterwards, Grahaem Brown announced a £10,000 reward for information leading to an arrest and conviction of his wife's killer.

Short told the audience: 'I cannot find a single policeman anywhere who has come across a crime like this. It is one of the most baffling cases I have come across ... so many things don't add up.'

More than eighty callers responded to the pro-gramme, including a professional house-breaker (who refused to give his name), who declared that no self-respecting burglar would break into a house like that.

The TV appeals and door-to-door interviews had yielded various leads. In particular, there were several cars seen in the vicinity of the murder – a small Fiesta or Metro parked 200 yards away at the Triangle at about 9.50 p.m. on the Monday night (10 April). Detectives also wanted to trace a brown Ford Escort-type car seen near the house and carrying three black men and one white man who were apparently trying to shield their faces.

In a separate incident, two women reported having been accosted by a man in the street within half a mile of the scene six weeks prior to the murder.

These incidents might just have been part of the 'noise' or background detail that surrounds all investi-gations. Nevertheless, every point would have to be sifted through and cross-checked before it could be discounted.

The killer had been very careful about not leaving clues. The packing tape was so commonplace that it couldn't be used to narrow the search. The handcuffs had no serial number or manufacturer's mark. I was surprised to learn how many pairs are imported and sold every year in the UK.

The police also prepared telephone 'wheels' – printed charts which had Hall Farm at the centre and plotted every call made in or out in the preceding weeks, showing the numbers, dates, times and duration radiating out like the spokes of a wheel. These are used to look for patterns and to check on the accuracy of witness statements. The police also searched for calls that didn't make sense, or that conflicted with what was known about Janet Brown's contacts and movements. Hundreds of pages of information had to be analysed.

I began looking at the maps, trying to become as familiar as possible with the area. Different people relate to landscape in different ways. This affects how they move through it. The significance of a map, for example, is different for a soldier than it is for a door-to-door salesman. A soldier is looking for cover, the salesman for customers.

The maps began as aerial survey charts and then narrowed down to concentrate on Spriggs Holly Lane and Hall Farm. The farmhouse was close to the lane, but the rear was exposed to open fields, hedgerows and clumps of trees. The nearest house was two hundred yards away.

Finally I began studying the floor plan of the house, in particular the extended lounge and the narrow bottleneck leading past the stairs into the rear lobby.

Opening a book of crime scene photographs, I noted how the tape had been wrapped around Janet Brown's head, covering her mouth and nose. The solid metal necklace was visible beneath her chin. It had a soft clasp at the back of her neck.

Looking at the injuries, it was clear the blows had been delivered with massive force. And the patterns of splashing and trickles down her body suggested she had been hit from two different angles. Given the narrowness of the area, he didn't have much room to swing. Would he have stopped and changed angles? Could there have been two attackers – or did she survive the initial attack, only to have the killer assault her again when she moved or whimpered?

There were smudges on the carpet. Where he had knelt perhaps, or put something down.

The post-mortem photographs showed bruises on her buttocks and face. The injuries to her back were caused by the handcuffs as she tried to get away, or twisted with her hands behind her as the weight of her body pressed her hands into her back. There were marks on her ankles, including broken skin. At some point these must also have been fastened.

The tape had been wrapped so tightly around Janet's face it was difficult to know if she had been beaten into submitting. More likely, he subdued her through fear alone.

I looked again at the scrap of tape found in the main bedroom. This was where the police suspected she had been bound. But, interestingly, the piece of tape didn't match either end of the tape used on Janet's face.

One of the post-mortem photographs revealed a blade of grass on Janet's body. A large arrow pointed towards it, drawing the eye's attention. This had clearly puzzled the pathologist and also the police.

Had the killer walked it inside? Had he left it there on purpose?

'*When was the garden last mown?*' I wrote in my notes.

I then began looking closely at other pictures in the series. According to the scene of crime report, two blades of grass had been found on the body and one on Janet's dressing gown.

The shots of Janet lying at the bottom of the stairs did not reveal the blade of grass on her torso. It first appeared in the photographs that were taken outside the house, where the forensic team had moved her body to give itself more room. Unwittingly, they had contaminated the body by laying the sheet down on the newly cut lawn. It was another dead end.

By the time I finished going through all the material it was close to midnight. The wind had picked up outside and I could just make out the swaying branches in the light from my study window. I didn't feel like sleeping yet. Too many thoughts were fighting for attention.

Closing my eyes, I tried to step back into the calm of an April evening at Hall Farm in Oxfordshire. I tried to picture Janet Brown arriving home from work and parking her car next to Roxanne's.

She dropped her papers in the study and made herself a cup of tea or coffee in the kitchen. Then she wandered upstairs to her bedroom to get changed.

Roxanne phoned. Janet made herself something to eat and watched TV in her room.

Everything I saw pointed to the fact that this wasn't a burglary gone wrong. This man came equipped for something else. He'd been watching the house. The lights were on and the curtains open. He saw Janet Brown make her way upstairs.

Perhaps he expected Roxanne to be there as well. Unless he'd been watching the house all day, he couldn't have known that she had made other plans.

How did he enter?

I couldn't be sure. The pattern of glass at the patio doors suggested it could have been broken from the inside, perhaps to make it look like a burglary.

I could be fairly certain about the timing. Janet Brown answered a phone call at 8.10 p.m. but didn't answer her husband's call twenty minutes later. Something happened in that time.

Perhaps Janet had been getting ready for bed. Her clothes were folded reasonably neatly and she wore a dressing gown. She might have been in the process of removing her jewellery and make-up.

At some point an interaction took place between her and her killer. Many women contemplate what they might do if attacked by a stranger. Often I hear them say, 'I'd punch him and kick him', or 'I'd scream at him to sod off'. But what often happens at the moment of attack is the victim loses all energy and offers no resistance. This isn't just a case of being paralysed by fear; there is a kind of passivity that overwhelms them.

Janet Brown showed no defence injuries and there were few signs of a struggle. This suggested that he either surprised her or he took control of her through fear rather than physical force.

He made her remove her dressing gown and then he played with her. Her hands may at first have been cuffed in front of her. She had a role to play – a script to act out. He will have needed to hear her talk, cajole, plead, or pretend that she found him attractive. Her jewellery was worn for him.

He forced her hands behind her to cuff them and

438

pushed her back onto the bed where the weight of her body pressing down on the manacles made indentations in her back and buttocks. It was enough to cut into her skin, indicating that he may have been lying on top of her.

At some point her ankles were also tied. Then he released her legs, perhaps so that he could try to penetrate her, or humiliate her, or make her move to another room.

Eventually, he took the brown packing tape and wrapped it nine times around her head, so tightly that she risked suffocation. Her terror must have been all-consuming.

This man was deeply excited at his control of another human being. He was also comfortable enough to stay with Janet for as long as he wanted. He didn't come for a quick and violent sexual coupling, ending in murder so he could obscure his identity. He came to seize and destroy her spirit; to refashion her in the same way that some owners will use systematic cruelty to break the spirit of a dog or a horse.

Why so much tape? A gag is normally used to silence someone, but this time it served a far more important purpose. It caused pain and alarm. It facilitated control. It allowed him to humiliate and degrade her. It lengthened the time that he could have her. This man wanted to savour Janet's terror and confusion. He wanted to prolong the experience for as long as possible.

The true significance of this mask, however, was to signal the end of the charade. When she couldn't speak or breathe Janet Brown knew she was going to die.

Perhaps, as part of his control, he had told her that he was going to wait to take Roxanne. If so, then

439

Janet's urge to warn her youngest daughter would have been immense. She would have wanted to get downstairs and somehow to draw attention to the house. It was her only chance to protect her daughter and save herself. She was willing to use her own death as the warning for Roxanne.

According to the pathologist, Janet would have suffocated if she hadn't been beaten to death. Unable to breathe, knowing she was going to die, she ran. Perhaps he'd just gone to the toilet. He may have wanted to ejaculate in a place where he could flush away any trace.

Janet ran downstairs. If she managed to reach the front door she would have found it chained and locked. Terrified and deprived of oxygen, she turned and headed for the back door. He intercepted her at the foot of the stairs. He was furious now. Anger overtook his thoughts of control. She had to be punished.

The first blows crushed her skull. The packing tape prevented some of the blood from splattering the nearby walls. The frontal injuries to her left eye and lower lip were possibly contra-coup injuries caused by a blow to the back of her skull forcing her face into the floor.

Why were the keys beneath her?

I wrote in my notes: '*She was either holding them or bending for them. Maybe she was being played with.*'

At some point during the fatal attack the killer paused to change position. Either that or he returned later to continue the blows.

Did he bring the handcuffs with him or find them in the house? Grahaem Brown remembered having seen a pair in the house years earlier, but he believed that they'd been thrown out.

I needed to be sure. If the killer had brought handcuffs with him, then he clearly expected to find someone in the house. Equally, he could have used the packing tape to bind Janet's hands and feet. The fact that he used handcuffs suggested that these were part of his sexual fantasy.

Why leave them behind? He had taken his other 'tools' with him. There are three possible reasons. One is that he always intended to do so because it made a rather dramatic statement. Secondly, the handcuffs were covered in blood and this put him off. Or thirdly, he lost the keys. I thought the third scenario was more likely. Both keys were out of sight beneath Janet's body. The only way to be sure that the killer had brought the handcuffs with him was to have the police visit the shop where the other handcuffs had been bought and check that these were not the same.

There were finger bruises on Janet's left leg, from her being pushed and held. The intruder had drawn the blinds in the bedroom but nowhere else in the house. I wrote in my notes: '*Had she been photographed?*'

After the attack, his hands were covered in blood. So, too, were his clothes. Even so, there seemed to be no real pattern of bloody footprints. Instead, the only traces of blood elsewhere in the house were the watery marks on the upstairs light switches. This person had sufficient self-control not to flee from the scene, but to wash carefully and then deliberately explore the house. Nothing had been ransacked or broken.

How did he manage to get past Janet's body at the foot of the stairs without putting his feet in the blood? He may have taken off his shoes, or found a way of covering them. This might seem like an overly elaborate precaution, but this man took great care. It is likely

441

that he had a change of clothes and a towel that he could stand upon. His probable use of the shower and the dressing room to change clothing suggested a thorough and leisurely tidying up after the killing. He couldn't go home to his wife or girlfriend covered in blood.

I jotted down further questions for the police. *'Where did Mrs Brown store her soiled linen? Where did she keep her underwear?'*

I knew from experience how intimate garments can be used to fuel fantasies. Perhaps the killer had taken a souvenir.

If this had been a burglary, as the police had assumed, then Janet Brown would have had to trigger the panic alarm when the patio doors were broken. If she'd been getting ready for bed, the logical thing to do would be to hit the panic button beside her. It seems she didn't do this. If anything, the half-turned key in the downstairs control panel suggested that it was the alarm near the front door that had been triggered.

It's possible that she managed to run that far with her hands cuffed behind her, but I doubt it. If she had triggered the alarm before she died, it meant her killer had cleaned himself up in a leisurely manner while the internal alarm screamed in his ears. That would take immense composure and self-control.

Similarly, he had no way of knowing whether the alarm was linked to a security firm or if a neighbour might hear it. This stretches risk-taking too far. The more likely scenario is that the killer triggered the alarm as his final act before leaving.

Only the external alarm could be heard from the road and it cut out after twenty minutes. We had a witness who heard it at around 10 p.m. If this is correct, then the killer spent nearly two hours in the house.

I hadn't set out to challenge the police assumptions. I had simply picked up the same pieces and recognized the anomalies in their interpretation. I had looked at the behaviour of both Janet Brown and her murderer and seen that the pieces could be fitted together to form a quite different picture.

I woke late the next morning and turned on the radio. The fourth item on the news announced that Janet Brown was being buried later that day – 13 June 1995. About a hundred mourners packed St Mary's, a tiny Norman church in Radnage.

The police used the occasion to issue a new appeal for public help. In particular they were looking for three drivers to come forward who were thought to have driven past Hall Farm on the night of the murder.

Several weeks later, I returned to Thame police station. The incident room seemed too hot and I worked in shirtsleeves. Michael Short and John Bradley were keen to hear my thoughts on the crime.

As I began the briefing, I was well aware of how dramatically my interpretation would differ from the currently held view of a burglary gone wrong. If the police were to accept my opinions, the investigation would have to take on an entirely new complexion.

'This is primarily the work of a sexual murderer,' I said, pausing to glance at my notes. 'He is a complex, aggressive sexual deviant. Someone with a very well-explored sadistic humiliation fantasy in which he imposes a passive, helpless role on the woman.

'You are most probably dealing with one man – an adult in this late thirties or forties. If there were two offenders, they are likely to be aged between fourteen and eighteen, but the way the house was used argues against it. I know the bludgeoning came from two positions, but that's more likely the same man twice – coming back when she moved.

'He has absolutely no idea how to break into a house professionally.

'The tape around Janet's face was more than a gag – it was part of the psychological torture and the fantasy he was enacting, and the role he had for her. It was planned for his pleasure.

'He was aware of his victims. He'd been watching the house. He may have come for both Janet and Roxanne.'

Short and Bradley appeared stunned. Both were family men who knew how Janet Brown's death had impacted upon a quiet rural area. The idea of a burglar killing a woman alone in her house had shocked the local community, particularly wives and mothers.

I had to go on. 'Two cars were parked in the drive. Even casual observation would show two women living at the house. Nobody knew Roxanne would be out that evening. She only made the decision that afternoon. On top of this, he came with enough paraphernalia to restrain two women.

'He either lives or works within a few miles of the house, or has done so in the past. He's likely to have come across Mrs Brown or Roxanne somewhere locally. He showed good knowledge of the house and its setting. He also knew how to make his way around the area in the evening, quite safe from discovery.

'He knew enough not to be concerned about being disturbed by neighbours. He knew that no man would be a regular part of their domestic setting, even though there were two cars in the drive. He was able to leave and get away without detection, and was undeterred by the alarm. He knew that he wouldn't be seen at the rear of the house because the land fell away at the boundary fence, effectively concealing him.

'He has transport. It is a relatively remote area to reach by foot, but fairly straightforward by car.'

If he had fled from the farmhouse on foot, there would have been a greater risk of being discovered with incriminating paraphernalia and of being recognized, given the strong possibility of his local history.

Having covered the physical elements of the profile, I began trying to give the detectives some inkling of the mind involved. 'The killer has a personality disorder and possibly a periodic psychosexual dysfunction.'

By this I meant that the offender had a core lack of empathy for other human beings. He didn't have the capacity to care or be touched by the terror in his victim's eyes, or her screams. Ultimately, if we could go back far enough in the killer's life, we'd find this started in his childhood, perhaps with serious abuse and certainly with inappropriate parenting.

Although genetic factors can sometimes play a part, it is very rare for someone to be born evil. Normally, it takes years of neglect and abuse to create a personality structure so damaged that it affects a person's ability to fit into society and maintain relationships.

This man had grown up focusing entirely on the needs and attentions of self. Other people existed only to serve his ends. He could camouflage himself with a skin of normality. Possibly he had reasonable social skills and was quite bright. He certainly wasn't mentally ill.

'What do you mean by "periodic psychosexual dysfunction"?' asked Short.

This is often a difficult concept to grasp.

'The killer wanted to dominate Mrs Brown sexually. Actual penetration isn't necessary to achieve such domination. Even so, I think this man has a problem in that regard. It's likely that in past sexual encounters and assaults, he's tried and failed to penetrate. As a result, he has developed themes of control and extended humiliation. He uses these to compensate or punish his victim for what he interprets as the ridicule he's suffered down the years.'

'So he can't get it up?' said Bradley.

'Not necessarily,' I said. 'It's quite possible he can have ordinary liaisons. It's just that he sometimes feels sexually inadequate and responds with planned aggression to keep it under control. That's why you shouldn't exclude a possible suspect just because he's married or has children.

'This man prepared for this – first in his imagination and then in his previous offending. That's why the murder of Janet Brown was such a polished affair. He brought special materials and spent a considerable time in social exchange. He had a mental storyboard drawn in his head. It shows in how he played with Janet and all of his subsequent actions.'

The details of his storyboard will have been built up over months and years – just as had happened with Colin Ireland, another moderately bright sexual sadist. New details will have been added and methods of control perfected.

'This man left very few clues behind. He has a forensic awareness. There was no wasted effort or un- necessary mess (except at the very end). This strongly suggests that he's done this before.

'This sort of expertise comes from practice. Check

446

the records for someone with a history of abduction and lengthy verbal exchanges, rape or attempted rape. In particular, look for these factors when combined with binding of the hands or feet, not for the abduction but for the assault itself.

'Go back as far as twenty years. Look at offences where the victim survived. In the later time frame, also look for unsolved murders with similar characteristics. If a victim statement shows the offender having difficulty with the sexual act, then this ought to have a high priority. The same is true of any such offender who has a geographical or occupational connection with this area.'

In one of the final points of the profile I suggested there was a strong likelihood that the killer immersed himself in pornography and, in particular, material that dealt with domination, crime and violence. His aggressive sexual and sadistic urges would not be constant. At times he'd be able to get by with just ordinary sex. At other times, due to stresses in his everyday life or periods of high arousal, he'd need to find an outlet for his deviancy.

'Pornography might satisfy this hunger when his drive is low, but it's only a matter of time before he needs to experience the real thing again,' I said. 'He will carry on. He won't stop after this. This man's core distortion is a preoccupation with violent sex and the depersonalization of women. It's like a hunger that constantly has to be satisfied. When he left Hall Farm, he took away with him the mental images – and perhaps even souvenirs – that will allow him to replay the scenes over and over in his mind while he masturbates and fantasizes.

'He's worried about getting caught, but at the

moment he thinks he's got away with it. As time goes on, his natural caution will diminish and his memory of Janet Brown will fade. By then his fantasy will have new elements and he'll want to practise them. That's when he'll start to look for other women to exploit – not necessarily to kill . . . at least not at first.

'The urge to have that same level of domination as he achieved with Mrs Brown may take some time to build. He'll also put off killing again if he thinks you suspect him, or that you're closing the net.'

There was a long silence when I finished the briefing. The two detectives were still trying to digest the ramifications. I knew the biggest shock had been the motivation. Up to that point they had been investigating a burglary that had gone wrong but if my analysis was accepted, the entire complexion of the investigation had to change. Right from the beginning, the public appeals for information had focused on a burglary rather than a sex crime.

The police had trawled through all of Janet's contacts and visitors to the house over the previous twelve months. These included potential house buyers, colleagues and tradesmen. They had also investigated the possibility of her having an undisclosed lover. Now the onus had to shift towards known sex offenders – particularly those who shared some of the features mentioned in the psychological profile.

Before leaving the station, I asked if the police could research several details. I wanted to know the customary height of the shower head in the en-suite bathroom. It was also vital to establish whether the killer had brought the handcuffs with him or found them in the house. The answer impacted enormously on the question of motivation.

I also wanted to know if any crushed or splintered glass had been found elsewhere in the house. Initially, Michael Short said it was no longer possible to answer this question. The carpets had all been cleaned. However, later I discovered that a fragment of carpet still existed. It had been cut away from beneath Janet Brown's body and taken away for analysis by scene of crime officers.

My understanding is that no fragments of glass were found on that piece of carpet. This tends to support the theory that the door was smashed from the inside.

Six months after the murder, Michael Short contacted me again. He'd been very disappointed by the public response to previous media appeals. What could he do to revitalize the case in the public's perceptions?

Information is the key to any investigation. Without help from the public, many serious crimes would never be solved. Unfortunately, when a case remains open for a long time, the flow of information slows to a trickle and it fades from people's minds.

I'd been involved in several police media appeals, including the Colin Ireland murders and the very recent killing of schoolgirl Naomi Smith. The appeals in each case were different, but based on core psychological principles. The aim is to engage the public – and sometimes the offender – by pulling certain psychological levers.

One particular appeal came to mind. Police from the north-east of England had been investigating the shotgun murder of a man outside a nightclub. They had good closed-circuit TV footage of the killing and had identified a prime suspect.

Unfortunately, he was known to be heavily armed

and had disappeared with the help of sympathetic or frightened contacts. He also had a very violent track record and had made it clear to police that he would shoot it out if cornered, taking down as many of them as he could. The police took his threats seriously and, after reviewing the material, so did I.

A tip-off from an informant had revealed the suspect was hiding in a woman's flat in a crowded area of the city. Clearly, any attempt to storm the address could have tragic consequences.

The informant also told the police that the suspect was a keen follower of *Crimewatch UK*. He'd certainly be watching the next programme to see if the murder was mentioned.

The police asked me if I could script an appeal for the programme. On the surface it had to appear like a typical *Crimewatch* segment, engaging the public and exhorting them to call the hotlines with any information. Yet the appeal also had to influence the mood of the suspect directly and reduce the risk of him shooting it out with police.

As the programme went on air, the police were waiting outside the flat.

The *Crimewatch* producer and presenters were made aware of the double purpose of this particular appeal. They had to use their presentational skills to drive the message home. The script I wrote for them had to help the suspect not to feel persecuted. The police weren't looking to win a macho stand-off or for an excuse to kill him. Obviously, the script said, something had happened outside the nightclub which had led to the shooting, but the police hadn't jumped to conclusions. They needed to hear all sides of the story before taking action. They also understood the pressure on someone who had become the subject of an armed national manhunt.

A few minutes after the broadcast, a detective contacted the flat. He continued the tone of the appeal, saying they wanted to talk, not shoot on sight. The suspect put down his weapons and walked out of the flat unarmed, giving himself up. The woman was unhurt.

'The problem with most appeals,' I told Michael Short, 'is they tend to be general shotgun blasts at the world, without any real focus on specific audiences.'

What normally happens is a victim's relative is put forward and makes a tearful plea to 'catch the monster who did this'. Although such appeals are heartfelt and emotional, they are effective only in a small number of cases. The vast majority of people watching a show such as *Crimewatch UK* have no connection with the crime; however, there are several quite distinct audiences who can be targeted, such as potential witnesses, the friends and family of the offender and the offender himself.

'So what audience should we be aiming at?' asked Short.

'Let's go over all of them first, then we can look at the right order and the correct emphasis.'

I had a briefing paper that I'd prepared several weeks earlier for the Naomi Smith murder appeal.

The fifteen-year-old schoolgirl had been sexually mutilated and had her throat cut only a hundred yards from her home at Ansley Common, a former mining village near Nuneaton.

I showed the paper to Michael Short and began explaining each point. 'The first target audience is the perpetrator. The aim of any media appeal must be to influence his mood, as well as his current and future actions.

'The second audience is his immediate family. A mother will almost never give up her child. Instead, she will tell herself, "It's a mistake. My boy wouldn't do that," or "I'll make sure he doesn't do it again," or "Giving him up isn't going to bring her back."'

For this reason, the media appeal had to carry a caring message, telling his family that he risked getting into more serious trouble if he continued to offend.

'The next audience is an accomplice or co-offender. Such an appeal has to be focused on self-interest and deal making. It can offer possible excuses for an accomplice. For instance, he didn't know how deviant, violent or dishonest the main offender was.

'The fourth target audience are distant family, friends, acquaintances and associates. These people have knowledge of the offender, but less emotional attachment to him. The approach has to be calmer and needs to appeal to their logic. It also has to overcome the sense of betrayal they may feel if they contact the police with information.

'The fifth target audience are the potential material witnesses; people who have knowledge about times, dates, places and events. It may be that they haven't come forward because they think their information is trivial or they might attract ridicule.'

The final two audiences were the general public and the broadcasting and publishing media. The latter were particularly important because they could keep the case in the public domain.

Having gone over the outline, I began discussing the specifics for a Janet Brown murder appeal. I told Michael Short he should be targeting group four (more distant acquaintances) and group five (locals or other potential witnesses who didn't realize they had important details, or were too shy to come forward).

I agreed to provide the basic structure of a script, leaving gaps for people's names and places. He could fill these in using local terminology. He also had to decide what aspects of the psychological profile he wanted to disclose.

That night at home I went over the case again – this time focusing on the characteristics of the people living around Hall Farm in the pretty villages and towns that dotted the landscape. Collectively, these people were 'Middle England' in all senses of the term.

Several hours later, I faxed a suggested script to Michael Short. It began with a direct appeal to the people of Thame and those communities within easy reach of Hall Farm:

> *Janet Brown lived as part of your community for ten years. Many of you knew her . . .* (screen photograph of Janet – various activities, locating her in the setting).
>
> *You will know that she was tragically and violently murdered during the evening or night of 10/11 April last year. Janet was a young-looking fifty-one-year-old mother of Zara, Ben and Roxanne.*
>
> *She was a quiet but eye-catching woman, a nurse in a group researching the causes of cancer . . .*
>
> *It is likely that the man who murdered her knows this area well. He has lived or worked here and may well still do so. I know that it's hard to accept that this man is a part of our comfortable and basically gentle community. It's equally hard to accept that you may actually know him, without realizing it.*

But Janet Brown – a warm, intelligent woman, a part of our community – was murdered here. Her murderer has brought fear and uncertainty to us.

It's most important that we find him, not only because of Janet's death and the ruin of her family, but because this man may possibly hurt someone else.

Most of us feel that we know the people around us well enough. We have grown up with them, worked in the same place as them, drunk in the same pub as them, seen them as people in the same street for so long that we take it for granted that they are more or less ordinary people, much as we are.

We can't easily think of someone we know as being a murderer because we think it would be obvious, or that we would instinctively dislike them.

Every man who has murdered grew up somewhere, among at least some people like us. Usually it is only with hindsight that we see the signs so clearly. If we do find ourselves becoming concerned or slightly suspicious about a particular man then we often doubt ourselves.

'Surely the police would have thought of that,' we tell ourselves, or 'I'm sure that someone else will have mentioned him.'

Often, people who turn out to have vital information hold back because they don't like to make a fuss or might be embarrassed if their suspicion proved to be groundless.

In a major police inquiry many of the concerns or suspicions phoned in turn out to have innocent explanations – which is quite natural. However, the investigating teams are very happy to receive and follow up dozens or even hundreds of such calls – because in one or two of them will be the tiny clue which finally brings the murderer to our attention.

I have explained how you may know of this man.
You may also, without realizing it until now, have
seen or overheard someone else say something which
is important in identifying him.

I then suggested the spokesperson give some very general guidelines from the psychological offender profile. This would help focus people's thinking before they contacted the police. Each element had to be explained carefully, so that any one point might trigger a response.

The script ended: '*I understand how difficult it may feel to actually make contact with me and I promise that everything will be in complete confidence. However, it is something that you really must do, because it may be your call that stops him from killing the next woman – who may be someone you know and care about.*'

The appeal aired in October and triggered renewed interest in the case, including a number of fresh leads.

I heard periodically from Michael Short and John Bradley over the next few months. In particular I gave advice on the offender's future behaviour and how those around him, such as his family, friends and colleagues, would see him.

When I was a police cadet, all those years ago, I went on a training march that included an ascent by a very muddy route of a place called Meon Hill in Warwickshire. At one point I found myself walking beside a young sergeant, who was keeping an eye on the cadets. As we laboured through the mud, scrambling out of ditches and over fences, he told me the story of Robert Fabian, one of the most famous detective inspectors in the history of Scotland Yard.

He told me that in Fabian's career there were only two major crimes that he failed to solve. One was the murder of a young nurse stabbed to death against the doors of Trinity Church at Stratford-upon-Avon, in Warwickshire. The other was the infamous witchcraft murder on Meon Hill between the villages of Upper Quentin and Lower Quentin.

'Every anniversary of the killing he'd come back here,' said the sergeant. 'He revisited the scene over and over – never able to let it go.'

Another cadet muttered, 'Silly old bugger.'

I didn't agree. I could entirely understand Fabian of the Yard coming back year after year. He was locked into these crimes. He couldn't let them go. Over and over, he kept asking himself, 'What did I miss? Where is the answer?'

This was how I felt about this crime. I kept wanting to go back, looking for something I might have missed.

Eight months after the murder, only four detectives were still working on the case. At the inquest into Janet Brown's death on 4 December 1995, Coroner Richard Hulett recorded a verdict of unlawful killing and made a new appeal for information.

'Bear in mind the horrible circumstances of this killing, bear in mind the terror of the victim. Someone must have washed the blood off themselves and either disposed of the clothing or washed it. They almost certainly behaved in what would have been a distressed fashion. That person – probably a male – is likely to have a wife, mother, girlfriend or landlady . . .'

In April 1996, on the first anniversary of the killing, a number of newspapers revisited the case. By then the police had interviewed 2,700 witnesses and taken 765 statements.

456

In one interview, Michael Short summed up his feelings.

'On balance, I don't think the motive was burglary,' he said. 'If a burglar did do it, it was not a half-decent one.'

Another officer revealed, 'Mrs Brown may have gone to bed naked and been woken by the sound of breaking glass but no woman goes to confront an intruder without putting something on. She would feel far too vulnerable.'

The thrust of the investigation had changed in the light of the psychological profile. As the police re-examined statements and alibis given earlier, several important suspects emerged. One man in particular had an offending background very similar to the one painted by the psychological offender profile.

Initially he had been eliminated because of an alibi. However, the police went back and discovered that it didn't stand up. They began researching his movements and lifestyle, trying to gather enough material to warrant interviewing him.

Unfortunately, this search was only partly productive. I had a call from the remaining senior detective asking if I could help them with an interview strategy. I wasn't hopeful. If their suspect was the killer, he was far too clever and careful to give up information easily. His confidence was already high. He knew that if the police could actually prove anything, they'd have charged him. He also knew, from past experience, that the safest course was to say nothing.

Unlike Colin Ireland, this killer wasn't a man who needed to be well regarded and respected by the police. He cared only about his self-preservation.

'If this man is the offender, he will acknowledge the

crime only if confronted with inescapable evidence and the realization that he *will* be convicted,' I said. 'Then he might offer an explanation if he thinks it could win him some mitigation.'

Despite my lack of optimism, I briefed the interviewing officers and told them to adopt a non-judgemental style.

'Let him think you understand how all this happened and that you sympathize. Tell him that you realize how problems can sometimes arise out of early experiences and rejections by women. Some of these women are very disparaging and cruel towards men. They treat them poorly and make them feel embarrassed over very common problems like premature ejaculation, or difficulty in maintaining an erection.'

As I feared, the formal interview proved unsuccessful and the suspect had to be released. The killer, whoever he is, remains out there.

I can still see him walking through the world, watching certain women and revelling in what he'd like to do to them. His urge is building and the only thing holding him back is the fear of getting caught.

Eventually, his hunger will overcome his natural caution. Then he will once again take his fantasy into the real world and find somebody to practise upon.

22

In the autumn of 1995 I had a telephone call from Rampton Special Hospital asking me to assess a patient who they felt was ready to come to Arnold Lodge on his way back to the world.

A few days later, as I pushed a shopping trolley through Tesco's, I suddenly remembered where I'd heard the patient's name before. Malcolm Harris, who first came to me because he had stolen women's underwear, had gone out of my life six years earlier and slid through the cracks of my memory.

My heart sank. What had happened to him? How much of his fantasy had he acted out?

Clearly, from the telephone call, Rampton had no idea that I'd dealt with Malcolm before. Would he remember me, I wondered? Yes. You don't forget a man who tries to take away your freedom.

On the following Monday, I arrived at Rampton and met with staff who had been treating Malcolm.

'How long has he been here?'

'Nearly four years.'

'What was the index offence?'

'He broke into a house and attacked a woman.'

I wanted to know more. Had he hurt her badly? Was

she raped? Was she alive? I stopped myself. These were questions the files would answer.

Sitting in a quiet office, I began studying the hospital paperwork. Malcolm had been staying in lodgings in Doncaster and had taken a coach to Leicester on a Sunday to see his mum. He broke the journey at Peterborough, had a few drinks at a pub and started walking around the town.

He told police that he came to a house with an open window. He knew a woman lived there because he could see knickers, bras and suspenders lying about. After watching for a while from outside, he climbed through the window.

Initially, he told police that he planned to rob the house, but under intensive questioning he admitted that he waited for the woman to get home. Then he attacked and tried to rape her. The police found him because he dropped his coach ticket as he fled the scene.

A part of me felt quite relieved – at least the woman had survived. Yet at the same time I realized how devastating such an attack could be. It could leave a victim and those around her damaged for the rest of their lives.

Psychiatric evidence had been given at Malcolm's trial and the judge had sent him to Rampton. Now he was being considered for transfer to a unit closer to the general community, with a view to release in due course.

There were several files of notes from the hospital, each formally prepared and filled out with care. I had arrived early so that I would have time to sit and read them all. I began looking at the nursing notes and assessments.

In general, the staff regarded Malcolm as being very pleasant and helpful. After a slow start, he had been encouraged to be reasonably open about his sexual fantasies and no longer tried to deny they had existed.

When asked if he understood why people might be worried about him, he said, 'Yes, they think I was dangerous.'

'Do you think they were right to be worried?'

'Yes.'

He spoke in the past tense because after four years at the hospital he now believed that he'd been cured.

'I'm OK now. Everything is better. I ought to be outside.'

Looking at the notes, I saw that Malcolm had undertaken a variety of programmes at Rampton. Some addressed his rape fantasies, while others dealt with alcohol use, anger control, social skills, relationship training, self-esteem, medication and family contact. He had moved through the system and impressed those who had the power to recommend his transfer out.

Over the years, the general concern for Malcolm had gradually given way to a sort of silence. Eventually this had been replaced by much more positive reports as he moved through all the necessary hoops.

Yet I couldn't see any deep-seated investigation of what happened inside his head. Where did he live in his psychosexual life? What did he fantasize about now?

The young man who entered the room looked very different from the one I had met six years earlier. I didn't recognize him physically. He was bigger and he walked with his shoulders back and his eyes up. His movements were co-ordinated and assured.

Gone was the shambling, enclosed and monosyllabic

461

twenty-four-year-old of the past. Malcolm had grown into a man who seemed relatively confident and self-possessed. He wore a pair of faded jeans and what looked like a new sweatshirt. His acne had cleared, but the pock-marked skin on his cheeks would always remind him of his adolescence.

A room had been set aside for the interview. It was a communal area, with armchairs, a TV in one corner and games such as table tennis and backgammon. A large window cast a square of light into the centre of the room. Specks of dust danced in the sunlight.

I quickly weighed up the security issue. Did I keep the door closed or open? The room had no alarm button. If something went wrong, I either had to mix it or get out. If I left the door open, we had no privacy. What was best?

I could see Malcolm watching me. A slight smile played on his lips. He knew what I was considering and it amused him. As far as he was concerned, if I left the door open I was scared.

Experience had taught me a lot over the years. I had sat opposite some truly dangerous men. In Malcolm's case his targets had always been women. Even so, I'd once tried to put him in jail.

I closed the door and his smile disappeared. I had sent him a message. I had no physical concerns about him.

'Hello, Malcolm, we've met before.'

'Yeah. I remember.' His tone of voice gave nothing away.

'It must raise interesting feelings to see me sitting here.'

'Yeah.'

'What do you remember about the last time we met?'

'You tried to have me put away.'

'Is that what I tried to do?'

'Yeah.'

'Let's just go back over that for a moment. What I tried to do was to get you into a hospital so that we could sort out your problems. Then you could go back and carry on your life.'

He said nothing.

'How long have you been here?'

'Four years.'

'If you had come into hospital then and we'd been able to help, where do you think you would have spent the last three or four years?'

He gave a wry smile. He knew what I was saying.

'Would you commit a rape now if you were out?'

'No.'

'How would you feel if a woman turned you down?'

'I would just walk away.'

'What would happen if you got pissed one night and saw a young girl in a tight miniskirt walking down a quiet, empty street? What would you do?'

'I'd keep under control. I'm here for rape fantasies, no other reason. I've had a test. Psychologists showed me films about rape and normal sex. I passed, OK. Sometimes I got erections, but not any more. That means I'm OK now.'

He wasn't challenging me to disagree with him. He was simply echoing what other people had told him. He could describe in detail how he had spent his time in Rampton and the various courses and programmes he had undertaken. His message through all of this remained clear. He had done his time. He didn't want to be here any more.

I pressed him further.

463

'How well do you get on with the other patients?'

'Good.'

'Any problems?'

'Yeah, sometimes. It's only natural in a place like this. People get on your nerves, or piss you off. But I just go with the flow.'

'What about the staff? Do you get on well with them?'

'Yeah. Some of 'em have been really good to me.'

He was able to name three or four who he felt had made a lot of positive inroads into his life. The occupational therapy sessions had gone well and he'd developed much better communication and social skills.

This was patently obvious simply by seeing the change in him. He was a new man, with a maturity that couldn't simply be explained by the passing of time.

'If you were to leave here and eventually make your way back into the community, where would you live?'

'In a flat.'

'What do you think the problems might be? You've been in hospital for quite a long time.'

'I might get lonely sometimes.'

'How do you think you'll cope with that?'

'Well, I'll have a social worker.'

'Yes.'

'And I'll get involved in some of the local social groups.'

The answers were delivered faultlessly. He made good eye contact and recognized the seriousness of the questions.

At the same time, his responses struck me as being too fast and too light – as though delivered by rote rather than reflected upon. He knew what answers were expected. These were questions that others had asked him before.

I knew this man. I had once listened to his sexual fantasies and recognized the risk he posed. That's why I knew there was a big gap between reality and the impression Malcolm worked to create. It wasn't that I had formed a negative opinion years before and was reluctant to see there had been a change. Even without my earlier knowledge, I would still have had a huge question mark over his veracity.

Nowhere in the files had I seen evidence that the psychosexual problem driving his original offending had been identified and fully dealt with. Where had it gone? How had it gone?

These were almost identical questions to those I'd asked about Jimmy Fordham and so many other patients since him. For somebody's deviant sexuality to be successfully treated there had to be evidence of a focused intervention. It wouldn't just disappear. Yet Malcolm made no reference to such an experience. Nor was there any real mention in the hospital notes and records.

I tried another approach. 'Women used to be quite important to you, didn't they? But I guess you don't get to see so many girls in a special hospital.'

'No.'

'Except on the ward. There are the nurses.'

He gave a big grin. 'Yeah.'

'How do you get on with them?'

'Oh, great.'

'Who do you work with?'

'Well, most days I see Sally, Barbara or Verity.'

'How do they figure in your life?'

'They have been really good to me. They're so nice. They've helped me a lot.'

465

'So what about sex? You're now thirty years old; you've got sexual needs like any man. Sadly, life hasn't treated you very well when it comes to getting girl-friends. I think that was part of your problem. Now you've been stuck in here for four years. How do you cope?'

'Well, how do you think?' There was a slight edge to the comment.

'I'd prefer it if you were to tell me.'

'Same as before, really.'

'In what way?'

'I have a wank. We all do it in here, only we don't talk about it.'

'How often do you wank?'

He shrugged. He didn't want to go in this direction.

'It must be a bit difficult in a place like this. You're on a ward. There's not much privacy. Where?'

'In the bog, in my room. It's only natural. We're all young blokes. It's not a crime.'

'When you do it, who do you think about?'

'Girls from magazines.'

'What about real people? It used to be better to have a real person to think about than just a picture of someone.'

'Yeah, I suppose so.'

'Who do you think about?'

'There's Sally and Barbara. Verity, too, sometimes.'

'Tell me about them.'

'Barbara is smart. She looks after herself. Verity is a bit younger and likes the lads looking at her. I think she'd be a bit of a tease if it came down to it. Sally is the quiet one. Deep as a puddle, I say. I reckon she's one of those birds who seem uptight until they let their hair down.'

His little word sketches centred on their appearance and personalities rather than professional skills.

'When you think about Sally, Barbara or Verity, what is the setting?' I asked.

I noticed a flash of recognition in Malcolm's eyes. At that moment he realized that I knew the truth. Up until then he'd been rattling off answers as if they were scripted. But he was bright enough to understand when his comments could hurt him.

'I don't know what you mean,' he said, eyeing me suspiciously.

'You're a reasonable man, Malcolm. You're plugged in to what's been happening here. I'm sure the psychologists and staff here have explained to you about psychosexual development and functioning. You know exactly what you did and why you are here. I want to know how you cope nowadays.'

'I don't have them fantasies any more,' he said defensively. He stared at his hands, rubbing his thumb across one palm. We both knew he was lying.

Malcolm couldn't be sure how much authority I wielded over his situation. The last time we'd spoken, I hadn't managed to get him detained. At the same time, he felt an enormous pressure not to lie to me because so far I'd been able to recognize it. Nobody likes being caught in a lie. For one thing, it's embarrassing.

'When you picture Sally, Barbara or Verity while you're wanking, tell me what you see.'

'It's nothing weird. We just have sex.'

'Tell me about it.'

He began describing his fantasy. I was amazed at the vividness and richness of his detail. He talked about the smell of them, how Sally wore perfume but Barbara seemed to prefer soap and deodorant. He knew

467

precisely what clothes each of them wore and when one of them included something new in her workday wardrobe.

Like the other men on the ward, Malcolm was completely tuned in to all the messages and movements made by the female members of staff. In particular, they loved the summer because the nurses wore fewer clothes. Some of them had tight tops and blouses, or light cotton dresses that were slightly see-through when they stood with their backs to the sun.

Malcolm knew immediately when any of the nurses had changed her hairstyle or the colour of her nails. He knew which of their skirts was tighter or shorter.

'What do you like Sally to wear?'

'Oh, she has this white dress with blue flowers stitched around the neck.'

'Why do you like it?'

'It does nice things for her tits. Sometimes, when she leans over to hand you something, you can see her cleavage and her bra.'

'What about Verity?'

'I like her blue skirt.'

'Why?'

'It's a bit tighter. It rides up her bum a little when she bends at the waist.'

'Do you think she knows that you're looking at her like that?'

'Of course she knows.'

'Why?'

'There's a dozen blokes on this ward. She likes showing off.'

'What would you like to ask her if you could?'

He paused to think about this. 'Whether she wears stockings or tights. I've always wanted to know that.

And last week she came back from holiday with a suntan. I want to know if her tits are brown too.'

All these details were very important – not just to Malcolm, but to the other young men on the ward. They soaked up every snippet of information during the day, preparing for those quiet moments, in the privacy of their rooms, when they could masturbate. Each of them had their own little fantasy scenarios that were played out in their minds.

Malcolm, too, was locked into his 'models'. His fantasies were so vivid because he kept adding to them with real-world details – the brief glimpse of cleavage, the way a dress moved when a woman walked, the colour of her nails . . .

'When you're wanking and thinking about a nurse, what pictures are you seeing?'

'We're making love.'

'Tell me about that.'

'It's normally in my room. It's quiet. There's nobody around.'

I could see him becoming slightly aroused at the thought. His skin tone had changed and his breathing quickened.

'How does she get into the bedroom?'

In the long silence that followed, I remained absolutely still, my face as expressionless as I could contrive. My eyes were focused but relaxed. I wasn't trying to 'stare him out'.

Finally Malcolm whispered, 'I push her in.'

'Then what happens?'

'I throw her on the bed and we do it.'

'What does she do?'

'She's struggling.'

'What then?'

469

'I hit her in the face a few times. Then I lift that white dress and squeeze her tits. I keep one hand on her throat while I get her knickers off. Then I shove and I'm inside her. She gets right off on that. She's moaning and writhing.'

'What happens afterwards?'

'I tell her to keep her mouth shut or I'll come back.'

He opened the palms of his hands, as if to signal, 'There, that's the lot.'

I knew this couldn't be right. Malcolm had painted the scene in monochrome. Where was the colour? Where were the tiny details he collected each day?

I went back over the fantasy and began unpacking it further. Although there were kidnap and rape elements, the fantasy also portrayed the nurse as becoming massively aroused by his manful taking of her.

His first account of the fantasy had a slight ambivalence, but with each new telling the picture became more vivid. Malcolm described taking off her stockings and using them to tie her up before raping her. When the nurse fought back, he grew angry and used his fists to keep her under control.

The degree of force varied, depending upon the person concerned. With Verity it seemed to be more aggressive and violent.

'It's just a fantasy,' he said, becoming defensive again. 'I wouldn't do it for real, Mr Britton. I got too much to lose.'

In desperation he began recounting another fantasy – this one involving caressing and gentle lovemaking. It lacked any of the richness or vivid description of his earlier story. Nor did it colour his cheeks and quicken his pulse.

It was obvious what had happened. Over the years

the psychology department had described to him healthy masturbatory fantasies. Malcolm was bright enough to parrot these, but he couldn't hide his true nature. His victim's distress was of far greater erotic value than images of a woman simply lying back and passively accepting her fate. He wanted her to fight. If she resisted he could beat her. It confirmed his conquest. In the sexual world that Malcolm inhabited, pleasure was only about *his* enjoyment.

Working to hold my voice free of either criticism or collusion, I probed this further. Eventually Malcolm relaxed and described the outside pressures and stresses that made him angry. These were more likely to trigger his abduction and rape fantasies.

For example, if someone on the ward was winding him up, or a new patient arrived who didn't respect his personal space, Malcolm would get angry.

One incident in particular had made him more aggressive than usual. He had quite fancied a patient from one of the female wards, but she had 'got off with another bloke'. His sense of betrayal and harsh opinion of the girl were very similar to those he'd expressed six years earlier about Jill, the woman who had gone to the police and complained that he was a peeping Tom.

'Since you've been at Rampton have they ever suggested ways of changing your fantasies?'

He shrugged. 'They used to get me to write them on scraps of paper and we'd talk about them.'

'OK. Do you understand that I have a problem here, Malcolm? When I met you six years ago you were fantasizing about raping and killing a woman. And now – after four years here – it seems to me that your rape fantasies are still the ones that turn you on.'

He grew very agitated.

471

'What has changed?' I asked.

Malcolm half rose and leaned forward, moving his face closer to mine. He wanted to frighten me. He looked at me as though I'd tricked him. He'd given away too much.

I didn't make a big movement. I simply shifted my weight forward, ready to stand. If he lunged, I could use the weight of his charge to turn him past me.

'I think it's better if we don't,' I said, looking directly into his eyes. For a moment he held the same pose, ready to strike. Then he lowered his eyes and rocked back into his chair. He grew surly and enclosed.

Finally I could see the man I'd known previously. He'd shown me that he still existed.

'Why do you say that if you left here, you wouldn't harm or rape a woman?'

He flicked at his fingernails. 'I keep telling them I would. They're not listening.'

Although he didn't use these words, obliquely he was saying: 'It's not my fault if guys like you fuck up. You're the experts. I've left enough clues for you. They've shown me all the porno films and pictures. I've had erections. They should have recognized it. That's why it's your problem, not mine.'

His lower lip curled. All the politeness and civility had gone. He hated me and all that I represented.

I didn't rise to any challenge. My manner didn't alter. 'How do you feel about your time here, Malcolm?'

He spat his reply. 'They've had their chance to fix me. I've done my time.'

Two things had happened. Malcolm accepted that he hadn't changed. He might just as well have uttered, 'I am who I am.' It wasn't his fault. How

472

could he change who he really was? Others were to blame.

This attitude is another example of the cognitive dissonance that often affects people who are faced with conflicting realities and desires.

Six years earlier I'd met a shy, inarticulate young man with low self-esteem who didn't want to talk about his problem because it made him feel awkward. He knew that his violent fantasies were not right by ordinary interpretation, which was why he tried to mask them.

When he got to Rampton he continued to be cautious and guarded. He worried about how people would view him. However, a subtle shift occurred during this time. He convinced himself that his violent rape and abduction fantasies weren't a problem after all.

If all these experts had failed to ask him the right questions or nail his lies, then it wasn't his fault. It wasn't up to him to volunteer information that might harm his chances of getting out. And if they all said he didn't have a problem any more, then he didn't. They'd said so.

His problem didn't embarrass him any more. He no longer cared that he was different. On the contrary, it was great. It marked him out as being special. This was how he had dealt with the sense of anguish at being caught and imprisoned in a special hospital. Instead of being ashamed of his deviancy, he regarded it as a triumph.

Of course, he could never discuss or display this. He learned quickly how the system worked. If he revealed the truth, they'd keep him locked up. The only reason he had told me was because he knew that I didn't just accept what he said. I saw through the lies.

I rose from my chair and closed the file. Malcolm didn't look at me as I said goodbye. A part of him already knew that he wasn't getting out of Rampton. Another part perhaps clung to the knowledge that last time I had failed to get him locked away.

I went to the nursing office and asked if Sally, Verity or Barbara was on duty. The senior charge nurse ran his finger down the roster. Verity was on the ward. The others were due in later.

'It won't take a minute. I'll page her,' he said.

From the desk I glanced out of the observation window and watched a woman approaching down the corridor. She had blond hair pinned back from her forehead. She was in her early thirties and wore a knee-length skirt and short-sleeved blouse. Her hospital identity tag was pinned to the breast pocket.

Verity glanced quickly at her boss for reassurance.

'Is something wrong?' she asked.

'I need to talk to you about Malcolm.'

Verity sat down beside her boss. She pushed her hair behind her ears and blinked nervously. I had a rueful sense of déjà vu, remembering a similar meeting with a young probation officer.

'Verity – may I call you that?'

'Yes.'

'I want to take you through my examination of Malcolm. He has just described a series of fantasies that he uses when he masturbates. These are very violent and feature women that he knows. One of those women is you.

'I'm not suggesting that you've done anything to encourage him. This isn't necessary in Malcolm's case. He reads things into your actions, your clothes and mannerisms.'

She frowned and looked at her boss.

'In his fantasy, Malcolm abducts you from a corridor, drags you into his room, ties you up with your stockings and then rapes you.'

'Oh, fuck,' said the charge nurse.

Verity was on autopilot. 'I don't wear stockings,' she said, her voice trembling.

'He knows your movements through the ward. He knows those places that are more isolated and private. He has been improving on this fantasy for months – feeding on every detail about your clothes, hair, smell and the way your body moves.'

'But I've never done anything,' she whispered, almost in shock.

'You didn't have to. I'm telling you this because he wants to act out his fantasy here. The only reason it hasn't happened is because he hasn't judged that the opportunity has been right. You haven't been in the right place at the right time.'

I warned them to be particularly vigilant over the next twenty-four hours. I had left Malcolm in a state of agitation and he'd already admitted that his fantasies were strongest when he felt under pressure.

The charge nurse agreed to explain the situation to Barbara and Sally. I also knew that nurses in key relationships with patients would have to be reassigned.

After Verity had left the room, the charge nurse asked me, 'Should I have seen this?'

'That depends. So many of Malcolm's actions were designed to draw these women in. He befriended them. He was helpful. Everyone thought it was evidence of progress.'

In a highly structured institution such as Rampton, a form of timelessness exists. It's easy to forget the full characteristics of the index offence because it's only referred to in outline. Instead, effort is focused on the small day-to-day gains – the new social skill acquired and the involvement in various groups.

People began to like Malcolm and he began to like himself. Quasi-parental feelings built up. Sadness for his early suffering and deprivation fuelled a growing belief that 'He won't let us down. We'll change him.'

Sadly, it doesn't work like that – not unless this faith and positive role modelling is backed up by deliberate and focused intervention.

Verity, Sally and Barbara had fallen into the compassion trap. They didn't continually check and challenge Malcolm's self-reports. They believed him because they wanted him to be better. They could see a person within him, behind the shell of deprivation, whom they wanted to reach out to.

'But I thought he wanted to get out of here?' asked the charge nurse.

'He does. But most of all he wants to act out his fantasy. His urge to rape and kill outweighs his desire for freedom. He also knows that once it happens, he's never leaving.

'For him that's not such a bad conclusion. He fits in here. He's got a few friends, of sorts. This is a comfortable place. He'll never have to worry about looking after himself – and sex is always in the air. Compare that with the sort of life he left on the outside. Nobody wants him and nothing is waiting for him out there.'

As I drove home that afternoon, I pulled in at a service station and bought a cup of coffee. Several long-haul coaches were lined up in the car park. Passengers spilled off and stretched their legs. It had been raining since I left Rampton and oil slicks gleamed in rainbow colours on the puddles. I thought of Malcolm getting off that bus four or five years earlier. He slid his bus ticket in his pocket and went walking through the darkened streets of Peterborough, looking in the lighted windows for a woman's silhouette.

As I've explained earlier, only a few people are evil from the moment they come into the world. Most of those who go on to injure and exploit have been distorted by what others have done or, more often, not done to them, usually in their younger years.

Despite their crimes, we all want these one-time victims to make good; to work through the dead weight of the past. We care for them and we feel enormous emotional surges of compassion for what has become of them. We work to help them change.

Nevertheless, we should never forget what the damage has made them become. Some of them are dangerous, often cunning, resourceful and deceitful. If we ignore this we leave others still at risk.

23

Malcolm Harris is not unique. there are too many cases like his, particularly if the right risk assessment procedures are not in place. For instance, Jimmy Fordham had convinced people that he was ready to go back into the world.

There had been two very similar incidents at Arnold Lodge. A young pregnant nurse had been seriously attacked while taking a patient on an escorted walk in the grounds. Another nurse was saved from strangulation only by a quick-thinking colleague who realized she had disappeared from a corridor.

In both of these incidents the patients denied any sexual intent and claimed to have been 'overcome by a sudden urge'. They were lying.

The first offender had followed the nurse's duty rota for days, carefully choosing to take her when the fewest experienced staff members were on duty. In the second case the 'spur of the moment' explanation didn't explain why he had set up a decoy story to woo the nurse before he attacked her.

These were symptoms of a much greater malaise at Arnold Lodge. The RSU had changed a great deal since my arrival ten years earlier. Not all of these changes were for the better.

By the mid-nineties the new regime that ran the Regional Forensic Service regarded people like myself as dinosaurs who wanted to undermine their push for savings and improved efficiency. I became increasingly unhappy when we couldn't persuade them that certain vital conditions had to underpin a truly effective forensic setting.

There seemed to be a growing tendency within the NHS to let the inexperienced view the organization in terms of flow charts and bed occupancy – as you might an international hotel chain. Hospitals and health care don't work this way. People like Malcolm Harris and Jimmy Fordham can't be shuffled around or treated as though time heals all wounds.

Although Jimmy's attempted rape had been thwarted, and nobody had been seriously hurt or died in the other incidents, it did lead to a local review and an attempt to clear out those on the Forensic Management Team who were not thought to be in tune with current thinking. I was not affected by this, but became even more deeply concerned at the management style then in place, which was characterized by authoritarianism and the covering up of problems.

Finally, in 1995, no longer able to ignore my concerns and frustrations, I resigned from the Forensic Management Team and reverted solely to looking after the psychology service, which I had headed since 1986. A year later I also withdrew from this, to focus on direct clinical work and research within the unit. I couldn't bear to see the service that I had helped nurture and build sinking in an organizational quicksand. It was very sad.

Later, Arnold Lodge made the headlines for all the

wrong reasons. A member of staff was stabbed and several patients escaped or absconded. The Secretary of State for Health became involved and ordered an independent inquiry.

I had mixed feelings. I had some affection for the RSU as an institution but, if left as it was, I could see it disintegrating. A management change might just save it.

I had two choices. I could watch from the sidelines and hope the inquiry found the true problems and made the right recommendations. Or I could accept its invitation to give evidence and make sure the problems were properly understood. I chose to give evidence. Having answered all I was asked, I left the inquiry feeling better about the future than I had for months; these people were looking neither to whitewash a problem nor to find a ritual sacrifice.

Unfortunately, this positive feeling didn't last. Shortly after my evidence there was another serious incident within Arnold Lodge. A patient detained because of the risk he posed somehow acquired a weapon and escaped. His absence hadn't been recognized by any of the existing security systems. It was almost a carbon copy of one of the incidents that had triggered the inquiry. This could and should have been prevented.

I wrote a letter to the chief executive of the Trust telling her of my concern over this copycat escape. I also asked her to close Arnold Lodge to further admissions until the inquiry had finished and its recommendations had been implemented. I sent a copy of the letter to the chairman of the inquiry.

An almighty battle ensued. The first salvo came from the corridors of power, claiming I had breached procedure by writing in such a way. Just as I was about to return fire, another serious incident occurred at Arnold Lodge. A patient given leave to visit a relative was found hanged.

The letter I wrote back to the chief executive contained the same advice I'd given earlier to the inquiry into Arnold Lodge. You cannot conduct or implement a treatment unless you have a proper assessment. In my view the risk assessment procedures had to be carefully re-examined.

Instead of reiterating my belief that the unit should stop admitting any new patients, I went a step further and asked for Arnold Lodge to be closed immediately and all the existing patients transferred. Alternatively, a new management team had to be put into place right away.

Silence followed. The new head of psychology was given instructions to make sure I adhered to the proper reporting procedures. The maverick label stuck.

Because I had been outspoken in my opposition to the regime at Arnold Lodge, people at the sharp end – the nurses and clinicians – were coming to me and expressing their unhappiness and their fears. They asked if I could speak on their behalf and insist on change.

Later that day I rang the chief executive. 'I don't want to put anything else in writing and add to your pressure,' I told her, 'but you must understand that unless you can make these changes within a few days I have no choice but to take it further.'

She listened intently and assured me that she knew about the situation.

Wheels were now in motion. Emmett Larkin, a senior clinician from another service, had been approached to become the clinical director at Arnold Lodge. Jim McDonald, a senior general manager with an extensive forensic nursing background, was also being recruited as director of operations and general manager for the forensic service.

Literally within days, most of the existing senior management left the service in the shake-out.

The new team quickly took Arnold Lodge out of Leicestershire's jurisdiction and into a different NHS Trust. By 2001 it should be part of a solely forensic trust – exactly what had been argued for at the very beginning. Much more importantly, McDonald and Larkin created and held together a new management team that completely transformed the functioning of the forensic service. Within eighteen months they had turned Arnold Lodge into a centre of excellence, the flagship from which staff are asked to go all over the world to show how it should be done.

This team is the best I have ever worked with. Instead of worrying about a culture of blame and concealment, we could get back to doing our real jobs.

'Do you know what the time is?' my secretary said, glancing at the clock as I arrived at the office.

I apologized for running late. I'd been to see a priest who was having an affair with a woman parishioner (a patient of mine). She had fallen in love with him and was now racked by guilt and convinced that God would punish both of them. The priest seemed to be playing both ends against the middle by telling her that he loved her but that he couldn't stop being a priest.

Diane handed me a bundle of phone messages. 'Mr Miller is waiting,' she said. 'You'll have to answer these later.'

Cameron Miller, a new patient, had been sitting in the waiting room for half an hour. Thankfully, he was the last appointment for the afternoon. He put down a magazine and stood as I arrived. 'I'm sorry I kept you,' I said. 'It's only a short walk to Main Lodge. We'll talk there.'

He had a dark, full beard and an olive complexion. His eyes were calm and alert, with the pupils dilated and looking jet black against the brilliant white that surrounded them. Overall, the effect was quite striking, even for a man of slightly less than average height.

He wore a tailored business suit and carried a briefcase. As we stepped outside, he slipped on a dark navy, knee-length coat and pulled the collar close to keep out the cold. It was late in the year and would soon be dark.

Main Lodge is a small, two-storey, red brick and sandstone building that had once been the gatekeeper's lodge at what is now the main entrance to the Towers Hospital. The hospital had taken its name from the magnificent twin brick towers that years ago had flanked the old entrance. Rising from a small hill and reachable along a sweeping ornamental drive, these towers had given the impression of continuity and resoluteness – reflecting the certainty of the city fathers that the best way to treat mental illness was to build such a hospital. Yet in reality such asylums cast a very bleak shadow across the lives of ordinary people. Many regard madness as being somehow contagious and being taken into 'the Towers' as akin to having the plague.

I can understand these irrational fears. In the early days, being diagnosed with mental illness often meant long years of confinement away from the public gaze.

Thankfully the treatment regimes and institutions had changed dramatically by the time I joined the service.

Main Lodge was part of the estate of the Regional Forensic Services. Initially it had been used as a clinical and administrative base, before Arnold Lodge was opened. Later it became an occasional outpatient clinic. I had to unlock two doors to get in and lock them behind us to prevent any unauthorized entry. The part-time offices were empty and we were alone in the building.

'Well, Mr Miller, come in and take a seat.'

He was plainly unimpressed by his surroundings, which were in need of new carpeting and a fresh coat of paint. He hung his overcoat over a chair and glanced casually at the clock. It was twenty minutes to four.

According to the referral letter Cameron had apparently run into problems in a relationship with a young woman, Julie. She had gone to see a social worker and spoken about his aggression. She felt that their love-making had become brutish and impersonal. He seemed to 'lose himself' and 'become an animal . . . I can't get close to him any more.'

None of these comments seemed to fit with the well-presented man sitting opposite me. He looked like a successful business manager or a junior executive on his way up the corporate ladder.

Having made the introductions, I explained to Cameron that I first wanted to get an overall under-standing of his difficulty and why he'd come to see me.

'From there we can move on,' I said. 'I want to get to know exactly who you are and what forces, processes and experiences have made you into who you are. I won't ask you anything just out of curiosity. Nor will

I judge you morally. If it gets too difficult or painful, you can call for time out.'

He relaxed a little and glanced at the clock again.

Apart from the brief referral note, I had no other paperwork on the case. I knew there had to be more, but it was obviously somewhere in the system and hadn't yet reached me.

It didn't bother me. I didn't particularly want to read what other people had said about Cameron. I wanted to hear it from him.

'Oh, that's a change,' he said, with only the slightest hint of sarcasm. 'I've seen dozens of people like you.'

'OK. So what is it that brings you to me?'

'Well, it's a very long story. It goes on for years.'

'I can accept that, but something must be happening in your life now that brings you here.'

He shrugged.

'Are you in work?'

'Yes.'

'So presumably you've taken time off to come here?'

'Yes, I have.'

'How long has it taken?'

'Two and a half hours.'

'That's a long trip. Something has to be going on to make it worthwhile coming to see me.'

'Well, yes.'

'So . . . ?'

'What do they say in the letter?'

'They talk about your relationship with Julie. There is a concern – I don't know if you share it – that you might want to hurt yourself or someone else.'

He didn't answer.

Cameron seemed quite hostile, as though he'd only

turned up at somebody else's behest; as though he was keeping a bargain.

'This is like a merry-go-round,' he said ambivalently. 'I've been in clinics all over the world. Now I'm here.'

'I can't make you any promises, Mr Miller, but you've come all this way, why not just talk to me a little. Nobody else is waiting. You have as long as it needs.'

He looked at the clock. His upper torso had begun to rock gently and I could see the tension in his shoulders.

'Are you all right?'

'Yes.' He didn't sound overly confident.

'Is there anything that I've said . . . ?'

'No.' His reply had a cool sharpness.

'Well, I can see that you're not altogether comfortable.'

'I'm fine.' He rocked back and forth.

Glancing down, I reread the referral note. A GP had written, '*I believe he sometimes carries a knife.*'

Oh great! I had just locked myself into Main Lodge with this man! There wasn't another soul within a hundred yards.

The room had grown darker as the light faded outside. I carried on talking to Cameron, but his attention kept drifting. Clearly something else was intruding into his thoughts. I needed to bring him back.

'Mr Miller . . . Cameron . . . tell me about Julie. She thinks something is going wrong. How long have you been together?'

'Four years.'

'Have they been good years? Do you love each other? Is there anyone else in your life or hers? Do you look forward to going home?'

'What is there to tell? We're together.'

He looked up at the clock again, growing more agitated. It was ten minutes to four.

'Julie says that you've become aggressive. It sounds as though she cares a lot about you.'

'Yes.'

'Do you care about her?'

'Not as much as she cares about me. She wants to get married and have kids, the whole lot.'

'And what do you think?'

'I'm not in love with her ... not in the same way.'

'So why are you together?'

'We just are.'

I pressed gently, trying to learn more about their relationship. Cameron still wasn't wholly concentrating on our discussion. He looked at the clock again.

'Mr Miller, something isn't right. Am I pushing into a sensitive area? Should we leave it till later? I don't want to bludgeon you into talking about things that you can't talk about yet. It's only our first day.'

He looked at the clock. 'No, it isn't that.'

'Have you got to be somewhere?'

'No, not really. How much longer will we be?'

'What's the matter?'

'What time do you make it?'

'Five to four.'

'Are you sure?'

'Yes. Why, what's wrong?'

'I don't want to be here at four o'clock.'

'Why?'

'You won't want me to be here.'

'I don't understand. What's so important about four o'clock?'

He paused, held my eyes for a moment, and then

looked past me. 'That's when I become a werewolf.'

Now I looked at the clock. What the hell was happening? Nothing in the referral note mentioned this. Was this man fragmenting? Did he have a profound psychotic illness that he'd masked until now? Had I done something to push him over the edge?

Although he was very calm, Cameron's breathing had become shallow and his skin pale. He rocked backwards and forwards.

I no longer thought about the knife. Werewolves don't need them. On the wall above my head, the red second hand circled. Black hands pointed to the twelve and four. Two minutes.

'It's not far off four,' I said.

'I know.'

'Are you going to be all right?' I tried to sound as calm as possible.

He didn't answer.

'Is there anything I can do now? Anything you can do?'

'You don't understand. I'm going to change, I'm a werewolf.'

The words sent a chill through me, but I had to be clear what he meant. 'Listen, Cameron, what's happened before? Are you going to be able to stay where you are? Do you need me with you or do you need space?'

The clock had ticked down to the final seconds. There wasn't time to flee. Main Lodge was empty. What a mess! If this was to be a physical acting out of a werewolf scenario, then it came down to Cameron and me.

Reflexively I summed up Cameron's physical size and strength. Even so, I knew it didn't really matter.

Big or small, if he slid into disinhibition, he'd doubtless become very powerful.

His hands began shaking and the fingers started to stiffen. From his lap they stretched out across his thighs. His knuckles were white and his fingers twisted inwards. His entire torso began to puff up and his eyes partially rolled upwards in their sockets.

I heard a guttural scraping sound – like the sound of a manhole cover being moved. It came from deep down in his diaphragm. The muscles in his shoulders bunched and his body tightened like a coiled spring. His head was cocked, his lips pulled back, away from his teeth. Slowly his eyes rolled down, the pupils dilated into blackness. He stared directly at me, or through me.

I heard him growl.

I sat extremely still, alert to his every movement. He had to be dissociating. How far would it go? Would he try to take prey?

If he comes off the chair, I have to match him for size, I told myself. He has to know, from wherever he is, that I'm not an easy mark.

At the same time, I knew that I shouldn't intervene or try to touch him. If he wanted to run, I'd give him a wide berth. But the doors were locked. He couldn't get out. There were three windows, all of them fastened.

Cameron had slipped onto the floor. He crouched there, on all fours, as if ready to spring. He tossed his head back and howled. It wasn't so much deafening as penetrating and I could feel the hair on the back of my neck rise.

He began to pull at his clothes, rolling his head from side to side like a dog trying to rid itself of a new collar.

Then he fixed his stare on me. He moved to face me.

His eyes were like black holes. He crouched to lunge. Here it comes, I thought.

Then, suddenly, the howling stopped. Cameron crumpled to the floor, thrashing his arms and legs for some ten seconds. Then he curled up into a ball, with his knees pulled up and his head down; he whimpered like a child in a nightmare. He rocked back and forth and after a minute he lay still, weeping.

I went to him, crouching down – not touching him or within arm's reach. 'How are you now?' I asked.

He seemed to look past me, unsure of where he was. 'I don't know.'

'Can you get back in your chair?'

He nodded.

Leaning heavily on the back of the chair, he dragged himself upright and sat down.

'How often does it happen?'

'Every day at four o'clock.'

'Any other times?'

'Sometimes.'

'Does it make a difference where you are?'

'Well, I make sure that I'm somewhere nobody can see.'

'Can you tell me what happened?'

'I'm a werewolf, I changed. Didn't you see?'

'What does that mean?'

'Surely you saw. I became a wolf – the wolf becomes me. We are one.'

'What happens to your body?'

'You saw it with your own eyes,' he said incredulously. 'I have the body of a wolf and the needs of a wolf. I am a wolf.'

Deliberately, I chose not to say, 'That isn't what I saw.' I hadn't forgotten the knife.

Cameron's breathing was laboured and his shirtfront stained with perspiration. He seemed exhausted, but I knew that I had his attention.

'You probably think that you're unique, Cameron,' I told him. 'And you probably think you're insane.'

He agreed with his eyes.

'From time to time people have these experiences. It doesn't mean that you're not entirely human or that it's not reversible. Something catastrophic is going on inside your mind. I need to find out what that is.'

'Others have tried.'

'Maybe. Where did you expect to be at four?' I asked.

'On the train. I would have locked myself in the toilet.'

Episodes like this don't happen on cue at particular hours, or times of the month, unless the subject has some degree of control. For this reason, I now didn't worry about Cameron attacking me. Four o'clock had passed.

'Has it always been like that?' I asked.

'No. In the early days, I'd go hunting.'

'What do you mean by the early days?'

He shrugged. 'Ten years ago.'

'I want to take you further back than that. I want to learn who you are and how you came to be this way. Is that OK?'

He nodded.

Werewolves aren't only found in horror films and fantasy books. They exist in real life. Known as lycanthropy, it is a condition in which a patient believes himself to be both a man and a wild beast. Under certain external conditions, the man 'becomes' the beast, or 'takes on' its true nature.

Although the werewolf is the best known, there are many far less common human–beast combinations. I've heard of were-bears, were-bats and were-badgers. I've also come across a man who believed that he changed into a panther; and a woman who thought she became a cat. There is undoubtedly a cultural symbolism and significance in the choice of animal. In the past some tended to be gender specific, but with greater female equality werewolves have become evenly distributed between the sexes.

Cultural influences have some other interesting effects in the mental health field. For example, there are fewer patients nowadays who persist in believing that they are Jesus Christ. This reduction can partly be explained by the use of prescribed psychotropic medication to treat delusions, but it also reflects the fact that religion doesn't play as big a role in people's lives as it once did.

Why do people choose to be animals? There is always some unique underpinning rationale behind the change. To discover what this logic is can sometimes be very difficult. It requires a willingness to stand in a patient's emotional shoes and see the world as they do.

Look at what they become. They don't turn into geckos or budgies or hamsters. Instead they become strong, predatory, liberated, fearless, frightening animals of one sort or another. This is because often these people need to have some form of expression and sense of power that their own background has never allowed them to develop in the ordinary way. They find a feeling of achievement and independence that is lacking in their normal lives. The surging internal wave of physical exhilaration at being a powerful and fearsome beast compensates for their sense of resentment and failure.

I didn't know if Cameron Miller fell into this category. I hoped so. The alternative was far darker.

The notion of the werewolf has long been embedded in folklore. Ghouls and vampires occupy distinct but similar niches in our cultural history in the sense that they elicit the same fears of physical and/or spiritual destruction.

Towards the close of the twentieth century we recognized the existence of certain abnormal people who gain pleasure, satisfaction or retribution from controlling, mutilating and killing others. These people have been labelled predatory serial killers. As each year passes and new examples emerge, we are learning more about how they develop, how they find their victims, what they do to them and, mercifully, how to catch them.

Against our expectations, we are constantly discovering that these people live blandly among us, often unrecognized for years. We look for depraved monsters in Victorian alleyways but don't look for them across the road in Cromwell Street or Rillington Place.

I have been asked many times if serial and predatory sexual killers are a modern phenomenon. Of course they're not, they've been with us from the beginnings of civilization; they just weren't understood then as we understand them today. In the past we called them werewolves, ghouls or vampires. We created myths about them, just as we still do, to an extent, with fictional creations such as Hannibal Lecter.

Today we make films that glamorize our serial killers and we give them exotic names such as the 'Gay Slayer' and the 'Midlands Ripper'. Some, like the 'Black Panther', are echoes from the past.

Certain elements are needed to create such myths –

great strength, animal ferocity, an attractive victim and the disappearance of the killer. Soon you have a central character that grows stronger and more brutal with each telling of the story. We add gloss and charisma to creatures that we fear because they fascinate us.

When seemingly ordinary people are arrested for these crimes, I suspect that they struggle to explain their actions. It is far simpler for them to say, 'Something inside of me took over,' or 'I became a beast.' So the legend grows.

Over time we forget the poor victims and focus on the 'shape-shifter' – a far more potent figure. He, too, is partially portrayed as a victim, one whose condition inspires fear and respect. This confirms his unsought isolation and justifies his anger and self-pity.

These aspects of lycanthropy are rarely recognized, yet they are of enormous significance to those who come to see themselves as werewolves.

Cameron Miller began relating his life story. He had been born in the Middle East thirty years earlier, the only son of a British oil financier. The family lived abroad, moving between various Arab countries and living in luxury expatriate compounds that seemed to isolate Westerners from the local culture and populace.

Cameron's mother, in particular, was frightened that her young son would come to harm if exposed to a society that she regarded as barbaric and heathen. For this reason Cameron spent long periods on his own, immersed in books and his own imaginary games.

In different circumstances his curiosity and verbal skills would have led him to become extremely gregarious, with good interpersonal skills and sensitivity, but because of his isolation he didn't become comfortable with other people. He grew accustomed to being alone rather than participating socially. It was like looking through a window at a party from the outside and seeing how the people moved between groups, smiling, chatting and pausing occasionally to reflect. Having only observed this but never experienced it, he didn't learn the essential social skills that most of us take for granted.

When Cameron was twelve years old he began to 'escape'. Without asking or telling anyone, he'd slip away from the compound and spend hours exploring the local souks and mosques. He embraced and soaked up the unfamiliar culture, with its blaring horns, exotic smells, flowing robes and calls to prayer. He had lived on the edge of these things for years but now he was there, in the midst of this incredibly vivid and lively environment.

Cameron had nobody to interpret or guide his perception of this new world. He became immersed in the foreignness of it all. In particular, he was impressed by the external, very visual manifestations of local religious and philosophical beliefs. These highly ritualized and symbolic displays of faith seemed to be an integral part of people's lives. This was very different from Cameron's limited experience of Christian beliefs, which tended to be downplayed by his parents and the churches. There were rarely open displays of religious ritual.

Side by side with this – again with hindsight – Cameron spoke of being deeply affected by the clear disregard for animal suffering in the souks and mosques. In the markets he saw live chickens, goats and sheep traded in the same way that we trade cauliflower. He saw them slaughtered openly, bled, disembowelled and carved up. Body parts such as eye-balls and testes were prized as delicacies. He didn't respond to this with repugnance, shock or fear. He was a blank canvas, upon which these events were the initial brush strokes.

By comparison, life in the compound and at home was very sanitized. Cameron's anxious and over-protective mother had cosseted him from birth. She was a pillar of the small British community and firmly believed that her son, above all else, had to be an Englishman. The fact that the family lived in an Arab country was an accident of fate, to be ignored and, where possible, shut out entirely behind high walls. This was to protect who they were as much as to guard against what might happen to them.

These incompatible strands of experience were juxta-posed when Cameron began exploring outside the compound.

As so often happens, it's not just the external world that impacts upon an individual. We each have our individual characteristics that influence how we see the world. If Cameron had been an ordinary, robust, uncomplicated youngster, being caught between these two vastly different cultures might have made no difference at all. Instead he had a strong artistic sensi-tivity. He was highly intelligent – not just academically, but in a socially insightful and delicate way.

Cameron's knowledge and attitudes had come mainly from books and films. He was able to read early and well and enjoyed a broad range of books, many of them literary classics. Again, he had nobody to inter-pret or aid his understanding of these stories. For him *Wuthering Heights* was a horror story rather than a romance.

Although intelligent, he wasn't sophisticated enough to pick up all the sub-plots or the nuances of character. Instead he took in the high-impact storyline – the plot became everything. Only later – and this caused him great problems – did he discover that the characters were far more complex than he imagined and even those he perceived as being heroic might in fact be pretty miserable people.

All of what Cameron described was a consequence of his cognitive development.

Jean Piaget, an immensely important Swiss researcher, spent his life studying the process of the child's mental development. Although other workers have produced many refinements and experimental exceptions, Piaget's main observations remain persuasive.

Between the ages of twelve and twenty-four months a child begins to search for novelty in the environment; to invent new ways of doing things and to have mental images and thoughts about objects that are not immediately present.

Over the next five years – during the Pre-operational Stage – the child develops the capacity to use symbols to represent objects and to assign them successfully to different groups. However, this is usually fragmented and strongly related to the physical appearance of objects.

Later – roughly between the ages of seven and eleven years – the child is able to perform mental operations, such as adding different groups of red blocks together and taking away any blue blocks from the table. Even this progress tends to remain related to tangible objects that are immediately present. Piaget named this the Concrete Operations Stage.

Finally the child develops the intellectual capacity to go beyond the physical appearance of the world and produce logical ideas of why things are as they are and how they relate to each other conceptually, whether the child is present or not. This is the Formal Operational Stage and seems to coincide with adolescence, between approximately twelve and fifteen years of age.

The capacity for formal operational thinking doesn't replace imagination or magical thinking or vivid daydreaming. Nor does it replace any strong feelings related to emotional distress, which may follow from defective perceptions or irrational reasoning about situations.

In Cameron's case, by the time he began secretly slipping away into the community, he was just reaching the point where the final stage of his basic cognitive capacity was beginning to open.

Because, up until this point, Cameron's understanding of the world at large had come mainly through books and the cinema, he had developed in a very passive way. He had seen little of what lay beyond the four walls of the compound.

For this reason, the impact of the new sights, sounds and smells was massive. It didn't overwhelm or frighten him because he approached it with the same passive involvement that he would when he read a book or watched a movie.

The difference, however, was that when he saw things in real life he didn't have to visualize descriptions of strange and unfamiliar locations. He could literally see, feel, smell and walk through this story. He didn't talk to people (he didn't speak their language) and he wasn't a character within the 'book'. He remained on the outside, looking in.

Walking through this book, he began to create his own stories to fit the scenes. His literary exposure fuelled these plots, which tended to be quite extravagant, with secret agents, spies and gallant heroes. That chicken seller on the corner has a secret past. He's in love with the woman behind the veil who watches from the window, who is really a kidnapped princess stolen from her cradle and raised by merchants.

The world had a completely new dimension for Cameron and it proved to be enormously exciting. He discovered it at a high absorption time in his childhood and it was all the more telling because he had done it secretly.

Over time he came to a deeper realization that people were moved by their own needs rather than by his thoughts. Just thinking them into particular roles and relationships would not determine what they actually did. They were uncontrollable and consequently they had to be watched.

Abruptly, with almost no notice, Cameron was sent back to England to a boarding school in the Home Counties. Now another new world demanded not his passive observation but full participation. Again, his only preparation for it came from books and his mother's memories. Externally, he greeted the news with eagerness. 'It's grand. I'm going to England; to Father's school.'

Totally compliant, he was packed off. As they all boarded the plane, his parents enthused about how much fun it would be and how his life's success would flow from it. Cameron waved goodbye to them from the school doorway.

Boarding school was to be a quiet catastrophe.

From the first moment of arrival, after being almost isolated from people he found there was no escaping them. Surrounded by students and teachers, Cameron rarely had a peaceful moment to himself.

Nothing marked him out as being different. He was bright and articulate; he could take part in classwork and didn't stand out as being particularly awkward in social gatherings. People wanted to be his friends; teachers asked him questions; he had to join in activities. Yet nobody realized that Cameron didn't want to be part of any of it.

Every effort was made to welcome and include Cameron, but this only increased the pressure. Each day was like a new assault on his senses; an overwhelming, continuous stimulation that he couldn't turn off. If it had been a book he could have marked the page, closed the cover and gone for a walk. This was real.

Cameron had always been a voyeur, watching the world from the outside. Now they wanted him to participate, to take a role. Cameron didn't know how. He had always looked through the window and never stepped inside. His heightened artistic sensitivity and social awareness exacerbated these problems. He wanted to be left alone, to re-establish a stillness in himself, but that was impossible in such an environment, no matter how idyllic it might seem to others.

How did he react?

He didn't truant or misbehave. Instead he began to fail academically, sinking quietly into the mire. The pastoral alarm bells began to ring loudly at the school. Here was a bright boy – on paper he should be getting straight As – so why was he failing?

Cameron's family was concerned and decided to move him to a new school. They put him through cramming courses in the summer in a bid to improve his grades. By now he spent virtually all his time in his room.

Cameron performed indifferently in his A-level exams. He managed to scrape into a university, although not the one family tradition required. He began his course the following October with high expectations of himself and visions of academic triumph.

Initially, it had seemed feasible. Unlike boarding schools, universities are places where it is possible to escape from people. Cameron could lock himself away for periods and emerge for seminars, lectures and tutorials. He wasn't socially phobic and could sit in rooms full of people, taking notes and asking questions.

An exciting feature of university life is normally the hothouse atmosphere of intellectual development. Usually this is characterized by intense political and social debate, sexual adventure, drug experimentation and alcohol use.

In such an environment, it wasn't long before Cameron began to lose his footing. The strategies he had developed for being in the world and understanding it, without having to take part, proved to be insufficient.

He tried to hang on but he couldn't. Increasingly he stayed in his room, sitting in silence and experiencing longer and longer periods of nothingness. He wasn't aware of any internal dialogue. He knew he had to keep going to lectures and producing assignments. He told himself, 'All I have to do is go outside. How hard can that be? Tomorrow I will.'

When an essay deadline approached, he said, 'I'll work all weekend. I'll make sure I do it this time.'

He often went so far as doing the pencil sharpening and preparation. Invariably, people would interrupt. They'd come looking for him, inviting him down to the Student Union for a pint. He made excuses but they wouldn't listen. 'Come on, Cameron, you can catch up tomorrow. All work and no play – you know what they say.'

Dragged out with the crowd, Cameron would massively overuse alcohol. It was like an anaesthetic, desensitizing him to having people physically and socially close. Being bright and articulate, he could carry on conversations and keep people entertained. None of those around him realized his inner torment and how much he hated the way they stood too close to him, or shook his hand, or kissed him on the cheek.

Privately, this introspective, passive, highly visual young man was beginning to have violent thoughts towards those who got too close. He found no chain of logic to this that made it easier to understand. He simply found that when the pressure began to build, if he used his aggressive imagination he felt better.

This quickly progressed to hurting himself – not self-mutilation, but abusing his body with food and alcohol. He would overeat and then starve himself or go on drinking binges. He then began to hurt himself on the furniture, punching the walls and banging his head into the door, sometimes marking himself quite heavily.

Despite all these barriers, a young woman found her way into his life, complicating things further. She fell in love with him and tumbled into the trap that I see so often in my clinical work. She was attracted by his vulnerability. To her, he seemed to be the ideal candidate for salvation and redemption – a broken doll that she would fix.

They began a relationship that Cameron was unable to consummate physically. He told himself they had a loving relationship and that sexual intercourse would be an acknowledgement of this. Instead, he felt massive shame and a certainty that he was a failure as a person, just as he'd failed as a lover.

According to his account, his girlfriend envisaged them spending the rest of their lives together. She imagined them finishing university, getting married, having a family – all the things she had dreamed about. Although Cameron didn't have the words to say this, the thought of having someone always with him, for the rest of his life, was the most frightening prospect of all.

He wanted to live in a world that didn't and couldn't touch him – to watch but not participate. For him, ordinary, interpersonal closeness between a man and woman was like being touched by a hot iron. He simply couldn't tolerate it.

Two things happened. First, he started to drop a shutter between himself and his girlfriend because he had to keep her away to stop his pain. He did this by becoming physically abusive. His intention wasn't to hurt her – the prime motivation was to reduce his own suffering.

Secondly, he found release in the beginnings of a dissociated state. He also started to have profound sleep disturbance and to show signs of depression, although not at a level that would trigger psychiatric intervention, but he remained anxious and couldn't put his thoughts together. Increasingly it became easier for him to sit in nothingness rather than to confront the world.

This 'emptiness' into which he escaped is difficult to

describe. He was able to sit alone, completely orientated in terms of person, place and time, and then to let everything gradually fade away. He could sit in his room for four, five, six hours at a stretch with no impatience or thought. Afterwards he had no recollection of having thought about anything.

One day Cameron hit his girlfriend. It wasn't an explosive rage or loss of temper. Instead, he responded to his own cold hopelessness. He could see no future, only pain associated with her being there.

His life was crumbling, along with, he thought, his sanity. He had been brought up, right from his earliest days, to know that certain things were expected of him – a path had been chosen by his parents that included a model education, academic achievement and a glorious career. There were implicit and explicit benchmarks and criteria that he was expected to meet. Set against this, he had the reality of his life. It didn't compete.

When Cameron hit his girlfriend, he upset her badly. From her point of view a vulnerable person had suddenly become a mad person and she was frightened. Nevertheless, she went back to him, wanting to sort things out. She didn't realize that Cameron had learned two important lessons when he struck her.

Violence drove people away from him and it could also remove his pain.

When Cameron failed his first year exams, there was a crisis meeting with his parents and the university administrators. As Cameron related the events to me, I could see a change in the family orientation. His mother had been portrayed as over-sensitive and smothering while his father had been sketched very lightly, as if he played little direct part in his son's life.

Now he suddenly came to life. There he was in the Dean's office, breathing cold retribution.

'What the hell are you doing? This is not what we expect. You're a disgrace to the family.'

The speech went on, littered with references to 'self-indulgent claptrap' and 'expectations'. As Cameron described his father, I saw a man with the angry, dispassionate tone of a senior civil servant casting some junior attendant into the darkness. Each sentence was a body blow to Cameron.

Submissive and apologetic, he listened to his father's harsh appraisal. 'Pull yourself together or you're not worthy of this family.'

Here was the external confirmation that he was a failure and it came from the highest source. From the beginning of his memory his father had been held out as 'that which you are to become'. Now the great man had spoken. No excuses were acceptable.

Cameron made another attempt at university – this time in America. He lasted a term and a half before finally leaving. The feelings of aggression had become much more solid and were now accompanied by violent masturbatory fantasies.

These fantasies were not sexual. He didn't imagine raping women or interfering with them. Instead his masturbatory release became conditioned to images of non-sexual violence. He simply fantasized about hurting people.

There were initially two threads to these fantasies. One was the anonymous stranger whom he visualized attacking and the second concerned specific people he had contact with. The latter was far more rewarding to him and of greater concern to me. He tended to fantasize about attacking people who caused him difficulty by giving him orders, such as a supervisor, or a traffic policeman at a road accident.

It was during this time that the first evidence emerged of a lycanthropic shift. Returning to America after a less than successful trip to see his family, Cameron arrived at JFK Airport in New York. His father's coolness still disturbed him.

'All I had wanted was to change my currency and to get away to my apartment,' he said. 'There was a woman in front of me in the queue. She kept complaining about the exchange rate and insisting that she should get more dollars. I looked at my watch. It was four p.m. I just wanted to get home.

'Just when she finished a man stepped in front of me. He said he had to get into Manhattan urgently. "I'm sure you won't mind me going first," he said, and then he put his money down on the counter. He didn't look at me once.'

I could see Cameron rerunning the pictures in his memory.

'The thing is, I didn't really mind. But then he smiled at the cashier as if to say, "What a sucker!" Something inside of me snapped.'

He paused. I looked into Cameron's dark eyes, waiting for the rest of the story. He looked up and realized I expected something more. 'Oh no. Nothing happened then. I didn't . . . you know.'

'But something did happen?'

'Yes. I just sort of started trembling. It was like looking out from the first crack in a cocoon. I thought, this must be how it feels to be a grub starting to emerge from that horrible little prison – about to become a glorious creature.

'I looked at the back of this man's head and I knew

he was nothing. He was totally insignificant. I could smell him standing there in front of me. I wanted him to look at me now – just turn his head and take one glance. Then he'd want to hide. He'd want to run. Inside me there was a great triumphant howl. Please look at me, I thought.'

Cameron's voice had grown deeper and it seemed as though he spoke to himself rather than to me.

'What happened?'

'He walked away, towards the taxi rank. It didn't matter. I was different now – more alive than I'd ever been. I could see all those people and they couldn't touch me at all, it was as if they were sheep. They were nothing compared to me.'

'Did this feeling stay with you?'

'I was OK until I got into the taxi queue. Then I felt disoriented and sick – I had to go to the lavatory. I threw up. I felt frightened. It literally scared the shit out of me. I knew something really important had happened, but I didn't understand it. A part of me knew it wasn't right, but it was *so* good while it lasted.'

'What did you do about it?'

He shrugged.

'Did you see your doctor?'

'And tell him what?'

'What happened then?'

'When I got home it was dark. I had a drink. I kept thinking about my father and how he looked down on me. He's a bastard. My mother is next to useless. I spent hours bunched up in tourist class, doing the right thing and going to visit them, and for what? More humiliation! Then there was the guy at the currency counter . . .

'I put on some really deep, pure, instrumental rock.

507

I lay back in an armchair and closed my eyes. My mind went for a night-walk in Central Park. But it wasn't me. I ... we ... This isn't making sense.' He sighed in frustration.

'Go on.'

'We couldn't see everything clearly. Everything narrowed down, like seeing through binoculars. But there was strength – real strength – nothing could take us. Whatever was out there was ours – we'd look till we found it. People ... humans ... they were nothing to us ... he lived off them.'

He paused and his body seemed to shiver with joy.

'I don't know what happened after that. I wasn't really there. But I know he'd been to the park. We must have gone. I felt very tired. Do you understand? Don't you see? That's when I knew I was becoming a werewolf.'

Cameron grew more relaxed in the month that followed his first visit. He still caught the train to Leicester and arrived in the early afternoon. He made sure he was well away by 4 p.m.

I'd done some reading on lycanthropes, wanting to find out what the latest literature had to say. Clearly, Cameron had suffered extensive personality disturbance or disintegration over a long period of time.

Most sufferers have great difficulty in the overall business of living. Yet this man had a good job, a house, a car and even a girlfriend. He showed few of the theatrical qualities that many lycanthropes display because they want to be acknowledged and appreciated.

'What do you think happened that evening in New York?' I asked.

'That's when he first showed up ... the first time I changed into a werewolf.'

'Is that the same thing as happened in my room?'

'No. It was slower. My body was changing but I didn't realize how. It's quicker now. I can feel the change properly. I know what I become . . . what I am . . . what I can do.'

'OK. Help me to understand this. Tell me everything that happens when you shift from man to wolf.'

'I feel the hair growing, thickening, covering me; even on my face. I want to tear off the human clothes. They're bad for me – especially the shoes. They hurt me and I can't sense the ground beneath my paws. My voice changes. I no longer talk like a man. I snarl and growl and howl. My face lengthens into a snout and my canine teeth grow. I am strong and lean. I can outrun all men and tear their flesh to the bone. I have the mind, the heart and the body of a wolf. That is what I am.'

'When you see these changes in the mirror, can you still recognize the man at all?'

He laughed scornfully. 'You can't see a werewolf in a mirror.'

'Tell me about the wolf. What sort is it?'

'I don't know.'

'Is it a Canadian timber wolf, an arctic wolf?'

'I can't tell you.'

He grew irritated because I seemed to doubt him. He was fully aware of the inconsistencies in his story, but these didn't worry him.

There was no indication that Cameron had studied or acquired a detailed knowledge of wolves and their natural history. It was sufficient that he knew the myths. The most important aspect of his body-shifting wasn't the physical change from man to wolf, but the sense of liberation this gave him. The wolf could run free. It could roam, hunt prey and kill.

The first time Cameron changed had been both terrible and awesome. Terrible because he knew that his ultimate safe retreat – his inner life – was no longer his to control. Awesome because never before had he felt so complete and so powerful. He was a feared predator, able to prowl through the night seeing but not seen. It was an echo of his solitary childhood when he explored the souks and bazaars.

Our everyday knowledge of werewolves might not be as well preserved as that of vampires, but we know there is a strong predatory element. A werewolf takes a victim not for sustenance or food but for the power that comes from stalking, controlling, killing and ripping someone apart. Our literature has often converted this into a romantic story about a poor wretch condemned to turn into a beast at every full moon. This minimizes the merciless, sadistic, narcissistic core of the werewolf. It also provides a cloak that some self-deceivers will hide behind, concealing their actions and urges from scrutiny.

On his fourth visit, Cameron brought with him a file of letters containing details of several mental health reports prepared after a court appearance. He'd been charged twice with assault and once with actual bodily harm.

The attacks had been random, increasingly violent and unprovoked. In each case Cameron had pleaded that they were drink-related and that he was seeking help for an alcohol problem. His family gave guarantees to the court and the attacks were treated as misdemeanours that didn't warrant a prison sentence.

I looked at the dates. All of the assaults occurred

over an eighteen-month period after Cameron left university. They also came after his body-shifting had started.

'These fights and assaults were a long time ago, Cameron. Can you tell me what happened?'

'It's complicated.'

'Why is that?'

'Well, it wasn't me – not as I am now – it was the wolf.'

'But you didn't tell the doctors who examined you?'

'No.'

'What did you say happened?'

He shrugged. 'I had too much to drink and I got into a fight. It's amazing what you can get away with if you wear a suit and have a nice accent. My parents were also pretty impressive.'

'What happens when you become a wolf, Cameron? You've told me how your body changes, but what happens then?'

'Different things.'

'How long does it last?'

'Not a whole night – only an hour or two.'

'Surely somebody must miss you if you change at four o'clock and go missing for two hours.'

'It's not just at four. It happens at other times.'

'When?'

'Maybe someone pisses me off – some macho hero strutting around the office, showing off and opening his big mouth. I think about really hurting him. I want to rip out his heart.'

'What happens?'

'I go somewhere quiet and masturbate while I think about killing him.'

'How often does this sort of thing happen?'

'Not every day. If I change like that, it won't happen again for three or four days.'

'So if someone puts you under pressure, the wolf comes.'

'If they piss me off.'

'But how is that connected with these assaults? These notes say the people you attacked were strangers.'

Cameron looked at me as though I couldn't possibly understand. He sighed and put the palms of his hands together. His fingers were slightly bent, as though he couldn't straighten them completely.

'OK, I'll try to explain. When I'm the wolf I don't care where I am, only that I have cover. Time isn't important to wolves. All that matters is the hunt. We watch and we wait. Eventually, someone will separate from the herd.'

'And then what happens?'

'Once I was staying at a hotel that looked like a big old house. Next door was a plot of open land. Someone had started building something and run out of money. It had thick bushes on two sides and a tree that overhung the footpath . . .'

Cameron's eyes had narrowed. He seemed to stare straight through me, looking at a scene in his mind.

'It's dark when I slip out of the hotel. I use the darker shadows of the trees to skirt the open ground. Nobody sees me. Inside the bushes, I scrape out a hollow in the earth. I need somewhere to come back and lie up.

'I can hear cats fighting and smell smoking fat from the kitchens. I wait for a while, but nobody comes along the footpath. I move out, sniffing the air.

'Along the street is an old warehouse. The freight containers are perfect cover. I stick to the shadows. I

512

sniff at the packing cases. With my front legs I lean on one and push it over. It's empty.

'Then I smell them – young, sweet, warm – two women in noisy shoes. They walk quickly towards the hotel. They're laughing to each other. One of them is wearing perfume. I can't take two. Be patient, another will come.

'Back in the bushes, I wait in my scrape. I put my head against the earth between my paws, listening to the rumble of distant cars. I watch the footpath.

'Another scent – this one sour and damp with sweat. A man, alone, his shoulders drooped. He's slow. His hands are down. He is mine!

'Quickly now! Before he reaches the light. I run at him and spring high, coming down upon him. He tries to shout, but it chokes in his throat. He fights – not many of them do. I can smell his fear and taste his blood . . .'

Cameron suddenly stopped and looked intensely at me. He shook his head.

'I don't remember what happened next. I've tried to remember but it just sort of fades away.'

'Until when?'

'Until I'm no longer the wolf. I'm lying in the bushes. My fingernails are bleeding.'

'You said that sometimes when the wolf comes you masturbate to violent thoughts?'

'Yes.'

'What happened this time?'

'I'd ejaculated in my pants.'

I had no way of knowing if Cameron was telling me the truth, or what he thought was true. Perhaps he was testing how I'd react to an extreme story. I had no reason to doubt him.

In court each victim had described their attacker as being like a wild animal that had clawed, scratched and growled at them with bared teeth.

After the worst of these attacks, his family helped him to leave the country and sent him to a clinic in Vienna where they hoped he could be treated. From there he went to a succession of psychotherapists, psychiatrists and psychologists in Switzerland, Germany and America.

He told none of them about becoming a werewolf. The only reason he had confided in me was that I'd seen it happen and he couldn't keep it a secret after that.

Several things about Cameron's story puzzled me. Since the attacks in his early twenties, how had he controlled the wolf for the following ten years?

Most lycanthropes experience longer and longer periods of dissociation and their propensity for violence gets worse. Yet according to Cameron, since his return to England he had kept his secret from everyone, including his current girlfriend, Julie. At the same time, he had managed to hold down a well-paid career and live independently in a flat.

The lycanthropy had never disappeared: it had never been treated. Neither had the violent masturbatory fantasies. So what had happened?

It may be that the mental health specialists whom Cameron visited during this time managed somehow to help him, even without knowing the true nature of his problem. This could explain how he'd moved from being almost totally fragmented and on the edge of psychotic breakdown in his early twenties to become the apparently successful businessman in front of me.

However, I suspected the answer had more to do with what happened at four o'clock each day.

As an intelligent man, Cameron knew the consequence of being caught if he attacked someone. Next time he'd go to prison, or worse, he'd be indefinitely detained if the true cause was discovered.

Because of this he had learned to hold an outline of control over the shift while still functioning in the real world. At four o'clock he could vent all the crucial energy and psychological pressure that built up inside him. As a result he was able to form superficial relationships, get a demanding job in information technology and turn it into a career.

Yet as he described his current life, I knew this could only be a façade. The Cameron Miller who now walked through the world was as limited a representation of the whole man as were the Soviet statues of the 'Motherland's heroic worker'.

Since university Cameron had been involved in several sexual relationships. None of his former girlfriends had been raped or subject to gross abuse, yet I had no doubt that they found an unexpected level of aggression that caused them disquiet. His current girlfriend, Julie, had described him as 'being like an animal' when they had intercourse. Cameron referred to it as 'the spirit of the wolf coming on me'.

The violent masturbatory fantasies that had helped Cameron to overcome his early sexual failure had continued and intensified over the years. During sex he fantasized about controlling, dominating and killing people, usually men. This allowed him to have some sort of sexual relationship with a woman and also ensured that he didn't become too emotionally involved with any of his partners.

His emotional volatility and intense anger had never gone away. Instead Cameron had learned to isolate himself from people and not to stay in one place for too long. Cameron still needed to be in touch with the wolf spirit and he still wanted to act upon his violent and predatory urges; however, he had never lost sight of the possible cost. That was why he came to see me.

I also suspected that he was struggling to maintain the status quo of the previous eight years. He was starting to fragment again and couldn't control the wolf.

During the history-taking Cameron had described himself as a telecommunications software consultant, working in a fairly specialized area. Not surprisingly, it was the sort of job that didn't involve other people. He could work with computers, cables and satellite links, keeping his own hours and company.

'Tell me a bit more about your job,' I asked him, wanting to understand how it was structured.

'Well, I sort out security coding for moving financial data about – company information, market movements.'

'How good are you?'

'I'm OK. The contracts are short. There is plenty of work. It's a hot area.'

'Do you work in a team or on your own? What's the set-up?'

I was now familiar with Cameron's physical responses and I could see him grow tense.

'I come in after the deal's worked out,' he said. 'I see how the current systems are configured – which is usually shit – and then I put one together that does the job. I do my work and feed it into the program. I liaise with users from the client company, but that's usually OK.'

'You must have some sort of manager,' I said.

His eyes grew blacker as though he could dilate his pupils at will. He didn't like this line of questioning. I expected this aspect of his life to be a problem area because it brought him into contact with people. I needed to know how he coped.

'So do you have a supervisor?'

'A few people,' he said tersely.

'How do you manage to deal with them?'

'All right, I suppose. I see them a couple of times a week.'

'Do you get on well with them?'

He laughed sarcastically. 'Not always.'

'Why?'

'You remember that day I first came to see you . . . the Wednesday afternoon?'

'Yes.' (How could I forget!)

'I was going to kill my boss.'

He spoke in such a matter-of-fact way that I wasn't sure if I should take him literally. He could see me wondering and reassured me, 'Oh, yes, I was really going to kill him. I had it all planned and rehearsed. I was going to stab him at his desk on Friday afternoon and then watch him die.'

'Why?'

'Because that's what he deserves.'

'What has he done to deserve it?'

Cameron described an incident six months earlier when a virus shut down an entire network of computers. He had written the software that had been contaminated.

'You should have seen my arsehole boss; he really put me down. He humiliated me in front of the whole liaison group. "It's not good enough, Miller," he said.

"You're a big disappointment. You're disgracing the company."'

Cameron's top lip curled as he repeated his boss's words. Significantly, these were almost identical to the words uttered by Cameron's father years earlier, when his son was struggling at university.

'What happened next?' I asked.

'He started riding me – every day on the phone and at our progress meetings. He wouldn't let up. I'm fucked because of him. I'll never get another contract.'

'He's blaming you unfairly?'

'That's what I just said.'

'Have you asked him why he's doing it?'

'No, but I've killed him over and over in my head.' He didn't try to hide the joy this gave him.

I told Cameron that I was interested in discovering why, after eight years of staying out of trouble, these violent thoughts and fantasies were pushing into his ordinary life. Surely he remembered what happened last time.

'This time I went looking for the wolf,' he said. 'I didn't just wait for him to come or try to hold him back.'

'Why?'

Cameron struggled to find the words. 'Do you know what it's like when I stab him in my mind? A part of me falls away and I'm open to the wolf. I'm not talking about my body changing, but my mind. The wolf comes inside and replaces my stupid quietness. It's like being plugged into the mains. My boss can't hurt me any more. He's a sheep waiting to be slaughtered. He's going to regret what he's done when I cut out his throat.'

'What changed your mind about killing him?'

'I came here.'

'Do you still want to kill him?'

'Not this week.'

'Are you still carrying a knife?'

'Yes.'

We sat for what seemed like a long time in quietness. Cameron seemed almost fatalistic about his prospects. I wondered how much longer he could walk this path.

Breaking the silence I told Cameron that we had another chance to put things right. He said nothing but I knew he was listening.

'Things began to go wrong for you many years ago. I can't rewrite the past, but I can try to help *you* change. It's going to be very painful. We'll have to look at areas that you've learned to close away.'

He nodded and gave me a weak smile. 'I've still got half a life left.'

My first task in treating Cameron was to help him understand how he came to be this way. The werewolf was a dissociated element of himself. Through the wolf he could encapsulate those aspects of himself that he couldn't express elsewhere.

The wolf didn't have to satisfy anyone's expectations. It was liberated and powerful. Similarly, Cameron felt he couldn't be blamed for what happened because the werewolf was not him – it was something that came *to* him.

Some of the more masculine characteristics that were exaggerated in the werewolf made him feel embarrassed, but I told him that this was OK and he shouldn't feel guilty. Even more importantly, he had to understand that although he bore the scars of his childhood, he wasn't the architect of what happened. Like a twig floating down a stream, he was carried along by a current over which he had little control.

Cameron desperately wanted to hear this. At the same time, he had terrible difficulty in accepting the possibility that his parents might have been to blame. As much as he hated his father's harsh words and condescending airs, he still loved him.

'Sometimes people unwittingly damage those they love,' I explained. 'They didn't mean to mistreat you. I'm sure they'd be horrified if they knew the truth.'

Just as Claire Brooks's mother had never intended that her belief system would damage her daughter, neither of Cameron's parents realized that their actions had impacted so negatively upon their son.

Cameron had been so emotionally mangled, it wasn't enough to speak to his intellect. I had to take him back into his childhood and let him express his feelings about his mother and father.

I pointed to an empty chair. 'Your mother is sitting there. What are you going to say to her?'

He looked at me uncertainly.

'I'm not here. What are you going to ask your mother?'

He thought for a moment. 'Why didn't you let me play with Ahmed? He was my age. I used to watch him out of the window kicking a soccer ball behind the staff cottages. Sometimes he'd wave to me. Why wouldn't you let me play with him?'

I motioned to the empty chair. 'What is your mother going to say? How does she answer?'

He replied for her. 'I was frightened you might get hurt. Ahmed seemed so rough when he played.'

'How could I get hurt?'

'You might have fallen off a swing, or tripped over.'

'All children trip over.'

'Yes, but you were my only one. My baby. I couldn't have any more.'

'Why didn't I go to the local primary school?'

'You had very good tutors.'

'Yes, but the other children went to school.'

'It was full of Arabs and Indians. You were always very quiet and sensitive. I used to read you poetry. Do you remember?'

'Yes.'

Using this same empty-chair technique, I had Cameron ask questions of his father. He wanted to know about the souks and bazaars. Why did the butchers bleed the carcasses? Why did some women wear veils?

More importantly, he asked his father why he demanded perfection from everybody.

Despite the failings of his parents, the cause of Cameron's problems didn't rest entirely with their unwitting actions. He also unconsciously played a part. A normal, robust, uncomplicated youngster would have survived this childhood and flourished. Cameron's intelligence, artistic sensitivity and acute social awareness made him much more susceptible.

Apart from helping him to understand this, I developed a parallel thread of the treatment to allow these features of his make-up to find fulfilment – something that hadn't happened so far in his life.

Cameron had developed an interest in what he called 'white magic'. This involved studying the legends and beliefs of ancient tribes and exploring the tenet that there is more to heaven and earth than can be explained by science. I encouraged him to continue his reading and soon his interests expanded to include philosophy and astrophysics. His mind was like a sponge and his appetite for new ideas voracious. He began looking at fundamental questions such as who are we, where do we come from, where are we going?

This exploration appealed to his intellect, but no-one in his small circle of acquaintances shared his interests. Most were nothing like him. Rather than enjoying abstract intellectual arguments about human existence, they were more interested in who should play up front for England with Alan Shearer. A night out with his friends entailed downing eight pints of lager, trying to pull a bird and grabbing a curry on the way home. Interestingly, these pastimes were far more closely related to the wolf side of Cameron's character than to his intellectual side.

I encouraged him to make contact with groups who shared his interests. This was obviously a very big step because Cameron had always tried to avoid getting close to people. To overcome his stress, I taught him how to manage distance and keep people far enough away to be comfortable. We drew up a timetable in his diary with carefully marked periods when he was to be alone. These were sacrosanct, with no exceptions. The stillness was fundamental.

Although the duration varied, it was never too long between periods of stillness. At the start they were quite close together and we gradually extended the gaps as the weeks passed.

Instrumental rock music had always been a great comfort to him and something that he associated with the most desirable mythical qualities of the wolf. Instead of listening to such music, I gave him relaxation tapes and taught him deep relaxation techniques.

Cameron proved to be remarkably good at monitoring

his muscle tension and relaxing his body. As these skills grew, I linked them with a thought-stopping regime for his violent imagery. Whenever he felt under stress, or angrily aroused, his mental images of taking bloody retribution were replaced by gentler, less destructive pictures.

Cameron learned not to be embarrassed or humiliated by his brief periods of silence at social gatherings. Such moments didn't signal poor social skills or attract criticism. Most people love to talk about themselves. All he had to do was direct a few well-chosen questions and he could happily listen to them chatting while he enjoyed a 'stillness' period. Another useful tool was to make sure that others knew that he had to leave at a particular time. This normally ensured that he could go without being pressurized into having one last drink or staying a bit longer.

Together we worked on teasing out the benefits and pleasures that most people get from the company of others. We also punctured many of the irrational beliefs and expectations that were associated with his symptoms. It wasn't an easy task. His interpretation of the world had been forged by enormous pain and he still tended to dissociate under the pressure of the consulting room.

In the months that followed, Cameron found it easier to be around other people and to control the stresses that came to bear on him. As this happened, the werewolf began to fade away and this element of his personality became integrated into his usual self-awareness. It wasn't a case of becoming a wolf less often – instead the episodes became less intense. At the same time the confidence and sense of self-worth that had been unquestionably part of the wolf became increasingly apparent in the man.

Eventually he reached the point where at four o'clock each day he would feel uncomfortable, but nothing more. He no longer posed a risk.

When I last saw him, six months later, he had started writing a book about 'white magic' and how ancient tribes dealt with death. He had left Julie and wasn't seeing anyone else. He didn't think he would ever fall in love.

24

In the course of my clinical work, I've had to deal with A number of stalkers and the people they shadow. The effect on a victim's life can be profound. They never know when they walk out of the door if somebody is watching, and never feel safe.

Often people make the mistake of thinking that most stalkers are jilted lovers, or the deluded fans of film or pop stars. A recent study by the National Institute of Justice in America found that 1.4 million people in the US are stalking victims every year. While a majority of the stalkers had been in relationships with the person they were stalking, a significant percentage had either never met them or were only vaguely acquainted.

Although there is a debate about how to classify stalkers, they normally fall into three broad categories: the delusional, the love-struck and the malicious.

The delusional stalker is the rarest. He (or she) suffers from a psychotic illness and falsely believes that the target is truly in love with them. All that is holding them apart are circumstances. In reality, the delusional stalker may have had very little if any contact with his victim, yet he believes they are in love or are destined to be together.

John Hinckley Jr, the man who tried to assassinate US President Ronald Reagan in 1981, was obsessed with the actress Jodie Foster. Even though they'd never met, he believed that if he impressed her enough she'd come to love him, as he loved her. He chose to do this by assassinating the President. The idea came from the movie *Taxi Driver* in which Foster starred as a twelve-year-old prostitute. In the film, the character played by Robert De Niro, a deluded loner, attempted to assassinate a US senator.

A patient of mine once presented a threat to Captain Mark Phillips and the Duke of Edinburgh because he was certain they were preventing the Princess Royal from being with him. By carefully studying her public appearances he convinced himself that she was privately communicating her distress to him through her 'waves and smiles'.

Delusional stalkers will often go to any lengths to persuade their target to follow their true but hidden feelings. Sometimes, in their minds, they create entire relationships that completely transform their lonely lives. Such an obsession can lead to violence if the stalker feels snubbed or rejected. He may also feel that someone close to his target such as a boyfriend or husband is standing in the way of them being together.

Love-struck stalkers fall into two categories. They can be former partners who simply 'can't let go'. They refuse to believe the relationship has really ended and will do anything to rekindle the romance. People invariably feel sorry for them – even the victims – yet often research into the background reveals that in the original relationship the stalker was controlling and emotionally abusive.

The other love-struck stalker is the unsophisticated

man or woman who simply wants the object of their passion to realize and return their love. They don't have the social skills or insight to court a partner in the usual way; instead they may focus on someone who once smiled at them, or said something nice to them.

These stalkers often live nearby. They take pictures and leave tokens of their love on the doorstep. They don't understand how they might frighten somebody. Instead they believe that somehow their beloved will recognize their feelings and perhaps return them.

Having an unknown admirer can be quite flattering. Anonymous Valentine's cards are a prime example. Even so, few people like being watched or followed. If they call the police they risk publicly humiliating their admirer, who may then be pushed into the next category – malicious stalking.

I remember treating a young woman whose life was being absolutely ruined by the attentions of a stalker. She had made a mistake that many women fail to recognize – she was careless with her eyes. A warm friendly glance was misconstrued and became the trigger for someone who read the innocent exchange very differently.

I'm not suggesting that women shouldn't look at or smile at people. They simply have to be aware of what effect they can have. Elise wasn't being flirtatious. She simply smiled at people and made eye contact when she said good morning.

Elsewhere in the company where she worked, on the factory floor, a young fork-lift truck driver had noticed Elise. Occasionally during the day she'd have to visit the main depot. She'd smile and say hello to anyone she met. She'd done the same thing for several years, unaware of how this young man was reacting to her –

building up his own ideas of what her gentle pleasantness really meant. At some point he established the belief that Elise was rightly his. She didn't encourage him – she couldn't have. She wasn't even aware it was happening.

One particular day she was walking home from work with a friend. As they chatted away, her friend said, 'That's the chap from work, isn't it?' He was waiting at a bus stop on the opposite side of the road.

In the weeks that followed Elise began to notice him every so often. He'd be standing on a corner or buying groceries at the local mini-mart. Obviously he lived nearby, she thought.

Soon the sightings came more frequently. Elise asked herself, why is he there? Is he waiting for someone?

Later she began thinking, is he really following me? Am I imagining this?

How many times before it is no longer coincidence?

On her visits to the factory floor she noticed him staring at her. It made her feel uncomfortable and she started trying to avoid going there. And even when she didn't see him, she sensed he was there, watching her. He began leaving her notes at work and putting them through her letter box. He knew where she lived.

Although he might sound like a love-struck young man, from the very beginning this man proved to be a malicious stalker. In his eyes, Elise was too cocky, too confident, too popular. Her smile was a teasing put-down.

He didn't bombard her with flowers and plead for a date. He wanted to punish her. He wanted to take an outwardly bright and vibrant young woman and destroy her psychologically.

When he didn't see her at work, he began seeking her

out during his lunch hour. He didn't break any company rules or regulations. He simply watched her from a distance – making sure that she knew.

She started to take sick-days off work. More hand-written notes were pushed through her door. 'You should be more careful,' he wrote in bold capitals. 'I don't think you're really sick.'

Another said, 'Who do you think you are? You can't get away from me.'

Elise didn't get angry. She became frightened. Her boyfriend told her, 'Don't be so silly. Why are you so upset? You're overreacting. He hasn't touched you. He's never said a word to you.'

Then her family began asking questions. 'So how did it start? You must have done something. Maybe you didn't even realize you were flirting?'

'But I wasn't flirting with him.'

'That's what I'm saying. Maybe you didn't realize.'

The notes became a little more sinister and he began using abusive language.

One of them read: 'You may have teased the others, but you're going to have to deliver to me.' Another revealed: 'I watched you looking out of the window after your mum went out on Thursday. Did you hope I'd come in? She goes out every Thursday night, doesn't she?'

The last note was more sinister. 'Well, tart, you wanted to be looked at by the lads – now you've landed a real man. And when I'm ready we've got a real date. You'll find out when. Keep yourself pretty.'

Elise called the police and got a sympathetic hearing. They made a few inquiries and the notes immediately stopped. Even so, they could do nothing more than warn him.

The following day, the aerial on her car was broken. On the day after, a car came hurtling along the street towards her and screeched to a halt. He simply sat behind the wheel and stared at her.

Elise was no wimp. Nor was she particularly robust psychologically. There came a point when this sort of terrorization finally broke her. The man didn't have to lay a finger on her. He made almost no direct verbal contact at all. His closest contact was the notes. Yet he grievously wounded Elise psychologically.

'I never know where he is,' she told me. 'I just know he's out there . . . watching me.'

She became like an animal in a cage. She didn't go out at night or at weekends. She left her job and moved to a different town.

This was a case that pre-dated the tougher anti-stalking laws that were introduced in Britain in 1997. It was one of the cases that led to the new law. The Protection from Harassment Act followed a series of high profile cases in which judges were powerless to act against stalkers. The legislation was devised to deal with stalkers who habitually frightened their victims and caused lasting psychological damage.

The main intention of a malicious stalker is to terrorize and threaten sexually and/or physically. He enjoys controlling his victim at a distance because of the exquisite power he feels he has over her. Some will send frightening 'gifts', such as intrusive photos taken with a long lens. Others kill and mutilate pets, leaving them prominently displayed. This sort of aggressive, sadistic predator often goes on to make direct contact.

One such man was Howard Simmons . . .

* * *

Sitting at the kitchen table each morning, Howard would slowly turn the pages of his local newspaper. He wore a cotton vest and ate from a bowl of cereal. A newly pressed shirt hung from one end of the ironing board next to him.

He paused when he reached the school sports section of the paper. There was a photograph of a beaming fifteen-year-old with blond pigtails. She held a netball above her head as if about to shoot for goal.

'Promising young netball player Zoe Campbell has been selected for the county under-seventeen team,' announced the caption. Howard took a pen from on top of the fridge and began making notes. He jotted down Zoe's school, what grade she was in and the colour of her school uniform.

Then he picked up a telephone directory and looked under the letter 'c' for the surname Campbell. There were six possible numbers and addresses close to the school. Howard wrote them on the same piece of paper and slid it into his wallet. Slipping on his shirt, he knotted his tie and left for work with his jacket slung over his shoulder.

Howard, aged twenty-eight, didn't like living in a seedy bedsit. The entrance hall was littered with junk mail and stank of rotting food from the bins outside. The couple downstairs kept their bicycles in the hall as well as a pram, making it an obstacle course.

Negotiating this every morning meant he started his day in a bad mood. He should have been with his wife and child. They had a nice council house with a big garden. Howard still paid the rent, but he no longer lived there. Suzie had thrown him out when she discovered he was still seeing Heather. To make matters worse, Heather had also dumped him when she discovered that he hadn't left his wife. He had tried to keep two women at two addresses and it hadn't worked.

In Howard's mind, he was the only real victim. Women expected too much from him. They wanted to own a piece of him. But he missed his daughter, Rosie. He only got to see her every second weekend.

Howard worked as a sales representative for a fabric company. He'd been there for the best part of a decade and his hunger to close the next deal had diminished. New salesmen had been promoted ahead of him, but Howard shrugged it off. He didn't particularly like the job, but it gave him a company car and a degree of unsupervised flexibility.

Later that day, on his rounds between fabric shops, Howard stopped at a phone box and took out the list of numbers he'd made that morning. He always chose phone boxes that were out of the way and rarely occupied.

He looked at his wristwatch. It was about lunchtime at school. The children would be in the playgrounds. Nobody answered at the first two numbers. The third had an answering machine and the fourth summoned a man's voice. Howard hung up immediately. He persevered. This was a hit-and-miss game.

Finally a woman answered.

'Have I got Zoe's home?' he asked.

'Yes, who am I speaking to?'

'Listen to me very carefully,' he said coldly. 'I've got Zoe. She won't get hurt – not unless you do something stupid. I want you to do exactly what I say.'

Almost paralysed by shock and fear, Zoe's mother tried to speak but no words came out.

'Are you listening to me, Mrs Campbell?' The voice had grown even more menacing. 'Do you understand me? She looks lovely in blue, doesn't she? Such a pretty school uniform.'

'Oh, my God. Please don't hurt her. Where is she? What have you done? Please let me speak to her.'

'And what lovely blond hair. You shouldn't tie it off her face. A ponytail doesn't suit her.'

'Oh, please, please. Just let me speak to her . . .'

'SHUT UP, BITCH!'

Howard knew exactly how to use his voice to gain control. Mrs Campbell had to be so frightened that she didn't question him, or begin to reason through what was happening.

She sobbed, 'Please let me talk to her.'

'SHUT THE FUCK UP!'

She flinched and began apologizing, pleading with him. Her emotional request to speak to Zoe was very similar to how a trained hostage negotiator would deal with the situation. Proof of life is an important aspect. In this case, Howard didn't have Zoe. He couldn't let her dictate things, so he screamed abuse and frightened her even more.

'DON'T YOU DARE QUESTION ME. Do as I say or she's in trouble.'

'Please, no, please don't hurt her.'

'You should let her wear her skirts shorter. She has such pretty legs. I bet she plays a lot of sport. Does she play a lot of sport?'

The mother sobbed, 'Yes.'

'Listen to me, Mrs Campbell. I'm going to ask you to do something for me. And I want you to remember that either you can do it, or Zoe can do it.'

'What do you mean? Please don't hurt her.'

'Shut up and listen! Either you do it, or she does it. Do you understand?'

'Yes.'

What alternative did she have? How could she be sure he had Zoe? She couldn't ring the school without hanging up. And if she put the phone down, she lost contact.

'Now, what are you wearing?'

'I beg your pardon?'

'DON'T PLAY GAMES WITH ME, BITCH!'

'Ah, oh, a skirt and a blouse.'

'What have you got on underneath?'

'Where's Zoe? Please, please don't hurt my little girl.'

'Either you do this, or she does. Remember? Are you wearing a bra?'

'Yes.'

'What colour is it?'

'White.' Mrs Campbell had started sobbing.

'Shhhhhhh, now listen to me. I want you to unbutton your blouse. You do it, or I make Zoe do it.'

'No, no, don't do that.'

'Unbutton your blouse. Have you done it?'

'Yes.'

'Now I want you to pull down your knickers. Don't put the phone down. Don't close the curtains.'

She suddenly wondered if he could see her. Was he watching the house? Did he have Zoe with him?

Calling on all his experience, Howard cowed and controlled Mrs Campbell, making her strip off her clothes. She had to masturbate and squeeze her breasts, while telling him in explicit sexual detail what she was doing.

Whenever she made the mistake of pausing or asking about Zoe, he reminded her that if she didn't do these things, her daughter would do them for him. Meanwhile he stimulated himself through the pocket of his trousers.

Normally Howard reached a point during such calls where he hung up and calmly walked away. He didn't want to stay on the line for too long. He couldn't be sure, for example, if Mrs Campbell had an answering machine that might record his voice; or if the number could be traced. Perhaps a passer-by would remember seeing him in the phone box.

But Howard had grown less cautious as he became better at controlling his victims. To get the same sexual return from his calls, he had to go a little further each time.

'Do you own an overcoat?' he asked.

'I'm sorry?'

'I want you to get an overcoat. Don't hang up and don't get dressed. You have thirty seconds. If you are not back at this phone in that time, then Zoe will have to do the rest for me.'

'No, please. I'll get it. Don't touch her.'

Mrs Campbell did as she was told.

Howard wanted more than before. He wanted her to put on the coat, get in her car and drive to a nearby children's playground. She had to walk through the gates and go to a picnic table.

'Then I want you to undo your coat. Remember I'll be watching. I've got Zoe. If you don't, she will.'

'Will Zoe be there? Will you let her go?'

'Do as I say.'

'Can I see her?'

'ARE YOU LISTENING? DO YOU WANT ZOE TO DO THIS?'

'No, no. I'm sorry. Please don't touch her.'

'You have ten minutes. Hang up now. Don't forget, I'm watching you.'

Mrs Campbell drove in tears to the playground. She

kept glancing in her rear mirror. Was he following her? She should have phoned the police but she was panic-stricken. She had only ten minutes. She had to save Zoe.

She sat for almost an hour at the picnic table – naked and crying – waiting for her child to be released. A passer-by called the police and comforted her until they arrived. Howard watched from a distance. He didn't stray close enough to see her nudity, but it was enough to see her bending to his will.

Zoe, of course, was safe and well at school. Every detail about her that Howard had used to convince her mother otherwise he had gleaned from a newspaper story.

Not every mother fell for his lies, but he had enough success to carry on. And it took nearly eighteen months for the police to catch him, when a woman with a mobile phone called 999 while she had him on the line. The police asked her to go along with Howard's demands and set up a wide net around the outdoor location he chose for her to expose herself. They scooped him up as he watched from the trees. Howard claimed that he was simply out for a walk, but the police managed to link him to the phone box and several other women were able to identify his voice.

Unfortunately, but not surprisingly, some of the victims were too traumatized or embarrassed to give evidence. With more evidence he might have received a longer jail sentence.

I first met Howard Simmons at an outpatient clinic three years later. A well-groomed man in a neat shirt and tie, he sat in the waiting room chatting to Diane, my secretary, and the other administrative staff.

Howard knew that women found him attractive. He had an easy charm and made them laugh. At the same time, he oozed confidence.

According to the introduction letter, Howard had been cured. He had served a prison sentence and another psychologist had concluded that he was better now. His phone stalking had been an aberrant episode and his prison sentence had taught him a lesson.

Despite this appraisal, someone thought it might be a good idea if a psychologist in the community could just keep an eye on him.

Howard expected me to rubber-stamp his recovery. He wanted to get back with his wife and two children. A son had been born while he awaited trial.

'Suzie wants nothing to do with me,' he said. 'But if you could sort of tell her that I'm OK now, then she'll have me back again. We'll be a family.'

'That's not the way I do things,' I told him.

'Why? Can't you give me some sort of certificate saying I'm cured?'

'Are you?'

I saw the flash of anger in his eyes, which he quickly concealed behind a genial smile. He chuckled as though I was teasing him.

What Howard couldn't possibly realize was how much I already knew about him. I knew about the index offence and had the reports from prison. I knew about his marriage and affair and the pressures these placed on him.

His enormous remorse and regret were writ large through all the reports. This man appeared to be truly sorry for what he'd done. Yet several pieces were missing in the case analysis.

For example, his explanation of why he terrorized

537

these poor women had been accepted with very little questioning. He had been under so much pressure – what with his wife and mistress both kicking him out of their lives – he simply cracked. It wouldn't happen again. He had reassured them of that, particularly with his obvious remorse.

I could find no reason to accept this. I didn't believe his explanation and I didn't believe he felt sorry for his victims. The only remorse Howard felt was for himself.

Howard tried a different tack. He began saying how much he respected the psychologist who had talked to him in prison. She had been very thorough, he said, and helped him a lot. He leaned forward and chatted to me like 'another man of the world'. His smooth, undeveloped face might be called handsome by some, but it lacked character.

'I don't want to offend you, Howard. I'm not here to put you down.'

'Well, why don't you believe me?'

'Because I know what you know.'

'What?'

'You are lying to me.'

He leaped to his feet, his eyes blazing. 'I'm not staying here for this. I don't have to put up with . . .'

'Well, that is up to you, Howard. I'll report back to the probation service. It may well be that the parole you received will have to be reviewed.'

He clenched his fists and grew red in the face. 'You can't do that. It's not fair. You're punishing me. I've already done my time. I've been punished for what I did.'

I could see him toying with the idea of physical intimidation, but he couldn't be sure about me. I might have been twenty years older and wearing glasses, but could I call his bluff?

Having been in the presence of seriously frightening and disturbed people such as Ray Knox and Malcolm Harris, I had nothing to fear. By comparison, Howard was a coward.

'If you want to go, please feel free,' I said, closing the folder in front of me. 'If you want to stay, that's also fine. Just remember one thing, I know you are lying.'

I knew Howard was a liar before he even walked through my door. I knew it from the history he'd given previously and his excuses for offending. None of this could be true because such terrible deeds do not come out of thin air. They did not start with the phone call to Zoe's mother, or the one or two that preceded it. They started much much earlier, with dozens and dozens of calls.

He probably began by dialling random numbers – hoping a woman would answer. Initially he would have tried to keep a victim on the line for long enough to get some idea of her age from her voice. Then he'd try to shock her with pornographic suggestions.

From the beginning there would have been an element of threat. 'I have seen you. I know what you look like.'

The poor women would panic and think, where?

From these early attempts, Howard quickly graduated to scanning the local newspapers, identifying stories and potential victims. The reports on school projects, field trips and sports days had proved to be a huge bonus. He now had a way of keeping his victims from hanging up.

All of this pointed to a sadistic psychosexual perversion, yet nowhere in the analysis of Howard's history and relationships was there any hint of sadism. I knew this couldn't be right. It has to start somewhere.

He sat down again, scraping his chair backwards and glowering at me.

'Will you stop calling me a liar,' he said petulantly.

I didn't like this man, but I had to put my natural anger to one side. He had terrorized dozens of women. Some might never recover from the emotional trauma. He had served a very short sentence and then been released, apparently reformed. It was a con.

He was still a danger. Perhaps it would have been better to let him walk out and for me to report to the parole board.

But could I prove what I was saying? Howard had served his time.

Instead I had to find a way of getting a psychological hook into him, rather than risk letting him get away. To bait the hook I had *his* family. He desperately wanted to be reunited with his wife and children.

'Most people when they first come to me hold things back, but in your case it's slightly different,' I said. 'You come to me with this history which has enormous holes in it. You haven't told the truth. We have to deal with that.'

Howard began complaining about how cruel life had been to him. It had put him in a situation where he had done something that was so out of character.

'I would never have called these women normally,' he said. 'I'm not a bad person. It's just circumstances, you know. I had these women screwing with my head. I'm disgusted at what I did. I really am.'

'Yes, you've said all this before. Now I want the truth.'

I began taking his history. I knew enough already to know when what he said about his background deviated from the truth.

The picture that emerged was of a man with a very high sex drive who had a great deal of success at seducing women. By his early twenties, he was often running several girlfriends in parallel. Occasionally he got caught out but there were always plenty more fish in the sea. Yet when he was twenty-six, one of these girlfriends persuaded him to marry her.

'Did you love her?'

'Yeah, I guess.'

'You don't sound particularly convinced.'

'I loved all of my girlfriends.'

'So why did you marry Suzie?'

'It seemed like a good idea. A lot of my mates were getting hitched. I'd been hanging around the same pubs and clubs for years, doing the same things. Suzie was really keen. She kept on at me about getting engaged.'

Suzie sounded like a girl who knew her own mind. Howard must have seemed like a reasonable catch because so many other girls wanted him. He had a steady job and most people thought he was charming.

Howard had told every woman he ever slept with that he loved her. He was very good at making promises and giving undertakings but he didn't know how to get out of them, so he just kept going. His notions of romance and marriage seemed to come from Hollywood films where the happy-ever-after ending normally involved a wedding dress and a 'Just Married' sign.

'What was your sexual life like with Suzie?'

'Ah, you know, pretty standard.'

'What do you mean?'

'She liked it, if that's what you mean. We were at it like rabbits when we first met.'

'And then?'

'Well, it's the same old story, isn't it? You get used to things.'

By the sounds of it, Suzie's sexual interests had been fairly mainstream, whereas Howard wanted to be more ambitious.

Marriage didn't stop him having other women. One, in particular, took a great interest in him. He met Heather through work and soon they were sleeping together. Even when she discovered that he was married, she didn't break off the affair.

'She wanted me to leave Suzie and live with her,' said Howard. 'She didn't say anything at first, then she started dropping hints.'

'What did you do?'

'I was caught in the middle. It's not easy trying to keep two women happy. Don't get me wrong – I loved both of them. Suzie had Rosie by then. I love being a dad. I couldn't leave her.'

'So why didn't you tell Heather?'

'I loved her too,' he said, certain that I understood his quandary.

In reality, Howard loved himself and the idea of two women wanting him gave him a sense of self-importance. It also helped satisfy his sexual needs.

Yet even two women weren't enough. He still had surplus capacity for the other women he was seeing.

There came a point when Suzie discovered these affairs and, according to Howard, 'She went bananas.'

'What did Heather say?'

'She was quite pleased about it. She said, "Your wife knows about us now – so move in with me."'

'Is that what you did?'

'Yeah.'

'How did that work out?'

'Terribly. I missed Suzie and Rosie.'

Somehow Howard managed to convince both women he was living with them, while bouncing between the two. He juggled his working hours, made excuses and kept up the pretence for nearly a month before being discovered.

Once Suzie and Heather knew the truth, they both kicked him out for good.

This much of Howard's history had come fairly easily and I had no reason to doubt him. He claimed that his abusive phone calls had started at about the time when he was being pulled between the two women. This was a lie. The true source lay in his past, perhaps in a former relationship. I suspected that someone had introduced Howard to sadomasochism and he'd enjoyed it enormously. This wasn't guesswork. The psychological literature gives many case studies that deal with sadomasochism and how it begins. I had also seen so many cases in the consulting room.

Howard claimed to have told me everything, but whenever I began digging deeper he grew uncomfortable. Each time I backed him into a corner or accused him of lying, he grew angry.

'I've seen the psychologist in prison,' he argued. 'She didn't treat me like this. She believed me.'

I decided on a direct course of action and threw the prison report on the desk. 'This is rubbish.'

'Why don't you believe me?'

'Because you haven't told me how this began.'

'Yes, I have.'

'No, because this started years before you were married. I don't know whether it ever touched your marriage or various affairs, but at some point you experienced sadomasochism in relationships with other women.'

Howard stopped himself swearing. He clenched and unclenched his fists, regaining control.

'I've told you everything.'

'You've had so many women, Howard, but one of them was special. What did she teach you?'

'I don't know what you're talking about.'

'It must have been exciting. You must have loved the feeling of being in control – the power to bring pleasure and pain.'

'You're sick.'

'And you're a liar.'

There are times in interviews when it's necessary to confront and accuse. This often happens when dealing with someone like Howard. I think the word psychopath is overused; I prefer to call him a 'serial liar' – somebody who finds it easier in any situation to tell a lie rather than the truth, regardless of whether it is important or not.

I had to deal with this directly. He had to understand that by continuing to lie he was digging himself into a deeper hole. This couldn't be done in just one or two sessions. It took weeks to win Howard's true history – almost to drag it from him amid his constant attempts to deceive.

Throughout his life Howard had needed to be in control of situations. He knew he was clever and he tended to classify most other people as mugs. I was somebody who didn't yield to him. At the same time, I made it clear that I wasn't going to harm or destroy him.

Normally I try to make patients feel as if there is something to be lost by not telling the truth. In

Howard's case I tried to give him a way of introducing new material without losing face.

'I'm not saying that you chose to become interested in sadomasochism,' I told him. 'I think that somewhere along the line you were exposed to it. Your sexuality was extended. You enjoyed it.'

It would have been easier if Howard had been an in-patient at Arnold Lodge. Then I could have seen him two or three times a week and had nursing staff influencing him twenty-four hours a day. As it was, I had an hour with him once a week. In that short period, I had to make an impact because otherwise, once he walked out of the door, he'd begin to filter out the things I said that he didn't want to hear or remember. I would become just another mug and he would assume control.

As much as I disliked him, I wanted to save Howard from himself. I also knew that unless I could intervene quickly, he was at risk of targeting women again. Only this time he was potentially more dangerous. He wouldn't make the same mistakes again.

Where did he fail last time? He lost control of his victim.

How could he stop it happening again? The one sure-fire way would be actually to abduct the child. When she said, 'Hello, Mummy,' down the phone then he'd have her mother completely, without question. He could also use the child to get closer – perhaps to gain entry to the house.

Even before he was caught, Howard had been moving closer to actual contact. This was a progression I'd seen many times before. It's why offenders move from stealing women's underwear to breaking into their houses, to rape and then to murder. Even someone as cowardly as Howard could kill if he believed a victim might identify him.

Mercifully he'd been caught. Carelessly he'd been let go. People often regard phone pests as being seedy and grubby. They don't attach a high enough concern to what they are capable of. Lesser offences such as this have been precursors to some of the terrible tragedies of our age. In 1972 an early warning was sounded about the predatory and sadistic sexual practices of Fred and Rosemary West.

The couple abducted, tortured and raped a seventeen-year-old former nanny in a terrifying ordeal. Her head was wrapped tightly in broad sticking plaster that covered her mouth, nose and ears. She was beaten with leather belts and in her hearing they discussed performing surgery on her vagina.

Fred told the teenager that he planned to keep her in the cellar so his friends could use her. When they finished she'd be killed and her body buried under the paving stones of Gloucester where there were hundreds of girls that the police would never find.

Look again at the year – 1972.

Mercifully the girl escaped and raised the alarm. Yet her ordeal ended as a relatively minor matter before Gloucester Magistrates' Court. Unbelievably, the Wests were allowed to plead guilty to the lesser charges of indecent assault and actual bodily harm while the rape charges were dropped. They were each fined £50 and left free for their passion to develop.

Twenty-two years later, I directed the police to the bodies in the basement of 25 Cromwell Street, and to others in and around Gloucestershire.

* * *

Two months after first seeing Howard, I finally began to unravel what happened in his history that set him on this path. The most important step was getting him to acknowledge that he was a liar.

When the first breakthrough came, he immediately gave his familiar whining account of how life had cheated and mistreated him. It wasn't his fault. Circumstances were to blame.

Even after this ceased, there were false starts. Howard eventually understood that one of the hoops he was supposed to jump through was to accept responsibility for what he'd done. He did so, but not with any sincerity. His remorse was empty.

Most great actors and some great deceivers can stimulate emotion at levels of intensity and accuracy that are almost impossible to recognize as being feigned. With a great deceiver the only way to discover the truth is to know the baselines of their normal behaviour. That way you can match the changes against new stimuli.

I knew, for example, that I could make Howard genuinely distressed by running the scenario of him losing his children and never seeing them again.

'How's Rosie going to feel when she's old enough to ask what Daddy did? How's she going to look at you?'

Angry tears washed across Howard's eyes. He wiped them away with the back of his sleeve. These were real tears. They set a benchmark for what I had to see elsewhere.

For example, I doubted if this man had ever felt genuine empathy for Mrs Campbell or any of his victims. This is what I hoped to see from Howard – genuine sympathy for the women he'd terrorized; a feeling for the injury he had inflicted.

However, this was easier said than done for Howard,

because the fear and humiliation of his victims were what had aroused him in the first place. That was why any sadness and disgust he felt about it now was directed at himself. He'd been caught. The world had treated him unfairly.

Deep down, the memory of actually making the phone calls still excited him.

As Howard began telling me the truth, he revealed a relationship in his late teens with a slightly older woman, Barbara. She had seduced him when he delivered a package to her house.

Barbara had a strong sex drive and an adventurous imagination. In particular she enjoyed sadomasochistic games and role-plays. She had pornographic videos and magazines, and would get Howard to tie her up and strap and bite her.

Howard had barely been introduced to straight sex, yet now he was becoming acquainted with the finer points of sadomasochism. He found himself responding to the scenarios she created. They excited him.

As time went by, Howard's masturbatory fantasies began to focus on sadism and control. When he married he had tried to introduce aspects of his fantasies into his sex life, but Suzie had regarded the games as being childish or perverted. The same had happened when he began his affair with Heather. She had no interest in being tied up and 'punished' for his enjoyment. Consequently Howard kept his masturbatory fantasies to himself and carried on his vigorous sex life.

Yet his interest in sadism and control continued to develop. Certain sorts of pornography helped his visualization, but soon this didn't give him the sexual return that he wanted. He was disappointed and angry that both his wife and his mistress had denied his needs. Yet he didn't have the courage to show the aggression towards them that he wanted to. They knew him and it would be ruinous if they told anyone else, or stopped their sexual favours.

Instead he found another way of getting women to be vehicles for his sadism and need for control. He just picked up the telephone and called them.

He started off in public phone boxes with a phone directory, he said, calling numbers at random. Most boxes don't have directories in them, so I put a question mark over this. More than likely he had a directory hidden somewhere and marked with a record of the calls.

Howard said he began making the calls after Suzie and Heather threw him out.

'They made me feel so rejected. It was cruel. They put me under so much pressure that I found myself doing these things. It was completely out of character.'

This was another self-justifying lie.

The pathology of a telephone sex abuser like Howard is very different from that of a rapist who breaks into a house and attacks a woman. The telephone abuser can often withdraw for a while and spin his wheels in masturbation for months on end before going back. The sexual rapist will normally need more frequent contact.

The rapist often *wants* an interaction with his victim, but doesn't always get this. The telephone abuser is almost guaranteed it. The rapist may want to push the woman into some little story suggesting affection perhaps, or enjoyment. He will have a very powerful visual image of what he wants to happen – a very strong sense of theatre.

The telephone abuser, however, has a far looser image. He can visualize entire rooms if necessary and doesn't really *need* to ask his victim for descriptions of what she is wearing. Instead, he is much more interested in the fear and arousal cues in her voice.

He has never seen her. She can fit any notion that he wants. He can make her blond, brown-eyed and tall. She can be wearing whatever he likes. And once he has control, she will say whatever he wants.

Sometimes he will ask for details of her physical appearance. If, by chance, the victim matches the woman in his fantasy then it will be a much richer experience for him. He'll want to keep her on the phone for longer.

After almost a year, Howard had come to terms with what he'd done. We did a lot of work helping him understand his sadistic urges and what caused them. We also redefined what feelings of pleasure were, and the importance of mutual enjoyment in a loving relationship.

Although I never met Suzie, I knew that her desire for sex and intensity of arousal didn't match her husband's. I encouraged Howard to discuss these things with her. Eventually Howard was able to do so.

He couldn't suddenly turn off his sexual appetite. Nor could a slate be wiped clean inside his head to remove his sexual deviance. All I could do was help reduce the energy that drove it and redirect it towards healthy – or at least legal – avenues.

Initially Suzie wanted nothing more to do with Howard, but she softened, listened and yielded. Surprisingly, I think her family smoothed the way because they didn't want the children to be separated from their father. I doubt if any of them realized the true extent of the abusive telephone calls.

Suzie wanted to provide for Howard sexually. She didn't want him to stray again. This didn't mean that she became a sadomasochist. Instead she worked to show more enjoyment in sex and her arousal fed into his pleasure.

A father had been restored to his family. A successful intervention had been made. Yet as Howard left my office for the last time I could give no guarantees about his future.

He wasn't a very likeable or attractive specimen of humanity. Eventually, I suspect, his wife will realize this. As her own sexuality opens up, she will see that Howard is self-centred and really only cares about his own needs.

Once Suzie appraises their relationship more objectively, I wouldn't be surprised if she leaves him. That's when the real test will come for Howard. It will be so easy for him to slip back into the belief that 'I am the victim, so I am going to punish.'

I have given him the mental tools to fight these thoughts and feelings. The rest is up to him.

25

The two detectives had travelled a long way down from the north to see me. Fog on the motorway had caused long tailbacks and they arrived at Arnold Lodge an hour late. I met them at the front gate and led them along the path to my office.

We sat in the seminar room. The more senior of the two detectives (I can't name them for operational reasons) looked as though he'd seen military service. He wore an old military tie and stood very straight as we shook hands.

Both men worked for the intelligence section of a Regional Crime Squad which specialized in compiling, analysing and sharing criminal intelligence between various forces. Its job is to keep track of organized crime figures, serial law-breakers and drug traffickers.

This included information about previous addresses, relatives, associates and known hang-outs, as well as intelligence gathered from surveillance and informants. Some of these 'people of interest' were in prison, in which case the database kept track of when they were due for release and information picked up from staff and other prisoners.

'We have a situation,' said the senior detective,

unbuttoning his coat. Loose change jangled in his pockets. 'Five days from now a man called Paul Tenon is going to walk out of prison. He's a nasty piece of work. He raped two women and one of them almost died. This guy should have got life instead of ten years.'

I was surprised. The Regional Crime Squad tends to be more concerned with gangs and drug cartels than straightforward sex offenders. Clearly something worried them.

The younger policeman, a detective sergeant, produced a file that described the rapes and also listed Tenon's prior offences. It was quite a track record. He had convictions for indecency, sexual assault, attempted rape and actual bodily harm. Now aged thirty-five, he had spent more than half his life in detention of one sort or another.

'There is nothing we can do to stop him being released,' said the senior detective.

I questioned this. 'If you can show he's a risk, surely you can stop him. You could argue that he has a psychological problem and have him transferred and detained at a special hospital.'

'It's too late for that,' said the senior detective. 'He's served his time and he's on the way out. It should have been done earlier.'

I couldn't quite see how I was supposed to help.

'Can you tell us the likelihood of Tenon offending again? Should we be watching him? If so, how closely?'

After giving me a detailed briefing, the detectives handed over a bundle of files that included reports from arresting officers, victim statements and Tenon's own version of events. There were also reports from prison officers and details of prison-based treatment programmes. I spent that evening learning all I could about a man who had very little to recommend him.

He had lived in Manchester all his life, except for when he was in prison. There was nothing at all about his father and the history of his mother was so thin it was merely a caricature. She had her first child in her mid-teens and three more by the time she was twenty-two. She worked in kitchens and hotels but was a convicted prostitute by the time her third child was born and seemed to have settled into that occupation.

Different boyfriends had beaten her up – sometimes in front of her children. According to one social worker this had 'deeply disturbed' Paul, who began bed-wetting at the age of five after witnessing such an assault.

He was the second born, with an elder brother and two younger sisters. All the children were eventually taken into voluntary care in 1970 because their mother was unable to look after them properly. There weren't any foster parents willing to take on four youngsters, so the children were split up. From the age of ten, Paul had no significant contact with any of his siblings.

He was regarded as being of average intelligence and a competent but indifferent pupil at school. He had adequate social skills but poor social insight. He was over-assertive and domineering towards girls, although sometimes regarded as a trophy boyfriend by younger girls competing for status at the school.

Paul was reported for several indecent assaults in his early teens, but his first recorded conviction was at the age of fifteen. The files had very few details. Apparently he'd been chatting to a girl working in a pet shop and later waited for her to finish work. He pulled her into an alley where he indecently assaulted her.

Sentenced to eighteen months in a juvenile detention

centre, Paul didn't cope well. Other inmates mocked him for being unable to 'persuade' the girl to have sex with him. Some chided him with chants of 'Can't get it up!' A psychiatrist who interviewed him at the home said Paul seemed to regard girls as 'prick-teasers who never deliver'.

On his release, he had a variety of odd jobs in Manchester, labouring on building sites and delivering leaflets. He didn't have any long-term romantic relationships, but had casual sex frequently. His 'seduction' techniques were very rough but few girls made formal complaints, primarily, I suspect, because of embarrassment and an irrational sense of guilt.

In June 1982, at the age of twenty-two, Tenon got chatting to a twenty-year-old woman who worked at a hamburger bar near his bedsit. 'I'll see you next time,' she told him as he left.

Two nights later Tenon followed her from the shop as she walked home. He pushed her into a derelict garage and beat her up.

Initially the girl complained that he tried to rape her, but Tenon denied this. He claimed that she'd been rude to him and he lost his temper. The girl didn't press the sexual assault allegations and Tenon was sent to prison for ABH (actual bodily harm).

Within a year of his release he had raped two women and was suspected of two other attacks. The offences took place within six weeks of each other and were carried out in a suburb several bus trips from his home. In each case he had 'bumped into' a young married woman – one in a large bookshop, the other in a super-market. The shops were close to each other and were reached by a brick footpath from an adjacent car park.

He followed one victim along the path before

555

pushing her through a broken fence into a disused yard. She cried out and fought. He punched her several times in the face, breaking her nose, before raping her.

A few weeks later he targeted a second woman, following her into the car park and bundling her to a junk-filled rubbish bay behind the supermarket. He pulled her hair back so severely it injured her scalp. Then he kicked her in the stomach and vulva before raping her.

I'd come across very similar histories to this in other sexually violent men I'd treated. I could also recognize in the victims a failure to accept that what happened to them was primarily sexual. They seemed to sense that it was anger, bitterness and hatred that drove their attacker. Sex was only part of the vehicle.

Even so, under the classifications we commonly use, Paul Tenon was undoubtedly a serial sex offender. The first question I had to ask was why he had been in prison for a decade and nothing had been done about it. It was not a question of him having to agree to treatment. He could have been directed to do so. This was nothing at all to do with the police. Their job was only to catch him. After that there is a whole system in place which is supposed to rehabilitate and treat sex offenders. If the system doesn't work, it fails the community as well as the man.

Treatment programmes for sex offenders are far more widely available these days than when I began to work in the forensic field. The core aim of these is to have the offender recognize his urges as deviant and feel true empathy for his victims. He has to take responsibility for what he's done. He also has to develop a behavioural and psychological set of techniques that deflect or deaden his deviant fantasies and practices.

Many offenders go through the motions of this – Malcolm Harris was one example – but without true motivation or developing commitment it is an empty exercise. Equally, it can take years of focused individual work in the intense atmosphere of a Regional Secure Unit to ignite a desire for normality in offenders who up until then have no willingness to change.

Unfortunately, the prison service has a limited number of special units that can offer this sort of intensive psychological support. At the same time, these units normally require a long period of residence for change to occur. Not every prisoner who would benefit has a long enough sentence.

In Paul Tenon's case he had refused to participate in any programme. It was quite likely, although I couldn't be certain, that his lack of co-operation had led to him serving his complete sentence rather than being paroled early. It also flagged him as a future risk. That was why his release date set alarm bells ringing for the Regional Crime Squad.

Tenon was due for release on 26 October – ten days away. As far as I was concerned he remained a profound risk to women. It wasn't a case of 'if' but 'when' he raped again.

As I pondered Tenon's release, I began thinking about an earlier police case I'd worked upon – a string of particularly violent sexual assaults in Merseyside. All of the young victims had been tracked through crowded streets by a man who managed to anticipate the short cuts they used.

He interrupted them quickly and violently, dragging them off the street into quiet corners. Normally the women were alone, but when confident and aroused enough he also attacked pairs. He used fear to control one victim while he assaulted the other. Some were so terrorized they lost control of their bodily functions and began closing down psychologically.

These attacks were not brief. This man took his time and seemed to know when to run. He disappeared easily into his surroundings without attracting attention.

The investigators asked me to provide a psychological analysis of the offences and they gave me a guided tour of the crime scenes. The assaults had taken place in the lee of churches, hospitals and public buildings, all different, but in each case the attack had occurred in a small, grassy, sheltered area within the larger site. On each occasion he was able to escape across green spaces and allotments and through the tight network of back alleys that threaded behind older terraced streets.

I took away copies of the paperwork, including aerial maps and street plans. I studied these at length, looking for psychologically significant features that the crime scenes had in common. Also, because it was a single series, I tried to find evidence for a pattern or trend in the geographical locations of the scenes themselves.

When I went back to present my findings, I advised the police to focus their resources on where the man would next offend.

'What do you mean?' asked the SIO. 'How can we possibly know that?'

I explained how the characteristics of the sites he'd used before could be mapped out to show his preferred locations. This also revealed that he was working in a geographical direction.

'I think there's a strong likelihood that he will attack in this area,' I said, marking a long ellipse on the map with my finger, running roughly south from the last assault and extending out over the end of the conurbation. I drew another from the first offence but running roughly north.

'You might check other divisions or forces in that direction as well. You're not looking for new offences there, but for older ones.'

'I still don't understand how you can predict the next location.'

'Don't just look at the victims. Concentrate on the scenes and the sequence. Each crime scene is tucked away near some public institution – a school, a hospital, a church . . . But the micro-scene itself – where he attacked these women – is not immediately in public view. It's hidden, or at least not open.

'There's always some vacant ground – grassy, packed earth with bushes. This is where he makes them lie down. And afterwards he always has a well-researched escape route. On the one occasion when he was chased by a passer-by, he easily managed to lose his pursuer in the alleys.'

I pointed to the map again. 'Now look at the locations plotted in sequence. It's not exactly a straight line, but if you allow for the meandering of both the main roads and the minor streets close to the scenes, they tend to run from the north or north-east to the south or south-west.'

'So you say if we extend the line in your ellipse that's where he'll strike next?'

'Yes. You can narrow the potential sites down by looking at public buildings, especially those pre-war or just after. Look for quiet grassy or earthy nooks, perhaps with bushes. They won't be obvious, but they'll be close to a quiet path. There'll be just enough foot traffic to provide him with a target.'

I suggested the police should pay attention to schools, churches, bus depots, hospitals and railway stations, especially where there were footbridges and paths.

One particular crime scene interested me. A woman had been attacked near a hospital and the location suggested a much more detailed knowledge of the area than quick research would allow. This man had taken his victim through a series of intricate short cuts straight to the place he wanted her.

I pointed to the map. 'A few years ago, there used to be a facility at this hospital for treating forensic patients. It's closed down now. Even so, it might be worth looking into. You might find someone willing to talk about old cases. They're not supposed to, but maybe you have ways and means . . .'

The implications of my advice were significant. If accepted and followed, it would mean a major police operation covering an enormous area. Decisions such as these involve many intricate policy and operational considerations.

I didn't hear from the investigation team again and I don't know the extent to which my analysis was acted upon, if at all. However, some months later I had a telephone call telling me that there had been another attack, allegedly by the same man. He had chosen a site near a railway station, in a small grassy space beside a footbridge. The station was at the southern end of the ellipse I had drawn during the last briefing.

Working as an outside consultant to the police is an honour, but it can have its frustrations. Naturally the same holds true in the forensic service. When I advise the police, I can only give an analysis or recommend a course of action. My advice has to be set against the overall priorities of the investigation and counsel from other quarters. Sometimes, even if we have the same pieces, we don't build the same picture.

In the case of Paul Tenon, I had a slight advantage – at least we knew his name and what day he was being released. I also knew where he'd be staying. The probation service had arranged a room for him at a hostel in Derby.

Having spent several evenings designing a strategy, I met with the detectives again in the library at Arnold Lodge. The bookshelves and journals gave everything a musty, academic air and I found myself talking in a subdued whisper.

Another DI had joined the two detectives who first briefed me. He was from the surveillance team and was there to listen rather than talk.

'Will he target another woman?' asked the senior detective.

'Oh yes.'

'Is there any way we can identify the likely target or the location?'

The answer was again yes, but with a lot of provisos and parentheses. It would take a massive amount of information that we didn't have.

Some sex offenders have a fixed preference for indoor or outdoor locations. Others, over a career, will move from one to the other. Some will tend to focus on parks, while others prefer railway embankments or places where they can watch houses, looking through windows at women.

From his past offending, I knew that Tenon favoured the outdoors, in particular recreation grounds, parks and footpaths. I also knew the age range and physical features of his previous victims.

Unfortunately, this wasn't enough. There were literally dozens of locations in Derby that fell into the favoured category. Similarly, there were hundreds of women aged between sixteen and forty who matched the loose profile of a potential victim. The police couldn't possibly protect them all.

'For me to narrow this group down means learning everything I can about this man's internal functioning. Obviously, I can't interview him. It's not in the notes. The only option left is to watch him.

'I think you should put him under surveillance day and night until you discover his pattern of local interests. Identify where he goes, what he does and who he sees.'

This wasn't just a case of keeping watch on him until a potential victim emerged. The police might not recognize her when the time came. Instead, they had to log and study his behaviour.

'I want to know every detail about him. Where he goes and when, for how long, what he looks at, who he talks to, what he wears. See how he uses his space. Each person has patterns and routines in what they do and where they go. This man will be no different. This area is going to be relatively new to him. It's not his old stamping ground. He'll investigate things first.'

Two days later Paul Tenon was released from prison. He carried a single old-fashioned suitcase and had a bus ticket to Derby. He walked from the coach terminal to a hostel that backed onto railway lines.

Police surveillance teams followed him every step of the way. Over the next two weeks I was briefed every few days. As operations went, the officers on the ground regarded this one as a chore. There was nothing exciting about watching a man go to the supermarket and then home again.

Some of their notes reflected their boredom:

3.30 p.m. – walked along high street, went into the Post Office. Presented benefit book and bought stamps at counter.

3.45 p.m. – stopped off at the supermarket. Bought a pint of milk.

6.25 p.m. – seen entering the Railway Hotel.

7.15 p.m. – left the Railway Hotel and walked home, browsed through private house windows fronting the street.

The officers hadn't understood the richness of detail that I needed.

'It's not just a question of him going out to the pub,' I explained at the next briefing. 'What was he wearing? Had he shaved? Did he carry anything? Did he walk slowly? What route did he take? Was it the shortest route? If not, why did he take the longer journey? Does he go along narrow streets or across open spaces? Did he pause anywhere on the route? Did he talk to anyone? Did you notice him looking down certain streets or at particular cars? When he got to the pub what did he drink? Who did he talk to? Who did he watch? Did he make eye contact with anyone? Did he acknowledge anyone? Did he sit with his back to the door? Were there any women in the pub? What were their ages? How did they dress?'

The questions went on and on. Finally the officers began to understand the wealth of data I required. It was my only way of understanding this man.

I had a similar series of questions about his hostel. I wanted to know who else lived there. Were there any women? What were the rooms like? Did he have a window overlooking other houses? Did he keep the curtains open or drawn? Did he talk to other residents? Had he made any friends?

A week passed and the surveillance reports continued to be faxed to me each day. The quality of information improved and particular aspects of Tenon's behaviour interested me.

Most people buy what they need for several days but he seemed to make a point of going to the supermarket every day, using it almost like an outing. Supermarkets, like leisure centres, can be beacons for sexual offenders because they allow predators to follow victims and watch them closely without drawing attention to themselves.

Tenon arrived at the store each morning, browsing through all the aisles. His basket contained only a few items – a loaf of bread, sardines, a can of baked beans . . . Despite this, he spent nearly an hour inside, far longer than necessary to buy so little.

The supermarket was a good distance from his hostel. There was at least one closer that he could have used. The one he chose was in a more affluent area of Derby and tended to attract a higher income clientele.

I asked the surveillance teams to pay close attention to the staff who worked at the supermarket. Did he look at anyone in particular? Did he speak to anyone or loiter around any of the checkouts?

Tenon's other daily trip was to the local library. He

normally went there after shopping in the morning. He sat on one of the comfortable lounge chairs and read copies of the *Sun* and the *Daily Mirror*.

There seemed to be a group of regulars who used the library. Some of them were unemployed and would scan the job vacancy pages. Others were retired or homeless, and some clearly used alcohol. The library was somewhere warm and dry where people could while away the hours until other venues opened, or the daytime soaps started on TV. There were fewer women in the library than the supermarket, but they tended to be the same faces each day.

After ten days the surveillance teams were getting frustrated at the lack of progress. Some of the senior officers from the 'command corridor' were asking questions about the cost. Surveillance is a fiercely expensive exercise, particularly if the imperative is not to let somebody know they're being followed. It can involve up to five teams at any one time, some on foot and others in cars and on motorbikes. To keep this up for ten days, around the clock, cost tens of thousands of pounds.

'There are so many different women that cross his path every day,' said the DI. 'Can you give us any idea of the sort of woman he might target?'

There was a danger in answering this question. If I encouraged the police to focus on a particular type of woman and I was wrong, then they might miss the real victim. Yet Tenon had revealed quite a lot about his internal functioning in his day-to-day activities.

He didn't seem to pay great attention to women in figure-hugging clothes or short skirts. These sexually confident, outgoing women often turn men's heads and capture attention, but not Tenon's.

If anything, he paid more attention to the quieter women who looked more homely or traditionally feminine, rather than being aggressively sexual or glamorous. From a sexual predator's viewpoint, they might also appear to be more pliable.

'Is there anyone who fits that description who works at the supermarket or in the library?' I asked.

'There's this girl,' said one of the officers, pointing to a name. 'She's a librarian. She's pretty, I suppose, in a bookish sort of way. She wears long skirts and cardigans – as though her grandmother dresses her for work.'

'Has he ever spoken to her?'

'Once or twice. He seemed to be asking after a book.'

'But you said he wasn't a great reader of books?'

'No. It's normally just the newspapers and motoring magazines.'

'OK. I want you to watch how he interacts with this woman. Where does he sit in the library? Can he see her working? Does he watch her movements? What are her hours? Where does she live? How does she get to and from work?'

I stressed to the officers that this didn't mean they should ignore other women he might come across. The librarian might not be the one. They couldn't afford to drop their guard.

I had a phone call from the SIO the following day. Tenon had visited the library later than usual. He arrived an hour before closing time and had been among the last to leave.

'He stood across the road and watched her locking up. Then she began walking home.'

'Did he follow her?'

'No.'

'Do you know where she lives?'

'Yes.'

'When he was in the library, did he talk to her?'

'No, but he sits in an alcove opposite the information desk. It overlooks the entrance so he can see people coming and going.'

'Does she work shifts?'

'Not really. It's usually nine to four. She works on a Saturday morning and has a half-day off during the week.'

'What day?'

'Thursday.'

'From the alcove he sits in, could he see her arriving at work?'

'I don't know.'

'Could you find out for me? I want to know if he can see the street where she turns off.'

The SIO came back to me within twenty minutes. From his vantage point, Tenon could look out of the window and see several streets branching off the main road, including the one the librarian used.

Within twenty-four hours, the Regional Crime Squad had provided me with a series of street maps and aerial photographs of the streets surrounding the library. Using the librarian's address, I could plot her most likely route home from work. I didn't think in terms of cars, but on foot. What were her likely short cuts? She was a local girl – she'd know the pedestrian bridges, vacant blocks and rights of way.

Recalling Tenon's previous attacks on women, I began looking for features that corresponded. Eventually I narrowed down the possible sites to one place – a short section of canal towpath. The trees were thicker and the undergrowth spilled out to narrow the path to only a few feet. Here it was possible for someone to hide, out of view, but still be able to see anyone coming or going from either direction.

This small area was the only place on her route that bore a direct similarity to the sites of the two earlier rapes.

The following morning I met with the police team.

'In evidential terms we haven't got enough to say this woman is clearly at risk,' I said. 'But I think he's chosen her.'

'Shouldn't we warn her?' suggested a young detective.

'And put the fear of God into her for no reason?' said another.

I could see their dilemma. They had no grounds to arrest Tenon. If they warned this woman off, he would simply find another. Unless they were prepared to follow him indefinitely, they couldn't identify, let alone start warning, each new potential victim.

The other option was to recruit the librarian into the operation. But it takes a very special personality to play such a role. Even with the right training beforehand, she could panic at the wrong moment and jeopardize her own safety as well as the operation.

'If she's the one, it will happen fairly soon,' I told them. 'I'd say in the next six days, perhaps a little longer. I think it's OK to stay with him. Keep up the surveillance but don't let him see you. At the same time, I would focus on this place.' I pointed out the section of towpath on a large-scale town plan. 'This is where she is most vulnerable.

'Whether you warn her is your decision. But if you want to catch this man, you can't let her change her routines. Nor can you afford to lose sight of her. This man has spent ten years in prison because his victims identified him. This time he might decide to remove that possibility. Her life could be in your hands.'

Nothing about this operation could be considered to be entrapment. The police hadn't enticed or encouraged Tenon by tantalizing him into an offence with a decoy. I seriously hoped that I was wrong about him. I wanted him to be a changed man.

At the same time I recognize how important it is for policing to be pre-emptive rather than only post-offence orientated. Yes, they have to catch criminals, but by preventing a crime they save the considerable anguish and trauma of the victims.

Five days later, Paul Tenon was arrested when he attacked the librarian on the towpath. The surveillance team arrived within seconds. The young woman, although shocked, suffered only minor bruises to her neck and arms.

Tenon pleaded guilty and was given a long prison term. The judge warned him that he risked spending the rest of his life in jail unless he could be successfully treated and rehabilitated.

26

Several years ago I wrote a book, *The Jigsaw Man*, that revealed how psychological offender profiling came into being in the UK. It was the first time I had ever stopped and logically assembled how I got to be where I am.

As I looked at the cases I had investigated and the patients who had graced my consulting room, one thing became absolutely clear. None of the victims ever woke up one morning and said, 'Today I'm going to be killed or raped or abducted or blackmailed.' We think violent crime happens to other people, not to us.

When Rachel Nickell took her little boy for a walk on Wimbledon Common, she didn't know that she'd meet her killer on one of the paths. And Samantha Bissett and her daughter Jazmine didn't know that by leaving the blinds open at night and the balcony door unlocked, they were inviting Robert Napper inside.

I can place both these women in categories that relate to the level of risk they faced – high, medium or low. This was something I had to do when I profiled their killers. I had to look at the victims' personalities and all the important variables and decide to what extent they had been 'selected' or if they were merely victims of opportunity.

I can't help but make these calculations today. I see young women coming out of hotels and chatting in cafés. I notice what they wear and how they use their bodies, faces and voices. I observe how they drive their cars and how they relate to each other.

Take, for example, three different women walking down the same street. Each wears certain clothes for particular reasons. The first likes to attract attention with bright colours and figure-hugging skirts. Being looked at makes her feel good. The second woman does completely the opposite. It's not that she is un-attractive, she simply doesn't like standing out in a crowd. The third woman wears comfortable clothes that suit her, without making any bold statements.

All three women drop into the same pub and each of them sees a completely different environment. The first looks at people laughing and joking at the bar. She smiles and thinks to herself, what a friendly place, I'll make friends here.

The second woman looks in the same bar and thinks, they're going to laugh at me. They'll make me feel bad.

The third woman pushes open the door and takes a perfectly realistic view. This place looks OK, she says to herself. There'll be good and bad here.

These are only pencil portraits, yet it's still possible to calculate the extent to which each of these women would be at risk from a sexual predator if one were sitting in that bar. And in just the same way that no two women (or children) are exactly the same, neither are any two predators. Their individual histories in-fluence exactly who they will prefer to take.

Many of the men I have encountered would be both angered and aroused by the first woman. They would describe her as a 'teaser' and say she was putting them down, even if she had not had any direct personal contact with them. This is the woman who is frequently caricatured by pornographers and consequently is very easily given a 'sexual object' label by the predator. This man needs some self-confidence but would not require social competence in order to build himself up for an attack on her.

The second woman often signals her vulnerability by her demeanour and hesitancy. She stands out like a beacon to the predator for whom control and domination are as important as sexual release itself; for whom control and domination may indeed be necessary before he can find sexual release. Her vulnerability may compensate for the gnawing self-doubt seen in some of these offenders; however, for killers such as Frederick West at the beginning of their careers, her defencelessness is a delight in itself.

Although the two types of women I have outlined above have particular risks of victimization, predators also attack other women. These men will sometimes develop a sexual assault fantasy in which the woman has some specific characteristic of clothing, hairstyle, facial shape, gait, posture, vocal quality or employment. Under these circumstances the particular feature becomes the most important factor in the search for a victim.

Of course these predators become impatient and highly aroused, and then they are more inclined to take risks. At this stage they seek not a special woman but any broadly suitable victim, and it is now that the risk to the third woman increases. Her usually adequate monitoring of her environment may be just not enough to protect her from the opportunist predator, or from the man who has gained personal knowledge of her and who has decided she is his. Only when she is mentally and physically prepared for this situation can she turn the balance back in her favour.

I don't make automatic judgements of risk factors. Their recognition follows from careful calculation based on decades of professional observation.

In my case, I try to use my knowledge to keep people safe. After twenty years working for the National Health Service, I retired after a road traffic accident in February 1998. Since then I've concentrated on helping people understand the nature of risk.

I know that it's not my place to tell every woman not to walk the streets alone at night, not to collect the milk in a skimpy dressing gown or not to leave her curtains open while she undresses. But if I can help a few individuals to understand how predators lock onto targets, then they may be less likely to become victims of crime.

The idea of pre-emptive policing isn't new. Unfortunately, it can sometimes be overshadowed by the clamour for tougher jail sentences and a more punishing penal regime.

The abiding rationale of my clinical work was to repair damaged lives, prevent crime and manage threat. These last two aims grew in importance because of the dreadful things I've seen.

In September 1995, while still advising on the Janet Brown investigation, I became involved in a police operation much closer to home. It was the largest surveillance and threat management exercise ever mounted in the UK. Most of the details must remain secret because the danger still exists, but the case has a resonance that continues to the present day.

An extremely violent man, who needed to control women and validate his own self-image through fear, was about to be released from prison after serving a long sentence. Unfortunately, just like Paul Tenon, he wasn't returning to society as a changed man. Instead he sought revenge. He had vowed to spend the rest of his life getting even.

In a covert operation lasting at least six months, I had to assess and train dozens of witnesses, police officers, probation service personnel and criminal justice employees, along with members of their families. All of them were possible targets and they had to learn how to recognize, prevent and, if necessary, respond to immediate danger if this man approached them.

One woman in particular, a past professional contact, was the highest probability target. Jackie was a bright, intelligent professional woman, who still bore the emotional and psychological scars of her last meeting with this man. I first met her in a seminar room at Arnold Lodge. She was about five foot four inches tall and wore a smart linen suit, tailored to narrow at the waist and make her shoulders look bigger.

She had once worked closely with the man who now threatened to kill her. She had tried to help rehabilitate him, but this had failed. Now he had set his mind to destroying her – first emotionally and then completely.

Jackie sat very still and listened intently. Her heels were pressed hard to the floor as though to stop her legs from shaking.

'Some people are very good at reacting instantly, Jackie, but more often the trauma of the moment sweeps away our capacity for rational response. That's why it's best to be prepared.'

'But he's not going to get close to me, is he?'

'Perhaps not. I hope not. What would you do if he did?'

'I'd hit the panic button, or they'll see him on the security cameras.'

'Yes. But no matter what happens, it's going to take a few minutes for the police to reach you. In that time *you* have to manage the threat.'

'Oh, my God!'

'Don't worry. I'm going to help you.'

I explained how this man would deliberately attempt to use his physical size and his words to control and intimidate her. No matter how confident she thought she was, she had no experience of anything like this. When that man confronted her, everything would be geared to making her paralysed and completely passive with fear.

'That's why we're going to rehearse,' I said. 'And we're going to do it over and over again, until you can reach into yourself and deal with him, no matter what pressure he puts you under.'

I began by setting up a role-play. It was evening. Jackie had come home from work. She had dropped her shoes in the hall and her bag by the phone table. There were no messages on the answering machine. She hung her jacket on the chair back and took an opened bottle of wine from the fridge. She mixed it with lemonade and put her earrings on the kitchen worktop. Then she sat in front of the TV to watch the local news.

'After a few minutes you hear a puppy crying in your garden. You put your slippers on and go out onto the front drive to see what's wrong. As you step outside you hear a voice from beside the front door. It's very quiet and very flat.

'"Hello, Jackie," it says.

575

'You turn to see Pete. He's standing between you and the house. Let's see what you do?'

I walked over to the door of the seminar room and leaned against it. Jackie stood in the middle of the room.

'Hello,' I said, giving her his cold smile.

'Er ... why ... what do you want?' She stumbled over the words and looked anxious.

'I SAID I'D BE COMING TO SEE YOU.' I didn't scream the words, but the volume made her flinch. I moved closer.

'Go away, Pete. You shouldn't be here. I'll phone the police. Get away from me, please ...'

'NOT THIS TIME, SLAG. I DON'T THINK THE PHONE WORKS – TRY IT – GO ON – INSIDE – TRY IT!'

This time I shouted, punching each phrase. My hands were held wide, shepherding her towards the door. Jackie had started shaking.

'Oh God ... Oh God, I don't know what to do.'

She cowered away from me, trying to avoid being touched. I drove her back towards the far wall without laying a finger on her. She was on the verge of tears.

'It's all right, Jackie. We'll stop there,' I said, letting my voice reassure her. 'Very few people are able to get it right first time.'

This may seem like a melodramatic approach, but we all tend to think in abstract terms about what we'd say in this sort of situation. However, unless we know the actual words and how to use our bodies and our voices, we can't make the abstract real. This can make the difference between getting hurt or not.

Jackie sat in a low vinyl-covered armchair with a

576

beech-wood frame. I wrote notes in black marker on a white board.

'*This man enjoys and feeds on your fear.*'

'He likes to feel he can hurt you with a quiet threat as much as yelling,' I said. 'The greater the fear he elicits the better he likes it. So if you're really showing great fear, he's not going to be touched with compassion – it's going to fuel him more.'

'*He reacts badly to aggressive challenges.*'

'We know this from his history. He will hit back if he thinks the balance favours him. It usually does.'

'*Confidence. Assertiveness. Self-assurance.*'

'You need all of these things, but not so much as to be confrontational or openly hostile.'

I knew that this might seem impossible to Jackie, that the balance was a difficult one to strike, given the way this man made her feel. But just as he used his face, posture and voice to frighten her, she had to use her body and voice to swing the odds back in her favour.

I began teaching her to keep her voice low and easy. At the same time, she couldn't sound like some 'nodding dog' counsellor, telling him, 'There, there, calm down now.'

She had to keep her shoulders level and not point at him. She should keep her hands at about waist level and *never* fold her arms.

She had to keep her face towards him, but at the same time stand with her body half-facing away. This was less confrontational, but just as importantly it was the best position to allow her to move away.

'Never turn your back,' I warned.

'Whatever he says to you, it's important to take him seriously. Don't brush him aside or patronize him. It's obvious that something has made him angry. Tell him you understand this. Why else would he have come all this way and put himself so seriously at risk? Clearly he feels that he has just cause. You don't know the exact reasons, but if he needs someone to push things along or get answers, you're willing to try.'

Jackie hadn't written anything down but had been following what I said. We tried again, starting with the same scenario.

'Hello, Jackie.'

'Hello, Pete. Are you all right?'

'What do you care? You grassed me up!'

'I've been a bit worried about you.'

'Don't you mean worried about yourself?'

'Yes, I am worried. Who wouldn't be? The police said I should look out for you. They came and put their electronics in. What's really going on, Pete? You're obviously upset. It must be pretty bad.'

'All because of you.'

'What's happened to make you read it like that? I want to see you able to put things together – to have it really good – without anyone on your back.'

'LISTEN, WHORE – DON'T FUCK WITH MY HEAD!'

She flinched and fell apart, but this run-through had been much better. It would take many hours of rehearsing various scenarios before she could maintain the plan.

Each potential target had a programme such as this. Some were much more confident, while others closed down initially. Eventually they all knew how to deflect and hold this man until support arrived. If Pete chose to confront them, he had a surprise coming.

A number of their addresses had a panic button

system installed, along with external cameras. If people failed to log in the correct code at the correct times, this would immediately alert the police. At the same time, their streets were to be regularly checked by patrol cars.

A massive surveillance operation was planned to run alongside the threat management. Most police stake-outs are clandestine affairs, with the idea being to gather information covertly or catch an offender in the act. This one had to be different, I advised. Instead of being invisible the police presence had to be obvious and continuous. They had to let this man know that every time he turned a corner, he was being watched.

The psychological rationale behind these tactics was that this man didn't want to go back inside. Yes, he wanted revenge and to make people fear him deeply, but not at the expense of his freedom.

Given what I'd learned about his personality, I suspected that he was quite fearful about a true 'man-to-man' confrontation. That's why he normally picked on women. He was a more sadistic version of the schoolyard bully, used to getting things his own way. Any open, confident show of strength would perplex him.

'If he thinks he'll get caught, he'll bide his time,' I said. 'He will make do with threatening pub talk and watching how nervous he can make people. This will give him pleasure.

'If he can be held in this loop long enough, his fear of getting caught will collide with his desire for revenge. If so, he'll begin to experience dissonance. He'll decide they're not worth it. They're too small for him to waste his energy on.

'At the same time, he'll realize that the longer he leaves them, the more exquisite their pain and uncertainty. The police are sure he is going to attack – why else the tight surveillance? He will prove how much he is in control by stringing them on and on.

'At some point during this period, other influences will begin to affect him. He'll meet new people and start enjoying being free of prison. Deep in his mind he'll still think, one day I'll go back and get them, but for the moment he can wait. His anger is no longer so immediate. The risk he presents will begin to diminish.'

The operation worked well. The massive and continual presence had the desired effect. Each time this man walked out of his flat, stepped on a bus, drank in a pub or shopped in a supermarket he would notice somebody watching him. They seemed almost to second-guess his movements, often arriving before him.

His interest in the potential targets began to wane and he seemed to find his feet. He appreciated his freedom rather than being preoccupied with the desire for retribution. Even so, he remained a danger. Much like Paul Tenon, he should have been successfully treated while in prison and, if not, detained indefinitely.

The advice I gave to Jackie and the other possible targets has become a blueprint for my own security. At the moment there are two individuals at large who have made threats against me.

One of them, a young man with a very troubled history, has promised to seek me out and teach me the error of my ways. He sends me letters to remind me that he hasn't forgotten who I am.

Another former patient phoned Arnold Lodge in the summer of 1999 saying that he intended to kill me. He dropped out of treatment about five years ago and now blames me for the collapse of his world. He has a history of violence and explosive rages and is impervious to the pain of physical conflict.

At one level threats like these are an occupational hazard. Most will fade away with the effects of medication, psychotherapy or boredom.

Unfortunately, in the second case, it isn't quite so easy. My colleagues at Arnold Lodge who have examined this man believe he should be taken seriously. The police have visited my home, made assessments and suggested safeguards.

However, as I've taught my clients and students, no system is invulnerable. There may come a time when I am face to face with an attacker. It has happened in my consulting room, but never on the outside. If his first one-to-one contact is to speak to me, then I know we can resolve his pain. However, if all else fails and my family is at risk, I won't hesitate to deploy whatever resources are available.

The work I do now has many facets. I organize courses that teach individuals how to be safe. I also teach groups such as nurses, doctors and administrators how to deal with danger. On a corporate level, I advise companies and other institutions how to organize their security to best effect. This includes running a crisis management consultancy which helps them deal with disasters, accidents and threats.

The crisis need not be criminal in nature. It may be an aggressive, unwelcome takeover, or a massive product recall, or an industrial accident in which people are hurt or die. I use psychological principles to evaluate the bureaucratic systems and the response strategies to make sure they are appropriate.

Part of this work involves risk audits. I've never

forgotten the abduction of four-hour-old Abbie Humphries from a maternity ward at the Queen's Medical Centre in Nottingham on 1 July 1994.

One of the hospital's twenty-nine security video cameras had captured grainy rear views of a bogus nurse in uniform. She was hunched over as if carrying something in her arms.

Unfortunately, the cameras were so badly positioned that the images became one of the most destructive aspects of the entire investigation. The quality was so poor that the photographs couldn't help identify the woman, yet they became the subject of heated debate over whether they should be released to the media.

The surveillance cameras at the Strand shopping precinct in Bootle had created a similar problem when James Bulger disappeared on Friday 12 February 1993. The grainy, time-coded images weren't sharp enough and the angle of the cameras was wrong. This made it impossible to pick out the faces or assess the ages of the boys with James.

Clear pictures and properly angled cameras might seem like basic requirements, but it's amazing how often the simple things are overlooked. Recently I was asked to conduct a risk audit on a newly built hospital. It had been designed originally for general cases, but was now being used by psychiatric patients. Several million pounds had apparently been spent on making it more secure.

One of the first things I noticed in a secure ward was a hatch in the ceiling. It could easily be opened and used to access the entire floor and areas beyond the secure sections. Elsewhere there were bedroom doors that weren't in direct view of the nursing stations, and security cameras were angled incorrectly.

I told the hospital manager that I needed to speak to a representative of all of the groups who worked on the ward.

'You mean doctors and nurses?' he said.

'Yes, and anybody else working on the ward.'

'There isn't anybody else.'

'How do you get your food?'

'The canteen.'

'Do you all go to the canteen?'

'Usually. I mean, occasionally we might get sandwiches brought up.'

'Who brings them?'

'The domestics.'

The penny dropped and the hospital manager admitted that cleaners and maintenance men were also regular visitors to the ward. Such staff are rarely even noticed, let alone addressed, because they work unsociable hours and perform unobtrusive tasks.

Two cleaning ladies were found. They were both in their late thirties to mid-forties and wore overalls. They were quite nervous about having been singled out and assumed they must have done something wrong.

I began asking them about their experiences on the wards. 'Has anything ever been said or done to you that you didn't like?'

They looked at each other. Nobody had ever asked them this. They didn't want to jeopardize their jobs.

Changing tack, I asked, 'Are there parts of the ward that are better or worse than others?'

'Oh, I don't like working down at that end,' said one of them. The other nodded.

'Why is that?'

'Well, there's nobody else there except the patients.'

'Yes?'

'Well, you know.'

'No, I'm not sure. Perhaps you could help me?'

'They touch me,' she whispered, suddenly unsure if she'd said too much. I tried to reassure her that I was simply trying to understand what happened and to make the wards a good place to work.

'You said they touch you?'

'Yeah. Some of the blokes try to feel me up. They say dirty things.'

'Like what?'

'You know – what they'd like to do to me. I don't like that, but I can cope. It's worse when they touch me. I don't like that.'

'What do they do?'

'Put their hands on my breasts and my bottom.'

'What do you do?'

'I tell them to sod off, of course.'

'When does this happen?'

'It always happens. Every time I go down there.'

'What does the ward manager say, or your supervisor?'

'I can't say anything, can I? I might lose my job.'

'Why?'

'I don't know. People don't like complainers.'

'Do you appreciate that you're the victim of what amounts to an offence?'

They both looked shocked.

'But it's all right, isn't it? You won't make trouble for us. I mean, I don't want to cause a fuss . . .'

I spoke to more of the cleaning staff and discovered similar stories. Despite being intimidated and sexually molested, none of them had ever filled out a critical incident report.

When I went back to the hospital manager he

reacted with dismay. 'Why didn't they come and tell us?' he said. His voice seemed to imply that it was somehow the cleaners' fault.

I was more interested in discovering what kind of system allowed a person who was being routinely sexually assaulted to feel too frightened to raise the issue with their supervisors.

Major changes were subsequently made to the reporting procedures at the hospital, which made all the employees feel safer. Changes were also made to the layout of the secure ward, exposing hidden corners and improving security.

I don't miss the working environment of Arnold Lodge, or the nature of the job. Nor do I regret seeing less of the police and the courts. However, there are some cases that still come back to me in quiet moments.

It concerns me, for instance, that the killer of Janet Brown is still at large and likely to strike again. Mercifully a line has been drawn under the names of Tracy Turner and Samo Paul, although I fear this same line underscores other deaths and assaults. Three weeks after the murder of Tracy Turner, a man was seen behaving suspiciously in the forecourt of a filling station in Balsall Heath, near Birmingham. He was posing as a journalist and enquiring about the red-light area in the city. This was where Samo Paul had been taken from in December 1993.

Alun Kyte, then aged twenty-nine, was a nomadic labourer and sometime painter and mechanic. When interviewed by police he denied being at the filling station, but a forecourt camera had filmed the scene. My psychological profile of the killer had strongly indicated his preoccupation with prostitutes and also that

Birmingham would be a focus. Yet instead of being interviewed extensively, Kyte was allowed to slip through the net before anyone learned that he worked as a trucker. This gave him a detailed knowledge of the trunk routes and back roads of the Midlands. He had also been seen with scratch marks on his face in early 1994.

Kyte remained at large until 1997 when he raped a woman at knifepoint in a Bristol flat. He was convicted and jailed for seven years. Only then did a routine DNA check link him to the death of Tracy Turner. It also emerged that he had boasted to other inmates of what he'd done to two prostitutes found dumped in Leicestershire. In particular, he described strangling Tracy Turner because she laughed at him during sex. He couldn't handle that.

'You don't pay for that sort of girl,' he told convicted killer Peter Baxter. 'That's why I killed her.'

The trial began at Nottingham Crown Court in February 2000. Prosecuting counsel, James Hunt QC, told the jury that Kyte had an 'unusual interest' in prostitutes and used them regularly. DNA tests had matched him with the semen found in Tracy Turner. A witness had also come forward claiming to have seen a passenger in the back of a car in Swinford (close to where Samo Paul was left) who appeared to be dead.

'These cases are linked in type, origin and disposal,' explained Mr Hunt, listing the similarities between the murders. He also pointed out how Kyte appeared to like the limelight. This fitted in with his posing as a journalist and boasting to fellow inmates about his crimes.

In the witness box, Kyte explained to the jury that

he might have had sex with one of the prostitutes, but he couldn't remember doing so.

'According to the scientists the DNA is mine, which means I must have had sex with her. You have casual sex. You meet people. You have one-night stands. You don't remember them. At the end of the day that doesn't make me a killer.'

He claimed the prison witnesses were lying in order to secure their own early releases. He then asked if he could have the artist's impression of a hitchhiker allegedly seen near to where Tracy Turner's body was found. He held it close to his face and said, 'I look nothing like the drawing. The only possible similarity is my receding hairline.'

The jury retired on Tuesday 14 March and returned a unanimous guilty verdict for both murders the following day. Kyte showed no emotion and stared straight ahead, ignoring shouts of hatred from the public gallery.

Sentencing Kyte to life imprisonment, Mr Justice Crane said, 'You cruelly killed these two unfortunate women. It is clear you despised them. It is you who deserves to be despised. You are plainly a very dangerous man.'

He added that despite some criticism levelled at the police, 'In my view the officers deserve a commendation and the thanks of the community.'

At a press conference afterwards, Assistant Chief Constable David Coleman of Leicestershire admitted that mistakes had been made. 'He could have been swabbed [earlier]. He wasn't and that's a matter of regret. We can't alter that . . . Different systems were in place at the time.'

Coleman also used the press conference to launch a

national appeal for more information about Kyte. His photograph, DNA swab and voice tape were being issued to other forces around Britain.

'[This] evil man travelled the length and breadth of the country committing crimes. He has taken the lives of two young women and is a dangerous and wicked man. I don't believe we have uncovered the full extent of his criminality. There is every reason to believe he may have been responsible for other serious attacks on women.'

As I read these words in the *Leicester Mercury*, I pondered the advice I'd given six years earlier. Apart from David Cox, very few of the policemen involved had wanted to see Tracy Turner and Samo Paul as victims of a serial killer.

After the sentencing, Mary Turner, Tracy's mother, told journalists, 'In the last six years I have built a brick wall around myself to try to make things fade into the background. In the last few weeks my whole world has just crumbled.

'I remember Tracy used to sit for a cuddle with me on the settee. She would put her arms around me and put her head on my shoulder. She was a prostitute but still my daughter . . . I loved her.'

EPILOGUE

When terrible crimes make headlines, we tend to
demonize the killers and paint the victims as being
sweet innocents, without ever knowing their true
nature. The real story is never so black and white.

I don't know the full history of Alun Kyte, but I suspect that if I could sit down with him in my consulting
room and unlock the details of his past, I'd discover
another sad tale of neglect and abuse. I'm not making
excuses for him. My profile of him showed an arrogant,
scornful killer; he had committed terrible crimes and
deserved to be punished.

Crime of course has many contributory strands –
poverty, unemployment, indifferent schooling, childhood
neglect and abuse, class inequity, disenfranchisement,
materialism, the loss of belief . . . These are vital issues
which our governments and democratic systems must
address.

The world seems to be a more dangerous place than
it was ten or twenty years ago. Partly this is true. It is
also the case that mass communications and greater
media coverage have meant that we *hear* and *see* more
about crimes – particularly those involving predators.

We cannot wrap ourselves in cotton wool or live behind high walls because of what may be outside. Statistically, the odds of being a victim of violent crime are still remarkably low. However, this is scant comfort to those innocent, delightful, vibrant people who account for the statistics.

I hope that through the course of these pages you have come to understand that victims come in all shapes and sizes. Some are just plain unlucky, others are careless and a few, like Ray Knox, grow up to have murder in their hearts.

Don't rush to judge them. All of them deserve the chance to pick up the pieces of their lives before it's too late.

If you take only one thought away with you from this book let it be the question, 'What can I do to help a child not to grow up like this?'

You have met some of my patients whose mistreatment during childhood partially determined the course of their lives. People like Claire, Jimmy, Tabitha, Malcolm, Cameron and, of course, Ray.

All were damaged or distorted as children and I had to treat the dangerous or vulnerable adult they became. This meant going into their dark places and finding the injured child. They had to trust me enough to hold my hand and find the path back.

It shouldn't be like this.

Over the past few years I've done a lot of work with children, but not perhaps in the way that I expected. I've been called upon more and more frequently to give guidance to the courts and Social Services departments as to whether certain children are at risk of sexual, emotional or physical abuse if they stay with their families. These are complex cases that often involve families that are unsophisticated and ill equipped to deal with the care system.

Where gross abuse has occurred and will continue, it is easy to argue for the child to be removed and taken into care. But I have never forgotten the sight of that small boy I escorted to the children's home when I was a young police cadet, nursing his stinging hand and looking at me as though I had betrayed him.

The sad fact is that thirty-five years on, even though we assume these institutions are now better, they probably aren't. What I have seen now is a much more institutionalized kind of abuse. So many of the prostitutes I have seen came out of the children's care system. So did many of the lads who had problems of interpersonal violence and impulse control.

Yes, they were damaged before they went into care. But I am absolutely certain that the care system exacerbated and accelerated the process. It didn't do the very thing that it was supposed to do – compensate for the neglect or abuse they had suffered at home.

Does that mean they shouldn't have been in care? Of course not, but it does make the choice of taking a child from their family a very difficult one.

What makes the difference for me is the knowledge that if they stay in the family environment, they have no chance at all. They are going to be seriously hurt or may even die.

If they go into the care environment, there is a chance that it will work out. And if they come out at the other end damaged there is a prospect that they will get to somebody else's consulting room and still make the journey to a reasonable life.

This may not seem like much of a choice. It's like asking a child, 'Do you want your hands cut off or your feet cut off? Well, what do you want to be – a runner or an artist? If you want to be a runner, keep your feet. If you are going to be an artist, hang on to the hands.'

The problems may seem enormous, but we can each try to help one person at a time. By all means save the whales, but don't forget to love and nurture each of our children.

I always remember the old story about a child walking along a beach, who is rescuing starfish that have been washed onto the sand by a storm. He can only carry a few at a time back to the water, yet there are thousands on the shore.

Somebody stops and says, 'You can't possibly hope to rescue them all. It's pointless.'

And the child says, 'Tell that to the starfish.'

INDEX

THE JIGSAW MAN
The Remarkable Career of Britain's Foremost Criminal Psychologist
by Paul Britton

'Riveting . . . Everyone should read it'
Frances Fyfield, *Observer*

Forensic psychologist Paul Britton asks himself four questions when he is faced with a crime: what has happened; who is the victim; how was it done; and why? Only when he has the answers to these questions can he address the fifth: who is responsible?

Paul Britton has assisted the police in over a hundred cases and has an almost mythic status in the field of crime deduction. His achievements read as though from the pages of Conan Doyle or Agatha Christie. What he searches for at the scene of the crime are not fingerprints, fibres or bloodstains – he looks for the 'mind trace' left behind by those responsible: the psychological characteristics that can help the police to identify and understand the nature of the perpetrator.

The Jigsaw Man is not only a detective story involving some of the most high-profile cases of recent years, but also a journey of discovery into the darkest recesses of the human mind to confront the question, 'Where does crime come from?'

'Britton has done hugely important work that saves lives. He is fascinating. His book is compelling'
Sunday Times

'A unique insight into the criminal mind . . . fascinating'
The Sun

0 552 14493 2

BRAVO TWO ZERO
by Andy McNab DCM MM

'The best account yet of the SAS in action'
James Adams, *Sunday Times*

In January 1991, eight members of the SAS regiment embarked upon a top secret mission that was to infiltrate them deep behind enemy lines. Under the command of Sergeant Andy McNab, they were to sever the underground communication link between Baghdad and north-west Iraq, and to seek and destroy mobile Scud launchers. Their call sign: *Bravo Two Zero*.

Each man laden with 15 stone of equipment, they patrolled 20km across flat desert to reach their objective. Within days, their location was compromised. After a fierce firefight, they were forced to escape and evade on foot to the Syrian border. In the desperate days that followed, though stricken by hypothermia and other injuries, the patrol 'went ballistic'. Four men were captured. Three died. Only one escaped. For the survivors, however, the worst ordeals were to come. Delivered to Baghdad, they were tortured with a savagery for which not even their intensive SAS training had prepared them.

Bravo Two Zero is a breathtaking account of Special Forces soldiering: a chronicle of superhuman courage, endurance and dark humour in the face of overwhelming odds. Believed to be the most highly decorated patrol since the Boer War, *Bravo Two Zero* is already part of SAS legend.

'Superhuman endurance, horrendous torture, desperate odds – unparalleled revelations'
Daily Mail

'One of the most extraordinary examples of human courage and survival in modern warfare'
The Times

0 552 14127 5

THE INFORMER
The Real Life Story of One Man's War against Terrorism
by Sean O'Callaghan

'The extraordinary story of an extraordinary man . . . His well-written book sheds an unprecedented light on the inner workings of the "Republican Movement"'
Conor Cruise O'Brien, *Sunday Telegraph*

In 1988 IRA terrorist Sean O'Callaghan walked into a Tunbridge Wells police station and gave himself up. Two years later, he pleaded guilty to all charges of which he was accused and received a sentence of 539 years. Since a teenager, he had been an active member of the IRA and had risen to be the head of their Southern Command.

But in 1996, he was released from prison by royal prerogative. For fourteen years he had been the most highly placed informer within the IRA and had fed the Irish Garda with countless pieces of invaluable information. He prevented the assassination of the Prince and Princess of Wales at a London theatre, he sabotaged operations, explained strategy and caused the arrests of many IRA members. He has done more than any individual to unlock the code of silence that governs the IRA, and by so doing, has made it possible to fight the war against the terrorists.

The Informer is the story of a courageous life lived under the constant threat of discovery and its fatal consequences. It is the story of a very modern hero, who is not without sin but who has done and continues to do everything in his power, and at whatever personal cost, to atone for the past.

'An extraordinary memoir of life within the murky world of Republicanism . . . filled with astonishing insights into the personalities and politics of the Provisionals. A huge leap forward in our understanding of the internal machinations of the Provisional Movement' Kevin Toolis, *Guardian*

'The best work in progress on the lethally sick, sad world of Republicanism . . . and a cracking story . . . O'Callaghan is one of the greatest friends of peace in Ireland' *Observer*

'A book of major significance . . . told with the suspence of a thriller' Mary Kenny, *Daily Express*

0 552 14607 2

BLACK HAWK DOWN
by Mark Bowden

A thrilling and visceral, no-holds-barred classic of modern war.

Late in the afternoon of Sunday, 3 October 1993, 140 elite US soldiers abseiled from helicopters into a teeming market neighbourhood in the heart of the city of Mogadishu, Somalia. Their mission was to abduct two top lieutenants of a Somali warlord and return to base. It was supposed to take them about an hour.

Instead, they were pinned down through a long and terrible night in a hostile city, fighting for their lives against thousands of heavily armed Somalis. When the unit was rescued the following morning, eighteen American soldiers were dead and more than seventy badly injured. The Somali toll was far worse – more than five hundred killed and over a thousand injured.

Authoritative, gripping, and insightful, *Black Hawk Down* is a heart-stopping, minute-by-minute account of modern war and is destined to become a classic of war reporting.

'Rip-roaring stuff, with one of the most gruesome battlefield wound treatments ever committed to paper'
Maxim

'One of the most electrifying, immediate and detailed accounts of a single battle ever told . . . the whole 24-hour nightmare seems like it's happening to you'
Later

0 552 14750 8

THE CUSTOM OF THE SEA
by Neil Hanson

On 5 July 1884, the yacht *Mignonette* set sail from Southampton bound for Sydney. Halfway through their projected one hundred and twenty day voyage, Captain Tom Dudley and his crew of three men were beset by a monstrous storm off the coast of Africa. After four days of battling towering waves and hurricane gales, their yacht was finally crushed by a ferocious forty foot wave.

The survivors were cast adrift a thousand miles from the nearest landfall in an open thirteen foot dinghy without provisions, water or shelter from the scorching sun. When, after twenty four days, they were finally rescued by a passing yacht, the *Moctezuma*, only three men were left and they were in an appalling condition. The ordeal that they endured and the trial which followed their eventual return to England held the whole nation – from the lowliest ship's deckhand to Queen Victoria herself – spellbound during the following winter.

This is the true story of the voyage and the subsequent court case which outlawed for ever a practice followed since men first put to the ocean in boats: the custom of the sea.

0 552 14760 5

SOME OTHER RAINBOW
by John McCarthy and Jill Morrell

On 17 April 1986 John McCarthy was kidnapped in Beirut. For the next five years he was cut off from everything and everybody he knew and loved, from family, friends and, perhaps above all, from Jill Morrell, the girl he was going to marry.

For five years, John McCarthy had to endure the deprivation – both physical and psychological – of captivity; the filth and squalor of the cells in which he was kept; the agony of isolation and repeated self-examination; and the pain of ignorance, of not knowing if those he loved even realized he was alive.

For Jill Morrell, the five years of John's captivity were a different kind of hell: the initial shock and disbelief; the gradual acceptance that John had been taken and that her life had changed irrevocably, that all their plans had been shattered.

But Jill refused to give up hope. For five years she and a group of friends worked ceaselessly on behalf of John and all the British hostages in the Middle East, until the extraordinary day in August 1991 when John McCarthy stepped down from an aeroplane at RAF Lyneham. A day when they could begin again.

This is their story, a remarkable account of courage, endurance, hope, and love.

'**Compelling and moving** . . . a beautiful story'
Anthony Clare, *Sunday Times*

'**An astonishing achievement:** while often wildly funny, it is also humbling, draining, exhausting and ultimately exhilarating to read'
Sue Gaisford, *Independent*

0 552 13953 X

THE GOD SQUAD
by Paddy Doyle

His mother died from cancer in 1955. His father committed suicide shortly thereafter. Paddy Doyle was sentenced in an Irish distrtrict court to be detained in an industrial school for eleven years. He was four years old . . .

Paddy Doyle's prize-winning bestseller, *The God Squad,* is both a moving and terrifying testament to the institutionalized Ireland of only twenty-five years ago, as seen through the bewildered eyes of a child. During his detention, Paddy was viciously assaulted and sexually abused by his religious custodians, and within three years his experiences began to result in physical manifestations of trauma. He was taken one night to hospital and left there, never to see his custodians again. So began his long round of hospitals, mainly in the company of old and dying men, while doctors tried to diagnose his condition. This period of his life, during which he was a constant witness to death, culminated in brain surgery at the age of ten – by which time he had become permanently disabled.

The God Squad is the remarkable true story of a survivor, told with an extraordinary lack of bitterness for one so shockingly and shamefully treated. In Paddy Doyle's own words: 'It is about a society's abdication of responsibility to a child. The fact that I was that child, and that the book is about my life, is largely irrelevant. The probability is that there were, and still are thousands of "mes".'

0 552 13582 8

A SELECTED LIST OF NON-FICTION TITLES AVAILABLE FROM CORGI BOOKS

THE PRICES SHOWN BELOW WERE CORRECT AT THE TIME OF GOING TO PRESS. HOWEVER TRANSWORLD PUBLISHERS RESERVE THE RIGHT TO SHOW NEW RETAIL PRICES ON COVERS WHICH MAY DIFFER FROM THOSE PREVIOUSLY ADVERTISED IN THE TEXT OR ELSEWHERE.

13878 9	THE DEAD SEA SCROLLS DECEPTION	Michael Baigent & Richard Leigh	£6.99
09806 X	WHAT DO YOU SAY AFTER YOU SAY HELLO?	Eric Berne M.D.	£5.99
99065 5	THE PAST IS MYSELF	Christabel Bielenberg	£7.99
13337 X	THE PROVISIONAL IRA	Patrick Bishop & Eamonn Mallie	£6.99
14750 8	BLACK HAWK DOWN	Mark Bowden	£5.99
14493 2	THE JIGSAW MAN	Paul Britton	£6.99
14465 7	CLOSE QUARTER BATTLE	Mike Curtis	£6.99
13582 8	THE GOD SQUAD	Paddy Doyle	£7.99
14239 5	MY FEUDAL LORD	Tehmina Durrani	£5.99
13928 9	DAUGHTER OF PERSIA	Sattareh Farman Farmaian	£6.99
12833 3	THE HOUSE BY THE DVINA	Eugenie Fraser	£8.99
14710 9	SIGNS IN THE SKY	Adrian Gilbert	£6.99
14760 5	THE CUSTOM OF THE SEA	Neil Hanson	£5.99
14185 2	FINDING PEGGY: A GLASGOW CHILDHOOD	Meg Henderson	£6.99
14694 3	VIEW FROM THE SUMMIT	Sir Edmund Hillary	£7.99
99744 7	CHARLES: A BIOGRAPHY	Anthony Holden	£7.99
14164 X	EMPTY CRADLES	Margaret Humphreys	£6.99
13943 2	LOST FOR WORDS	Deric Longden	£5.99
14544 0	FAMILY LIFE	Elisabeth Luard	£6.99
13356 6	NOT WITHOUT MY DAUGHTER	Betty Mahmoody	£5.99
12419 2	CHICKENHAWK	Robert C. Mason	£7.99
54536 8	SHE MUST HAVE KNOWN: THE TRIAL OF ROSEMARY WEST	Brian Masters	£6.99
13593 X	SOME OTHER RAINBOW	John McCarthy & Jill Morrell	£6.99
14127 5	BRAVO TWO ZERO	Andy McNab	£6.99
14137 2	A KENTISH LAD	Frank Muir	£7.99
14288 3	BRIDGE ACROSS MY SORROWS	Christina Noble	£5.99
14607 2	THE INFORMER	Sean O'Callaghan	£6.99
14330 8	THE TEMPLAR REVELATION	Lynn Picknett & Clive Prince	£7.99
14550 5	PURPLE SECRET	John Röhl, Martin Warren, David Hunt	£5.99
14709 5	THE YAMATO DYNASTY	Sterling and Peggy Seagrave	£7.99

All Transworld titles are available by post from:
Bookpost, PO Box 29, Douglas, Isle of Man, IM99 1BQ
Credit cards accepted. Please telephone 01624 836000,
fax 01624 837033, Internet http://www.bookpost.co.uk
or e-mail: bookshop@enterprise.net for details.
Free postage and packing in the UK. Overseas customers: allow
£1 per book (paperbacks) and £3 per book (hardbacks).